Managing Development

Globalization in the 1990s provided both opportunities and challenges for developing and transition economies. On the one hand, it offered the chance to achieve economic growth through active involvement in an integrated and liberalized world economy, but on the other, it led to an increase in vulnerability to external shocks and volatility, as demonstrated quite dramatically by the Mexican peso crisis of 1994–5 and the Asian financial crisis of 1997–8.

This book brings together an international team of contributors, including Barbara Stallings, Choong Yong Ahn and J.C. Ferraz, to analyze the different methods employed to manage globalization and development, as well as to examine the challenges of development and transition strategies at the beginning of the twenty-first century.

Junji Nakagawa is Professor at the Institute of Social Science, University of Tokyo, Japan.

Routledge studies in development economics

1 **Economic Development in the Middle East**
   Rodney Wilson

2 **Monetary and Financial Policies in Developing Countries**
   Growth and stabilization
   Akhtar Hossain and Anis Chowdhury

3 **New Directions in Development Economics**
   Growth, environmental concerns and government in the 1990s
   Edited by Mats Lundahl and Benno J. Ndulu

4 **Financial Liberalization and Investment**
   Kanhaya L. Gupta and Robert Lensink

5 **Liberalization in the Developing World**
   Institutional and economic changes in Latin America, Africa and Asia
   Edited by Alex E. Fernández Jilberto and André Mommen

6 **Financial Development and Economic Growth**
   Theory and experiences from developing countries
   Edited by Niels Hermes and Robert Lensink

7 **The South African Economy**
   Macroeconomic prospects for the medium term
   Finn Tarp and Peter Brixen

8 **Public Sector Pay and Adjustment**
   Lessons from five countries
   Edited by Christopher Colclough

9 **Europe and Economic Reform in Africa**
   Structural adjustment and economic diplomacy
   Obed O. Mailafia

10 **Post-apartheid Southern Africa**
   Economic challenges and policies for the future
   Edited by Lennart Petersson

11 **Financial Integration and Development**
   Liberalization and reform in sub-Saharan Africa
   Ernest Aryeetey and Machiko Nissanke

12 **Regionalization and Globalization in the Modern World Economy**
Perspectives on the Third World and transitional economies
Edited by Alex E. Fernández Jilberto and André Mommen

13 **The African Economy**
Policy, institutions and the future
Steve Kayizzi-Mugerwa

14 **Recovery from Armed Conflict in Developing Countries**
Edited by Geoff Harris

15 **Small Enterprises and Economic Development**
The dynamics of micro and small enterprises
Carl Liedholm and Donald C. Mead

16 **The World Bank**
New agendas in a changing world
Michelle Miller-Adams

17 **Development Policy in the Twenty-First Century**
Beyond the post-Washington consensus
Edited by Ben Fine, Costas Lapavitsas and Jonathan Pincus

18 **State-Owned Enterprises in the Middle East and North Africa**
Privatization, performance and reform
Edited by Merih Celasun

19 **Finance and Competitiveness in Developing Countries**
Edited by José María Fanelli and Rohinton Medhora

20 **Contemporary Issues in Development Economics**
Edited by B.N. Ghosh

21 **Mexico Beyond NAFTA**
Edited by Martín Puchet Anyul and Lionello F. Punzo

22 **Economies in Transition**
A guide to China, Cuba, Mongolia, North Korea and Vietnam at the turn of the twenty-first century
Ian Jeffries

23 **Population, Economic Growth and Agriculture in Less Developed Countries**
Nadia Cuffaro

24 **From Crisis to Growth in Africa?**
Edited by Mats Lundal

25 **The Macroeconomics of Monetary Union**
An analysis of the CFA franc zone
David Fielding

26 **Endogenous Development**
Networking, innovation, institutions and cities
Antonio Vasquez-Barquero

27 **Labour Relations in Development**
Edited by Alex E. Fernández Jilberto and Marieke Riethof

28 **Globalization, Marginalization and Development**
Edited by S. Mansoob Murshed

29 **Programme Aid and Development**
Beyond conditionality
Howard White and Geske Dijkstra

30 **Competitiveness Strategy in Developing Countries**
A manual for policy analysis
Edited by Ganeshan Wignaraja

31 **The African Manufacturing Firm**
An analysis based on firm surveys in sub-Saharan Africa
Dipak Mazumdar and Ata Mazaheri

32 **Trade Policy, Growth and Poverty in Asian Developing Countries**
Edited by Kishor Sharma

33 **International Competitiveness, Investment and Finance**
A case study of India
Edited by A. Ganesh Kumar, Kunal Sen and Rajendra R. Vaidya

34 **The Pattern of Aid Giving**
The impact of good governance on development assistance
Eric Neumayer

35 **New International Poverty Reduction Strategies**
Edited by Jean-Pierre Cling, Mireille Razafindrakoto and François Roubaud

36 **Targeting Development**
Critical perspectives on the Millennium Development Goals
Edited by Richard Black and Howard White

37 **Essays on Balance of Payments Constrained Growth**
Theory and evidence
Edited by J.S.L. McCombie and A.P. Thirlwall

38 **The Private Sector After Communism**
New entrepreneurial firms in transition economies
Jan Winiecki, Vladimir Benacek and Mihaly Laki

39 **Information Technology and Development**
A new paradigm for delivering the internet to rural areas in developing countries
Jeffrey James

40 **The Economics of Palestine**
Economic policy and institutional reform for a viable Palestine state
Edited by David Cobham and Nu'man Kanafani

41 **Development Dilemmas**
The methods and political ethics of growth policy
Melvin Ayogu and Don Ross

42 **Rural Livelihoods and Poverty Reduction Policies**
Edited by Frank Ellis and H. Ade Freeman

43 **Beyond Market-Driven Development**
Drawing on the experience of Asia and Latin America
Edited by Makoto Noguchi and Costas Lapavitsas

44 **The Political Economy of Reform Failure**
Edited by Mats Lundahl and Michael L. Wyzan

45 **Overcoming Inequality in Latin America**
Issues and challenges for the twenty-first century
Edited by Ricardo Gottschalk and Patricia Justino

46 **Trade, Growth and Inequality in the Era of Globalization**
Edited by Kishor Sharma and Oliver Morrissey

47 **Microfinance**
Perils and prospects
Edited by Jude L. Fernando

48 **The IMF, World Bank and Policy Reform**
Edited by Alberto Paloni and Maurizio Zanardi

49 **Managing Development**
Globalization, economic restructuring and social policy
Edited by Junji Nakagawa

Managing Development
Globalization, economic restructuring and social policy

Edited by Junji Nakagawa
ISS Institute-Wide Project Research Series
Institute of Social Science, The University of Tokyo

LONDON AND NEW YORK

First published 2006
by Routledge
2 Park Square, Milton Park, Abingdon, Oxon OX14 4RN

Simultaneously published in the USA and Canada
by Routledge
270 Madison Ave, New York, NY 10016

Routledge is an imprint of the Taylor & Francis Group

© 2006 editorial matters and selection, Junji Nakagawa; individual chapters, the contributors

Typeset in Baskerville by Wearset Ltd, Boldon, Tyne and Wear
Printed and bound in Great Britain by MPG Books Ltd, Bodmin

All rights reserved. No part of this book may be reprinted or reproduced or utilized in any form or by any electronic, mechanical, or other means, now known or hereafter invented, including photocopying and recording, or in any information storage or retrieval system, without permission in writing from the publishers.

British Library Cataloguing in Publication Data
A catalogue record for this book is available from the British Library

Library of Congress Cataloging in Publication Data
A catalog record for this book has been requested

ISBN 0-415-36410-8

Contents

List of figures   xi
List of tables   xii
List of contributors   xv
Preface   xvii
Acknowledgments   xix

Introduction: managing development – globalization, economic restructuring and social policy   1
JUNJI NAKAGAWA

PART I
Globalization and global governance   15

1 **Managing global risks and creating prosperity: the role of the IMF and regional financial architectures**   17
HAIDER A. KHAN

2 **Globalization and economic development: the role of multilateral development banks**   42
MASAHIRO KAWAI

3 **Is the international trade regime contributing to liberalization in developing countries?**   86
KAZUYORI ITO

4 **The governance of global issues through regionalism: NAFTA as an interface between multilateral and North–South policies**   108
ISIDRO MORALES

x *Contents*

PART II
Financial crises and restructuring 137

5 Financial sector development in Latin America and
    East Asia: a comparison of Chile and South Korea 139
    BARBARA STALLINGS

6 Restructuring the financial and corporate sector: the
    South Korean experience 162
    CHOONG YONG AHN

7 Economic performance, crisis and institutional reforms
    in East Asia and Latin America 191
    AKIRA SUEHIRO

8 Business groups as an organizational device for
    economic catch-up 217
    KEUN LEE

9 Will inward internationalization foster economic
    development in Latin America? 234
    JOÃO CARLOS FERRAZ, AIRTON VALENTE JR. AND
    MARIANA IOOTTY

10 Determinants and effects of foreign direct investment
    in transition economies 261
    YUKO KINOSHITA AND NAURO F. CAMPOS

PART III
Social policy in transition 287

11 Latin American social security reform in the 1990s 289
    KOICHI USAMI

12 Welfare states in East Asia: similar conditions, different
    past and divided future 306
    YASUHIRO KAMIMURA

13 Characteristics of the Central European welfare system 333
    TAKUMI HORIBAYASHI

    Index 355

Figures

4.1	US imports from Canada 1981–2003 annual rate of growth	118
4.2	US exports to Canada 1981–2003 annual rate of growth	119
4.3	US imports from Mexico 1981–2003 annual rate of growth	119
4.4	US exports to Mexico 1981–2003 annual rate of growth	120
7.1	Economic and social restructuring programs in Thailand (1997–2001)	205
9.1	FDI in privatizations and M&A, percentage over value of transactions, 1990–9, by target country	249
11.1	Most common health model in Latin America	294
12.1	Government expenditure on social security and welfare (as % of GDP)	308
12.2	Government expenditure on health care (as % of GDP)	309
12.3	Government expenditure on education (as % of GDP)	309
12.4	Economic level and social expenditure	310
12.5	Aging and social expenditure	310
12.6	Aging and public health expenditure	311
12.7	Diagram of welfare state–civil society trajectories	327

Tables

1.1	External debt outstanding (US$ billions)	26
1.2	Net capital flows (% of GDP)	27–8
2.1	Organization of multilateral development banks (as of December 2001)	44–5
2.2	Regional breakdown of poverty in developing and transition countries	53–4
	a Population living below $1 per day (at 1993 PPP), 1981–2001	
	b Population living below $2 per day (at 1993 PPP), 1981–2001	
2.3	Benefits and costs of globalization	57
2.4	New and old Washington Consensus	60–1
2.5	First- and second-generation reforms	63
2.6	Net ODA receipts of developing countries (US$ million)	68
2.7	Comprehensive Development Framework: prerequisites for sustainable growth and poverty reduction	70
2.8	Progress on Poverty Reduction Strategy Paper (PRSP), January 2005	72
A2.9	Country Progress on Poverty Reduction Strategy Paper (PRSP), January 2005	80–1
5.1	Latin America and East Asia: financial depth, 1990 and 2003	144
5.2	Chile and Korea: financial development, 1990 and 2003 (% of GDP)	149
5.3	Chile and Korea: ownership of assets in banking sector, 1994 and 2003 (%)	151
5.4	Chile and Korea: financial performance of banking sector, 1995/6–2004 (%)	153
5.5	Chile and Korea: access to finance, 1997 and 2000–1 (%)	154
6.1	Debt/equity ratio in the manufacturing industry (%)	165
6.2	International comparisons of manufacturing firms' profitability (%)	165

6.3	Non-performing loans (ending March 1998) (trillion won)	165
6.4	Changes in loan classification standards	166
6.5	Sample estimates on NPL ratio and NPL company (listed) ratio with interest coverage ratio less than 100%	168
6.6	Major economic indicators (1996–2001)	169
6.7	Changes in foreign exchange reserves (US$ million)	169
6.8	Changes in the number of financial institutions during 1998–2001	174
6.9	Number of bankruptcies: 1994–2002	175
6.10	Five major principles of corporate restructuring	176
6.11	Implementation of restructuring MOU as agreed between the top four chaebols and creditor banks	178
6.12	Injection of public funds by end May 2002 (billion won)	179
6.13	Use of public funds for financial sector by source and support type (November 1997–May 2002) (billion won)	180
6.14	Change in number of employees at domestic financial institutions	180
6.15	Corporate performances (1995–2001) (%)	182
7.1	Summary table of comparison of East Asia, South Asia and Latin America: 1980s and 1990s	194–5
7.2	Performance of the social protection policies under the Thaksin government (as of September 2004)	209
9.1	Evolution of structural reforms in Latin America 1970–95	237
9.2	National regulatory changes, 1991–2003	238
9.3	Latin America: evolution of consumer price index (December to December % variation)	238
9.4	Selected indicators of FDI and international production, 1982–2000 (US$ billion)	239
9.5	M&A to FDI ratio (%)	240
9.6	FDI outward/inward flows in US$ million and as % of gross fixed capital formation, 1989–94, 1995, 2000	241
9.7	FDI outward/inward stock, selected years, countries and regions, in US$ million and as % of GDP	244
9.8	Geographical distribution of FDI flows, trade, domestic investment and technology payments, 1998–2000 (annual average, %)	245
9.9	FDI inward stock, by industry and region, 1988, 1999 (in US$ billion and %)	247
9.10	The largest 500 Latin American companies, 1990–2000, by sector of origin (number, sales in US$ million and %)	248
9.11	Privatizations in Latin America 1990–9 in numbers and US$ million	249
9.12	M&A in Latin America 1990–9 in numbers and US$ million	249

xiv *Tables*

9.13	The ownership of the largest 500 Latin American companies, 1990–2000 (number, sales in US$ million and %)	250
9.14	The role of M&A and joint ventures in chemical industries in the Mercosul	251
9.15	Participants in M&A in chemical industries, by ownership (1985–99)	251
9.16	Exports and imports of foreign firms – 1995, in US$ billion	252
9.17	Share of foreign companies in the sales of the largest companies of Brazil (%)	253
9.18	FDI stock and inflows by sector	253
9.19	FDI stock by industry, 2002 (%)	254
9.20	FDI stock in Brazil, by home country	255
9.21	Corporate networks of Japanese affiliates in selected American countries, 1999	256
9.22	Sales, investment and R&D: US TNCs and affiliates in 1999 (US$ billion)	257
9.23	Brazil: necessary efforts to advance in S&T	259
10.1	Determinants of FDI: fixed effects	270
10.2	Determinants of FDI	273
10.3	Determinants of FDI: GMM	275
10.4	Determinants of FDI: FE model	276
10.5	The impact of FDI on growth in transition economies, 1990–8	278
A10.6	Definition of variables	281
A10.7	Summary statistics	281
11.1	Socio-economic indicators in Latin America	291
11.2	Comparison of social insurance systems in Latin America	293
11.3	Latin America and the Caribbean: urban unemployment	301
12.1	Introduction of social security schemes in East Asian countries	312–15
12.2	State–labor relations in the regime formation periods	317

Contributors

Choong Yong Ahn is President, Korea Institute for International Economic Policy. Currently on leave from Department of Economics, Chung-Ang University, Korea.

Nauro F. Campos is Reader (tenured Associate Professor), Development Economics, University of Newcastle, UK.

João Carlos Ferraz is Director, Division of Productive Development, Economic Commission for Latin America and the Caribbean, United Nations (ECLAC-UN); Senior Lecturer, Instituto de Economia, Universidade Federal do Rio de Janeiro (on leave), Brazil.

Takumi Horibayashi is Professor, Faculty of Economics, Kanazawa University, Japan.

Mariana Iootty is Researcher, Instituto de Economia, Universidade Federal do Rio de Janeiro, Brazil.

Kazuyori Ito is Lecturer, Faculty of International Relations, University of Shizuoka, Japan.

Yasuhiro Kamimura is Lecturer, Faculty of Social Sciences, Hosei University, Japan.

Masahiro Kawai is Head of the Office of Regional Economic Integration, Asian Development Bank, as well as Special Advisor to the ADB President; Professor, Institute of Social Science, University of Tokyo (on leave), Japan.

Haider A. Khan is Professor, Graduate School of International Studies, University of Denver, USA; Visiting Professor, CIRJE, Graduate School of Economics, University of Tokyo, Japan.

Yuko Kinoshita is Economist, International Monetary Fund.

Keun Lee is Professor, School of Economics, Seoul National University, Korea.

Isidro Morales is Dean, School of Social Sciences, Universidad de las Américas-Puebla, Mexico.

Junji Nakagawa is Professor, Institute of Social Science, University of Tokyo, Japan.

Barbara Stallings is Director and Research Professor, Watson Institute for International Studies, Brown University, USA.

Akira Suehiro is Professor, Institute of Social Science, University of Tokyo, Japan.

Koichi Usami is Senior Research Fellow, Institute of Developing Economies, Japan.

Airton Valente Jr. is Research Specialist, Banco do Nordeste, Brazil.

Preface

The chapters in this book are the result of an international joint research project, titled "Managing Development and Transition in a Globalizing World: A Comparative Analysis of Economic Policy Reform and Corporate Behavior in Developing Countries and Former Socialist Countries (hereinafter 'MDT')," organized by the Institute of Social Science (ISS), University of Tokyo, as part of its Institute-Wide Project Research. It aimed at exploring the opportunities and challenges of globalization facing developing countries and countries in transition from the 1990s through the early years of the twenty-first century.

The MDT started in November 1999, when the ISS invited researchers from Brazil, Argentina, Korea and the United States to discuss the research framework, major topics and the target countries of the project. Based on the result of this brainstorming workshop, the MDT was launched in 2000 with the financial support of the Japan Foundation Center for Global Partnership (CGP). Through four workshops (September 2000 (ISS), February 2001 (Rio de Janeiro), March 2002 (ISS), and July 2002 (ISS)), two public symposia (September 2000 and July 2002 (Sanjo Conference Hall, University of Tokyo)), and one project seminar (March 2002 (ISS)), we developed ideas and discussed draft papers and final papers.

This book is, therefore, the result of a continuous and multidisciplinary learning process. As project leader of the MDT, I'd like to express my deep gratitude to those who contributed to this book, as well as to those who actively participated in the process and gave us valuable insights and comments: Aurelijus Dabusinskas (CERGE-EI, Charles University, the Czech Republic), George DeMartino (Graduate School of International Studies, University of Denver), Hilda Eitzen (ISS), Mitsuhiro Furusawa (Ministry of Finance, Japan), Alicia Girón (Instituto de Investigaciones Económicas, Universidad Nacional Autónoma de México), Ananta Gondomono (University of Indonesia), Irene Grabal (Graduate School of International Studies, University of Denver), Michael Herrmann (UNCTAD), Takeo Kikkawa (ISS), Akio Komorida (ISS), Tadeusz Kowalik (Polish Academy of Science Institute of Economics; Warsaw

Socio-Economic School), Natenapha Wailerdsak (Institute of Oriental Culture, University of Tokyo), Yoichi Tajima (Faculty of Foreign Studies, Tokyo University of Foreign Studies), late Yuichi Tsukamoto (University of São Paulo), Shin Yasui (Faculty of Business and Commerce, Keio University).

The MDT would not have been possible without the support of the Japan Foundation Center for Global Partnership (CGP) and the Institute of Social Science, University of Tokyo. Kiyomi Hyoe, Eriko Sase, Masahiko Asano and Yuri Usami provided tireless secretarial, logistical and editorial assistance throughout the process of preparing the workshops, international symposia, Project Seminar, papers and the final manuscript.

Junji Nakagawa
Tokyo, Spring, 2005

Acknowledgments

The Author and publisher would like to thank the following for permission to reproduce previously published material:

Choong Yong Ahn (2003) "Restructuring the Financial and Corporate Sector: The South Korean Experience," ISS Research Series (11): 89–119.

João Carlos Ferraz, Airton Valente, Jr. and Mariana Iootty (2004) "Will Inward Internationalization Foster Economic Development in Latin America," ISS Research Series (13): 71–94.

Takumi Horibayashi (2003) "Characteristics of the Central European Welfare System," the *Journal of Social Science*, 55(1): 169–88.

Yasuhiro Kamimura (2003) "Towards a Comparative Study of East Asian Welfare States," the *Journal of Social Science*, 55(1): 189–206.

Haider A. Khan (2003) "Managing Global Risk and Creating Prosperity: The Role of the IMF and Regional Financial Architectures," ISS Research Series (11): 15–39.

Yuko Kinoshita and Nauro F. Campos (2004) "Agglomeration and the Locational Determinants of Foreign Direct Investment in Transition Economies," ISS Research Series (13): 137–59.

Keun Lee (2004) "Business Groups as an Organizational Device for Development and Transition," ISS Research Series (13): 55–70.

Isidro Morales (2003) "The Governance of Global Issues through Regionalism: NAFTA as an Interface between Multilateral and North-South Policies," the *Journal of Social Science* 55(1): 27–52.

Barbara Stallings (2003) "Domestic Capital Markets in Latin America and East Asia: An Alternative to Foreign Capital?," LAEBA Working Paper No. 15, December.

Akira Suehiro (2004) "Economic Performance, Crisis and Institutional Reforms in East Asia and Latin America," ISS Research Series (13): 13–34.

Koichi Usami (2003) "Latin American Social Security Reform in the 1990s," the *Journal of Social Science* 55(1): 153–67.

Introduction
Managing development – globalization, economic restructuring and social policy

Junji Nakagawa

Background: opportunities and risks of globalization

Globalization in the 1990s provided both opportunities and challenges for developing and transitional economies. While globalization offered the chance to achieve economic growth through active involvement in the integrated and liberalized world economy, it also increased their vulnerability to external shocks and volatility (Grindle 2000). In consequence, stakeholders at every level of the development and transition process – international organizations, national governments and the private sector – had to review their strategies in order to adjust to the new world economic environment. As the Mexican Peso Crisis of 1994–5 and the Asian Financial Crisis of 1997–8 showed dramatically, the cost of maladjustment was not only very high but it also affected many more stakeholders than before, due to the contagious effects of crises.

By globalization, we refer to the increasing integration of economies around the world, particularly through trade and financial flows (IMF 2000). Globalization is not a new phenomenon. Some analysts, such as Frankel (2000: 47–8), argue that the world economy was just as globalized 100 years ago as it is today. But today global commerce and financial services are far more developed and deeply integrated than they were at that time. The most striking aspect of this new trend is the integration of financial markets, which has been brought about by the innovation of telecommunication and information technologies in the past two decades.

Developing and transitional economies can achieve rapid economic growth if they succeed in making full use of globalization. However, promoting trade, investment and financial flows is not an easy task. Even if they succeed in promoting trade and attracting investment, many disrupting factors such as exchange rate fluctuation and short-term capital flight may endanger national economies. In sum, globalization has made the rewards as well as the challenges of managing development and transition far greater than they used to be.

During the 1990s, international financial institutions and influential actors in the industrial world (the US and UK, in particular) promoted a common policy package for developing and transitional economies in their economic policy reform. Varyingly referred to as structural adjustment, neoliberalism, or the Washington Consensus,[1] the package emphasized the role of the market in development and transition, with reduced governmental intervention. Although there have been alternative state-centered approaches, such as the one presented (with many caveats) in a much-discussed World Bank study of East Asia (World Bank 1993), the Asian financial crisis seems to have undermined the attractiveness of this alternative path. With the adoption of a market-oriented transition strategy in the former socialist countries since 1989, endorsed by the IMF, the World Bank and the European Bank for Reconstruction and Development (EBRD), this approach has acquired almost universal reach.

Nonetheless, the crises of the 1990s showed that the market-oriented approach is not a panacea. Rather than a one-size-fits-all solution, it is necessary to tailor-make economic policies to fit each country. In particular, the institutional arrangements – both at the national governmental level and at the individual corporate level – must be taken into account, since these reflect the historical and structural legacy of each nation. While some aspects of the new market-oriented approach may have much to offer, stakeholders in the developing and transition economies must consider each aspect carefully, rather than adopting them as a whole just because they fit the current ideological paradigm. They should also take into account the available international evidence on the timing and sequencing of policy reform, which can make a great difference in their impact.

One of the greatest challenges of globalization concerns social policy. The crises in the 1990s hit the poor the most (World Bank 1998: 80–5), and governments in crisis had to reconsider their traditional social policy framework. Some, including those in formerly socialist countries in Central and Eastern Europe, conducted market-based reform of social security, while others introduced and/or strengthened social policy within a broader framework of social safety nets. International financial institutions such as the IMF and World Bank played a significant role in these policy reforms. However, the content of the reforms as well as their sequencing varied, reflecting each country's historical, institutional and structural background.

Based on these premises, this book analyzes the challenges of development and transition strategy at the beginning of the twenty-first century. We will be examining international prescriptions and the strategies of international institutions, national governments and the private sector. This multi-layer analysis is justified by two facts. First, market-based policies have different implications for each level of stakeholders, as a result of which one policy taken by one level of stakeholders will produce different expectations and outcomes for the other levels of stakeholders. Second, development and transition is a comprehensive and interactive process, in which each level of stakeholders has a different role that must be coordinated and fine-tuned, reflecting the different historical, institutional and structural background of each economy.

The target regions of the analysis are East and Southeast Asia, Latin America, and Central and Eastern Europe, focusing on middle-income countries such as Korea, Thailand, Mexico, Chile, Argentina, Brazil, Hungary, Poland and the Czech Republic (hereafter "target countries"). Despite the strong converging force of the market-based policy package, the three regions differ in the way they have applied the policies, reflecting differences in state-private sector relationships as well as differences in the trajectory of their economic policy and private-sector behavior.

This book consists of three parts. Part I deals with globalization and the resulting framework of global governance, focusing on the multilateral and regional framework for managing development and transition. Part II turns to economic restructuring, where national governments and the private sector have been struggling to meet the changing economic environment. Focuses are on such fields of economic restructuring as financial sector restructuring, corporate restructuring and foreign direct investment (FDI). Part III deals with social policy reform in the three target regions. Together, they provide a thorough overview of the challenges confronting developing and transitional economies at the beginning of the twenty-first century. The remainder of this introduction presents a brief description of each of the subsequent chapters. The final section offers a concise summary of the main messages of the book.

Challenges to global governance

Part I deals with the multilateral and regional framework for managing development and transition. Globalization in the 1990s deeply influenced the existing multilateral framework for global governance, and many proposals were made to renovate it either by improving the existing framework or by establishing supplementary regional frameworks. The four chapters in this part of the book examine these challenges and proposals for reinventing global and regional framework for managing development and transition in the twenty-first century.

Haider Khan (Chapter 1) deals with the IMF and regional financial architectures. Financial liberalization and financial crises in the 1990s posed a new set of challenges to these institutions. One critical challenge relates to the policy diagnoses and policy prescriptions they give to national governments on how to conduct financial liberalization. In addition to neo-classical prescriptions, these institutions came to put much more emphasis on institutional and structural underpinnings supporting a liberalized financial sector.[2] A second challenge concerns crisis management. Most agree that crises are inevitable even when national governments introduce stringent prudential regulation of the liberalized financial sector. One realistic measure to deal with financial crises is to build up monitoring and early warning mechanisms at national, regional and multinational levels, and to work out a procedure for dealing with bankruptcy and liquidation in a swift manner. This leads us to the discussion of an alternative regional financial architecture to supplement the IMF.

Based on the theory of evolutionary economics, Khan presents a case for a hybrid form of global financial architecture (GFA) that allows for the existence and co-evolution of regional financial architectures (RFAs) with the IMF. The most important steps ever taken in this direction are a series of regional financial initiatives after the Asian Financial Crisis: the Manila Framework Group Meeting, the ASEAN surveillance process, the ASEAN+3 surveillance process and the Chiangmai Initiative. This modest beginning needs to evolve into a workable RFA, and this requires both the willingness of the IMF that the RFA should have a certain degree of autonomy, and the viability and cooperation at the national level among the members of the RFA. A set of realistic reforms of the IMF together with the formation of RFAs will, he concludes, offer the best chance for the global economy to achieve both stability and prosperity.

Masahiro Kawai (Chapter 2) discusses the changing role of the multilateral development banks (MDBs), including the World Bank and regional development banks. He starts from the fact that these organizations are now facing a challenge greater than ever before, to enable poorer countries to catalyze successful integration into the global economy and, at the same time, help reduce poverty, income inequality and the socioeconomic tensions created by such integration. Globalization can be a driving force for economic growth, poverty reduction and global income inequality reduction, if accompanied by complementary policy and institutional reforms and a better investment climate. This is where the MDBs must play a new role as "knowledge banks" and "public goods-providing banks," in addition to their traditional function as "money banks," financing development and crisis-resolution. They must provide knowledge on best practices fine-tuned to the specific needs of a particular country. Also, provision of certain types of international public goods by the MDBs can be essential to the economic development of developing countries. Some examples of such public goods include: transportation infrastructure that goes across borders; containment of communicable diseases; environmental protection; prevention of serious impacts of natural disasters hitting several countries; and containment of conflict that has the potential to become a cross-border issue.

Focusing on the World Bank, Kawai analyzes a series of its recent initiatives toward this new direction, such as the Comprehensive Development Framework (CDF) and Poverty Reduction Strategy Papers (PRSP).[3] He puts emphasis on the fact that these initiatives are comprehensive and long term, and require an active role of an effective, transparent and accountable government. He concludes that development assistance provided by the MDBs needs to extend well beyond the "Washington Consensus," to address multi-dimensional policy considerations, including the realignment of policies and institutions to maximize its effectiveness.

Kazuyori Ito (Chapter 3) asks whether and to what extent the GATT/WTO contributed to political democratization and economic liberalization in the target countries. He argues that the GATT did not lead these countries to trade liberalization because many of them were not members, and those who were members were allowed to maintain protectionism. Nonetheless, he argues, protectionism and state intervention led to ever-growing economic distortions, which contributed to the eventual collapse of the authoritarian, protectionist regimes in the 1980s in Latin America. Ito calls this the indirect convergent function of the GATT. The WTO, with its worldwide membership and broader issue coverage, has pressed the MDT countries to harmonize their economic policies with those of developed members and has provided technical assistance to achieve this goal. At the same time, however, due to the differences in historical, institutional and regional backgrounds, the target countries have pursued different paths of democratization and liberalization, and the WTO has provided flexibility to allow this. Thus, Ito concludes, the WTO has had a diversifying effect. The future challenge for the WTO is how to promote active involvement of the target countries in the WTO framework without marginalizing them.[4]

Isidro Morales (Chapter 4) focuses on regional economic integration, particularly the North American Free Trade Agreement (NAFTA), as a key strategy for advancing and expanding a regulatory framework for global governance. As the current proliferation of regional trade agreements shows,[5] regional economic integration has become an important means of promoting trade and investment liberalization. NAFTA was unique in the sense that it was considered by the US to be an interface between multilateral and bilateral trade/investment policies, and between a North–South agenda.

To make its balance-sheet, Morales argues, the NAFTA has made the protectionist pressures of the US more manageable, though some deep-rooted protectionist interests persist, as in the case of decades-old softwood lumber dispute between the US and Canada. Also, NAFTA has disproportionately empowered private investors vis-à-vis governments by means of the investor-to-state dispute settlement procedure under Chapter 11. He finally discusses the possibility of deepening and widening the NAFTA. Again, the US priorities will be a decisive factor.

Financial crisis and restructuring

The opportunities and risks of globalization were felt more seriously in the financial sector than elsewhere in the economy. In their efforts toward financial liberalization, most of the target countries relaxed external and internal financial controls in the 1990s, and their domestic financial systems became far more integrated into the world financial market. At the same time, relaxing financial controls often led to macroeconomic instability (Caprio *et al.* 2001) and intensified competition between local and foreign financial institutions, in which the latter more often prevailed over the former. Without adequate regulation and control, however, the liberalized financial sector might become more vulnerable to exogenous shocks and turbulences, which was dramatically shown by the crises in Mexico, Asia, Russia and, most recently, Argentina.

The first two chapters in Part II deal with this issue. **Barbara Stallings (Chapter 5)** begins with a comparative analysis of financial sector development and restructuring in Latin America and East Asia, focusing mainly on Chile and South Korea, which have the most successful domestic financial sectors in their respective regions. The most interesting point is the increasing convergence between the financial systems in these two economies, which would not have been expected a decade ago. Chile has shown that Latin American countries can match East Asia in the size of financial markets, but it grew in ways that were more typical of best practices found in Anglo-Saxon countries than those of the Asian tradition, such as tight and opaque links between finance, government and firms. Korea has now taken the lead in Asia of moving in a similar direction, due to both the financial crisis of 1997–8 and a longer-term trend of financial liberalization that dates from the 1980s.

An important remaining difference concerns the question of credit access for small and medium-size enterprises (SMEs), in which Korean SMEs enjoy better conditions, perhaps attributable partly to the continuation of government controls in Korea, and partly to commercial banks' new focus on profitability. Since finance for SMEs is a topic of great interest for most Latin American countries, she concludes, Korea's experience in this area might provide some insight for that region. Likewise, Chile's successful management of its market-based financial sector over the last two decades could offer useful lessons for Asia.

As a follow-up to Stallings' general argument, **Choong Yong Ahn (Chapter 6)** provides an empirical study of financial liberalization, financial crisis and financial restructuring in Korea. Expanding on Stallings' analysis, Ahn describes what Korea has accomplished in terms of restructuring its financial and corporate sectors since the crisis of 1997. A special focus is given to how Korea has cleaned up the non-performing loans accumulated in the financial sector. Because of the intertwined nature of the financial and corporate sectors, he also addresses several important restructuring issues of still highly leveraged corporations, which are so critically linked to the creation of sound and robust financial institutions.

Corporate restructuring and FDI

Globalization in the 1990s offered both opportunities and risks to the private sector in the target countries. However, the challenges to the private sector, as well as its responses, varied in each country, reflecting the different historical, institutional and politico-economic backgrounds. One of the responses commonly pursued by the target countries was corporate restructuring and promotion of FDI, though the results of these initiatives varied, depending on many factors. The following four chapters in Part II deal with these issues.

Akira Suehiro (Chapter 7) conducts an extensive comparison of East Asia and Latin America with respect to the role of private firms and economic reforms in overcoming the crisis. In Latin America, economic liberalization was based on "first generation Washington Consensus" policies, which centered on macroeconomic changes (Williamson 1990), and governments hardly touched on corporate restructuring. As a result, many state enterprises and large local firms were taken over by leading multilateral corporations. By contrast, economic reforms in East Asia after the crisis of 1997 put a priority on institutional development, or "second generation Washington Consensus" policies.

Nonetheless, in practice, Suehiro argues, corporate reform in East Asia has not always been conducted according to that prescription. Taking Thailand as an interesting example, he describes how a reformist government was replaced by a neo-populist, inward-looking one, which took the teeth of the Anglo-American model of corporate reform. This is, of course, not the end of the story. He concludes that East Asian countries and Latin American countries are facing a fundamental problem of how to coordinate their internal requirements with globalization in order to achieve sustainable growth.

Keun Lee (Chapter 8) analyzes family-controlled business groups as an organizational device for development and transition. He argues that the classical separation of ownership and control is an exception rather than a principle, and that it is more common around the world to have family-controlled firms often taking the form of business groups. He then poses two questions: why are these business groups developing in so many countries, and what went wrong with many of them?

Concerning the first question, Lee presents a "developmental device" view of business groups, whose main strength is to facilitate entry into formerly monopolized markets by mobilizing financial resources, technology and brand names. On the other hand, Lee's answer to the second question provides a rather cautious assessment of the role of business groups in development and transition. Based on an in-depth analysis of Korean business groups (chaebol), he asserts that while the business groups are effective in responding to market failure or economic catch-up, these benefits come with long-term risks. Specifically, the benefits of economic value creation by the business groups tend to decline over the long run as institutions evolve and markets mature. Family-controlled business groups tend to be subject to increasingly serious agency problems resulting in value-destroying, inefficient investment drives, and finally, the existence of business groups in an economy might hamper the sound development of a competitive market economy by distorting and manipulating the course of liberalization and deregulation.

The last two chapters deal with FDI as a key engine for development and transition. However, their messages are not as promising as those expected by most policy makers in the target countries. In many cases, FDI inflows have been disappointingly low. Even when FDI inflows have been positive, the form and content of FDI have been such that their innovative effects are limited, and they often create market distortions. This poses a serious challenge to policy makers, namely, how to attract innovative and non-market distorting FDI inflows.

Ferraz, Valente and Iootty (Chapter 9) examine how and to what extent economic liberalization has influenced ownership change and brought inward internationalization of companies in Latin America. After illustrating the global and regional trend in the internationalization of capital, they analyze ownership change in Argentina, Mexico, Chile and Brazil in the 1990s, featuring privatization and mergers and acquisitions (M&A), which led to significant ownership restructuring and changes in corporate control in the region.

As a result, they observe, Latin America is facing a development paradox since history tells us that local capital and local innovation capabilities have been crucial features of successful and sustained economic and social development. They conclude that policy makers in the region are facing challenges as to how to promote a national regime of incentives and regulations inductive to activities that generate qualifying jobs in a context of open economies and ownership internationalization.

One of the important policy questions for developing and transitional economies is what the host government can do to attract FDI. **Yuko Kinoshita and Nauro Campos (Chapter 10)** try to answer this question by examining the locational determinants of FDI in 25 transition economies in Central and Eastern Europe by utilizing panel data between 1990 and 1998.

They tested three categories of determinants: country-specific advantages such as low-cost labor, large local market, skilled labor force, sufficient infrastructure and proximity to the West; macroeconomic policy and policy that facilitates business operation; and the agglomeration effect of foreign investment. To test their weight in the determination of FDI location, they adopt the generalized method of moments (GMM) technique proposed by Arellano and Bond (1991), with a fixed-effects model as the supplementary method for comparison.

The results of the regression analysis can be summarized as follows: (1) Agglomeration effects are the most significant determinant of FDI inflows in the region. The effect is greater in CIS countries than in non-CIS countries, perhaps due to insufficient information about local conditions. (2) The degree of external liberalization is another strong determinant in non-CIS countries. (3) Poor quality of the bureaucracy in the host country is found to be a deterrent factor, even after controlling for agglomeration effects. This last finding has important policy implications as to what the host government can do to attract FDI. Once a host country secures macroeconomic stability in its early stage of transition, the institutional dimension of the transition process (such as improving bureaucratic quality) becomes more important when a country tries to promote FDI. This conclusion is reinforced by the analyses of Suehiro (Chapter 7), Lee (Chapter 8), and Ferraz *et al.* (Chapter 9) on East Asia and Latin America.

Challenges to social policy

Until the end of the 1980s, the three target regions proceeded along different paths in the field of social policy. In Latin America, under corporatist governments such as the Valgas Administration in Brazil (1930–8) and the Peron Administration in Argentina (1946–55), social insurance systems were developed so that by the 1970s almost all workers in the formal sector had been covered. In contrast, East Asia, except Japan, was characterized by low social expenditures, and the social insurance systems offered limited coverage, supplemented by family support. Central European social policy under the communist regime was an inseparable part of a total political and economic system. In return for political subjugation, people were provided by the party-state with "full and quasi-obligatory employment, universal social insurance and a highly developed, typically company-based system of services and fringe benefits" (Esping-Andersen 1996: 9). In the 1990s, however, these regions implemented drastic reforms of social policy, and one of the common causes was the market-based prescription provided by the IMF and the World Bank. Did this result in convergence of social policy in these regions? Or, did regional differences persist due to institutional and other legacies peculiar to each region? The three chapters in Part III deal with this issue.

Koichi Usami (Chapter 11) analyzes social security reform in Latin America in the 1990s. According to Usami, this reform, especially in pensions and health care, allowed the incorporation of the private sector into the formerly public social insurance system. Many Latin American governments also tried to introduce market principles into social security policy. This process went in the same direction as the economic policy change, as it shifted from the import substitution industrialization model to the market-oriented model. In addition, weakened labor unions lost their power to sustain the former public social security policy. International financial institutions such as the IMF and the World Bank supported this process through austerity programs. Under these circumstances, social security reforms have been achieved by strong "delegative democracy" type governments (O'Donnell 1997: 293–7).

However, Usami asserts, there has not been a complete shift in Latin American social security system to a market model. In the case of pension systems, most countries adopted a combination system, which introduced a private capitalization system into a reformed public pay-as-you-go system. At the same time, political legacies constrained the reform, as in the case of slow medical insurance reform in Argentina or slow pension system reform in Brazil. He finally observes the active role of civil society in the implementation of urgent anti-crisis social assistance in crisis-hit Argentina. With the demise of labor unions, the Latin American social security system of the twenty-first century needs a new social power for its reform and implementation, and civil society itself will have to bear this burden.

Yasuhiro Kamimura (Chapter 12) conducts a comparative analysis of East Asian welfare states. The economic crisis of 1997–8 promoted the debate on the welfare systems of the region. The policy prescriptions of international financial institutions, however, split between the one-size-fits-all approach and the country-specific approach. He, therefore, tries to overcome this split by answering three questions: Why have the social expenditures in the region been kept much lower than those of the advanced welfare states? Has the region followed a single trajectory of welfare development which can be labeled as the "East Asian welfare model?" Which direction(s) are the welfare systems of East Asian countries marching towards? How are they located in relation to the reform trajectories of the advanced welfare states?

His answer to the first question is that the young population structure of the region has enabled it to save on the cost of social welfare. However, he emphasizes, low expenditure does not mean that the welfare systems in the region are embryonic. There have been various social security schemes in the region, public, communal and private. Concerning the second question, he concludes that it is difficult to identify the "East Asian welfare model" common to all countries in the region. Taking Asian NIES before 1980s, for example, there was a wide difference in the development of social security schemes, according to whether inclusionary corporatism had been established or not. Finally, concerning the third question, he observes that the welfare systems of East Asian countries are changing, stimulated by democratization and economic crisis. The magnitude and direction of the change, however, seem to vary among countries, depending on the character of democratization and the legacy of inclusionary corporatism.

Takumi Horibayashi (Chapter 13) analyzes the characteristics of the Central European welfare systems, focusing on those of Poland, Hungary and the Czech Republic. After describing the main features of the traditional communist welfare systems in these countries, he traces the formation and transformation of welfare systems since the political change of 1989. In the early stage of the reform, emergency measures were introduced to deal with the social costs of transformation such as mass unemployment, widespread poverty and deteriorating living standards. This process overlapped with a transition to the three-tier system prevalent in Western Europe, consisting of social insurance plans, universal benefits and social assistance policies. Then, since the mid-1990s, the neo-classical approach to social policy, inspired by the World Bank, became visible in the region, the core of which was comprised of two elements: the targeting of welfare benefits provision to the truly needy, and the privatization of the pension system in Hungary and Poland. The Czech Republic maintained its public pension system because it did not face serious financial problems.

Although the neo-classical approach has become a notable element of post-communist social policy in the region, he concludes, it has failed to permeate deeply into society due to the legacies of the communist era. People continued to expect a strong commitment to welfare from the state, and have resisted attempts by post-communist welfare regimes to move toward a more residualist welfare state. Finally, he poses an important question for future research. Now that the three countries have joined the EU, their future social policy and welfare system depend not only on their own choice but also on the EU's choice: whether they seek a "European social model" or they aim only to be a winner in global economic competition.

Challenges of globalization: a continuing agenda

Globalization in the 1990s brought about more challenges than opportunities for developing and transitional economies in many cases. Stakeholders at every level of development and transition sought to find ways to adapt to the changing international economic environment, which necessitated rethinking the adequacy of their traditional strategies and institutions. A market-based policy package for economic restructuring, often accompanied by market-based social policy reform and promoted by the international financial institutions and major actors in the industrial world, became one of the most important guiding principles in this process. While providing a number of benefits, it was far from being a panacea. Rather, it had to be modified and reformulated to meet the different historical, institutional and structural settings of each country. Based on empirical and comparative analyses, this book will show the readers varied approaches taken in the target countries.

The message of the book is simple. There is no single, universal prescription for managing development and transition. Each country must invent its own optimal level of state-market relationship. Financial and corporate restructuring was a common feature of the 1990s. However, its content and sequencing differed considerably, as did its effectiveness in achieving growth, stability and equity. Social policy had to be reformed in the direction of privatization, but to varying degrees. In sum, the challenge was to tailor an optimal strategy for development and transition, taking into consideration specific historical, institutional and structural settings of each economy, rather than to adopt a universal prescription.

The challenge is not over. Though some of the countries that experienced serious crises in the 1990s have recovered, many are still struggling to find better ways for managing development and transition. These processes must be analyzed continuously. Based on further empirical analyses, models of best practice must be sought, rather than a single, universal model. This book, therefore, is not an end in itself. Rather, it must be the first step for finding better ways for managing development and transition.

Notes

1 The best-known exposition of these policies is contained in the book by John Williamson (1990), in which he introduced the term "Washington Consensus." In the wake of the Asian Financial Crisis, several policy items were added to the prescription; these were sometimes referred to as the post-Washington Consensus. See, for example, Rodrik (2001) and Chapters 2 (Kawai) and 7 (Suehiro) of this volume. Recently, Williamson (2003) has published a new volume, entitled "After the Washington Consensus."
2 This new focus has led to the establishment of standards and codes of good practice on data dissemination and transparency in monetary and financial policies. See Uzan (2001).
3 For a concise explanation of the PRSP, see IMF (2003).
4 As is shown by the failure of the 2001 WTO Cancún Ministerial Conference to set the modalities of the Doha Development Agenda, this is no easy task, given the strong distrust of developing countries as to the welfare-enhancing effect of the WTO. See Howse (2001: 365–8).
5 The number of regional trade agreements reported to the GATT/WTO more than doubled after January 1995 (from about 120 to 250). See WTO, Regional trade agreements [http://www.wto.org/english/tratop_e/region_e/region_e.htm].

References

Arellano, M. and Bond, S. (1991) "Some Tests of Specification for Panel Data: Monte Carlo Evidence and an Application to Employment Equation," *Review of Economic Studies*, 58: 277–97.
Caprio, G., Hanson, J.A. and Honohan, P. (2001) "Introduction and Overview: The Case for Liberalization and Some Drawbacks," in G. Caprio, P. Honohan and J.E. Stiglitz (eds) *Financial Liberalization: How Far, How Fast?*, Cambridge: Cambridge University Press.
Esping-Andersen, G. (1996) "After the Golden Age? Welfare State Dilemmas in a Global Economy," in G. Esping-Andersen (ed.) *Welfare States in Transition*, London: Sage Publications.

Frankel, J. (2000) "Globalization of the Economy," in J.S. Nye and J.D. Donahue (eds) *Governance in a Globalizing World*, Washington, DC: The Brookings Institution.
Grindle, M.S. (2000) "Ready or Not: The Developing World and Globalization," in J.S. Nye and J.D. Donahue (eds) *Governance in a Globalizing World*, Washington, DC: The Brookings Institution.
Howse, R. (2001) "The Legitimacy of the World Trade Organization," in J. Coicaud and V. Heiskanen (eds) *The Legitimacy of International Organizations*, Tokyo: The United Nations University Press.
IMF (2000) *Globalization: Threat or Opportunity?*, IMF Issue Brief, April, Washington, DC: IMF.
—— (2003) *Poverty Reduction Strategy Papers: A Factsheet*, September, Washington, DC: IMF.
O'Donnell, G. (1997) "Democracia delegativa?" in G. O'Donnell (ed.) *Contrapunto*, Buenos Aires: Paidós.
Rodrik, D. (2001) *The Global Governance of Trade as if Development Really Mattered*, New York: UNDP.
Uzan, M. (2001) "The Process towards the New International Financial Architecture," in J. Coicaud and V. Heiskanen (eds) *The Legitimacy of International Organizations*, Tokyo: The United Nations University Press.
Williamson, J. (1990) *The Progress of Policy Reform in Latin America*, Washington, DC: Institute for International Economics.
—— (ed.) (2003) *After the Washington Consensus: Restarting Growth and Reform in Latin America*, Washington, DC: Institute for International Economics.
World Bank (1993) *The East Asian Miracle: Economic Growth and Public Policy*, New York: Oxford University Press.
—— (1998) *East Asia: The Road to Recovery*, Washington, DC: World Bank.

Part I
Globalization and global governance

1 Managing global risks and creating prosperity

The role of the IMF and regional financial architectures

Haider A. Khan

Introduction

The Asian Financial Crisis (hereafter AFC) and the contagion it created unleashed a process of questioning the wisdom of the standard recipe of the Washington Consensus. This is still continuing; but the real costs of the crises have forced on the policy agenda the question of what kinds of national and international policies and institutions are appropriate during the current period and in the foreseeable future. In this chapter, I will discuss the problems of national macroeconomic policies and governance within a framework of overall global and regional financial architectures. Whether state capacities exist for the formulation and implementation of national economic policies may depend in large measure on the kind of global and regional financial architecture in existence.

The methodological approach adopted here is that of evolutionary economics. The institutions I discuss and the alternatives I propose are all path dependent. They all also depend on a supporting structure of complementary institutional network (CIN).[1] Global financial architecture (GFA) and Regional financial architecture (RFA) both depend on their respective CIN within a global system of nation states. Given the real interdependence within the system, all actors have some stake in sustained growth and stability with equity. Thus the central argument of this paper is that sustainable policies at the national level require a supporting network of GFA and RFAs. Such national policies in their turn can contribute to the sustainability of the GFA and RFA. It can be shown that following an evolutionary theory of international financial institutions, two broad types of possible Global Financial Architectures can be identified.[2] In this paper, following Khan (2002c) the first is called an *overarching type*, exemplified by the classical gold standard and the defunct Bretton Woods system. The second is called a *hybrid form* that allows for the existence and coevolution of some Regional Financial Architectures as well. The changing roles of the IMF and national economic policies can be examined within these two possible financial architectures under globalization.

The role of structural unevenness in the global economy is particularly important to recognize within the proposed framework of analysis. The range of economies, the types of polities, the institutional capacities and resource endowments including technological progress and capacities for innovation all vary widely. A simple system of gold standard or adjustable peg or free and flexible exchange rate together with free multilateral trade under, say, the WTO arrangement may therefore be simplistic. It may better serve the needs of one group of actors, for example, the advanced economies with well-developed financial services sectors, than some others. How best to achieve a synchronized growth and development regime that is perceived to be fair by all is indeed a challenging problem. The GFA is defined here as a system of global financial arrangements for international payments with specific rules and procedures for the member nations to follow. If there exists a similar institutional arrangement at the supranational but regional level only then I call it an RFA. It will be seen that one attractive solution to the problem of global unevenness is to design a GFA which also includes a number of RFAs as an integral part of the global financial system.

An important initial distinction also needs to be made between the crisis management and crisis prevention tasks of GFA and RFAs. Of course, prevention, as the old bromide goes, is better than cure. Therefore, the GFA and RFAs are to be judged optimal in the sense of achieving the highest probability of prevention subject to the constraints of the system. However, it is not clear that the best GFA and RFAs from this perspective are also the best in promoting growth or managing crisis. For example at one extreme, an autarchic system may never have a crisis, but may not promote much growth. If there is a crisis because of domestic moral hazards and adverse selection problems, it may be difficult to manage because capabilities do not exist for crisis management under the assumption that these crises are rare events. But there could be GFAs and RFAs that can potentially develop the capacity for both better crisis management and crisis prevention. In a world of bounded rationality and institutional uncertainty, there may be considerable room for improvement along both the dimensions in an evolutionary sense. However, in such a world the application of the pragmatic principle of prudence would support the development of crisis management capacities at all times, since it will be difficult to prevent crises entirely under any type of open economy GFA and RFAs. The main goals, pragmatically speaking, are to minimize financial and economic instabilities while facilitating global payments, trade and investments.

Globalization, marketization and the role of global capital markets[3]

Globalization of financial markets has increased the flow of various types of capital across the borders. Observers have cautioned about the adverse effects on market stability. Indeed, even as marketization of finance across borders proceeds rapidly substantial instability is manifest in the global financial markets. As resistance to further marketization without regulation grows, the instabilities are likely to spread and result in political and social instabilities as well.[4] For this reason alone, it may be wise to adopt a new and more pragmatic approach to GFA that can help policy making for greater well-being in the nations of the world. As mentioned before, this will help prevent a third type of crisis: a political and social crisis. The developments in Indonesia during the AFC illustrate how suddenly such crises can break out. The evolutionary theory developed here actually suggests a pragmatic path-dependent institution-building approach to a hybrid GFA. But the process is likely to be quite complex.

It is because of such complexities that the term "globalization" which is so much in vogue today has to be used with caution. When viewed historically, it appears that globalization is a contradictory process of international economic integration that was severely interrupted by the First World War, the Great Depression and the Second World War. The emergence of the Bretton Woods framework can be seen as a way to integrate the world with respect to trade while controlling the flow of private capital. The demise of Bretton Woods has set in motion forces of capital account liberalization that are often the most visible aspects of "globalization." However, even this process is fraught with new instabilities as evidenced by the Mexican and – more recently and even more dramatically – by the Asian Financial Crisis. At the same time integration of trade even within the standard neoclassical Heckscher–Ohlin–Samuelson model would imply a fall in the wages of unskilled workers of the North thus increasing inequality there (Krugman 1996). The South is supposed to experience a more equalizing effect through trade; but empirically, there is very little evidence of this happening. Therefore, it is necessary to treat the rhetoric of globalization with caution. At best, we are experiencing a "fractured" globalization. Integration of financial markets, for example, can lead to great benefits for all in a truly liberal world of equal actors. However, in a world of unevenness the evolutionary paths may lead to crisis unless institutions are designed properly. Leaving everything to the markets may produce the supreme irony of ultimately leading to crises which prevent some very important capital and commodity markets from functioning.

For these reasons, it is best to ask what roles the global capital markets are supposed to perform in a world of free capital mobility. The functions are variously described, but mainly emphasize the transfer of resources from savers to investors globally. In addition, the agglomeration of capital, selection of projects, monitoring, contract enforcement, risk sharing and pooling of risks are also mentioned. All these are legitimate functions of capital markets. However, despite much talk the crucial problem of handling various kinds of risks and the inability of simple free markets with international capital mobility are nearly always elided. What are some of the most important of these risks?

Exchange rate risk refers to the possibility that a country's currency may experience a precipitous decline in value. This risk is present in any type of exchange rate regime, with full or even partial currency convertibility. Both floating exchange rates and pegging a currency to another single currency, or even a basket of currencies present such exchange rate risk to various degrees.

Capital flight risk refers to the possibility that both domestic and foreign holders of financial assets will sell their holdings whenever there is an expectation of a capital loss. Exchange rate risk is one possible avenue through which such expectations may be formed. As with many types of expectations formation mechanisms, in a world of nonlinearity, bounded rationality and uncertainty, a Keynesian type of short-termism takes over. Investors head for the exit simply on the basis of short-term calculations of possible loss, and herd behavior is a likely outcome. Financial distress follows for the hapless country from which capital thus exits in a hurry. In the extreme situation of large short-term liabilities, the affected economy may land in a full-blown financial or even economic crisis.

There is thus a systemic risk of financial fragility associated with the above risks, and the stability of the financial and political institutions. This type of systemic risk raises the possibility of a financial meltdown. In case of the AFC, the risk of financial fragility increased over the 1990s through maturity mismatch of loans. The fact that many of the short-term loans were in foreign currencies without risk-sharing mechanisms such as currency swaps in place, created further exchange rate risk, which also increased the potential systemic risk. This is consistent with the view of Knight (1998), who affirms that although globalization has brought about spectacular increase in the flow of capital to emerging markets, the AFC demonstrates that it can also create financial instability and contagion. Under fairly realistic conditions, the banking system of emerging economies can respond in ways that worsen the impact of adverse shocks, causing severe macroeconomic repercussions and exacerbating systemic financial and economic fragility.

In the case of the AFC, we also witnessed a fourth kind of risk for vulnerable economies that others have also recognized.[5] This is the risk of contagion.[6] Some countries were unnecessarily victimized simply because expectations moved against their economic prospects as their neighbors experienced financial fragility and capital flight. This has important implications for both global and regional financial architecture. Both GFA and RFAs should try to minimize the contagion risk. Contagion can happen even without much financial and trade openness. However, the more integrated with the rest of the world, or even a region, an economy is, the more is the risk of contagion. There is some theoretical support for this last proposition in specific markets that are being globalized. For example, some argue that the globalization of securities markets can promote contagion among investors by weakening incentives of gathering costly country-specific information because the marginal benefit of gathering information may be decreasing as securities markets become more global in scope.[7]

The key problem which underlies the above risk scenarios, long recognized by the practitioners before theorists started to study it, is that given informational problems and the cost of building enforcing institutions, capital markets are almost always incomplete. Thus classical theorems of welfare economics no longer apply even within a closed economy. In a world of open economies these problems become more severe, and are directly related to the lack of global institutions of governance. The recognition of this point underlies the various proposals advanced so far. There are already many proposals for GFAs on the table.[8] Even a partial cataloging will have to include the many national proposals (e.g. US, UK, French and Canadian), private proposals such as Soros' credit insurance agency, Edward's specialized agencies, Bergsten's target zones and so on, and other international proposals. Among the international proposals could be included the IMF proposals, G7 and G22 proposals. Although they vary in scope and degrees of political realism, they share one feature in common. All of them fall into the *overarching type* of GFA category.

Although many of the proposals for GFA are possible theoretical solutions, the evolutionary approach looks at path dependence and sequential selection processes as crucial. We need to recognize that the actual evolution of such institutions of financial governance will depend crucially on coordination among the actors, in particular among some key actors in the global system. This leads us to the consideration of an evolutionary structural theory of GFA and RFAs.

An evolutionary theory of GFA: two evolutionary types of GFA

In order to motivate the discussion, we can return to some aspects of the AFC. In distinguishing among the countries that managed to survive the AFC and those that did not, John Williamson, one of the proponents of the "Washington Consensus," pointed out that whether or not these countries had liberalized their capital accounts could be construed as crucial. Those that had not, survived.[9]

All Asian crisis countries had accepted the IMF's Article VIII obligations, as evident from the historical documents. But as some have pointed out, liberalizing the trade and liberalizing the financial sector have different policy implications.[10] In line with the discussion in the previous section, theoretically, one should carefully distinguish the welfare impacts of financial market liberalization in an uneven world from such impact in a smooth world of equals with information symmetry. Indeed, next to unevenness, the most critical element is the role and the presence of *asymmetric information*. In a financial market, gathering, selecting, using and providing information are central to its proper functioning, yet it is precisely here that market failures from asymmetric information can arise.[11]

But the evolutionary structural theory goes further than simply cataloging moral hazard and adverse selection problems. On the *explanans* side are also *the asymmetries in the size, structure and capabilities of the economies and polities*. These asymmetries constrain some polities, particularly the economically disadvantaged ones, from developing as quickly as possible in an equitable manner. The recent UNCTAD report on the poorest underdeveloped countries points this out empirically.[12] The theoretical significance of these features of the real world is that no uniform set of rules can work for all the economies and polities in the world. A fortiori, it follows that for GFA and RFAs to serve these poor countries as well as the rich countries equally well, special provisions should be in place.

It may appear that the least developed countries are only a special case. But that is not the case. The NIEs, the European social democracies, Japan and so on, each in its own way, is also different. This poses the real theoretical challenge: how can we even attempt to theorize in the face of such diversity? The way out is through a consideration of the basic needs of the system and asking if these can be satisfied better under arrangements that are different from the IMF and the "Washington Consensus."

Recent work by Barry Eichengreen and others shows that it is possible to move beyond the post Bretton Woods situation.[13] In contrast with the conservative Meltzer report, all of these authors emphasize the need to strengthen the IMF in certain dimensions. However, not all of them recognize the crucial need also for the RFAs and the role they can play in creating an enabling environment for the state to implement beneficial economic policies. A completely evolutionary theory of GFA recognizes the need for RFAs from both an *evolutionary* and a *structural* perspective. Given the lack of political resolve, a point made forcefully by Eichengreen among others, there is little chance of creating *institutional structures* in the manner of the 1944 Bretton Woods agreement. The recent path of the world economy does not lead to this immediately. At the same time, the recent path does not lead only to neoliberalism. It is possible to both reform the IMF, as Eichengreen suggests, and to create new RFAs to complement such reforms. Thus this theory leads to the question of identifying a spectrum of GFAs. Most important among these are those that combine the GFAs like a reformed IMF with appropriate RFAs.

Formally, the heuristic argument presented above can be established via a careful consideration of *path dependence* during evolution of the GFA. In order to do this in a conceptually rigorous manner, the concept of *path dependence* itself has to be refined and formalized in a specific way. I have developed this idea elsewhere, and will only sketch the conceptual path to be followed briefly.[14] Briefly, there can be completely deterministic (CD), completely stochastic (CS) and partially deterministic (PD) characterizations of path dependence. Eschewing the formal apparatus of graph theory and neural network dynamics which can be used to describe these rigorously, we can simply say that in deterministic path dependence there is only one choice of path. Everything is as it should be, since there are no bifurcations at any point in history. In fact, we can make a stronger statement. At *no* point in history is there even a *possibility* of even a bifurcation. Most people will see this as an extreme, and in the case of human institutional design, perhaps as an unrealistic case.

The purely stochastic case is all *random mutation*. Again, there is no way that conscious choice can play a role here. Blind chance determines the outcome. The last type of path dependence, that is, the PD variety, leaves some room for evolution to be a result of at least some kind of boundedly rational human activity. In this case, a complex set of human activities including learning and improving policy-making capabilities can influence which network of paths are followed over time. While the number of available paths at any point in history may be large, they are never infinite. Therefore, combinatorial mathematics will in most cases show the existence of the most likely evolutionary outcome. However, the caveat that large, seemingly random fluctuations (e.g. a war) can throw these calculations off is always a (rare) possibility.

Fortunately, barring such events as wars, revolutions, complete meltdowns of financial systems and so on, there are not at present an unmanageably large number of outcomes that are possible for the GFA. In fact, if we are willing to assume a continuum with nothing but an overarching *global* architecture for international finance with regional impurities added as another type, we have just two types of possible evolutionary outcomes for the institutional history of GFAs from a theoretical point of view. In terms of Aoki's theory of comparative institutional analysis framed in evolutionary game theory, there are multiple institutional equilibria; but the selection process specified here leaves only two broad types of equilibria to be considered.[15]

The first type, which can be created at special evolutionary moments, can be called *Overarching GFAs*. Gold standard under the UK hegemony and Bretton Woods under the threats of a postwar depression are two examples. Recent history does not support the hope that such events are about to happen again. Therefore, a second type of evolutionary path resulting in a hybrid form should be recognized. This is the hybrid coexistence of a GFA together with one or many RFAs. We can call this type a *hybrid GFA* for shorthand reference. Once again, Asia after the AFC is a good place to begin the analysis.

In the Asian case, as many have observed, the financial sector liberalization followed the pre-AFC GFA by default. There were some short-term gains of the policy, but ultimately it resulted in severe instability. More generally, as Kaminsky and Reinhart show,[16] based on the episodes of 76 currency crises, of which 26 are also characterized by banking crises, financial sector liberalization can result in a boom-bust cycle by providing easy access to short-term financing. Proponents of liberalization suggest some sort of micro sequencing in order to prevent such adverse consequences. With some variations, the most commonly suggested sequence is: improve the quality of regulation, make sure it is enforced and then improve the supervisory mechanisms. Once the markets are liberalized, the level of a bank's minimum capital requirements can be brought closer to what the *Basle Accord* requires.

As one author, who, of course, does not use the same terminology as developed here, nevertheless points out, there is a contradiction in this type of GFA arrangement.[17]

But when the Asian crisis countries liberalized the financial sector in the 1980s, the aforementioned preconditions (assumptions) were not in place. Yet, they were rushed to liberalize by the IFI. Ironically, when at the early stage the policy showed favorable impacts, for example higher economic growth, greater access to financial services, the IFI applauded it. But when the crisis hit, the very same countries previously praised were swiftly placed into the category of those with misplaced development strategies. All of a sudden, nothing was right with these countries. When confronted with such an embarrassing contradiction, the international institutions are quick to claim that they actually *saw* the faults, and had *already reminded* the governments about the existing flaws (e.g. weak banking system, unsustainable exchange rate system, and widespread corruption).[18]

An IMF recommendation during this period led to the increase in interest rates. Because of the common prescription under the GFA, this occurred in all Asian crisis countries. Such high rates created more moral hazard and adverse selection problems, thus showing that the incentive system has indeed been altered, and led to the undertaking of bad risk by the banking sector. As Azis correctly points out:

> Under these circumstances, the amount of investment credits going to risky sector rose (adverse selection), the incidence of bail out in the absence of free-exit scheme also increased (moral hazard), and the subsequent banks' franchise values (expected returns) declined. All these are precisely what the "pre-conditions prior to liberalization" are expected to avoid. Thus, the implicit logic is inherently self-conflicting, i.e., expecting bank's prudent behavior while allowing "franchise value" to fall. The suggested preconditions, although seemingly logical, simply do not match with the prevailing institutional conditions.[19]

Azis points out further:

The IMF persistently argued for liberalizing the sector and meeting the pre-conditions simultaneously. A study by the Fund on the sequencing of capital account liberalization using the case of Chile, Korea, Indonesia and Thailand, for example, stresses the importance of proper sequencing if benefits from the liberalization are to be achieved and the risks to be minimized. The study also argues that financial sector liberalization, especially capital account liberalization, should be a part of a coordinated and comprehensive approach, in which the sequencing of regulatory and institutional reforms is critical. The design of macroeconomic and exchange rate policies should also play a vital role (Johnston *et al.* 1997). While intuitively making sense, such conclusions are too broad, far from being practical. No one would argue against the importance of making liberalization policy (or any policy for that matter) consistent with the prevailing macroeconomic policy. But how you do it remains unanswered. The information contained in such a study is of limited value to policy makers. Yet, while many countries still had problems to meet the stated preconditions, they were pushed to accelerate the liberalization policy by recommending one or two new measures to safeguard. <u>More often than not, these measures are based on the practice of developed countries that have different institutional conditions</u> [emphasis mine].[20]

Here the author correctly pinpoints the failure to recognize unevenness as a key feature of the failure of the IMF to prescribe the correct medicine. In fact, the IMF did much worse: it prescribed the wrong medicine, a set of measures that worsened the impact of the AFC. This situation illustrates the danger of being in the grip of a (pseudo-) universalistic theory that simply cannot be applied in the real world of unevenness without serious distortions that may cause great harm. An alternative is to work with our type-two hybrid combination of GFA and RFAs. Again, Asia can be used as an illustration. There are many aspects one could focus on; I choose to look at the debt and capital flows situation prior to the crisis in specific countries.

As both Tables 1.1 and 1.2 show, the borrowing in short-term market and the increased flow of foreign capital both occurred almost simultaneously in these countries. As the real exchange rate appreciated, competitiveness suffered, and vulnerability to sudden reversals of capital flows increased. It must be emphasized that these were systemic features that went largely unnoticed by the IMF or the private sector. As is well known, in a nonlinear system the vulnerability to sudden shocks is a logical possibility. In case of Asia, this became an empirical reality of nightmare proportions.

With most debtors being in the corporate sector during the AFC, the capacity to invest became severely constrained. The debt-deflation scenario

Table 1.1 External debt outstanding (US$ billions)

	1990	1991	1992	1993	1994	1995	1996
ASEAN-4							
External debt	144.3	166.1	180.9	194.1	221.8	257.0	274.5
Short-term debt	25.7	33.8	41.7	49.6	58.2	69.8	80.4
(% of total debt)	17.8	20.3	23.0	25.6	26.2	27.2	29.3
Long-term debt	118.6	132.3	139.2	144.5	163.6	187.2	194.1
(% of total debt)	82.2	79.7	77.0	74.4	73.8	72.8	70.7
Indonesia							
External debt	69.8	79.9	88.3	89.6	96.6	116.3	118.1
(% of GDP)	65.9	68.4	69.0	56.6	54.6	53.3	52.0
Short-term debt	11.1	14.3	18.1	18.0	17.1	24.3	29.3
(% of total debt)	15.9	17.9	20.5	20.1	17.7	20.9	24.8
Long-term debt	58.7	65.6	70.2	71.6	79.5	92.0	88.8
(% of total debt)	84.1	82.1	79.5	79.9	82.3	79.1	75.2
Debt-service ratio	30.9	32.0	31.6	33.8	30.0	33.7	33.0
Malaysia							
External debt	16.0	18.1	19.8	23.2	24.8	33.2	31.6
(% of GDP)	37.6	37.9	34.6	37.1	37.5	40.3	38.1
Short-term debt	1.9	2.1	3.6	6.9	6.2	7.3	7.5
(% of total debt)	11.9	11.6	18.2	29.8	25.0	22.0	23.7
Long-term debt	14.1	16.0	16.2	16.3	18.6	25.9	24.1
(% of total debt)	88.1	88.4	81.8	70.2	75.0	78.0	76.3
Debt-service ratio	10.3	7.7	6.6	7.7	7.7	6.1	6.0
Philippines							
External debt	30.3	32.2	33.3	35.7	39.3	39.5	45.7
(% of GDP)	69.1	71.5	62.3	66.1	61.3	53.2	56.0
Short-term debt	4.4	4.9	5.3	5.0	5.7	6.0	6.3
(% of total debt)	14.5	15.2	15.9	14.0	14.5	15.2	13.8
Long-term debt	25.9	27.3	28.0	30.7	33.6	33.5	39.4
(% of total debt)	85.5	84.8	84.1	86.0	85.5	84.8	86.2
Debt-service ratio	27.0	23.0	24.4	25.5	18.5	15.1	15.4
Thailand							
External debt	28.1	35.9	39.5	45.7	61.1	68.1	79.0
(% of GDP)	32.9	36.4	35.5	41.7	45.3	47.0	49.9
Short-term debt	8.3	12.5	14.7	19.7	29.2	32.2	37.3
(% of total debt)	29.5	34.8	37.2	43.1	47.8	47.3	47.2
Long-term debt	19.8	23.4	24.8	26.0	31.9	35.9	41.7
(% of total debt)	70.5	65.2	62.8	56.9	52.2	52.7	52.8
Debt-service ratio	16.9	13.0	13.7	18.5	15.6	11.7	14.5

Sources: Compiled by the author with data from International Financial Statistics (1997); World Debt Tables (1996).

became the reality because the price effects of depreciated exchange rates did not occur until much later, if at all. Hence, the initial currency crisis became first a more general financial crisis and then a full-blown economic crisis. In Indonesia it also became a social and political crisis.

The AFC showed that the composition of capital flows matters. The fact

Table 1.2 Net capital flows (% of GDP)

	1983–8	1989–95	1991	1992	1993	1994	1995	1996	1997
China									
Net private capital flows	1.2	2.5	1.7	−0.9	4.5	5.6	5.2	4.7	3.7
Net direct investment	0.4	2.9	0.9	1.7	5.3	5.9	4.8	4.6	4.3
Net portfolio investment	0.2	0.2	0.1	–	0.7	0.7	0.1	0.3	0.2
Other net investment	0.5	−0.6	0.7	−2.6	−1.5	−0.9	0.2	−0.3	−0.8
Net official flows	0.3	0.5	0.3	0.8	0.9	0.4	0.3	0.2	−0.1
Change in reserves	−0.4	−2.2	−3.7	0.5	−0.4	−5.6	−3.2	−4.0	−4.5
Indonesia									
Net private capital flows	1.5	4.2	4.6	2.5	3.1	3.9	6.2	6.3	1.6
Net direct investment	0.4	1.3	1.2	1.2	1.2	1.4	2.3	2.8	2.0
Net portfolio investment	0.1	0.4	–	–	1.1	0.6	0.7	0.8	−0.4
Other net investment	1.0	2.6	3.5	1.4	0.7	1.9	3.1	2.7	0.1
Net official flows	2.4	0.8	1.1	1.1	0.9	0.1	−0.2	−0.7	1.0
Change in reserves	–	−1.4	−2.4	−3.0	−1.3	0.4	−0.7	−2.3	1.8
Malaysia									
Net private capital flows	3.1	8.8	11.2	15.1	17.4	1.5	8.8	9.6	4.7
Net direct investment	2.3	6.5	8.3	8.9	7.8	5.7	4.8	5.1	5.3
Net portfolio investment	n.a.	n.a.	n.a.	n.a.	n.a.	n.a.	n.a.	n.a.	n.a.
Other net investment	0.8	2.3	2.9	6.2	9.7	−4.2	4.1	4.5	−0.6
Net official flows	0.3	–	0.4	−0.1	−0.6	0.2	−0.1	−0.1	−0.1
Change in reserves	−1.8	−4.7	−2.6	−11.3	−17.7	4.3	2.0	−2.5	3.6
Philippines									
Net private capital flows	−2.0	2.7	1.6	2.0	2.6	5.0	4.6	9.8	0.5
Net direct investment	0.7	1.6	1.2	1.3	1.6	2.0	1.8	1.6	1.4
Net portfolio investment	–	0.2	0.3	0.1	−0.1	0.4	0.3	−0.2	−5.3

continued

Table 1.2 continued

	1983–8	1989–95	1991	1992	1993	1994	1995	1996	1997
Other net investment	−2.7	0.9	0.2	0.6	1.1	2.5	2.4	8.5	4.5
Net official flows	2.4	2.0	3.3	1.9	2.3	0.8	1.4	0.2	0.8
Change in reserves	0.5	−1.1	−2.3	−1.5	−1.1	−1.9	−0.9	−4.8	2.1
Thailand									
Net private capital flows	3.1	10.2	10.7	8.7	8.4	8.6	12.7	9.3	−10.9
Net direct investment	0.8	1.5	1.5	1.4	1.1	0.7	0.7	0.9	1.3
Net portfolio investment	0.7	1.3	–	0.5	3.2	0.9	1.9	0.6	0.4
Other net investment	1.5	7.4	9.2	6.8	4.1	7.0	10.0	7.7	−12.6
Net official flows	0.7	–	1.1	0.1	0.2	0.1	0.7	0.7	4.9
Change in reserves	−1.4	−4.1	−4.3	−2.8	−3.2	−3.0	−4.4	−1.2	9.7

Source: Compiled by the author with data from *World Economic Outlook* (December 1997).

that there were sudden reversals of capital flows during 1997 and 1998 led many to believe that most capital flows in the region were of portfolio investment type. Reversals of such capital can strain the region's financial system sufficiently to cause or exacerbate its collapse. However, while it is true that portfolio investment was on the rise, data indicate that foreign direct investment (FDI) remained the largest in all Asian crisis countries. As shown in Table 1.1, in all Asian crisis countries foreign debts increased persistently until the onset of the crisis. These are debts of the private sector from foreign private lenders. Regional monitoring with the help of a theory such as the one proposed here could have caught the problem and a regionally, ultimately globally, coordinated solution could have been attempted. But this was never a possibility under the then existing circumstances. We now know that financial and balance-of-payments crises became interlinked precisely because of the existence of foreign-currency-denominated liabilities (foreign debt) in the domestic financial system.[21] This hindsight can be used to develop RFAs in Asia, Latin America and a few other regions.

In Asia, a "Washington Consensus" policy mix of monetary tightening and fiscal restraints was imposed as part of the IMF conditionalities. The experience during the Mexican Crisis in 1995 had convinced the Fund that such a policy mix was appropriate for Asia as well, despite the fact that the pre-crisis conditions in Asia were quite otherwise.[22] Another element emerged in Asia that was indeed new. The IMF suggested a rather radical and fundamental change in the countries' institutional structure.[23] In the event, neither set turned out to have been well-conceived.

As already observed, the Fund's insistence on severely tightening the monetary policy by raising the interest rates turned out to be incorrect and counterproductive. Its arguments for remaking many institutions in Asia did not make evolutionary sense although all would agree that ending corruption, curtailing special business privileges and imposing the practice of good governance, including good corporate governance, were good overall goals.[24] But quite apart from the well-known fact that this falls outside the Fund's mandate, such adjustments at the time could result in further instability. In the words of Morris Goldstein, an ex-IMF staff member: *"both the scope and the depth of the Fund's conditions were excessive.... They clearly strayed outside their area of expertise.... If a nation is so plagued with problems that it needs to make 140 changes before it can borrow, then maybe the fund should not lend."*[25] Although not a conscious advocate of the evolutionary theory advanced here, Goldstein's long experience and solid sense of institutional matters led him to the right conclusions in this matter.

Before leaving the question of the analytical distinction between the two types of GFAs, it is instructive to ask whether the theory of the second best is relevant in making this distinction. Although the language of evolutionary theory is different, this can be done in a way that throws further light on why the hybrid form is important. In a first best world without frictions, information problems and market imperfections, an overarching GFA is indeed optimal. However, once we depart from any of these we are in the second best world. Interestingly, given these imperfections, at least along some dimensions, a hybrid architecture with RFAs can (locally) improve upon the surveillance problems that an overarching GFA will face. As long as local information gathering and monitoring can be improved under a (local) RFA, there is an advantage to having an RFA. In the world of second best, this can be called "the principle of localism."[26]

Towards a workable hybrid GFA: RFAs, the IMF and national policy management during transition

But how is the transition towards a hybrid GFA to be effected? What conceptual modifications are necessary to the way in which we have become accustomed to thinking under the present institutional order? The present and following sections are all intended to answer these questions. The present section will consider some general issues and the possible formation of RFAs while the following two will address how the IMF can be modified and what such a modified IMF together with an Asian RFA could have done to handle the situation before, during and after the AFC.

If the argument presented so far is valid, then several propositions can be accepted. First, there may be more than one evolutionary possibility; so there may not be a unique, global optimum set of institutions. Second, the goal of achieving stability and sustainable growth in a world of scarce resources leads to exercising prudence as a principle, particularly when costs are distributed unevenly over space and time. Third, a combination of global institutions with regional and national level institutions may provide more public good than focusing simply at the global level. The case for RFAs has so far rested implicitly on the third proposition. I now wish to elaborate more on this point and link it to the formulation of national economic policies and institution building at the national level as well. It is best to focus again on a concrete case such as post-crisis Asia to give substance to the formal argument.

Since the crisis, the IMF, the World Bank and the national policy-making bodies have been in intense consultation. The individual East Asian economies have taken numerous measures such as improving bank supervision, allowing greater exchange rate flexibility and so on to inoculate themselves against future capital account shocks. However, most of them are still vulnerable to large negative capital account shocks. The national strategy of having a very large stock of foreign reserves to deal with large capital flight may work. But it is an extremely expensive strategy. No one can foretell how frequent such crises may be, and how expensive; but if the past is any guide, even infrequent crises can be quite expensive to manage in this manner. This is not to say that such measures should not be taken. On the contrary, these measures are and should be a part of the transitional national management strategy. However, more is clearly needed. It seems that following this logic, an increasing number of East Asian policy makers are realizing that although they may not have the capacity to change the international financial architecture immediately, creating a regional financial architecture may be an attainable goal. There can be a whole range of regional financial cooperation policies leading to more permanent institution building. These could begin with a peer review process such as the G7 process. Using this as the reference point, a move to mutual liquidity provision and some form of enforcement mechanism could be adopted. These could be enhanced through exchange rate coordination and an enhanced surveillance process. Ultimately, such a process could evolve into an RFA that could have its own institutional and organizational structure.

In the Asian case, such an evolutionary process has already started. The most important steps taken so far are: the Manila Framework Group Meeting, the ASEAN Surveillance Process, the ASEAN+3 Surveillance Process, and the Chiangmai Inititative-related Surveillance Process.

It can be said that the performance of the Manila Framework Group as a mechanism for regional financial cooperation and regional financial surveillance has not yet reached its potential. The reasons are related to institutional incapacity which has prevented the parties from specifying clearly the objectives of information exchange and surveillance. Consequently, no priorities, targets and rules have been set for the process of information exchange and surveillance. Most importantly, there is no actual peer review process; the surveillance process seems to be simply general discussion of the global and regional economic outlook. Finally, there seems to be no attempt to formulate any country-specific or region-wide recommendations for policy actions – a point to which I will return at the end.

The other processes also have much room for improvement and actual prospects for improvement, as shown by the Chiangmai Inititative-related Surveillance Process. In addition to an expanded ASEAN Swap Arrangement (ASA) that includes all ASEAN members and a network of bilateral swap agreements among ASEAN countries plus China, Japan and South Korea, the initiative has opened the door for further discussion about concrete policy coordination and institution building. In so far as the swap arrangements are concerned, currently 10 percent of the swap arrangements can be disbursed without IMF involvement.

Even with this modest beginning, there is now a need for the swap-providing countries to formulate their own assessments about the swap-requesting country. Costs of such information gathering can be economized through regional cooperation. Such a move will also make it possible to pre-qualify members for assistance if and when the need for such assistance arises. This will also help fight contagion and prevent capital flight when actions are taken promptly before a crisis point is reached because of avoidable delays. Acting in accordance with the principles of prudent management stated earlier, there could be a regular policy dialogue at the deputy minister level. Finally, at the organizational level, the evolutionary approach could lead to the establishment of an independent surveillance unit to serve as the core of an RFA, and to lead the policy dialogue. The proposed policy dialogue process should pay particular attention to the root problems in East Asia's weak financial systems (e.g. prudential supervision, risk management and corporate governance), and actively promote the development and integration of long-term capital markets. At this point, it is not essential to pinpoint any further the precise organizational blueprint for such an RFA; but the point that the process underway can result in an appropriate institutional structure with proper organizational design is important to grasp. Evolutionary economic theory suggests that an open architecture will be better able to absorb future shocks, learn from them and modify itself.[27]

There are two key aspects of such an interrelated architecture that will crucially affect the workability of a possible RFA in Asia or in any other region. First, the willingness of a reformed IMF to permit the RFAs to have a certain degree of regional autonomy. For this the complementarity and burden-sharing aspects of the GFA with RFAs need to be recognized. This is a special case of complementary institutional network (CIN). Second, and another instance of CIN, is viability and cooperation at the national level. A slogan accompanying globalization is that the nation state can no longer act on its own. This may be true in certain areas of macroeconomic policy, but on a wide range of issues from tax policies to environmental policies the national governments can, within limits, formulate and implement policies. In the area of finance, even under WTO rules, there are possibilities of not only policy maneuvering but also of institutional reform and new institution building. In addition to addressing such matters as prudential supervision, risk management and corporate governance, the need for building other institutions for risk sharing, human development and policy dialogues within the nation loom large as tasks during the transitional management at the national level.

One final observation regarding the creation of an RFA within Asia is necessary before moving to a discussion of the future of the IMF in the next section. To put it in the most concrete and perhaps provocative way, could the Chiangmai Initiative foreshadow an East Asian Monetary System?

The AFC has led to a collapse of the dollar pegging most of the economies in East Asia had before the crisis. The East Asian economies prefer a certain amount of exchange rate stability due to their multilateral trade dependence. They also see some advantages to be gained from coordination against speculative attacks, and preventing competitive devaluations in the region. However, fixing rates with respect to one another like the EMS earlier also carries dangers. Furthermore, the US dollar is still the most important vehicle currency in the region. Therefore, whether something like a yen bloc, or even an Asian Currency Unit (ACU) can be created in the near future is doubtful.

At the same time, the experience of the AFC points towards closer coordination and a concerted effort to reduce volatility in the currency and financial markets. Since there are asymmetries among the countries in the region, the more advanced countries need to take the lead and ensure that in times of asymmetric shocks, the less advanced countries will have resources to call upon. Thus any kind of step towards an RFA will have to involve adequate reserves and the ability to provide liquidity and other resources to countries that need these in times of crisis.

The changing role of the IMF within a hybrid GFA

In this section I want to address what is perhaps the most important institutional and policy question that arises from the proposal for a hybrid GFA. What will be the role of the IMF, and how will this new role differ from its present or neoliberal role? As mentioned already, the handling of the AFC by the IMF has raised important issues of global governance. The Fund has been criticized by the left, the right, and also the center. I have already alluded to some of the ways in which the IMF will need to change its ways if the hybrid form of GFA I am suggesting here is to become a viable option for institution building. Elsewhere, I have pointed out the need for adhering to some basic principles as the IMF transforms itself in an "extended panda's thumb" manner.[28] Chief among these principles are the principle of symmetry and the principle of burden sharing. These are described briefly below:

1   *The principle of symmetry*, that is, the surplus and deficit countries should be treated equally. However, it was not realized in the past; nor is it likely to be realized in the near future. However, there are various ways to pursue this as a goal even under the current setup of the IMF. If serious efforts are made to follow this principle by a reformed IMF, that will be an important step towards a new and better GFA.
2   *The principle of burden-sharing*, that is, during episodes of crisis management, the IMF will share the management burden with the RFAs and through them also with the affected countries and their neighbors.

It should be kept in mind that in keeping with the "extended panda's thumb" argument both the principles recognize the practical impossibility of the IMF being transformed into a global central bank in the near future. What the IMF cannot do now and will not be able to do in the foreseeable future is to follow Bagehot's dictum to lend freely against good collateral at a high interest rate in time of crisis. Unless SDRs become the commonly accepted and easily expandable means of settlement, this role will remain foreclosed. It is unlikely that the principal shareholders of the IMF will allow such a change to occur.[29] Also, compared to a national central bank dealing with a problematic domestic financial institution, the IMF has a limited ability to force corrective action. Yet, there will clearly be a role for IMF lending, and the consequent moral hazard will need to be recognized. But just as the moral hazard from having fire fighters ready to fight fires does not compel thoughtful communities to abolish fire stations, the global community also cannot abolish the IMF, or reduce its resources simply because there is a moral hazard problem associated with such institutions. The second principle above, the principle of burden sharing with the RFAs, national governments and the private sectors should go some distance towards both increasing the overall resources available, and mitigating the moral hazard.

While the Fund cannot now, or even in the near future, be expected to act as a global central banker, pressures for increasing the net supply and poor country allocations of SDR will have beneficial effects. Even if the increases are not significant in the short run, the tendency will keep alive the eventual goal of forming a global central bank, as Keynes had envisioned. More practically, putting pressure on the IMF to emit new SDRs in order to finance the stabilization of primary (and perhaps other) commodity prices will lead to benefits for both the developing and the developed countries in the intermediate run. The stabilization of these prices will help many developing countries avert balance of payment disasters. Furthermore, to the extent that the unusual price increases, such as the oil price increase in the 1970s, create general inflationary pressures, such pressures can also be averted. A smooth international transactions pattern will thus be consistent with domestic price stabilization as well.

In addition, the Fund can make a concerted effort to manage the private creditors. Most important from the point of view of managing crises will be the incorporation of new provisions on loan contracts so that orderly workout procedures become feasible. The Fund can also lend into arrears as a means to provide debtor-in-possession financing. Such a provision, along with more direct measures vis-à-vis the creditors, can help to bring the creditors to the bargaining table during a crisis.

Such measures to manage the creditors should also be complemented by increased surveillance of financial markets. Strengthening supervision is one aspect. Arriving at independent assessments of financial risk is another, related aspect of moving in this direction. However, it is important to realize that even after adopting this stance, the risk of crises will still remain. Not all crises can be foreseen, much less prevented. The best that can be done is to draw the countries, the private sector and the RFAs together in an effort to strengthen the financial structures, including information gathering and processing capabilities. A cooperative structure where the Fund recognizes the need for hybridity will also help to reduce the reaction time.

Reducing the reaction time can help only if the policies undertaken cannot do much harm even if they are not successful in achieving their positive aim. The IMF has been correctly criticized for suggesting a "one-size-fits-all" policy package. Here again, a changed institutional structure with a more flexible IMF will mean a case-by-case approach where the RFAs will play a significant role. National economic policies such as requiring borrowers to unwind positions in increasingly risky situations, curbing excessive foreign borrowing, limiting portfolio investment, cautionary policies towards derivatives and off-balance sheet items may need to be examined as serious policy options. Tobin tax, or individual country taxes of the Chilean variety should also be given serious consideration. The mantra of free capital movements together with the refrain that there is no alternative needs to be revised appropriately to incorporate the available tools that the Fund can help countries use to mitigate the risks arising from such capital movements.

It is not clear that the Fund can do much in instituting a more stable exchange rate regime. The pegged rate system, advocated among others, surprisingly, by the *Wall Street Journal*, will create one-way bets for speculators. Free floating, on the other hand, can lead to disasters when exchange rates collapse suddenly instead of finding a new stable equilibrium. Such perverse dynamics was observed during the AFC, particularly in the Indonesian case. Neither currency boards nor perfect flexibility can prevent vulnerable currencies from collapsing. Rather, a managed float before any signs of crisis appear together with a prudent management of the financial and real sectors would seem to be both pragmatic and feasible at this point. Strengthening the capacities of central banks will have better pay off here than urging the IMF to twist the arms of the countries through conditionalities.

In Asia, in addition to the high interest rate standard recipe, the IMF seized the crisis as an opportunity to dismantle what remained of the particular mix of institutions that had historically evolved to create the so-called "Asian Model of Development." Widespread and massive bank closures, enterprise restructuring, opening up sectors to foreign ownership, tearing down labor institutions in the name of flexibility and attacks on living standards seemed to be a part of an overarching agenda. This type of radical restructuring under duress is not the way to apply the principles that are being advocated here.

In spite of widespread criticism from many quarters, the IMF remains committed to capital account liberalization as an ultimate goal. The AFC and similar crises have merely given it pause to consider proper sequencing before liberalization. The structural evolutionary theory together with the "extended panda's thumb" argument point to a more nuanced, less global approach. Some economies may be ready for capital account liberalization; others are not. The IMF needs to distinguish among them carefully, and not adopt capital account liberalization as a principle enshrined in its revised Articles of Agreement.

It goes without saying that proper sequencing, better monitoring and management of debt, greater transparency in both government and private sector operations and more effective regulation of domestic financial institutions are all desirable policy goals. Also desirable are domestic tax policies that do not encourage excessive reliance on short-term capital inflows. However, in a world of unevenness some countries may also require temporary capital controls through various means. The IMF, instead of taking a dogmatic approach that says "no" to any form of capital control, should set up facilities for examining the impacts of different alternatives. In doing so, it should also pay attention to the principle of symmetry so that the borrowing countries do not always and everywhere have to take the initiative. At the same time, both capital inflows and outflows need to be controlled to some extent.

A reformed IMF together with the RFAs could take the lead in providing the overall framework within which individual countries could pursue policies most advantageous from a systemic point of view. For example, as alluded to already, the hybrid GFA could have a framework agreed to by the member countries of the IMF so that when a crisis hits lenders would be subject to credit standstills and orderly workouts. This would clearly force the creditors to shoulder some of the responsibility for the crisis.

Such an arrangement, in all likelihood, would also reduce the need for large IMF loans. Another part of the new IMF responsibilities could be the collection of a global Tobin tax. Although no panacea, such a tax would almost certainly reduce returns to very short-term capital movements. A further consequence of a Tobin tax could be a somewhat more stable exchange rate system. Adoption of a securities transactions tax is also not a far-fetched idea. Even Lawrence Summers wrote academic articles before he joined the government advocating modest taxes on these transactions.[30] As any international monetary economist knows, the "impossible trinity" of international capital mobility, fixed exchange rate system and an independent monetary policy cannot all be pursued together. Slowing down short-term capital movement need not prevent long-term capital from flowing across borders. However, fixed exchange rates must be given up if countries are still to pursue independent monetary policies. Thus, a return to the old IMF is neither necessary nor desirable. The transformation of the IMF as a handmaiden of the neoliberal agenda in the 1980s shows that something like an "extended panda's thumb" process was already at work in the post Bretton Woods system IMF. Given sufficient political wisdom and will that process can be reversed towards creating a transformed IMF that can serve the cause of financial stability for global prosperity much better than it has done during the last decades of the twentieth century. This new IMF will adopt a more flexible approach towards national policies. It will recognize that in periods that seem to be leading towards a crisis there may need to be policy shifts such as a shift towards some types of capital controls. The present Articles of the IMF actually allow some forms of capital controls when countries are in distress. Instead of dismantling, these provisions have to be made realistic and applicable whenever the financial system seems vulnerable. Thus flexibility and context-dependent policy making will be the key features of a hybrid system. To begin with, debt rescheduling, moderation in fiscal-monetary policy mixed with an expansionary bias for most economies and gradual restructuring of corporate sectors with strengthening of standards and corporate governance are steps that the IMF can encourage the economies to take without interfering directly with policy making in specific countries.

Other measures that the IMF can allow or even encourage national governments to pursue could include requiring lending institutions to hold different levels of provisions for countries with different estimated levels of riskiness measured by such factors as the state of the banking system and the level of reserves relative to short-term debt. As many have observed, risk assessment by the credit rating agencies also leaves much to be desired and could be improved if the IMF provided some guidance and input. Another, more practical measure would be to impose different levels of taxation on earnings from overseas investments with different maturities. Although as stated in the previous sentence, it will not be so sensitive to individual country risk, it will nevertheless curb some of the tendencies towards short-termism. It should be mentioned that the Basel Committee regulations in effect during the AFC may have been a culprit in this respect. These regulations gave a lower weight to short-term foreign lending (20 percent) for capital adequacy purposes than for loans with a maturity period of over one year (100 percent). A new IMF could make such rules less biased by coordinating its guidelines with BIS, and being guided by a better theory than the one underlying the Washington Consensus.

Summary and conclusions

The history of financial crises shows that they cannot be prevented once and for all in a monetary economy with unpredictable ebbs and flows in capital movement. This history also shows that financial markets have short memories and limited long-term learning capacity. Thus there needs to be – within the limits of human fallibility – a well-designed set of institutions capable of dealing with the tendencies towards financial instability and crisis.

In times of crisis, there are well-meaning suggestions of radical institutional restructuring that fade away when the immediate crisis is over. Only a few farsighted or worrying types may still voice lingering concerns. The AFC, the proposals for an *overarching type* of GFA – to use the terminology developed here – and the subsequent fate of these proposals is a case in point.

Given these features of the real economic world, an evolutionary approach admits of multiple evolutionary equilibria, and a need for realistic institutional design that recognizes path dependence without the disabling and in most cases incorrect slogan that there is no alternative. Such an approach applied to recent economic history leads to the identification of two broad categories of global financial architectures. The *hybrid* variety advocated here on the basis of both realism and systemic efficacy would nevertheless involve much institution building that is always fraught with the danger of politics-gone-awry.

The dismantling of Chilean capital controls in 1998 is a case in point. In this particular instance, a balance of payments crisis prompted the loosening of capital controls instituted earlier. It can be argued that the situation of policy and institutional reversal occurred because the interest groups favoring liberalization following a particular world view were strengthened.[31] Such interests in Chile included at that time holders of foreign exchange, exporters, foreign creditors and investors, and the IMF and other international financial institutions. Thus the political problems of coalition building and ensuring the least cost cooperative outcome need attention. The limited achievements and remaining problems that can be seen from the Asian example discussed here should provide concrete motivation to think further about such problems of designing institutions in the real world currently.

From the policy perspective, it is important to know if the existence of an Asian RFA would have helped in any way during the AFC. This is really a counterfactual question which asks: suppose there existed an RFA for Asia during the AFC, how would it have responded to the crisis that would have been different?

In contrast with the behavior of the IMF, within the proposed hybrid GFA, a regional financial architecture, had it been present, could have done at least the following on the basis of applying an evolutionary theory of financial instabilities under globalization:

1 Through constant regional monitoring, it would have sensed the danger ahead of time. Even a regional monitoring unit alone would have been able to do better than the IMF team in Asia.
2 Through constant formal and informal contact with the officials in member governments and the private sector, it would have sized up the possible extent of the problem earlier and better than did the IMF.
3 Through prompt and early action, it would have provided liquidity to the system, and punished bad management in coordinated measures with the national governments.
4 It would have been able to start regional discussions about bankruptcy and work out procedures by keeping in close touch with the history and legal issues facing particular countries.
5 It would have been in a position to use both moral persuasion and toughness to keep both regional creditors and debtors in line.

The fundamental requirement for this, however, was an actually existing RFA with enough liquidity and technical expertise. The Asian Development Bank provided quite a bit of liquidity to Korea in particular, but did not even have a monitoring unit when the crisis broke out. Furthermore, the autonomy and integrity of any future RFA, in Asia and elsewhere, are issues that need discussion. The relationship between the RFAs and the IMF also needs to be further specified. These are matters that are of necessity evolutionary by nature. In this paper, I have tried to specify some principles that may help in selecting the more beneficial evolutionary path.

Once there is a regional financial architecture for Asia, for instance, it could be a regional lender of last resort. It could also perform effective surveillance functions. In addition, it could promote financial and corporate restructuring that is necessary, but almost impossible for the IMF to do. Finally, in the event of a future crisis, a more timely response could come from such an RFA already in place.

The proposed "extended panda's thumb" argument points to the possibility of using our knowledge and ingenuity to utilize existing institutions together with some new ones to achieve desirable goals. In case of the GFA, this argument strengthens the case for developing the hybrid variety. Using both the existing global institutions such as the IMF, albeit in a modified form, and building upon existing regional initiatives may offer a better chance of creating a beneficial makeshift hybrid GFA than the textbook type pie-in-the-sky schemes correctly dismissed by Eichengreen. However, Eichengreen does not consider the role of RFAs in his otherwise excellent analysis. One way to read the present paper is to see it as filling this gap by using the "extended panda's thumb" principle along with other arguments. A set of realistic reforms of the IMF together with the formation of RFAs will offer the best chance for the global economy to achieve both stability and prosperity.

Notes

1 For a rigorous statement in terms of evolutionary game theory, see Aoki (2000), and also Khan (2002c).
2 For specific models and arguments see those developed in Khan (2001 and 2002c). Khan (2001) formalizes various types of path dependence. In Khan (2002c) a specific argument called "the extended panda's thumb" is advanced to urge the utilization of the existing IMF with some modifications in a new, hybrid GFA.
3 This and the next section draw heavily upon Khan (2002c).
4 See Polanyi (1944) for a classic discussion of marketization of money, labor and land, and the resulting resistance that he calls "the double movement."
5 See for example, Knight (1998).
6 Of course, the risk of contagion is always present whenever a financial crisis breaks out. Whether actual contagion is observed depends on a number of factors including the domestic economy's ability to fight off speculative attacks.
7 See for example, Calvo and Mendoza (1999).
8 As Eichengreen (1999) documents, these range from individuals to national to international agendas.
9 Williamson (1998).
10 See for example, Bhagwati (1998).
11 Stiglitz has been one of the pioneers of such "information theoretic" approach. For further analysis, see Stiglitz (1994).
12 See UNCTAD (2002), particularly sections 5 and 6.
13 See in addition to Eichengreen (1999) cited earlier, Azis (1999), Khan (2004a, b), Sachs *et al.* (1996), Sachs and Woo (2000), Summers (2000), Tobin and Ranis (1998), Yoshitomi and Ohno (1999).
14 See Khan (2001 and 2002c). A more readily available exposition is given in chapter 8 of my book, *Global Markets and Financial Crises* (2004a).
15 See Aoki (2000: 43–59), particularly his discussion of institutions as a kind of codification of evolutionary equilibrium strategies, 57–9.
16 See Kaminsky and Reinhart (1999).
17 Azis (2002).
18 Azis (2002: 3).
19 Azis (2002: 3).
20 Azis (2002c: 3–4).
21 See Krueger (2000).

22 Tobin and Ranis (1998) were among those who believed that the IMF programs in Asia were based on the Fund's experiences with Mexico in 1994.
23 Azis suggests: "The experience with policy adjustments of this kind in Eastern Europe and the former Soviet Union (from communism to market economy) had inspired the Fund to do the same thing in Asia" (2002: 7).
24 See Khan (1999a, b, 2001) on Asian corporate governance reform, and the sketch of an evolutionary theory.
25 *New York Times*, 21 October 2000.
26 I am grateful to Barbara Stallings for very helpful discussion on this point.
27 Although the terminology used is different, Kuroda and Kawai (2002) describe the case for strengthening regional financial cooperation in East Asia in terms that lend support to the "open architecture" view with a regional component advanced here from an evolutionary perspective.
28 See Khan (2002c).
29 However, this should not be ruled out completely. Pressures for increased supply of SDRs will be beneficial in specific ways as argued below.
30 See Summers and Summers (1989).
31 See Dean (1998).

References

Aoki, M. (2000) *Information, Corporate Governance, and Institutional Diversity*, Oxford: Oxford University Press.

Azis, I.J. (1999) *Do We Know the Real Causes of the Asian Crisis? Global Financial Turmoil and Reform: A United Nations Perspective*, Tokyo: The United Nations University Press.

—— (2002) "Financial Sector Liberalization and the Asian Financial Crisis: The IFI Got it Wrong Twice," Working Paper.

Bhagwati, J. (1998) "The Capital Myth," *Foreign Affairs*, May/June, 77(3): 7–12.

Calvo, G.A. and Mendoza, E.G. (1999) "Regional Contagion and the Globalization of Securities Markets," NBER Working Paper No. W7153.

Dean, J. (1998) "Asian Financial Crisis," in B.K. MacLean (ed.) *Out of Control*, Ottawa: Canadian Centre for Policy Alternatives and Toronto: James Lorimer & Co.

Eichengreen, B. (1999) *Toward a New International Financial Architecture: A Practical Post-Asia Agenda*, Washington, DC: Institute for International Economics.

Johnston, B.R., Darbar, S.M. and Echeverria, C. (1997) "Sequencing Capital Account Liberalization – Lessons from the Experiences in Chile, Indonesia, Korea, and Thailand," IMF Working Paper WP/97/157.

Kaminsky, G.L. and Reinhart, C.M. (1999) "The Twin Crises: The Causes of Banking and Balance-of-Payments Problems," *American Economic Review*, 89(3): 473–500.

Khan, H.A. (1999a) "Corporate Governance of Family Businesses in Asia: What's Right and What's Wrong?" ADBI Paper No. 3.

—— (1999b) "Corporate Governance in Asia: Which Road to Take?" paper presented at 2nd high level symposium in ADBI, Tokyo.

—— (2001) "A Note on Path Dependence," unpublished manuscript.

—— (2002c) "The Extended Panda's Thumb and a New Global Financial Architecture: An Evolutionary Theory of the Role of the IMF and Regional Financial Architectures," University of Tokyo CIRJE Discussion Paper No. 2002-CF-163.

—— (2004a) *Global Markets and Financial Crisis: Asia's Mangled Miracle*, Houndmills and New York: Macmillan/Palgrave.

—— (2004b) *Innovation and Growth in East Asia: The Future of Miracles*, Houndmills and New York: Macmillan/Palgrave.

Knight, M. (1998) "Developing Countries and the Globalization of Financial Markets," IMF Working Paper WP/98/105.

Krueger, A.O. (2000) "Conflicting Demands on the International Monetary Fund," *American Economic Review*, 90(2): 38–42.

Krugman, P. (1996) *Pop Internationalism*, Cambridge, MA: The MIT Press.

Kuroda, H. and Kawai, M. (2002) "Strengthening Regional Financial Cooperation in East Asia," revised paper presented in the seminar on regional economic and financial cooperation, April.

Polanyi, K. (1944) *The Great Transformation*, New York: Rinehart & Co.

Sachs, J.D., Tornell, A. and Velasco, A. (1996) "Financial Crises in Emerging Markets: The Lessons From 1995," *Brookings Papers on Economic Activity*, 1: 147–98.

Sachs, J.D. and Woo, W.T. (2000) "Understanding the Asian Financial Crisis," in W.T. Woo, J.D. Sachs and K. Schwab (eds) *The Asian Financial Crisis: Lessons for a Resilient Asia*, Cambridge, MA: The MIT Press.

Stiglitz, J.E. (1994) *The Role of the State in Financial Markets*, Proceedings of the World Bank Conference on Development Economics 1993, Washington, DC: World Bank.

Summers, L.H. (2000) "International Financial Crises: Causes, Prevention, and Cures," *American Economic Review*, 90(2): 1–16.

Summers, L.H. and Summers, V. (1989) "When Financial Markets Work Too Well: A Cautious Case for Securities Transactions Tax," *Journal of Financial Services Research*, December: 261–86.

Tobin, J. and Ranis, G. (1998) "The IMF's Misplaced Priorities: Flawed Funds," *The New Republic*. Online: http://www.thenewrepublic.com/archive/0398/030998/tobin030998.html (accessed 20/3/1999).

UNCTAD (2002) *Report on Least Developed Countries*, Geneva: UNCTAD.

Williamson, J. (1998) "Capital Mobility, Contagion and Crises," unpublished paper.

Yoshitomi, M. and Ohno, K. (1999) "Capital Account Crisis and Credit Contraction: Towards a Better Management of Systemic Currency Crisis," paper presented at ADB Annual Meeting, Manila, 29 April.

2 Globalization and economic development

The role of multilateral development banks

Masahiro Kawai

Introduction: what are multilateral development banks?

There are a number of multilateral development banks (MDBs) in the world. The World Bank is a global MDB, while the Asian Development Bank (ADB), the Inter-American Development Bank (IDB), the African Development Bank (AfDB), and the European Bank for Reconstruction and Development (EBRD) are major regional MDBs (see Table 2.1).[1] These MDBs typically have two groups of members: one group includes developing countries that need external official financing for their economic development and, hence, are potential borrowers from the MDBs; another group consists of developed countries that have the capacity to finance the development needs of the former group and, hence, are potential creditors.

Financing for the construction of economic infrastructure such as transport, power generation and distribution, and irrigation and water supply has been sought by MDB borrowing members and was once a mainstay of MDB operations for those who lacked such infrastructure for economic development. More recently, the upsurge of financing capacity in the private capital markets has led MDBs to withdraw from some infrastructure financing in favor of private sector financing. The financial crises in the emerging market economies in the 1990s and the first five years of the 2000s have also posed new challenges for the MDBs in crisis prevention, management and resolution from developmental perspectives. The World Bank's relationships with the International Monetary Fund (IMF) as well as with regional MDBs are also focus issues.

The MDBs are in need of reforming their operations, particularly in order to enhance their aid effectiveness in assisting developing countries' development, growth and poverty reduction strategies in the context of globalization. The organization of this chapter is as follows. The next section reviews the functions of the MDBs. The third considers the issue of globalization and its impact on economic development and poverty reduction. The fourth focuses on the effectiveness of development aid. The fifth takes up the World Bank's approach to aid, development and poverty reduction. The sixth examines agendas for MDB reform. The final section provides concluding remarks.

Functions of the multilateral development banks

A common characteristic of multilateral development banks (MDBs) is that they are financial institutions with the objectives of financing long-term economic development and providing policy advice for economic and institutional reform in their developing members. The former objective includes: (1) the financing of projects needed for long-term development of hard infrastructure and institutions; (2) the provision of fiscal support to developing members that need to pursue policy and institutional reforms – often, but not necessarily, as a result of financial and economic crises; and (3) the funding of economic reconstruction after disasters such as wars, conflicts and natural disasters. The latter objective involves advice in a wide range of financial, sectoral and institution-building activities, technical assistance and training, and research and analytical work for the client countries.

The World Bank

The World Bank Group is the only global MDB, which includes the IBRD, IDA, IFC and MIGA. It is a global institution in the sense that its membership is open to all members of the IMF, another global international financial institution.

The *International Bank for Reconstruction and Development (IBRD)* was created together with the IMF following the 1944 Bretton Woods meetings held by the Allied Countries at the near-conclusion of World War II. Its initial task was to provide financing for the reconstruction of war-torn countries in Europe and then Japan. Its role was subsequently expanded to cover wider development financing especially as the decolonization process gathered pace. Over time the majority of the World Bank's project operations have been concentrated in developing-country members.

The IBRD has been operating as a money bank by raising funds from the international capital markets at AAA terms and by lending such funds to members at more favorable terms than are available to them in the market. Considering the need to provide more concessionary (or "soft") financing to the poorest members, the World Bank established the *International Development Association (IDA)* in 1960. The IDA receives donated funds from richer members and lends such funds to qualified low-income countries at zero interest with a lengthy grace period and repayments over 40 years. Since then the IBRD has been lending funds to upper middle-income countries and the IDA to qualified lower middle-income and low-income countries.

Table 2.1 Organization of multilateral development banks (as of December 2001)

Organization	World Bank Group				Asian Development Bank	
	IBRD	IDA	IFC	MIGA	OCR	ADF
Year Established	Dec. 1945	Sept. 1960	July 1956	April 1988	Aug. 1966	June 1974
Head Office	Washington, DC (USA)				Manila (Philippines)	
Objectives	Sustainable economic development and poverty reduction through concessional loans and technical assistance (TA).		Economic development through investment and loans to the private sector.	Promoting private FDI through guarantees against non-commercial risks.	Poverty reduction with focu on sustainable economic development, social development and good governance through loans and technical assistance.	
Membership						
Number	183	162	175	155	60	
Eligibility	IMF members	IBRD members			ESCAP members and non-regional developed UN members	
Capital (million)	$189,505	SDR 8,647	$2,450	$1,957	$43,834	$19,963
Shareholders (%)						
USA	16.9	20.9	24.1	16.5	15.9	16.7
Japan	8.1	18.7	6.0	6.8	15.9	37.6
Germany	4.6	11.0	5.5	3.8	4.4	6.5
England	4.4	7.3	5.1	4.6	2.1	4.3
France	4.4	7.3	5.1	5.1	2.4	4.8
Canada					5.3	7.1
Loans						
Annual (million)	$10,487	$6,764	$5,357	$2,000	$3,977	$1,362
Outstanding (m)	$118,866	$86,572	$10,909	$5,179	$28,659	$14,832
Terms of Lending						
Interest Rate	LIBOR + 75–80 bp	zero	Market rate	–	LIBOR + 60 bp	1.0% (grace period)/1.
Maturity (years)	15–25	LLDC & IDA-only: 40 Others: 35	8–12	Within 15	15–30	24 or 32
(grace period)	(3–5)	(10)		(20)	(3–7)	(8)
Service Charge	–	0.75%	–	0.50–1.25%		
Commitment fee	0.75–0.85%	–	0.50–1.00%		0.75%	
No. Professionals		3,436	825	65		749

Source: Ministry of Finance, Japan.

The role of multilateral development banks   45

_merican Development Bank Group			African Development Bank		European Bank for Reconstruction and Development	Reference: IMF
		IIC	AfDB	AfDF		
FSO	MIF					
959 Dec. 1959	Jan. 1993	Mar. 1986	Sep. 1964	June 1973	April 1991	Dec. 1945
gton, DC (USA)			Abidjan (Cote d'Ivoire)		London (UK)	Washington, DC
mic and social pments of l and south can countries h concessional	Promoting private investment through assistance to small sized firms.	Economic development through investment and loans to private SMEs.	Economic development and social progress of African member countries through loans.		Economic transition of the central and eastern European countries through loans, investment, guarantees and TA to private firms and privatizing SOEs.	Monetary cooperation, exchange rate stability, ST financing for BOP imbalances.
	28	38	77	26 plus AfDB	60 plus EC and EIB	183
embers, and gional IMF ers						
59 $9,480	$1,231	$704	$28,495	$14,231	EUR 20,000	SDR 213,700
50.8	40.6	25.8	6.9	12.2	10.0	17.4
5.6	40.6	3.5	5.7	14.2	8.5	6.2
2.4	2.4	2.0	4.3	10.0	8.5	6.1
1.8	–	–	1.8	3.6	8.5	5.0
2.2	1.2	3.2	4.8	2.8	8.5	5.0
3.1						
1 $443	–	$128	$1,099	$1,472	EUR 3,656	SDR 7,680
1 $6,637	–	$381	$8,554	$7,602	EUR 6,327	SDR 50,300
1–2%		Market rate	7.16%	zero	LIBOR + 50–600 bp	– SBA, EFF: 3.07% – PRGF: 0.5% – SBA, EFF: 3–10 PRGF: 10 (5.5)
25–40	Case by case	5–12	20	50	5–15	
(5–10)		(5)	(Max 5)	(10) 0.75%		
0.5%		0.50–1.00%	1.00%			
1,243		53		587	613	1,799

Recognizing the role of private sector investment in the development process, the World Bank established the *International Finance Corporation (IFC)*, a lending institution to operate exclusively in the private sector, which provides loans and equity investments for suitable projects. In 1985, the World Bank initiated a second agency to support private sector investment, the *Multilateral Investment Guarantee Agency (MIGA)*, to offer investment insurance. The objective is to enhance the flow of capital and technology for productive purposes to developing countries under conditions consistent with their developmental needs.

The initial operational focus of the World Bank strongly reflected the conditions of the founding countries and their key representatives, creating an essentially North Atlantic and European institution. In one sense this was natural because the United States and Western European coalition was a major driver of European economic reconstruction. In addition, in terms of personnel, competent professional staff with adequate technical and analytical skills was available only in these countries. Over time, however, the World Bank Group has attracted highly qualified professional staff from all over the world, including from developing countries.

Regional development banks

While the lending focus of the World Bank shifted towards developing countries, US–European dominance made the "developing" post-colonial African, Latin American and Asian members feel that their economies should obtain complementary support that would give them greater priority for development. Consequently, moves began for establishing new regional development banks to provide additional assistance to Latin America, Africa and Asia. Later, when the trading and investment arrangements under the Council for Mutual Economic Aid (COMECON) broke up, a need arose to found a new regional development bank for the transition economies in the former Soviet Union and nations of Central and Eastern Europe.

The *Inter-American Development Bank (IDB)* was established in 1959. It began operation as an essentially North–South American partnership with the United States as its largest shareholder (30 percent), followed by Japan (5 percent) and Canada (4 percent). From the beginning the IDB adopted both Ordinary Capital (OC) loans and Funds for Special Operations (FSO) loans, the latter of which emphasized concessional terms. In 1983, IDB members created the Inter-American Investment Corporation (IIC) to provide loans and investments to private small and medium-sized enterprises (SMEs) at market rates. While the United States, Canada and Japan are important developed-country members, many Latin American countries are among the top ten shareholders, including Argentina, Brazil, Mexico, Venezuela, Chile and Colombia.

The *African Development Bank (AfDB)* was created in 1964 based on the principle of self-sufficiency. While it did not admit non-African member countries initially, it later decided to enlarge membership by including non-regional developed countries. Many African countries are among the top ten shareholders, including Nigeria (as the top donor), Egypt, South Africa, Cote d'Ivoire and Morocco. Major developed country donors are the United States, Japan, Germany and Canada. The AfDB introduced African Development Fund (AfDF) loans for the poorest members on concessional terms.

The *Asian Development Bank (ADB)* was established in 1966 under the leadership of the Japanese government. Modeling itself closely after the World Bank, it welcomed members from North America, Europe and the Pacific. Japan and the United States have been the largest shareholders with equal shares (16 percent). The ADB also includes major developing-country members, notably China (third) and India (fourth), although China joined later and India refrained from borrowing for many years. The ADB adopted an arrangement with its Ordinary Capital Resource (OCR) loans and Asian Development Fund (ADF) loans, with the latter on very concessional terms. ADF finance is used only in the poorest countries or where there are special circumstances that require a high level of concessionality. In order to operate more directly with the private sector, the ADB established a private sector lending division to facilitate private investment by sponsoring venture and capital funds.

The *European Bank for Reconstruction and Development (EBRD)* was established in 1991 in order to foster private sector investment in the transition economies in Central and Eastern Europe and in the former Soviet Union – or Commonwealth of Independent States (CIS) countries. Unlike other MDBs, the EBRD incorporates a political mandate for promoting democracy and an exclusive economic mission of assisting transitions from planned to market economies. It is not required to make sovereign loans or loans with government guarantees. The top ten shareholders are all major industrialized countries – such as the United States, Japan, France and Germany – except that Russia is the seventh largest shareholder.

MDBs as banks for development, poverty reduction, reconstruction and crisis-resolution

The objectives of most MDBs, including those of the World Bank, IDB, ADB and AfDB, are to help developing countries achieve sustainable economic development and poverty reduction. These objectives are only implicit for the EBRD in its special mandate to foster economic transition and democracy. The MDBs also function as banks for economic construction in post-conflict countries as well as for structural reform in crisis or non-crisis developing countries.

Sustainable economic development

Economic development is often captured by both increases in per capita income and improvements in social conditions. It also involves a series of societal transformations at all levels, that include:

- Shifts of economic resources (capital, labor and management skills) away from traditional rural sectors towards industrial and services sectors, particularly in urban areas;
- Greater weight of private sector economic activity;
- Emergence of an educated middle-class population in urban areas; and
- Institutional developments that support the functioning of a market-based economy, including a newly defined role of the government, the rule of law, a sound financial system, human development – in terms of education, health and nutrition – and economic infrastructure.

In previous decades, the international development community focused on physical capital accumulation and construction of hard infrastructure (1950s–60s), improvements in social conditions in areas such as education, health and nutrition (1970s), management of macroeconomic and structural policies (1980s), and institution-building and human development (1990s) as the most important elements affecting economic development. In the aftermath of the collapse of the socialist system in Central and Eastern Europe and the former Soviet Union, the international community has begun to stress the need to set up sound institutions for a market economy. As a result, the MDBs are now increasingly concerned with public sector governance, social sector protection, human development, environment protection and infrastructure sectors with an emphasis on policy and institutional reforms.

Poverty reduction

Today, poverty reduction has become the overarching objective of many MDBs. Following the World Bank's *World Development Report 1990: Poverty* there has been a fundamental re-orientation of development assistance toward addressing poverty by focusing on growth, productivity, human capital and income distribution. This report argued that the principal elements of an effective poverty reduction strategy are: (1) rekindling economic growth, particularly labor-intensive growth, which should provide opportunities for the poor to become more productive; (2) increasing government expenditure on education and human capital to equip people to take advantage of those opportunities; and (3) provision of a social safety net for those who are left behind. The 2000/2001 WDR, subtitled *Attacking Poverty*, refocused on poverty but from wider, multi-layered perspectives and recommended three actions: (1) promotion of opportunity; (2) facilitation of empowerment; and (3) enhancement of security.

The basic approach assumes that economic development in any meaningful sense cannot be achieved without resolving the problem of poverty. The established view sees poverty reduction as not only raised and increasing income and consumption but also high achievement in education, health, nutrition and other areas of human development. In this sense, economic development represents "a transformation of society, a move from old ways of thinking, old forms of social and economic organization, to new" (Stiglitz 2000).

Transition to a market economy

Transition to a free market is another important objective for countries that were once socialist economies. Replacing a planned economy with a market requires wholesale institutional change, including market infrastructure and institutions that support the underpinnings of a market economy, legal systems that facilitate and protect market transactions, and social sector protection mechanisms to absorb risks associated with market adjustment. The EBRD was created to specifically address the transition issue for Central and Eastern Europe and CIS countries, while the ADB also handles transition economies in East Asia and Central Asia. Some countries – namely those in Central and East Asia – are undergoing both economic development and economic transition at the same time. A comprehensive strategy is needed for these nations in order to minimize the transition costs without incurring undue risks of labor dislocations and worsening poverty.

Economic reconstruction

The MDBs play an important role in reconstructing economies damaged by wars, conflicts and natural disasters.[2] Recent activities in this area include those in Kosovo, East Timor, Afghanistan, Iraq and the tsunami-affected countries in the Indian Ocean. Economic reconstruction in these countries entails nation-building, starting from the establishment of a functioning government, basic economic and social infrastructure, and a whole set of market infrastructure and institutions.

Crisis response and resolution

A crisis is an event that marks a serious discontinuity in a country's performance or policies or that might require exceptional support from the International Financial Institutions – particularly the IMF, the World

Bank and relevant regional MDBs. Examples of such events include an imbalance of payments, interrupted debt service payments, a financial sector collapse, a loss of fiscal control and rapid inflation, a sudden and sharp drop in economic activity, a loss of capital market access, abrupt policy reversals, political turmoil and natural disasters.

Once a crisis occurs, it is important to prevent it from evolving into a full-blown economic crisis, by maintaining market confidence through economic stabilization and putting into place needed policy reforms. In response to a crisis, the IMF, the MDBs and bilateral donors often provide liquidity support to contain it. Liquidity from the IMF is added to foreign exchange reserves, while resources from the MDBs are directed to fiscal support to be mobilized for counter-cyclical fiscal policy programs, bank recapitalization, social sector protection or speedy recovery from the crisis.

MDBs as money, knowledge and public goods banks

The MDBs are often said to perform three different, though related, functions. Each MDB serves as a:

- money bank,
- knowledge bank, and
- public goods bank.

As money banks, or development finance institutions, the MDBs primarily provide long-term funds for development to their client countries at rates more favorable than those available in the market. The capital-scarce poor countries are particularly in need of this type of financing, and even some middle-income developing countries need additional financing due to their limited access to international capital markets. Second, as money banks, the MDBs provide fiscal support for policy, institutional and structural reforms either at times of financial and economic crises in developing countries or in the absence of such crises. This type of financing, that is, a structural adjustment loan, used to be accompanied by "policy conditionality" and often by IMF programs.[3] Third, the MDBs provide financial assistance for economic reconstruction when civil war, natural disasters or other events devastate an economy. Recent examples include Kosovo, East Timor, Afghanistan and, more recently, Indian Ocean countries hit by the tsunami.

As knowledge banks, the MDBs provide economic analyses, policy advice and technical assistance by mobilizing global or regional knowledge on best practices (and bad examples and failed attempts as well) on particular issues – financial sector supervision, corporate governance, pension schemes, anti-corruption measures, water and forestry resource management – and tailor them to the specific conditions and needs of a particular developing country. The MDBs act as knowledge banks either in conjunction with their roles as money banks, as public goods providing banks or independently of any such functions. The MDBs, particularly the World Bank, are increasingly emphasizing knowledge, because without it they cannot identify high-value added investment projects (i.e., those projects that induce significant policy and institutional reforms) nor can they provide effective policy advice to their client countries.

Another important role of the MDBs is the provision of international public goods. An international public good is any good, service, system of rules or policy regime that generates shared benefits for the participating countries as a result of coordinated actions by the participating countries and organizations. Provision of certain types of international public goods by the MDBs can be essential to the economic development of developing countries. Some examples of such public goods include: transport infrastructure that goes across borders; containment of communicable diseases; environmental protection; prevention of the serious impacts of natural disasters hitting several countries simultaneously; and containment of conflict that has potential to become a cross-border issue. The World Bank is best suited to provide global public goods, while the regional MDBs are best suited to provide respective regional public goods.[4] Global, regional and national public goods are often complementary to one another and, hence, cooperation both among the MDBs – particularly between the World Bank and the regional MDBs – and between the MDBs and the national governments is essential.

Globalization, growth and poverty reduction

In recent years, there has been a wide range of criticism against international organizations, such as the WTO, the IMF, the World Bank and several regional MDBs which promote economic liberalization and globalization. These organizations are now facing a greater challenge than ever before to achieving their shared objective of enabling poorer countries to catalyze successful integration into the global economy and, at the same time, help reduce poverty, income inequality, and the socio-economic tensions created by such integration.

Poverty reduction

Most MDBs have shifted their overarching objectives to poverty reduction. Even the IMF has begun to focus on poverty reduction as an important objective for low-income developing countries.[5] Poverty reduction is hard to reject, even for many market-oriented economists.

Strategies for poverty reduction

There are basically two views on poverty reduction. The mainstream view sees systematic poverty reduction as possible only through sustained economic growth and productivity increases. Without economic growth, there will be no systematic poverty reduction. The other view argues that economic growth does not necessarily alleviate poverty and that poverty reduction is possible through microeconomic interventions that target the poor, such as community-based social programs, micro-credit schemes, and provision of social services that are essential to the poor. According to this perspective, poverty reduction requires a marked increase in the provision of basic services for the poor in the areas of education, health and nutrition, and marked attention to the social foundations for the development process.

A balanced position would be that while sustained economic growth is needed for systematic poverty reduction, growth is only a necessary – though not a sufficient – condition for countrywide poverty reduction. In order for economic growth to lead to poverty reduction, growth must be accompanied by a higher demand for unskilled labor. Economic growth accompanied by the development of unskilled labor-intensive sectors, particularly in light manufacturing and agriculture, is likely to result in poverty reduction. Poverty reduction is only possible through raising the rate of return on assets the poor have or have access to, such as unskilled labor and small plots of land. Once market-based growth and development is achieved, key social goals will also be achieved over time.[6]

Measuring poverty

Poverty is often measured by the number of people – or the share of such people in the total population – living below a certain threshold level of income or consumption, such as $1 a day or $2 a day. Though there are several problems associated with these measures,[7] the general trend is captured by World Bank data summarized in Table 2.2.

Table 2.2 reveals that between 1981 and 2001, there was some reduction in poverty worldwide. The most successful region has been East Asia and the Pacific, whether China is included or excluded, while other parts of the developing world, particularly Sub-Saharan Africa and to some extent Latin America and the Caribbean, have shown disappointing performance. The table indicates that there are still 1.1 billion people in the world living on less than $1 a day and 2.7 billion people on less than $2 a day.

Poverty reduction is also accompanied by improvements in various social and human conditions concerning education, health and nutrition. Some of these are captured by the Millennium Developmental Goals (MDGs), which the international community has endorsed:[8]

- Eradicate extreme poverty and hunger – by halving, between 1990 and 2015, the proportion of people whose income is less than $1 a day and who suffer from hunger.

Table 2.2 Regional breakdown of poverty in developing and transition countries

a. Population living below $1 per day (at 1993 PPP), 1981–2001

Region	Population covered by at least one survey (%)	Number of people living on less than $1.08 per day (millions)					Headcount index (%)				
		1981	1990	1996	1999	2001	1981	1990	1996	1999	2001
East Asia and Pacific, inc. China	90.8	795.6	472.2	286.7	281.7	271.3	57.7	29.6	16.6	15.7	14.9
China		633.7	374.8	211.6	222.8	211.6	63.8	33.0	17.4	17.8	16.6
Europe and Central Asia	81.7	3.1	2.3	19.8	29.8	17.6	0.7	0.5	4.2	6.3	3.7
Latin America and the Caribbean	88.0	35.6	49.3	52.2	53.6	49.8	9.7	11.3	10.7	10.5	9.5
Middle East and North Africa	52.5	9.1	5.5	5.5	7.7	7.1	5.1	2.3	2.0	2.6	2.4
South Asia, including India	97.9	474.8	462.3	428.5	431.1	428.4	51.5	41.3	36.6	32.2	31.3
India		382.4	357.4	399.5	352.4	358.6	54.5	42.1	42.2	35.3	34.7
Sub-Saharan Africa	72.9	163.6	226.8	271.4	294.0	315.8	41.6	44.6	45.6	45.7	46.9
Total	88.1	1,481.8	1,218.5	1,096.9	1,095.1	1,092.7	40.4	27.9	22.8	22.2	21.1

Table 2.2 continued

b. Population living below $2 per day (at 1993 PPP), 1981–2001

Region	Population covered by at least one survey (%)	Number of people living on less than $1.08 per day (millions)					Headcount index (%)				
		1981	1990	1996	1999	2001	1981	1990	1996	1999	2001
East Asia and Pacific, inc. China	90.8	1,169.8	1,116.3	922.2	899.6	864.3	84.8	69.9	53.3	50.3	47.4
China		875.8	824.6	649.6	627.5	593.6	88.1	72.6	53.4	50.1	46.7
Europe and Central Asia	81.7	20.2	22.9	97.4	112.3	93.5	4.7	4.9	20.6	23.7	19.7
Latin America and the Caribbean	88.0	98.9	124.6	117.2	127.4	128.2	26.9	28.4	24.1	25.1	24.5
Middle East and North Africa	52.5	51.9	50.9	60.9	70.4	69.8	28.9	21.4	22.3	24.3	23.2
South Asia, including India	97.9	821.1	957.5	1,029.1	1,039.0	1,063.7	89.1	85.5	81.7	78.1	77.2
India		630.0	731.4	805.7	804.4	826.0	89.6	86.1	85.2	80.6	79.9
Sub-Saharan Africa	72.9	287.9	381.6	446.8	489.1	516.0	73.3	75.0	75.1	76.0	76.6
Total	88.1	2,550.0	2,653.8	2,673.7	2,737.9	2,735.6	66.7	60.8	55.5	54.4	52.9

Source: World Bank, *Global Poverty Monitoring*.

Note

The numbers are estimated from those countries in each region for which at least one household survey was available during the sample period (for many countries more than one survey was available). The proportion of the population covered by such surveys is given in the first column. Survey dates often do not coincide with the dates in the above table. To line up with the above dates, the survey estimates were adjusted using the closest available surveys for each country and applying the consumption growth rate from the national accounts. Using the assumption that the sample of countries covered by surveys is representative of the region as a whole, the numbers of poor are then estimated by region. This assumption is obviously less reliable in the regions with the lower survey coverage. The headcount index is the percentage of the population below the poverty line.

- Achieve universal primary education – by enrolling, by 2015, all children in a full course of primary schooling.
- Promote gender equality and empower women – by eliminating gender disparities in primary and secondary education preferably by 2005, and in tertiary education by no later than 2015.
- Reduce child mortality – by reducing by two-thirds, between 1990 and 2015, the mortality rates among children under five.
- Improve maternal health – by reducing by three-quarters, between 1990 and 2015, the maternal mortality ratio.
- Combat HIV/AIDS, malaria and other diseases – by halting and beginning to reverse the rising trend in HIV/AIDS, malaria and other serious diseases by 2015.
- Ensure environmental sustainability – by integrating the principles of sustainable development into country policies and programmes and reversing the loss of environmental resources; by reducing by half, by 2015, the proportion of people without sustainable access to safe drinking water and basic sanitation; and by achieving, by 2020, a significant improvement in the lives of at least 100 million slum dwellers.
- Develop a global partnership for development – by addressing the special needs of the least developed countries.

Impact of globalization on growth, poverty and income distribution

Implications of globalization for developing countries have attracted considerable attention among policymakers, international organizations, academics and researchers, mass media and civil society from both developed and developing countries. While globalization appears successful in raising living standards for a large number of people around the globe, there is a fear that its benefits are distributed unevenly in favor of the rich, that it has been widening the income disparity between rich and poor nations as well as between the rich and the poor within nations, and that it makes many developing countries vulnerable to the vagaries of global capitalism. Opponents of globalization often argue that it has harmed developing countries by increasing poverty and widening income inequality across countries and within countries.

A preponderance of the statistical evidence appears to support the proposition that a group of "globalizing" developing countries that have integrated their economies with the rest of the world has achieved faster economic growth and significant poverty reduction. A statistical assessment of global poverty conditions and global income inequality is complex because it involves various types of aggregation problems. Nonetheless, if countries are population-weighted and incomes and consumptions are expressed at the internationally comparable PPP dollar – which is a well-accepted procedure for many economists – then the data demonstrate there have been improvements in poverty reduction and reductions in income inequality at the global level.[9]

Growth, poverty and global inequality

Nonetheless, experts agree that there is no definitive relationship among globalization, economic growth, poverty and income inequality. It is also hard to establish that globalization is always good for growth, for the poor and for fair income distribution (Birdsall 2002).

As noted by Dollar (2002), five successful countries – China, Vietnam, India, Bangladesh and Uganda – have all benefitted from increased integration in terms of faster economic growth and significant poverty reduction, while many Sub-Saharan African countries have failed to integrate themselves with the world economy, to grow or to reduce poverty. Faster growth and significant poverty reduction in low-income Asia contributed to a reduction of global income inequality while slow growth in Africa contributed to a rise in global inequality. The net result is a modest global decline in inequality with the former outweighing the latter.

This finding about the average is important, but it would be more informative to uncover what is happening behind the average. The relevant questions are why have certain countries such as China, India, Vietnam and Bangladesh been successful in generating growth and poverty reduction under globalization and why have others such as Sub-Saharan countries not done so. The issue here is not only whether and how countries have implemented external liberalization policies and other complementary policy reforms – such as domestic deregulation and institution building – but also how they have nurtured private sector-led development, particularly private investment in labor-intensive manufacturing industries, under globalization.

National income inequality

One of the common claims about globalization is that it leads to greater inequality within countries and hence fosters social and political polarization. Dollar finds that changes in national income inequality are not related to any of the measures of integration. For example, greater trade integration is associated with rises in national inequality in some countries and declines in others. Among the five successful countries that have actively pursued integration with the international market, only two (Vietnam and Uganda) have revealed an improvement in national income distribution in favor of the poor.

One may argue that national income inequality induced by globalization may be a natural phenomenon that takes place anyway in the course of economic development and structural changes. Labor, capital and other productive resources naturally migrate away from less productive sectors of the economy to more productive ones. Income inequality facilitates such resource re-allocation and would eventually disappear in the long run. So it appears that there is nothing to worry about. Nonetheless, to the extent that rising income inequality becomes a source of social tension, there is room for public policy to play to mitigate the negative effects of globalization through social protection and investment in education and health.

Policy implications of globalization

On balance, globalization can be a driving force for economic growth and poverty reduction, if accompanied by complementary policy and institutional reforms and a better investment climate. On the other hand, globalization may aggravate national income inequality and can be disruptive, by producing winners and losers and widening their gap.

Maximizing the benefits and minimizing the costs of globalization

There is no way to stop the globalization process. Doing so would be highly counterproductive. To the extent that globalization provides significant benefits as well as costs, policymakers should focus on how to manage the process of globalization, by maximizing its benefits and minimizing its costs. Table 2.3 summarizes the benefits and costs of globalization for developing and developed countries.

Table 2.3 Benefits and costs of globalization

	Benefits	*Costs*
Developed countries	• Greater efficiency of resource allocation • Increased consumer benefits	• Pressure for domestic industrial adjustment and dislocation • Potential for greater domestic income inequality • Potential for loss of policy autonomy
Developing countries	• Access to developed countries' product markets, capital, technology and knowledge • Greater efficiency of resource allocation if accompanied by structural reforms	• Potential for greater domestic income inequality • Greater vulnerability to external shocks

The discussion in this section has focused on "real" globalization, that is, integration through trade and foreign direct investment (FDI) with the international market. In practice, it is quite important to make a clear distinction between "real" and "financial" globalization, the latter referring to integration through financial sector opening and capital account liberalization. Financial globalization calls for greater care on the part of policymakers, because it amplifies shocks and turbulence affecting a country. Sequencing of liberalization, provision of financial safeguards and the choice of exchange rate regime are some of the added policy issues that the authorities must pay attention to.

Implications for developing countries

If a developing country wishes to benefit from globalization, it must liberalize trade and foreign direct investment (FDI) regimes, pursue a variety of complementary structural reforms – including privatization, deregulation and increased competition – and strengthen policy capacity to manage economic and social risks due to globalization, including social protection and financial safeguards. Simply maintaining sound macroeconomic policy and pursuing external liberalization and domestic deregulation is not enough for this purpose. A country must go beyond the "Washington Consensus" (see below) and focus on wide-ranging reforms of institutions and policy frameworks and strengthen market infrastructure so as to be able to benefit from globalization at smaller costs. In addition, the country must set market friendly environments for private sector activity, particularly private investment, by ensuring political and social stability, increasing business predictability, establishing the rule of law and intellectual property rights and providing necessary industrial infrastructure.

At times, globalization can be disruptive, by forcing certain industries to shrink, which may call for public policies – social protection, training of displaced workers and investment in education – to mitigate these negative effects. Provision of social safety nets is clearly an important component of globalization policy and the associated market reforms – it cushions the damage done to the most severely affected, it helps the momentum of these reforms and it avoids a backlash against the distributional and social consequences of globalization. Where informal social safety nets based on families and communities play an important role, the public sector must find a complementary mechanism to support the existing informal arrangement.

Implications for developed countries

The developed countries can help developing countries benefit from trade and investment openness by maintaining a sound economic and financial management, open market access to their exports of agricultural and labor-intensive manufacturing products, and providing capital to developing countries. The developed countries must be ready to accept industrial adjustment on their part by making their labor markets more flexible. Provision of technological, organizational and management know-how through foreign direct investment (FDI) is crucial to enabling developing countries to accumulate knowledge and participate in the innovation process. All of these have been noted as important ways to encourage the economic development of developing countries in the context of "policy coherence for development" (see Fukasaku et al. 2005).

Essentially, developed countries must pursue policies that are conducive to the economic development and poverty reduction of developing countries, by maintaining stable macroeconomic and financial conditions, liberal trade and investment regimes and open market access, steady flows of long-term risk capital – such as FDI – to developing countries, and steady transfers of production technology, management know-hows and organizational skills. Such policies, if combined with their official development assistance (ODA), can be quite effective in inducing market-based growth and development in developing countries.

Given that many developing countries have problems in their initial conditions – low levels of infrastructure, unattractive geography, poor health and agricultural conditions – the developed countries, by providing ODA, can assist them to overcome these unfavorable initial conditions and pursue private sector-led development. ODA can have a greater positive impact on the recipient economies if it stimulates private investment, total factor productivity and economic growth.

The post-Washington Consensus and developmental agendas

The World Bank is often blamed, together with the IMF, for forcing developing countries to pursue liberalization on both the domestic and external fronts too hastily or prematurely, through imposing "policy conditionality" attached to their loans. The liberalization cum openness approach is often called the "Washington Consensus." The consensus emphasizes that once prices are right, sound macroeconomic environments are ensured, an open trade and FDI regime is achieved and government involvement in productive activity is minimized (see Table 2.4), economies will grow and develop.

The "Washington Consensus" is the "lowest common denominator of policy advice being addressed by the Washington-based institutions to Latin American countries as of 1989" (Williamson 2000).[10] It emerged as a set of policy prescriptions designed mainly for Latin American countries in the 1980s that suffered from external debt problems resulting from bad macroeconomic management. The World Bank introduced adjustment

Table 2.4 New and old Washington Consensus

Washington consensus (Old)	Post-Washington consensus (New)
Objective: Standard economic goals of maintaining low inflation, fiscal discipline, a viable balance of payments, economic growth, domestic and external liberalization and equitable income distribution.	Objective: Institutional reforms to support market-based economy and promote development and poverty reduction while securing macroeconomic stability.
Maintaining macroeconomic stability 1. *Fiscal discipline*: Public sector budget deficits should be small to be financed without recourse to the inflation tax. Public expenditures should be redirected from politically driven areas (defense, indiscriminate subsidies, white elephants) towards areas with high economic returns and the potential to improve income distribution (primary health, education and infrastructure). 2. *Monetary policy discipline*: Low inflation through money supply control. 3. *Tax reform*: Broadening the tax base with improved tax administration and lower marginal tax rates to sharpen incentives and improve horizontal equity without lowering realized progressivity. 4. *Exchange rate discipline*: A unified exchange rate (at least for trade transactions) set at a level sufficiently competitive to induce a rapid growth in non-traditional exports.	**Maintaining macroeconomic stability** 1. *Fiscal policy*: Limited fiscal deficits. Increased domestic savings through fiscal discipline. Increased educational spending, especially at the primary and secondary level. Reinvestment of public resources in well-designed social programs. 2. *Monetary policy discipline*: Low inflation through an independent. central bank. 3. *Tax reform*: Tax system reform, introducing, among other elements, a land-use tax that takes ecological considerations into account. 4. *Exchange rate policy*: No "one-size-fits-all" exchange rate regimes, bringing back floating rates or using fixed rates as nominal anchors. Maintenance of competitive exchange rates.
Three pillars of structural reform building **A. Abolition of protectionist policies** 5. *Trade liberalization*: Replacement of quantitative trade restrictions by tariffs and progressive reduction of tariffs to a uniform low rate in the range of 10–20 percent. 6. *Financial liberalization*: Abolition of preferential interest rates for privileged borrowers, achievement of a moderately positive interest rate, and market-determined interest rates.	**Structural reform and institution** 5. *Trade and investment liberalization*: Continued liberalization of trade and foreign direct investment within multilateral and regional arrangements. 6. *Financial system reform*: Well-sequenced liberalization of the financial system. Effective regulatory/supervisory frameworks to be put in place, and consolidation of banking supervision.

Table 2.4 continued

Washington consensus (Old)	Post-Washington consensus (New)
7. *Foreign direct investment liberalization*: Abolition of entry barriers of foreign firms and opportunities for competition between foreign and domestic firms on equal terms.	7. *Capital account liberalization*: Well-sequenced liberalization of capital account to maximize its benefits and minimize the costs.

B. Deregulation

8. *Deregulation of domestic markets*: Abolition of regulations that restrict entry of new firms or competition, and adoption of regulations that can be justified by solid criteria such as safety, environmental protection or prudential supervision of financial institutions.	8. *A competitive market economy*: Creation of a competitive market economy through privatization and liberalization, including the labor market.
9. *Property rights*: Provision of secure property rights.	9. *Redefining property rights*: Provision of access to property rights for all society members.

C. Abolition of government intervention

10. *Privatization of public enterprises*	10. *Institution building*: Creation of strategic institutions such as independent central banks, strong budget commissions, an independent, non-corrupt judiciary and regulatory/supervisory agencies to support sound competition.
11. *Reduction of the government size*	11. *Good governance*: Clean government without corruption, absorbing social risks.

Note
Produced by the author from Williamson (1990, 1994, 2000), etc.

loans in the early 1980s in exchange for which the recipient government would accept "policy conditionality" for the purpose of macroeconomic stabilization (fiscal discipline), liberalization of trade and FDI, deregulation of domestic markets and market-oriented structural reforms – like privatization of public enterprises. With one exception – the protection of property rights – the "Washington Consensus" ignored the potential role that institutional reforms could play in accelerating economic and social development and poverty reduction.

The international community is now increasingly realizing that these prescriptions based on the "Washington Consensus" alone cannot achieve economic development and poverty reduction in the medium term unless domestic policies and institutions are adequate and supportive of the functioning of a market economy. In other words, the deregulation and opening of the economy does not automatically guarantee the emergence of a healthy market economy. For this, a set of structural underpinnings supporting market-based activity needs to be developed, including the rule of law, effective bankruptcy procedures, a well functioning financial system and competition policy to limit the monopoly powers of privileged firms. These require the active role of an effective and accountable government. Part of the reason for the failure of Russia's economic transition in the 1990s can be attributed to inadequate attention given to institutional aspects of transition and development.

The post-Washington Consensus states that maintaining stable macroeconomic conditions and liberalizing and opening the economy would not be enough to make the economy develop; these must be supported by complementary structural reforms and institutional underpinnings. Developing good institutions is key to successful economic development. "Institutions" are "the rules of the game" (North 2000), including organizational rules, formal laws and informal conventions sanctioned by members of society. Among them, public sector institutions are the most critical and governance the most important to economic development.

This view also reflects the lesson that while the first-generation reforms were successful to some extent, deeper progress requires second-generation reforms (Table 2.5). The latter reforms go much deeper in terms of the nature of reforms and country stakeholders involved.

Effectiveness of development aid

Enhancing aid effectiveness

Impact of aid on savings, investment and growth

In the early literature on the effectiveness of aid, foreign aid was perceived as an exogenous variable to the financial resources of the recipient country, which would eventually contribute to growth.[11] The simplest hypothesis was that each dollar of foreign resources in the form of aid would result in an increase of one dollar in total savings and investment. The underlying theoretical framework was the Harrod–Domar growth model or the two-gap model. In the Harrod–Domar model, foreign aid was considered to raise both savings and investment by relaxing a savings constraint. In the two-gap model, foreign aid would contribute to greater savings or imports or both by relaxing savings and/or import capacity constraints. In this simple world, fungibility of aid resources was not allowed for, and aid for consumption was not considered in this aid-effectiveness analysis. In a later model, these two factors were incorporated and the impact of aid on economic growth was empirically analyzed.

Table 2.5 First- and second-generation reforms

	First-generation reform	Second-generation reform
Main Objectives	Macroeconomic stabilization (lower inflation and smaller budget deficit) and selected structural reforms to promote economic growth.	Improvement of competitiveness and social conditions, while maintaining macroeconomic stability.
Instruments	Budget cuts, tax reform, price liberalization, trade and foreign investment liberalization, deregulation, social funds, autonomous contracting agencies, some privatization.	Civil service reform, labor reform, restructuring of social ministries, judicial reform, modernizing of the legislature, upgrading of regulatory capacity, improved tax collection, large-scale privatization, restructuring of central-local government relationship.
Actors	President, economic cabinet, central bank, multilateral financial institutions, private financial groups, foreign investors.	President and cabinet, legislature, civil service, judiciary, labor unions, political parties, news media, central and local governments, private sector, multilateral financial institutions.
Main challenges	Macroeconomic management by insulated technocratic elite	Institutional development that is highly dependent on middle management in the public sector.

Source: World Bank, *World Development Report: The State in a Changing World*, 1997, 152.

Over the last few years, a new set of aid-effectiveness studies have appeared. First, these studies work with panel data for a number of years and a large number of countries. Second, measures of economic policy and institutional environments are included directly in the reduced form growth regressions alongside traditional macroeconomic variables, reflecting recent shifts in thinking over development assistance. Third, the endogeneity of aid and other variables is often addressed explicitly. Fourth, the aid–growth relationship is often allowed to be non-linear.

Importance of good policies and institutions

Following the new approach to the effectiveness of aid, a World Bank report on aid effectiveness (World Bank 1998) concluded that official aid achieved growth and poverty reduction only if it induced a country to reform economic policies and institutions.[12] Collier and Dollar (2002) conclude that countries with *strong economic policies* – defined as low inflation, budget balance or surplus and trade openness – and *high quality institutions* – defined as the rule of law, effective public bureaucracy and minimal incidences of corruption – benefit the most from aid by achieving the highest growth rates. Moreover, ideas (or knowledge) are more effective than financial flows in generating reforms and in improving the quality and efficiency of public services. The report concludes that "well-designed assistance can help countries find the policies that they need, and help communities improve important public services that make for a better life today and contribute to long-term development."

By now it is clear that economic development involves a multi-dimensional transformation of society; to the extent that funds are fungible, "the net benefit from financing any individual project is ... the net benefit of the marginal government program" (Stiglitz 1999). What determines the success or failure of development assistance is not the choice of a particular project, but the whole set of policies and institutions adopted by the recipient country, including its own governance structure.

Emerging consensus

The international community seems to share a consensus that development aid works under the following conditions:

- *The right policy environment in the recipient countries.* This means that recipient countries must commit themselves both to peace and political stability and to sound macroeconomic, structural and social policies, good governance, and the rule of law. The resulting enabling environment would attract private capital, particularly foreign direct investment, which complements official aid.
- *Recipient country ownership of development.* Strong country ownership of

its own development strategy is instrumental because without it policy and institutional reforms for economic development and poverty reduction cannot be effective.
- *Donor coordination of assistance efforts.* The donor community needs to pursue harmonization of policies and procedures in order to reduce transaction costs and focus its assistance efforts on the countries with sound economic management and good governance.
- *Donor–recipient partnership.* The donor community and recipient countries must work together, by involving other stakeholders, in achieving the common goals of economic development and poverty reduction as the only objectives. This reflects the past experience that aid-effectiveness is reduced when aid is tied to other often politically motivated objectives of donors.

To achieve this, the MDBs need to be important development partners and enhance efficiency and effectiveness of their activities.

East Asian development experience

The early successful globalizers in East Asia – including the high-income industrializing economies (Singapore, Hong Kong, Korea and Taiwan) as well as the middle-income ASEAN countries (Malaysia, Thailand, Indonesia and the Philippines) – have achieved rapid economic development and remarkable poverty reduction over the last 30 years. China and Vietnam have been following similar patterns of development. East Asia's historical experience reveals that three essential elements contributed to their successes:[13]

- Political stability, sound policies, right institutions and national ownership;
- Outward orientation with a focus on private sector development and the investment–trade nexus; and
- Effective development assistance.

Political stability, sound policies, right institutions and national ownership

First, political stability, sound policies and right institutions played an essential role in the economic development process in East Asia for two to three decades leading up to the financial crisis in 1997–8. Needless to say, the crisis has revealed inadequacies and weaknesses of economic governance systems, particularly in the financial and corporate sectors across crisis-affected East Asia, which should have been strengthened through appropriate regulatory and supervisory frameworks in a way commensurate with the pace of globalization. Nonetheless, the East Asian economies until the age of financial globalization had institutional capabilities that facilitated sustained growth, rapid development and poverty reduction. Important was the presence of sound policies, workable institutions and stable and predictable policy regimes.

In addition, the East Asian states had clear national ownership over long-term economic development programs, liberalization and deregulation and structural reforms. Rigorous implementation of policy and institutional reforms backed by national ownership was an important driver of successful economic development. Strengthening institutional capacities and human resources was indispensable in their efforts to enhance national ownership.

Outward orientation with private sector-led investment–trade interactions

Second, the East Asian economies embraced the notion of globalization by adopting outward-oriented policies with emphasis on private sector development and investment–trade linkages. Many of them initially focused on import substitution and then shifted to export promotion. A major mechanism for export sector growth was through expansion from sales in domestic markets to sales in international markets. Successful domestic market development that was made possible by product and factor market integration and the creation of spatially concentrated clusters of firms, supplier networks and distribution systems was thus a basis for successful export expansion. Export expansion in turn helped each economy overcome the limits of the domestic markets and the foreign exchange constraints, and promoted learning and technology upgrading, economies of scale and production networks. It was also accompanied by liberalization of imports, foreign direct investment (FDI) and use of foreign technologies and ideas. Formation of regional trade–FDI linkages has been a natural consequence of their market-based, outward-oriented policies.

These East Asian economies emphasized the role of investment – in capital equipment, human resources and market knowledge – and its nexus with trade as a basis for sustained economic development. Their governments focused on the creation of a favorable investment climate, reduction of the risks and uncertainty of investment activity and ensuring the availability of finance for productive investment opportunities. Their pro-growth development strategy was supported by the mutually reinforcing interactions between investment and trade. Investment – by both domestic firms and foreign multinationals – and trade stimulated each other, thereby contributing to output growth. Output growth in turn stimulated further investment and trade.

Effective ODA

Third, external development assistance was used effectively in East Asia. As Table 2.2 indicates, the number of people living in extreme poverty – below $1 per day at 1993 PPP – in East Asia declined substantially from 470 million in 1990 to 270 million in 2001. The amount of official development assistance (ODA) that East Asia received during this period totaled US$113 billion, or less than US$10 billion per year on the average (Table 2.6). This ODA performance in East Asia is outstanding – in achieving rapid economic growth and poverty reduction – in comparison to any other part of the developing world. For example, a total of US$192 billion was disbursed as ODA in Sub-Sahara Africa during 1990–2001 but the number of poor rose (from 230 million to 320 million) rather than declined.

The reason behind the successful ODA performance in East Asia was that it was used as a catalyst to support the broad, nationally owned development programs.[14] These programs focused on overcoming the unfavorable initial conditions – particularly low levels of industrial and social infrastructure such as power, telecommunications, transport, water, health and education – of the recipient countries, providing them with a basis for pursuing private sector-driven, outward-oriented, pro-growth strategies. ODA in East Asia essentially helped create a favorable investment climate and interacted positively with the recipient countries' political stability, stable macroeconomic policies, predictable business environments and right institutions.

Lessons for other developing countries

There are three challenges and lessons for low-income countries in East Asia and other regions. First, trade and investment openness is key to success. Second, developing economies need to enhance domestic institutional and entrepreneurial capacities to proactively respond to favorable external environments. Third, ODA can effectively support this process if combined with efforts to improve domestic policies, institutions, governance, human resources and capacities, and industrial and social infrastructure.

These lessons from the East Asian experience may not be readily transferable to other developing countries because of East Asia's favorable geography and some initial conditions. But what matters is not the amount of money to be used, but how external aid helps the country's own development programs, in building government capacities and institutions for development.

Table 2.6 Net ODA receipts of developing countries (US$ million)

Region	1990	1991	1992	1993	1994	1995	1996	1997	1998	1999	2000	2001	2002
East Asia and Pacific	**8,655**	**8,020**	**10,574**	**10,180**	**10,266**	**10,962**	**8,670**	**7,486**	**9,095**	**12,980**	**8,626**	**7,438**	**7,340**
Far East Asia[a]	7,277	6,649	9,077	8,612	8,482	9,095	6,889	5,930	7,444	11,553	7,809	6,657	6,631
Oceania	1,378	1,371	1,497	1,568	1,784	1,868	1,781	1,556	1,651	1,426	817	781	709
EAP, excluding China	6,478	6,021	7,524	6,909	7,041	7,432	6,023	5,431	6,638	10,586	6,894	5,967	5,864
Europe and Central Asia	**1,441**	**2,356**	**2,348**	**3,809**	**3,043**	**3,378**	**3,463**	**2,982**	**3,342**	**6,009**	**6,055**	**4,825**	**7,222**
Europe	1,441	2,241	2,283	3,411	2,189	2,294	2,189	1,764	2,007	4,608	3,736	3,353	5,508
Central Asia	0	115	65	398	854	1,084	1,274	1,218	1,334	1,401	2,319	1,472	1,714
Latin America and the Caribbean	**5,304**	**5,998**	**5,581**	**5,606**	**5,724**	**6,459**	**7,566**	**5,530**	**5,688**	**13,298**	**4,966**	**5,998**	**5,112**
North and Central America	2,821	2,999	3,005	2,520	3,115	3,507	3,131	2,397	2,607	4,311	2,219	2,945	2,368
South America	2,049	2,576	2,215	2,747	2,155	2,620	2,752	2,528	2,365	8,251	2,354	2,624	2,430
Unspecified	434	423	361	339	454	333	1,683	605	716	736	393	429	314
Middle East and North Africa	**11,566**	**12,062**	**9,098**	**6,866**	**8,257**	**5,853**	**8,096**	**5,447**	**5,322**	**5,433**	**4,544**	**4,841**	**6,117**
Middle East	4,373	5,076	3,735	3,129	4,357	2,884	4,748	2,525	2,237	2,405	2,337	2,484	3,329
North of Sahara	7,193	6,986	5,363	3,737	3,900	2,970	3,347	2,922	3,084	3,029	2,207	2,357	2,788
South Asia	**6,058**	**7,967**	**6,627**	**5,281**	**7,144**	**5,238**	**5,184**	**4,341**	**4,903**	**4,581**	**4,330**	**5,939**	**6,749**
Sub-Saharan Africa	**17,452**	**17,697**	**19,122**	**17,330**	**18,822**	**18,420**	**16,119**	**14,245**	**13,900**	**12,325**	**12,693**	**13,729**	**18,615**
Total[b]	**57,282**	**61,865**	**61,437**	**57,053**	**60,646**	**59,610**	**56,636**	**48,686**	**51,353**	**63,637**	**50,386**	**52,003**	**61,611**

Source: Compiled by the author from OECD, *DAC Journal Development Co-operation*, 1994–2004 (Paris).

Notes
a Far East Asia includes Myanmar.
b Total includes other unspecified countries.

The World Bank approach: CDF and PRSP

The World Bank's approach now extends well beyond the traditional "Washington Consensus," the agreed set of measures that are typically called for in the first stage of policy reform.[15] To accelerate the process of economic development and poverty reduction, deeper policy and institutional reforms are necessary – hence the reason behind the need for the second-generation reforms. These reforms focus on improving the quality of investments in human development, promoting the development of sound and efficient financial markets, enhancing the legal and regulatory environment, upgrading the quality of the public sector and consolidating the gains in macroeconomic stability thorough fiscal strengthening. Such institutional reforms take time and are complex. A well-functioning market economy cannot be created overnight.

Comprehensive Development Framework (CDF)

The Comprehensive Development Framework (CDF) has been put forward by the World Bank under the leadership of its former president, James Wolfensohn. This initiative suggests a broad, holistic and long-term approach to development. It supports a balanced approach to development in line with each country's specific current needs, and seeks to respond to a broader development agenda through stronger partnerships in order to achieve greater development effectiveness. Table 2.7 summarizes its conceptual framework. Its approach can be summarized as follows:

- A *comprehensive, long-term approach* to development. The approach has to be holistic in nature, addressing the multidimensional nature of sustainable, equitable growth and poverty reduction. Such an approach involves promoting macroeconomic stability, a transition to open markets, good governance and sound institutions, investing in people through education and health, protecting the environment and creating a business climate to attract foreign and domestic investments.
- *Country ownership* is an objective in itself and a necessary condition for sustainability of development and poverty reduction efforts. Country-owned reforms, based on broad societal foundation and participation, are more likely to survive periods of hardship.
- *Partnership* of all development actors, with country governments at the apex, and external partners participating where they add value and have a comparative advantage, to ensure efficient use of development resources.
- *Outcome focused, linked to performance* and built on *transparency* on the part of donors and recipient countries alike.

Table 2.7 Comprehensive Development Framework: prerequisites for sustainable growth and poverty reduction

The Activities of Partners in the Development Process	Structural				Human		Physical				Specific Strategies			
	(1) Good and Clean Government	(2) Justice System	(3) Financial System	(4) Social Safety Net and Social Programs	(5) Education and Knowledge Institutions	(6) Health and Population	(7) Water and Sewerage	(8) Energy	(9) Roads, Transportation and Telecommunications	(10) Environmental and Cultural Issues	(11) Rural Strategy	(12) Urban Strategy	(13) Private Sector Strategy	(14) Country Specific Headings
Government - National - Provincial - Local														
Multilateral and Bilateral Institutions														
Civil Society														
Private Sector														

Source: Wolfensohn (1999).

Focus on country ownership

It is alleged that policy and institutional reforms for economic development and poverty reduction cannot be effective without strong country ownership. Such reforms often require elimination of rents on the part of privileged sectors, firms and individuals so that they are likely to encounter political resistance. Hence, for it to be successful, the government must be committed to such reforms. If the political base of the country is strong, the reforms can be successful – as in the case of Korea under Kim Dae-Jung. If the political base is weak, on the other hand, the reforms encounter difficulties – as in the case of Indonesia. Unilateral conditionality that is imposed upon a country from external forces would not work without strong country ownership. To deepen country ownership, consultation processes involving parliaments, business community, academics, news media, labor unions and civil society are important, thereby encouraging participation and forming a broad-based coalition for reform.

Poverty Reduction Strategy Paper (PRSP) initiative

In the low-income developing countries, the CDF and the Poverty Reduction Strategy Paper (PRSP) have become recognized as the major instruments to focus on pro-poor growth. The PRSP is a new process through which the developing-country government describes its own detailed and comprehensive strategy for poverty reduction. It is an element of the Country Assistance Strategy (CAS) – the World Bank's business plan that is the main forum for Bank–client interaction – and a basis for the CDF. The PRSP describes a country's macroeconomic, structural and social policies and programs to promote growth and reduce poverty in a framework of enhanced country ownership, transparency and stakeholder participation, while presenting an assessment of associated external financing needs and major sources of financing required. It also provides a decision point prerequisite to the Highly Indebted Poor Countries (HIPC) Initiative. It is linked to the Poverty Reduction Support Credits (PRSCs) of the World Bank and the analogous Poverty Reduction Growth Facility (PRGF) of the IMF. PRSC is provided in support of a PRSP, in early stages of implementation, for the express purpose of enabling the country to pursue the poverty reduction strategy it has laid out.[16]

As of January 2005, 43 countries had finalized PRSPs and 13 others had prepared Interim-PRSPs (see Table 2.8 and Appendix Table 2.9). For the middle-income countries, PRSPs are not required, but their governments are encouraged to produce PRSP-like documents.

Going beyond the CDF and PRSP

There is no doubt that the PRSP initiative has made a positive contribution to settling coherent frameworks for economic development and

Table 2.8 Progress on Poverty Reduction Strategy Paper (PRSP), January 2005

Poverty Reduction Strategy Paper (PRSP) (43)	Albania, Armenia, Azerbaijan, Benin, Bhutan, Bolivia, Bosnia and Herzegovina, Burkina Faso, Cambodia, Cameroon, Chad, Djibouti, Ethiopia, Gambia, Georgia, Ghana, Guinea, Guyana, Honduras, Kenya, Kyrgyz Republic, Lao PDR, Madagascar, Malawi, Mali, Mauritania, Moldova, Mongolia, Mozambique, Nepal, Nicaragua, Niger, Pakistan, Rwanda, Senegal, Serbia and Montenegro, Sri Lanka, Tajikistan, Tanzania, Uganda, Vietnam, Yemen, Zambia
Interim Poverty Reduction Strategy Paper (I-PRSP) (13)	Bangladesh, Burundi, Cape Verde, Central African Republic, Congo, Cote d'Ivoire, Dominica, Guinea-Bissau, Indonesia, Lesotho, Macedonia FYR, Sao Tome and Principe, Sierra Leone

Source: World Bank.

poverty reduction in low-income countries. But simply introducing a new procedure will not change the reality of developing countries unless it is accompanied by substantial improvements in the way in which the international community and the developing countries approach the development agenda. Most important is for the developing countries to articulate their own long-term development programs and put the PRSP in this context so as to utilize external aid in the most effective way.

World Bank Instruments

The World Bank has two main categories of lending instruments: investment loans and development policy loans. Investment loans have a long-term focus (five to ten years) and provide financing for specific development projects. Development policy loans have a short-term focus (one to three years) and provide quick disbursing funds for policy and institutional reforms.

Investment loans

Investment loans provide financing for a wide range of activities aimed at creating the physical and social infrastructure necessary for sustainable development and poverty reduction. Over the past two decades, investment loans have, on average, accounted for 75 to 80 percent of all Bank loans.

The nature of investment loans has evolved over time. Originally focused on hard infrastructure and engineering services – such as irrigation, communication and transportation – investment loans have come to focus more on institution building, social development and building the market infrastructure needed to facilitate private sector activity. Projects range from urban poverty reduction (involving private contractors in new housing construction, for example) to rural development (formalizing land tenure to increase the security of small farmers); water and sanitation (improving the efficiency of water utilities); natural resource management (providing training in sustainable forestry and farming); post-conflict reconstruction (reintegrating soldiers into communities); education (promoting the education of girls); and health (establishing rural clinics and training health care workers).

Funds are disbursed against specific foreign or local expenditures related to the investment project, including pre-identified equipment, materials, civil works, technical and consulting services, studies and incremental recurrent costs. Procurement of these goods, works and services is an important aspect of project implementation. To ensure satisfactory performance, the loan agreement may include conditions of disbursement for specific project components.

Development policy loans

Development policy loans provide quick-disbursing assistance to countries with external financing needs, to support structural reforms in a sector or the economy as a whole. They support the policy and institutional reforms needed to create an environment conducive to sustained and equitable growth. Over the past two decades, development policy loans – previously called adjustment loans – have accounted, on average, for 20 to 25 percent of total Bank lending.

In June 2004, the World Bank replaced the previous adjustment loans of different types – such as structural adjustment loans (SALs), sectoral structural adjustment loans (SECALs), programmatic structural adjustment loans (PSALs), and rehabilitation loans (RILs) – by development policy loans (DPLs). While the DPL has consolidated these separate lending instruments into one, the older formats are still effective for the ongoing and pre-appraised projects. Development policy operations in PRSP countries may continue to be called "Poverty Reduction Support Credits (PRSCs)," because this is by now a well-established "brand name." The main core of the DPL is the former SAL and SECAL.

The former SAL was introduced in 1980 and the former SECAL in 1984. The SAL was a policy-based loan extended for the purpose of reforming the client economy as a whole, while the SECAL was a policy-based loan extended for the purpose of reforming certain sectors of an economy. They were fast-disbursing loans in exchange for the implementation of certain policy changes called "conditionality." The programmatic structural adjustment loan (PSAL) was introduced later to assist governments in forestalling potential distortions and in implementing long-term reform that addresses systemic social, structural and institutional issues.

The PSAL has supplied funds directly to the treasury of the recipient country once criteria were met, with renewable stages (tranches), continuation generally being contingent on satisfactory use of the previous tranch. The government has been able to use the funds for poverty reduction purposes as it sees fit.

Long-term structural focus and "conditionality"

The development policy loan (DPL) has three main features: country ownership, long-term focus and evolved conditionality. On country ownership, the World Bank moves away from a very prescriptive list of policies that were part of the early adjustment loans – that used to focus largely on fiscal discipline, trade liberalization, market deregulation – to a much broader range of issues. DPL operations now generally aim to promote competitive market structures (for example, legal and regulatory reform), correct distortions in incentive regimes (taxation and trade reform), establish appropriate monitoring and safeguards (financial sector reform), create an environment conducive to private sector investment (judicial reform, adoption of a modern investment code), encourage private sector activity (privatization and public-private partnerships), promote good governance (civil service reform) and mitigate short-term adverse effects of development policy (establishment of social protection funds).

As many of these issues involve longer-term structural change, the DPL encompasses a much broader and longer-term focus of this work. In this sense, the Bank is increasingly finding it useful to use programmatic operations, which assist a government program with a series of loans, each building on the preceding loan to support sustained and sequential structural and/or social reforms. As a result, "policy conditionality" is no longer an imposition by the Bank on the borrowing country but rather has now evolved into a mutual commitment device which holds borrowing governments accountable for reliably making progress toward their own poverty reduction strategies and the international community reliably providing financial support to help achieve these results.[17]

Funds are disbursed in one or more tranches into a special deposit account. Tranches are released when the borrower complies with stipulated release conditions, such as the passage of reform legislation, the achievement of certain performance benchmarks, or other evidence of progress toward a satisfactory macroeconomic framework. Funds may be disbursed against a *positive list* of specific imports needed for the operation, or subject to a *negative list* of prohibited expenditures – for example, military and luxury items.

MDB reform agenda

MDB reform proposals

A wide range of criticisms on the role of the MDBs comes both from the left and the right.[18] Those on the left claim that the MDBs are a vehicle for globalization that is dominated by multinational corporations, large private banks and financial institutions, imposing needless "conditionality" and hurting the poor. Those on the right claim that the MDBs are ineffective in alleviating poverty in poor countries and are crowding out private investment in middle-income countries. Several committees have been seeking ways and means to reform international organizations, including the MDBs.[19] The G7 countries have also been proposing measures to reform the MDBs.

Meltzer Commission's proposals

The so-called Meltzer Commission (International Financial Institution Advisory Commission 2000) made some of the most radical recommendations. They include:

- The World Bank should get out of loans and move to grants and small technical assistance programs for the poorer countries – to become a "World Development Agency."
- The World Bank and the regional MDBs should withdraw altogether from lending to middle-income countries with investment grade ratings or per capita income over $4,000 and scale back lending to countries with per capita income over $2,500.
- The World Bank should focus its operations on poverty reduction for African nations, and the IDB and ADB should take over World Bank tasks in their respective regions.
- The MDBs should be precluded from financial crisis loans.[20]
- The MDBs should adopt a performance-based assistance in order to ensure that aid resources are used effectively.

G7 proposals

Considering the important role of the MDBs in the promotion of economic development and poverty reduction, the G7 countries have been trying to improve the delivery and effectiveness of the MDBs' aid since 2000. Reform proposals were put forward in a report produced by the G7 Finance Ministers in Rome (2001), and transmitted to the Heads of State and Government. They can be summarized as:

- *Coordination.* The MDBs must improve coordination, at the country and institutional level, in order to achieve a more selective approach

to development issues, while promoting greater complementarity and avoiding undue overlapping or duplication of efforts.
- *Internal governance.* The MDBs must enhance internal governance, accountability and transparency in order to strengthen their role in the fight against poverty and retain institutional credibility.
- *Review of lending instruments and pricing policies.* The MDBs must review their lending instruments and pricing policies in order to focus on operations targeted at poverty reduction, to be selective in countries with access to private capital, and to enhance the development impact of the resources available.
- *Focus on good governance.* In their assistance to recipient countries, the MDBs must put good governance at the top of their list of activities, with particular focus on public sector management, accountability and anti-corruption measures.
- *Focus on financial sector reform.* The MDBs must help developing countries strengthen their financial sector, particularly in developing institutional capacity and appropriate strategies to meet international standards and codes.
- *Focus on the provision of international public goods.* The MDBs must become more involved in the provision of international public goods to accelerate development and poverty reduction.

Some of these G7 proposals have already been addressed, such as the review of lending instruments by the World Bank.

Articulation of development strategies for MICs, LICs and HIPCs

A "one-size-fits-all" approach would be inappropriate, particularly when the recipient countries are diverse in their income levels, stages of institutional development and policy capacities. The MDBs face several challenges in their relationships with middle-income countries (MICs) and low-income countries (LICs), particularly highly indebted poor countries (HIPCs).

Middle-income countries

Though the Meltzer Commission recommended that the MDBs should get out of middle-income developing countries – largely emerging market economies – there is a strong case for the MDBs to stay engaged.[21] First, although many middle-income countries have investment grades at normal times, their access to the international capital markets is often unstable and volatile as well as quite limited and costly at the time of global market turbulence or crisis, thereby exposing them to financial vulnerability. Thus the MDBs must continue to assist middle-income countries at the time of financial and economic crisis when access to international capital markets tends to be blocked. Second, despite their relatively healthy economic conditions, these nations have large populations of poor people. Being home to nearly 80 percent of the world's poor, they need external financing for those projects targeted at reducing poverty. Third, lending is an important instrument to induce recipient governments to pursue policy and institutional reforms – together with their policy commitments – for achieving internationally desirable policy goals, including human and social development, environmental protection and good governance.

Nonetheless, there is no clear instrument to serve as a middle-income country counterpart to the PRSP. There are tentative indications that this will take the form of a "Letter of Development Strategy (LDS)" or a "Letter of Development Policy." The LDS (or equivalent) can serve as a cornerstone of a constructive development partnership once it evolves, like a PRSP, into a comprehensive development strategy prepared by middle-income countries themselves and presented to the international community. At this point, it is not clear if the actual form would be as structured as that of the PRSP; it might vary in accordance with the widely varied circumstances of this group of countries (see Akiyama and Akiyama 2001).

Low-income countries

For low-income countries, achieving the Millennium Developmental Goals (MDGs) would be a great challenge for their poverty reduction and human and social development, which the MDBs can help greatly. For these countries, country ownership of development programs and reforms, partnership among major stakeholders and performance-based allocation of development resources should be the most important priorities. The World Bank's PRSP process is an important coordinating vehicle for these efforts. Performance-based allocation that is currently used by some MDBs to allocate concessionary loans need to ensure consistency across MDBs and other donor institutions.

For highly indebted poor countries (HIPCs), debt relief is an integral part of the external assistance package. Eliminating unsustainable debt would be needed for these countries to get on a development path. But simply eliminating debt would not be enough for development and poverty reduction. The most significant challenges arise because many poorest countries, particularly those in Sub-Sahara Africa, often lack the necessary prerequisites and institutional capacity – such as functioning government and economic institutions, basic human resources and basic education and health facilities – to be able to mobilize resources effectively. The international community and the MDBs need to explore more creative mechanisms to induce them to launch effective policy and institutional reforms and capacity building. Given that a performance-based approach is unlikely to direct a large sum of aid resources to these countries, workable initiatives need to be developed in partnership between donors and recipients in order to ensure that limited aid – mainly in the form of grants – be well targeted.

Other challenges

MDB coordination

Greater coordination among the MDBs in producing coherent country strategies is underway. One way to ensure this coordination is to encourage consultation by holding a coordinated country strategy meeting among the MDBs and with major stakeholders. Some healthy competition among the MDBs is desirable at the intellectual level as long as their collective outcome can lead to mutually consistent and coherent strategies with the promotion of economic development and poverty reduction. With undue competition at the strategic and operational levels, however, an appropriately rigorous approach taken by an MDB to policy reform and pricing could be undermined. There needs to be strong coordination among them.

A Memorandum of Understanding (MOU) has been agreed upon between the World Bank and each MDB so that their activities are well coordinated. Their presidents hold a regular meeting every year. Operational vice presidents in each of the regional MDBs and their World Bank counterparts meet regularly to discuss operational cooperation, including dispute resolution. Similarly, several key senior managers in the MDBs meet regularly to discuss their fields of responsibility, share information and experience, and seek coherence in approaches. MDBs also coordinate with other international organizations such as the IMF, the United Nations Development Programme (UNDP), the OECD and the WTO. Such efforts continue to be important.

Regional MDBs should focus more on the provision of regional public goods and regional issues that would not be covered by the World Bank. A regional approach taken by the ADB, such as the Greater Mekong Sub-Regional Program and ASEAN+3 financial cooperation, would be a good example for such provision. Of particular relevance is the provision of public goods or economic infrastructure that would cover several countries within a region, where the relevant MDB can play a significant facilitator role in promoting inter-governmental cooperation. Sharing of regional knowledge, good practices and key experiences by regional MDBs is certainly quite useful in providing regional public goods in an effective way. A greater challenge would be the case where public goods cover two or more regions because more significant coordination by the MDBs would be necessary.

Poverty reduction and the Article of Agreement

Although poverty reduction has become the most prominent overarching objective of many MDBs, it is not one of the purposes stipulated in the World Bank's Articles of Agreement. Poverty is not even mentioned there. The World Bank has addressed this problem through a creative redefinition of the term "development" which it has a mandate to promote. Poverty reduction is such an accepted objective now that its legal underpinnings have not been questioned, but the World Bank may need to strengthen its legal basis on this issue.

In response to the changing economic environments at the regional and national levels, regional MDBs must also sharpen their own development strategies in a way that serves most effectively for their clients while embracing poverty reduction as the most important overarching objective. This necessitates a sharpened focus on the provision of regional public goods so as to complement the operations of the World Bank, which should focus on the provision of global public goods.

Concluding remarks

The multilateral development banks are financial intermediaries that channel financial resources they raise in the international capital markets to developing countries at concessional terms. In this sense, taken together they function as a "money bank." Recently they have intensified their non-lending activities in recognition of the critical importance of ideas or knowledge, even more than financial assistance, in generating the necessary reforms to achieve sustainable development, economic transition and poverty reduction. Thus, the MDBs, as a group, have increasingly functioned as a "knowledge bank." They have put an increasing emphasis on policy advice based on international best practices, technical assistance and training and research and analytical work. The group of MDBs is also functioning as a "public good-providing bank" because globalization has increased the demand on MDBs to provide international public goods.

While recent research shores up continued relevance of the "Washington Consensus," this paper has argued that the old consensus reforms are not enough. Development assistance needs to extend well beyond the "Washington Consensus," to address multi-dimensional policy considerations, including the realignment of policies and institutions to maximize its effectiveness. The MDBs need to work jointly and with the developing countries as well as with other stakeholders. They need to focus on their essential comparative advantage to benefit their developing member countries.

Appendix

A2.9 Country Progress on Poverty Reduction Strategy Paper (PRSP), January 2005

Countries/regions	Interim-PRSP	PRSP	PRSP progress report
Albania	May 2000	November 2001	May 2003; April 2004
Armenia	March 2001	November 2003	–
Azerbaijan	May 2001	April 2003	May 2004
Bangladesh	March 2003	–	–
Benin	June 2000	December 2002	–
Bhutan	–	August 2004	–
Bolivia	January 2000	March 2001	–
Bosnia and Herzegovina	October 2002	March 2004	–
Burkina Faso	–	May 2000	Sep. 2001; Sep. 2002; Dec. 2003
Burundi	November 2003	–	–
Cambodia	October 2000	December 2002	August 2004
Cameroon	August 2000	April 2003	April 2004
Cape Verde	January 2002	–	–
Central African Republic	December 2000	–	–
Chad	July 2000	June 2003	–
Congo, Dem. Rep. of the	March 2002	–	–
Cote d'Ivoire	January 2002	–	–
Djibouti	June 2001	March 2004	–
Dominica	November 2003	–	–
Ethiopia	November 2000	July 2002	December 2003
Gambia, The	October 2000	April 2002	–
Georgia	November 2000	June 2003	–
Ghana	June 2000	February 2003	March 2004
Guinea	October 2000	January 2002	April 2004
Guinea-Bissau	September 2000	–	–
Guyana	October 2000	May 2002	December 2004
Honduras	April 2000	August 2001	December 2003
Indonesia	March 2003	–	–
Kenya	July 2000	March 2004	–
Kyrgyz Republic	June 2001	December 2002	April 2004
Lao PDR	March 2001	June 2004	–
Lesotho	December 2000	–	–
Macedonia, FYR	November 2000	–	–
Madagascar	November 2000	July 2003	July 2004
Malawi	August 2000	April 2002	October 2003
Mali	July 2000	May 2002	April 2004
Mauritania	–	December 2000	March 2002; June 2002
Moldova	Nov. 2000; Apr. 2002	May 2004	
Mongolia	June 2001	July 2003	
Mozambique	February 2000	April 2001	February 2003
Nepal	–	May 2003	–
Nicaragua	August 2000	July 2001	Nov. 2002; Nov. 2003

A2.9 continued

Countries/regions	Interim-PRSP	PRSP	PRSP progress report
Niger	October 2000	January 2002	July 2003
Pakistan	November 2001	December 2003	–
Rwanda	November 2000	June 2002	June 2003
Sao Tome and Principe	April 2000	–	–
Senegal	May 2000	May 2002	–
Serbia and Montenegro	–	February 2004	–
Sierra Leone	June 2001	–	–
Sri Lanka	–	December 2002	–
Tajikistan	March 2000	June 2002	March 2004
Tanzania	March 2000	October 2000	Apr. 2001; Mar. 2003; Apr. 2004
Uganda	–	March 2000	March 2002; August 2003
Vietnam	March 2001	May 2002; Nov. 2003	November 2003
Yemen	December 2000	May 2002	–
Zambia	July 2000	March 2002	March 2004

Source: World Bank

Notes

1 In addition, there are several sub-regional MDBs, including the Andean Development Bank, the Arab Bank for Economic Development in Africa, the Caribbean Development Bank, the East African Development Bank, the Islamic Development Bank, and the West African Development Bank.
2 After all, the World Bank was created as a post-war reconstruction bank for Europe and other economies damaged by World War II.
3 As will be explained in a later section, this situation is changing as a result of the introduction of development policy loans that replaced various types of adjustment loans.
4 The "principle of subsidiarity" rests on the notion of "fiscal equivalence," which indicates that the decision-making jurisdiction should coincide with the region of spillovers, so that those affected by the public good determine its provision decision. See Olson (1969).
5 The IMF transformed the Enhanced Structural Adjustment Facility (ESAF) into the Poverty Reduction and Growth Facility (PRGF) in 1999, by underlining the importance of poverty reduction in IMF programs in poor countries. The World Bank also renamed the Structural Adjustment Credit (SAC) the Poverty Reduction Support Credit (PRSC) in 1999.
6 See also McCawley (2002).
7 Measurement of per-capita income (or consumption) and its interpretation, however simple it appears at first sight, can be fraught with problems. For example, the poverty headcount in developing countries is very sensitive to: the precise level of the poverty line because income distribution in the vicinity of developing-country poverty lines is typically flat; the PPP conversion rate used because the implied consumption basket may be inappropriate for the poor

due to the inclusion of many non-essentials that are cheap in developing countries but are irrelevant to the poor; and the assumed rate of change in the consumption of the poor – which tends to be overestimated particularly in Asia – because there are large discrepancies between consumption estimates from household expenditure surveys and estimates from the national income accounts. In addition, the application of a $1 (or $2) per day standard to both urban and rural areas in a given country may be misleading because of differences in consumption baskets. Based on some of these observations, Wade (2002) claims that the margin of error is so large that we do not have definitive knowledge as to whether there has been real progress on poverty reduction, and that the number of people in extreme poverty may be significantly higher than the World Bank's estimate.

8 The Millennium Declaration was adopted by all the United Nations member states at the United Nations Millennium Summit in September 2000. The goals formulated in the chapter on development were taken up by UN Secretary-General Kofi Annan when he presented his "Road Map for the Implementation of the Millennium Declaration" to the UN General Assembly in September 2001. Annan identified and quantified *inter alia* eight measurable development goals with 18 targets. They are known as the MDGs.

9 Dollar (2002) identified five statistical trends in growth, poverty and income distribution in the developing countries: (1) *Poor country growth rates have accelerated.* During the period 1980–97, the population-weighted average growth rate of the poorest one-fifth of countries in 1980 (4 percent per capita per annum) has been higher than that of the richest one-fifth of countries (1.7 percent per capita per annum). This is in contrast with the experiences for the prior two decades (1960–80), where the growth rate for the poor group (1.8 percent) was lower than that for the rich group (3.3 percent). (2) *The number of poor people in the world has declined significantly, the first such decline in history.* Over the period 1977/78 to 1997/98, there has been a large net decline in the number of poor due to massive poverty reduction achieved in China and India, which more than offsets an increase in poverty in sub-Saharan Africa. (3) *Global inequality (among citizens of the world) has declined modestly over the last 20 years.* Measures of global inequality, such as the global Gini coefficients, have declined modestly since 1980, reversing a 200-year-old historical trend toward higher inequality. Rapid growth in Asia (China, India, Bangladesh and Vietnam) has been a force for greater global equality because that is where the majority of the world's extreme poor lived in 1980 and they benefitted from the growth. (4) *There is no general trend toward higher or lower inequality within countries; in particular, among developing countries inequality has decreased in about as many cases as it has increased.* There is no pattern of rising or declining inequality within countries, though there are some notable cases in which inequality has risen. (5) *Wage inequality is rising worldwide.* There is a general pattern of rising wage inequality, that is, larger wage increases for skilled and/or educated workers relative to those for unskilled and/or less educated workers. This trend does not contradict the preceding one because wages are a small part of household income in developing countries, which make up the bulk of the world in terms of countries and population.

10 It must be noted that the "Washington Consensus" as defined by John Williamson (1990) does not include complete capital flow liberalization or full currency convertibility on the capital account, though it includes FDI liberalization.

11 See Hansen and Tarp (2000).

12 See Burnside and Dollar (2002). But Hansen and Tarp (2000) claim that aid and good policies can independently increase the recipients' growth rates. See also papers in Tarp (2000), Lesnik and White (2000) and Easterly (2003) for

criticisms of the Burnside–Dollar exercise. McGillivray and Morrissey (2000) discuss the issue of fungibility.
13 Some of these elements, but not all, and others have been analyzed by the World Bank (1993). See also Fukasaku et al. (2005).
14 The World Bank, the Asian Development Bank and Japan are major aid donors in East Asia. See Kawai and Takagi (2004) for the assessment of Japan's ODA in recent years.
15 As Williamson (1994) himself acknowledges, there were many policy issues on which different views existed, including: speed of trade liberalization; capital controls; need to target the current account; pace and extent of inflation reduction; smoothing of business cycles; incomes policy and wage and price freezes (sometimes called "heterodox policies"); elimination of indexation; correction of market failures; size of tax revenue and public sector spending as a ratio of GDP; desirability and extent of deliberate income redistribution; role for industrial policy; diverse models of a market economy – Anglo-Saxon laissez-faire, European social market economy or Japanese-style responsibility of the corporation to multiple stakeholders; and priority of population control and environmental preservation.
16 The first one was given to Uganda in May 2001.
17 This change reflects the recognition that a large number of structural adjustment loans (SALs) in African and other low-income countries were a failure. In these countries, "policy conditionality" was not effective as an instrument for reform and non-compliance with "conditionality" rarely punished in any effective or consistent way (Killick 2004). See also Gilbert et al. (1999).
18 See Krueger (1998) and Banerjee and He (2003) for these issues.
19 See Task Force on Multilateral Development Banks (1996) for earlier issues.
20 Also supporting this recommendation, Nunnekamp (2002) suggests a transfer of the PRGF from the IMF to the World Bank.
21 See also the Commission on the Role of the MDBs in Emerging Markets (2001), which was co-chaired by José Angel Gurria and Paul Volcker.

References

Akiyama, T. and Akiyama, S. (2001) "International Development Assistance: Where It Is Today and How We Got There, with Specific Reference to the World Bank," Mimeo., October.

Banerjee, A.V. and He, H. (2003) "The World Bank of the Future," *American Economic Review (AEA Papers and Proceedings)*, 93(2): 39–44.

Birdsall, N. (2002) "A Stormy Day on an Open Field: Asymmetry and Convergence in the Global Economy," in D. Gruen, T. O'Brien and J. Lawson (eds) *Globalization, Living Standards and Inequality: Recent Progress and Continuing Challenges*, Proceedings of a Conference held in Sydney on 27–8 May, Sydney, Reserve Bank of Australia and Australian Treasure: 66–87.

Burnside, C. and Dollar, D. (2002) "Aid, Policies, and Growth," *American Economic Review*, 90(4): 847–68.

Collier, P. and Dollar, D. (2002) "Aid Allocation and Poverty Reduction," *European Economic Review*, 46(8): 1475–500.

Commission on the Role of the MDBs in Emerging Markets (2001 "The Role of the Multilateral Development Banks in Emerging Market Economies," Washington, DC: Carnegie Endowment for International Peace.

Dollar, D. (2002) "Global Economic Integration and Global Inequality," in D.

Gruen, T. O'Brien and J. Lawson (eds) *Globalization, Living Standards and Inequality: Recent Progress and Continuing Challenges*, Proceedings of a Conference held in Sydney on 27–8 May, Sydney, Reserve Bank of Australia and Australian Treasure: 9–36.

Easterly, W. (2003) "Can Foreign Aid Buy Growth?" *Journal of Economic Perspectives*, 17(3): 23–48.

Fukasaku, K., Kawai, M., Plummer, M.G. and Trzeciak-Duval, A. (2005) "Policy Coherence towards East Asia: Development Challenges for OECD Countries," *Policy Brief* No. 26, Paris: OECD.

Gilbert, C., Powell, A. and Vines, D. (1999) "Positioning the World Bank," *Economic Journal*, 109(459): F598–F633.

Hansen, H. and Tarp, F. (2000) "Aid Effectiveness Disputed," *Journal of International Development*, 12: 375–98.

International Financial Institution Advisory Commission (2000) "International Financial Institutions Reform: Report of the International Financial Advisory Commission," Mimeo., March, Washington, DC: US Congress.

Kawai, M. and Takagi, S. (2004) "Japan's Official Development Assistance: Recent Issues and Future Directions," *Journal of International Development*, 16: 255–80.

Killick, T. (2004) "Politics, Evidence and New Aid Agenda," *Development Policy Review*, 22(2): 5–29.

Krueger, A.O. (1998) "Whither the World Bank and the IMF?" *Journal of Economic Literature*, 36(4): 1983–2020.

Lesnik, R. and White, H. (2000) "Aid Allocation, Poverty Reduction and the *Assessing Aid* Report," *Journal of International Development*, 12: 399–412.

McCawley, P. (2002) "Asian Poverty: What Can Be Done?" *Economic Analysis and Policy*, 32(2): 123–39.

McGillivray, M. and Morrissey, O. (2000) "Aid Fungibility in *Assessing Aid*: Red Herring or True Concern," *Journal of International Development*, 12: 413–28.

Meltzer, A.H. (2001) "The World Bank One Year after the Commission's Report to Congress," Mimeo., 8 March, Carnegie Mellon University.

North, D.C. (2000) *Institutions, Institutional Change and Economic Performance*, New York: Cambridge University Press.

Nunnenkamp, P. (2002) "Targeting Aid: What the World Bank Has (Not) Achieved," *Journal of International Economic Studies* (Korea Institute for International Economic Policy), 6(1): 87–111.

Olson, M. (1969) "The Principle of 'Fiscal Equivalence': The Division of Responsibilities among Different Levels of Government," *American Economic Review*, 59(2): 479–87.

Stiglitz, J.E. (1999) "The World Bank at the Millennium," *Economic Journal*, 109(459): F577–F597.

—— (2000) "Development Thinking at the Millennium," in B. Pleskovic and N. Stern (eds) *Annual World Bank Conference on Development Economics 2000*, Washington, DC: World Bank.

Tarp, F. (ed.) (2000) *Foreign Aid and Development: Lessons Learnt and Directions for the Future*, London and New York: Routledge.

Task Force on Multilateral Development Banks, Development Committee (1996) *Serving a Changing World: Report of the Task Force on Multilateral Development Banks* (15 March), Washington, DC: IBRD and IMF.

Wade, R.H. (2002) "Globalization, Poverty and Income Distribution: Does the

Liberal Argument Hold?" in D. Gruen, T. O'Brien and J. Lawson (eds) *Globalization, Living Standards and Inequality: Recent Progress and Continuing Challenges*, Proceedings of a Conference held in Sydney on 27–8 May, Sydney, Reserve Bank of Australia and Australian Treasure: 37–65.

Williamson, J. (1990) "What Washington Means by Policy Reform," in J. Williamson (ed.) *Latin American Adjustment: How Much Has Happened*, Washington, DC: Institute for International Economics.

—— (1994) "In Search of a Manual for Technopols," in J. Williamson (ed.) *The Political Economy of Policy Reform*, Washington, DC: Institute for International Economics.

—— (2000) "What Should the World Bank Think about the Washington Consensus?" *World Bank Research Observer*, 15(2): 251–64.

Wolfensohn, J.D. (1999) "A Proposal for a Comprehensive Development Framework," Manuscript, 21 January, Washington, DC: World Bank.

World Bank (1990) *World Development Report 1990: Poverty*, Washington, DC: Oxford University Press.

—— (1993) *The East Asian Miracle: Economic Growth and Public Policy*, Oxford and New York: Oxford University Press.

—— (1997) *World Development Report 1997: The State in a Changing World*, Washington, DC: Oxford University Press.

—— (1998) *Assessing Aid: What Works, What Doesn't and Why*, Washington, DC: Oxford University Press.

—— (2000) *World Development Report 2000/2001: Attacking Poverty*, Washington, DC: Oxford University Press.

3 Is the international trade regime contributing to liberalization in developing countries?

Kazuyori Ito

Introduction

In managing the stability and development of a national economy, the appropriate level of government regulation of market transactions has always been a central question. Although it is true that market regulation policies have been adopted intensively in Western countries since the late nineteenth century, the socialist and developing countries that appeared on a large scale in the last 50 years have shown an unprecedented adherence to state leadership in managing economic and social development. Since the late 1970s or early 1980s, however, these countries have been confronted with the great transformation of their economic systems from state-centered to market-oriented. While voluminous debates have surrounded this drastic change in development strategy, this chapter examines whether and to what extent the international trade regime[1] (the General Agreement on Tariffs and Trade (GATT) and the World Trade Organization (WTO)) contributed to economic liberalization in these countries. To sketch the complex functions served by the trade regime will be helpful in clarifying the relevance of international norms and rules to the domestic policymaking process in these countries.

It is convenient to divide the postwar period into two; *before* and *after* the mid-1980s, when most of the developing and socialist states began shifting their development strategies toward liberal market economic regulatory environments. The international trade regime has served dual functions in each period. The next section reveals that the dual functions of the regime *before* the 1980s were "to tolerate deviation from liberalization principles" and "to stimulate spontaneous liberalization." The former function originates in the tolerant and exceptional treatment granted to developing countries that needed to restrict trade and to protect infant industries. In this respect, the international trade regime exercised very little direct influence on the removal of restrictive regulations to international trade. At the same time, however, we can identify the latter function of the regime in this period. It was the very tolerance of protectionist measures under the old regime that paved the way to macroeconomic crises in these countries. The international trade regime functioned, in an unexpected manner, as a precondition for leading these countries toward radical liberalization in the 1980s.

In addition, it is important that the international trade regime has facilitated trade in goods and services among advanced industrial countries, and has contributed to the dramatic increase in the amount and value of international trade. This gradually formed an external environment of "globalization" or "internationalization" of commercial activities that has raised the opportunity cost of rejecting involvement in the free trade circle and missing out on the advantages of gains from trade that reduced transport costs and lowered tariff barriers have engendered.[2] This is another indirect effect of the international trade regime on domestic economic policy choices in these countries.

The third section examines the dual functions of the regime *after* policy reform; "integration and harmonization" and "technical assistance and preferential treatments." The former function is premised on the improved comprehensiveness of the regime in membership and issue coverage as a result of active participation by the developing and transitional countries. It is, however, the unprecedented organizational, normative and ideological unity of the international trade regime that requires the latter function. Most of the developing countries lack the financial and human resources or experiences necessary to harmonize their economic institutions and policies with international norms and, therefore, to implement and administer WTO obligations effectively. Therefore, the regime implicitly obliges advanced industrial countries to provide technical assistance and preferential treatments to developing and transitional countries. These correlative requirements of harmonization and technical assistance will continue to catalyze the unprecedented interaction between the international trade regime and policymakers in developing countries. We can never fully understand the highly internationalized character of the liberalization processes in these countries without paying attention to the dual functions of the international trade regime.

In this way, this chapter will examine how the international trade regime has legally and politically affected the process of liberalization in the developing and transitional economies, with the emphasis placed on a regime's dual, apparently conflicting, functions. In the concluding section, several aspects of divergence among developing countries will be presented briefly.

Before policy reform: the dual functions of the regime

In this section, it is argued that, while developing and transitional countries have entered into the economic liberalization process in the 1980s, the international trade regime did not explicitly foster this process. Rather, it induced them to stick to, rather than abandon, their market-intervening development policies through a general tolerance for deviation from free-trade obligations. At the same time, however, this generous attitude of the regime has paradoxically provided, in an indirect manner, an essential precondition for leading these countries toward the drastic liberalizing reform. This dual feature of the international trade regime will be examined below.

Existing theories about the function of the international trade regime

There exist two systemic theories that attempt to explain country-level trade liberalization in the anarchic world where centralized authority is absent and commitments to cooperate are not guaranteed. The first is the "theory of hegemonic stability," which claims that the presence of a single dominant state leads to collectively desirable outcomes for all countries in the international system (Snidal 1985: 579). Charles Kindleberger contends that the maintenance of free-trade regimes can be directly attributed to the leadership provided by the dominant state, Britain in the mid-nineteenth century and the United States in the mid-twentieth century, for example (Kindleberger 1981). Without hegemonic leadership, there may not be sufficient provision of a facilitating environment for free trade. Since such an environment is a public good,[3] everyone benefits from a stable, low-risk international trade environment, but it is expensive to maintain. According to this theory, it is indispensable for the maintenance of an open international trade regime,[4] though these public goods, once provided by a benevolent hegemonic state,[5] are available for other countries to "free ride." In sum, hegemonic stability theory claims that the cooperative actions of trade liberalization can be possible thanks to the unilaterally provided public goods supporting the establishment of an international trade regime. As for the developing and transitional countries, they were able to keep restrictive trade practices as long as the stable international trade system was provided by American hegemony in the latter half of the twentieth century, but they began liberalizing after the dominant power of the United States began to decline in the 1970s. Therefore, the theory of hegemonic stability cannot explain why these countries shifted their economic policies from restriction to openness, and how the international trade regime influenced this process.

To account for the survival of the international trade regime and the continuation of cooperative behavior given the decline in American hegemony, there evolved an alternative school of thought: "Liberal-Institutionalism." Robert Keohane contends that, in many of the issue areas of international relations, countries share common interests, the realization of which render all the members better off if all (or most) cooperate. They do not share incompatible interests, the satisfaction of which by one country will be the loss of another.[6] Even if common interests exist, however, countries might be unable to cooperate and to reach a Pareto-optimal solution when nothing would guarantee the prevention of any country from "defecting" from cooperation and gaining extra benefits. In order to overcome this failure (aptly modeled as a Prisoners' Dilemma), countries develop institutional mechanisms that inhibit cheating by providing information, reducing transaction costs and raising the cost of defecting. Thus, by means of constructing an appropriate international trade regime, countries are able to open their economies and reach mutual gains without worrying about the sudden closure of trading partners' markets. With respect to the developing and transitional countries, however, they were not satisfied with the "mutual gains" that would be obtained by cooperating with advanced industrial countries. Rather, they sought a privileged position in which they could foster the growth of their own industries, through protection from international competition, in order to catch up with developed countries. Therefore, even if active participation in, and full compliance with, the international trade regime could bring the developing and transitional countries some "absolute gains," such gains were not sufficient for them to accept full involvement in the regime, since they were interested in "relative gains" vis-à-vis advanced industrial countries.[7] We have to conclude that the institutionalist approach to the international trade regime is unable to explain the cause of liberalization reforms in the developing and transitional countries.

What, then, is the appropriate description of the political functions served by the international trade regime in the liberalization process in these countries? My argument is that the "dual functions" of the regime must be considered; the first was, a visible and direct function which helped these countries to reinforce their state-interventionism; the second, an invisible and indirect function which nonetheless constituted a factor behind their ultimate turn toward market liberalization. The rest of this section will describe these dual functions in turn.

The direct function of the regime: tolerance for deviation

From the beginning of the GATT, advanced industrial countries as well as developing countries have been allowed to adopt several exceptional measures to protect domestic markets from foreign competition.[8] But developing countries, in pursuit of "relative gains" against developed countries, demanded further exceptional treatment from the major obligations of the GATT. During the Cold War, Western developed countries were eager to incorporate newly independent countries into the Western camp by securing participation of these countries in the GATT. The need for the "enclosure" of the Third World necessitated advanced industrial countries making substantial compromises on exceptional treatment. Consequently, developing countries remained virtually outside the fundamental GATT obligations and maintained a highly restrictive trade system for several decades. Most socialist countries, on the other hand, did not intend to be members of the GATT. Thus, the fundamental GATT obligations to liberalize trade were meaningless for most of its members.

The reason developing countries desired trade restrictions are found in the prevalent strategies of centrally planned and domestically driven industrialization. In the 1950s, most developing countries were highly specialized in the production of primary commodities for export, while importing manufactured products. Policymakers in these countries regarded these strategies as indispensable to overcoming specialization in primary commodities, improving domestic productive capabilities and industrializing domestic economies. Countries, it was believed, facilitated industrialization by protecting their domestic "infant" industries. A market-oriented system was thought to harm their economies' development, and governmental intervention in domestic and international markets was regarded as indispensable for the management of the national economy through strategic industrial policies (Krueger 1995: 3–8). A number of developing countries adopted the import substitution industrialization policy, though some countries in East and South East Asia abandoned the strategy relatively early, and shifted to export-oriented industrialization. Despite this bifurcation, however, almost all policymakers in developing countries sought to retain manipulative instruments to intervene in markets, especially by means of restrictive measures. The GATT, while enshrining a fundamental principle of trade liberalization, was required, for the reasons described above, to accept the state-interventionism of developing countries, and allowed many exceptions to the rules. The following are notable.

Balance-of-payments restrictions

Although Article XI of the GATT prohibits member countries from adopting quantitative restrictions, Article XII prescribes that each state may restrict the quantity of imports in order to safeguard its external financial position and its balance of payments. Because the conditions for applying restrictive measures of Article XII are rather strict, developing countries demanded mitigation of the requirements, leading to the attachment of a separate provision on balance-of-payments restrictions for developing countries at the 1954–5 Review Session, namely, Article XVIII: B. Under this provision, developing countries are permitted to use quantitative restrictions in order "to ensure a level of reserves adequate for the implementation of its programme of economic development," which means restrictions are almost always possible.[9] In addition, periodic reviews by CONTRACTING PARTIES[10] over all restrictions under the Article gradually became ritual and meaningless. Moreover, developing countries adopting import-substitution policies failed to increase export earnings to support import-substituting industries which demand foreign exchange for importing capital equipment and intermediate goods (Krueger 1995: 8–9). Since most developing countries suffered from constant foreign exchange shortages, Article XVIII: B was quite easy to apply. In fact, from 1974 to 1987 developing countries declared almost 3,500 quantitative restrictions under the balance-of-payments exception (Finger and Winters 1998: 376–7).

Non-reciprocity

While Article II of the GATT requires member countries to maintain tariffs below the levels of "scheduled" concessions, it is one of the major principles of the GATT to incrementally reduce the existing general level of tariffs through periodic multilateral negotiations, or "rounds." In addition, such negotiations are supposed to proceed on a reciprocal and mutually advantageous basis, as declared in Article XXVIII *bis*. Developing countries, however, were naturally very reluctant to offer tariff concessions that are equivalent in value to those offered by developed countries, since they felt they had to maintain high tariff barriers to protect domestic infant industries that confronted import competition. In the 1954–5 Review Session, developing countries demanded exceptional treatment to the principle of reciprocity. This demand was accepted and materialized in Article XXVIII *bis*: 3, which reads that "the needs of less-developed countries for a more flexible use of tariff protection to assist their economic development" shall be taken into account.[11]

This does not mean that developing countries cannot benefit from mutual tariff concessions among advanced industrial countries, since Article I of the GATT ensures any advantage granted by any member shall be accorded unconditionally to all other members (General Most-Favored-Nation treatment: MFN). As a result, most developing countries became bystanders in round negotiations, while free-riding on outcomes. Until the Uruguay Round began, less than 30 percent of all the tariffs in developing countries were on the GATT's reduction schedule. By contrast, 80 percent of developed countries' tariffs were scheduled for reduction (Finger and Winters 1998: 368). Average tariff rates in developing countries were also higher than those of developed countries, which were close to zero at the beginning of the Uruguay Round.

Special and differential treatments

The main purpose of exceptional GATT treatment was to obtain permission for import-decreasing restrictions in developing countries. It had become obvious, however, by the end of the 1950s, that the import substitution strategy would not be sufficient for promoting economic development, because it led to shortages of foreign exchange necessary for importing intermediate goods. Thus, it became important to dramatically increase export earnings. This led to the demand for the non-reciprocal opening of advanced industrial markets through preferential tariff rates. This meant active, unilateral, and non-reciprocal trade liberalization by advanced industrial countries in order to give developing countries more improved access to their markets. The UNCTAD II of 1968 declared the establishment of the "Generalized System of Preferences (GSP)." Later, in 1971, the CONTRACTING PARTIES of the GATT finally waived the provisions of Article I (MFN) for a period of ten years, making possible the implementation of the GSP. At the same time, another decision also waived Article I, allowing developing countries to accord preferential treatments with respect to products originating in other developing countries. In sum, by the end of 1971, the MFN was invalidated not only in North–South trade but also in South–South trade (Carreau and Juillard 1998: 276). These two provisional waivers were made permanent in the so-called Enabling Clause of 1979, and plenty of preferential tariff reductions were adopted by developed countries. The Enabling Clause also authorized exceptional treatment for developing countries in GATT rules dealing with non-tariff trade barriers, such as the Subsidies Code, the Government Procurement Code and the Standards Code. Accordingly, developing countries received a wide variety of "special and differential treatments," which exempted them from the obligation to liberalize non-tariff measures and regulations.

The non-reciprocal, preferential treatment was so tolerant that policy-makers in developing countries found it possible to maintain tariff and non-tariff measures, sheltering domestic markets from exposure to international competition in a GATT-consistent manner. Thus, it is clear that the international trade regime did not compel or persuade policymakers in developing and transitional countries to liberalize their economic systems; rather, its direct function was to tolerate and even encourage them to deviate from fundamental GATT principles and engage in intense market-control policies.

The indirect function of the regime: stimulating spontaneous liberalization

A variety of factors have been pointed to as causes for the trend toward reduced market intervention in developing and transitional countries since the 1980s. Frequently mentioned are the following: a growing sense of disillusionment with past development strategies in the face of a deep economic shock caused by the global recession in the early 1980s; the financial, political and ideological pressure exercised by international creditors like the IMF, the World Bank and transnational private banks; the dissemination of neoclassical economic ideas among officials, technocrats and academic economists in developing countries, many of whom were trained in North American universities.[12] On the contrary, considering the role of the GATT described above, the international trade regime seems to have been quite irrelevant, or even detrimental to the shift toward market liberalization. Here I reveal, however, another aspect of the dual functions of the international trading regime, which indirectly pushed them toward drastic reforms.

Inviting macroeconomic collapse

Under the import-substitution strategy, developing countries had to import capital equipment and intermediate goods, while restricting imports of consumer goods. However, they were doomed to suffer from foreign exchange shortages, since their export earnings were insufficient to finance imports. Things worsened for several reasons. First, nominal exchange rates were fixed at unrealistically over-valued levels in order to import capital goods or commodities less expensively, which disadvantaged exporting sectors. Second, foreign aid and investment devoted to export-promotion was quite limited. Finally, domestic import-substituting producers with monopoly positions in the sheltered market were free from competition in the world economy, which resulted in perpetually low competitiveness. Foreign exchange shortages and the resulting large current account deficits threw most developing countries into debt to international financial institutions and transnational private banks.[13] This made these countries vulnerable to crisis when the early 1980s global recession dried up international loans and raised interest rates in international financial markets. This enabled international financial institutions, other creditors and neoclassical economists to intervene in the economic policies of developing countries. Indeed, these actors exercised direct influence on the correction of the misguiding policies. In this respect, the drastic policy reform toward economic liberalization in developing countries seemed to take place completely outside the international trade regime.

But we should also pay attention to the indirect functions served by GATT practices. As the trade regime tolerated the maintenance of import restrictive measures and, despite such conduct, ensured automatic MFN benefits, the cost of pursuing market-control policies was kept to a minimum. Without the generous tolerance for free-riding on the fruits of the GATT, such market-controlling development strategies might have been abandoned much earlier before it led to destructive fiscal imbalance and macroeconomic collapse. In other words, the GATT, through a series of self-contradictory protectionist exemptions, functioned as an essential precondition for enabling drastic liberalizing reforms in developing countries. By no means was this paradoxical consequence intended, the international trade regime could be said to have contributed in an indirect and unexpected way to the pivotal policy change in developing countries.

Evoking broad opposition to the protectionist policies

According to classical international trade theory, unilateral trade liberalization is sufficient for a country as a whole to become better off. The principle of reciprocity or mutuality, asking for trading partners' equivalent concessions, has an affinity with mercantilist ideas that detest importing foreign products without obtaining equivalent opportunities to export. Reciprocity as a principle of international trade, however, has important *political* implications. When bargaining is reciprocal, exporters in a country will support the concession by their government in order to obtain concessions from other governments. Accordingly, a country's export coalition will be a strong constituency for trade liberalization.[14]

As an effective political instrument, reciprocity was not available in developing countries, since the GATT exempted developing countries from the principle of reciprocity. Therefore, even if policymakers felt the need for trade liberalization, they could not find enough domestic supporters to push the effort forward. On the contrary, they have been confronted with protectionist requirements from interest groups, which were strengthened by the official recognition of non-reciprocity.[15] Protectionist rent-seeking activities, even when aimed at pursuing self-interest, and irrelevant to the development of infant industries or national interests, became extremely hard to turn down (Hudec 1987: Ch. 9). Politicians and government officials in developing countries had to continue economically irrational market controls such as restricting imports, managing inefficient state-owned enterprises, and subsidizing noncompetitive domestic producers. Consequently, most developing countries suffered from large fiscal deficits and increased money supply, which invited inflation. Thus, *even if* politicians and policymakers in developing countries were aware of the destructive effects of market-intervention policies, the international trade regime hindered them from changing their policies toward liberalization. Indeed, in many developing countries, elaborate relationships of patronage or corruption were reinforced between politicians and import-competing sectors, which sought parochial benefits from protectionism at the expense of long-run national development. As a consequence, macroeconomic deterioration as evidenced in fiscal deficits and high inflation finally aroused broad domestic opposition. We should note that the realization of drastic liberalizing reforms in this way would be attributed in part to the international trade regime, which encouraged politicians and protectionist beneficiaries through the extension of non-reciprocal treatment. This was a major indirect function of the international trade regime.

Promoting globalization

At least among advanced industrial countries, the international trade regime has facilitated and promoted trade liberalization. Multilateral negotiations worked fairly well along the principle of reciprocity to promote substantial reduction of tariffs in these countries. In addition, revolutionary progress in transportation and communications has reduced transaction costs in international trade. These promoted "globalization," which has dramatically increased international trade.[16] Accordingly, the opportunity costs of insulating a country from the world economy have risen. Enterprises in a country with high tariffs and other restrictions cannot take advantage of less expensive products in world markets. Nor can they transfer stages of their production processes overseas, because high trade barriers make inter- and intra-firm transactions very costly. Thus, import restrictions deprived domestic industries of advantageous opportunities, strategic perspective and, consequently, international competitiveness. Furthermore, notwithstanding the existence of the MFN clause, it was rather difficult for competitive industries in developing countries to obtain substantial concessions from advanced industrial countries, unless their government would offer meaningful concessions. Consequently, the industries in developing countries with specific types of comparative advantage were precluded from getting into the large markets of advanced industrial countries. The loss of these potential GATT benefits was so remarkable that some policymakers and entrepreneurs in developing and transitional countries, realizing these opportunity costs, carried on a vigorous campaign for liberalizing reforms. This fostered the decline of those who clung to "statist" development strategies.[17] Accordingly, the international trade regime exercised an indirect and exogenous influence on the shift of political opinions about desirable economic policies for development.

To sum up, the visible and direct function of the international trade regime before policy reforms was to encourage policymakers and private sector actors in these developing countries to concentrate on, and cling to, market-intervening and protectionist policies by exempting these countries from most of the obligations of the GATT. On the other hand, the regime indirectly influenced the shift of economic policies in these countries by leading to fiscal and monetary crises, evoking wide social opposition to the systems' poor economic outcomes, and promoting an alluring global free-trade system. We should note that these dual functions of the regime, which were, in fact, both sides of the same coin, jointly contributed to policy reforms in these countries, although these complicated and hidden functions of the regime have not yet been well explored.

After policy reform: the dual functions reversed

The emerging domestic conditions of the developing and transitional countries described in the previous section, combined with the rapid erosion of their bargaining position caused by changes in the international political environment, namely the end of the Cold War, led these

96 *Kazuyori Ito*

countries to deep integration with the international trade regime. On the other hand, the process of integration entails another problem that may once again differentiate the position of developing and transitional countries inside the regime from that of advanced industrial countries. This contradictory character of the contemporary international trade regime will be explained in this section.

The primary function: integration and harmonization

Once developing countries decided to abandon market-control policies and to open up their economies to the rest of the world, policymakers increasingly came to see the advantages in working within the GATT. An agreement to launch a new round was reached in 1985 with the strong support of developing countries. Indeed, they participated in the Uruguay Round with unprecedented aggressiveness.

Lowering walls for trade

The Uruguay Round Balance-of-Payments Understanding encourages the tariffication of existing quantitative restrictions and the gradual phasing-out of balance-of-payment measures. Developing countries had already recognized the need to get rid of such restrictions as a necessary step in the process of policy reform and by June 1996 only three developing countries, Tunisia, India and Pakistan, maintained import restrictions declared under Article XVIII: B (Finger and Winters 1998: 376–7). In addition, developing countries agreed at the Uruguay Round to reduce their tariff rates by an average of 8 percent, whereas advanced industrial countries reduced theirs by an average of 3.2 percent.[18] In the Uruguay Round, developing countries were not bystanders, nor free-riders on developed country tariff reductions, but were, for the first time, active participants, willing to offer concessions on their side.

New issues

The United States was eagerly seeking to extend GATT rules into such "new issues" as enhancing trade in services, liberalizing trade-related investment regulations, and improving protection of intellectual property rights. In contrast to the "traditional" issues dealt with under the GATT, namely the removal of border trade restrictions such as tariffs and quantitative limits, these "new" issues are seeking to coordinate numerous behind-the-border policies formerly regarded as a matter of domestic jurisdiction (Haggard 1995: 2). Most developing countries approved of incorporating these new issues, because they faced strong incentives to coordinate their domestic regulations with those of advanced industrial countries in order to regain access to foreign investment and borrowing markets. In addition, since the final package of a series of agreements in the Uruguay Round had to be accepted in its entirety ("single undertaking"), developing countries were able to exchange the acceptance of new issues in exchange for concessions from advanced industrial countries in such areas as agriculture, textiles and clothing, which were politically volatile issues in developing countries. In this way, agreements were made that expanded the scope of the international trade regime dramatically and stimulated further integration and harmonization of domestic economic institutions in each country.

Tightening up the discipline

As some developing countries began to export their products in great volume, advanced industrial countries faced strong demands for the protection of threatened domestic industries. The policymakers had recourse to GATT rules regulating "unfair" trade such as dumping and subsidies (antidumping and countervailing duties, or "ADs and CVDs"). On the other hand, since the GATT rules regarding safeguards were difficult for developed countries to employ, developing countries were, in turn, encouraged to carry out voluntary export restraints (VERs), whose legality was dubious in the GATT system. Furthermore, the Congress of the United States passed the 1974 Trade Act containing Section 301, as amended by the Omnibus Trade and Competitiveness Act of 1988. This legislation sought to force other countries, through threat or imposition of sanctions, to liberalize or coordinate their policies concerning new issues with those of the United States. In order to reduce these unilateral or bilateral pressures exercised by advanced industrial countries, in particular by the United States, developing countries sought to clarify and tighten the discipline regarding ADs, CVDs and safeguards, and to strengthen the GATT machinery of dispute settlement (Haggard 1995: 43–4). This pursuit of discipline resulted in clarified and tightened agreements in these areas.

Aggressive participation by developing countries transformed the GATT into a truly global and comprehensive trade regime. The organizational character of the regime was strengthened as well, which led to the establishment of the WTO. Member countries have generally showed respect for, and compliance with, the rules of WTO agreements. The increased use of the WTO dispute settlement procedure by developing countries represents the diffusion of rule-oriented approaches.[19] In addition, the Trade Policy Review Mechanism (TPRM) enables the periodic collective assessment of member countries' trade policies and practices covered by WTO agreements. Pressures from other countries will contribute to the coordination of trade policies through future WTO agreements.

For those countries recently admitted to the WTO, transitional economies in particular, the accession procedure is an important opportunity for harmonization. When a country submits a request for accession a working party is established, and the submitted memorandum about the foreign trade system and relevant legislation of the applicant country is examined in detail. If the examination in the working party is sufficiently advanced, member countries may initiate bilateral market-access negotiations, the result of which will apply to all other members through the MFN clause. This accession procedure helps policymakers in each applicant country to ensure that their laws and regulations conform to WTO agreements.

Therefore, as a result of the economic liberalization reform in the developing world, the international trade regime achieved a global and comprehensive character. Member countries have clearly recognized that they should comply with the rules and procedures of the regime, and the developing and transitional countries in particular have become aware of the benefits of compliance. By complying with the rules of the WTO, policymakers in these countries are able to arrange a favorable environment for foreign direct investments, to weaken domestic political forces requiring protection and to check and contain unilateral and bilateral pressures from advanced industrial countries. Accordingly, the integration and harmonization, *without deviation from fundamental principles*, of each country's economic institutions, regulations and policies with multilaterally negotiated norms have become the primary function of the international trade regime.

The complementary function: technical assistance and preferential treatments

The fact that developing and transitional countries have become important constituents of the international trade regime indicates that, without ensuring their confidence in, and satisfaction with, the regime's operation, the organizational process as a whole could break down at any time. Such a condition is considerably different from that of the former GATT regime, which developed countries could manage autonomously. This change in organizational character was already realized at the 1999 Seattle WTO Ministerial Conference that failed mainly because of disagreement between developing and developed countries. Recognizing the crisis of the regime, advanced industrial countries initiated confidence-building measures within the WTO, and the General Council decision of the WTO in May 2000 supported these initiatives.

Capacity building

As explained above, each country is required to coordinate and harmonize their non-tariff domestic institutions with international norms. But those countries lacking in financial and human resources, or lacking the requisite experience in administering or implementing WTO obligations, find it difficult to fully and quickly harmonize their regulations.[20] Thus, a number of WTO agreements prepared "special and differential treatment" for developing and transitional countries, permitting transition periods for full implementation. Most of these treatments expired by the end of 1999, but many developing members requested their extension (WTO 2001: 24). To help policymakers in those countries to improve their ability to fulfill their WTO obligations, advanced industrial countries have arranged various capacity-building programs. The Integrated Framework (IF) is one of the most important institutional mechanisms for the delivery of trade-related technical assistance to least developed countries (LDCs).[21] In addition, several developed countries supported the creation of the Advisory Center on WTO Law, which assists developing and LDC members to use the dispute settlement procedures in order to promote adherence to WTO provisions.

Market-access improvements

Since 1974, major developed countries have provided unilateral duty-free treatment to a number of goods from developing countries (GSP). Some of the GSP programs have recently been extended: the EU "Everything but Arms (EBA)" program; the United States' African and Caribbean access programs; and Japan's 99 percent initiative for industrial products (WTO 2001: 41–2). Although these preferential systems were provided, developing countries often lack the domestic capacity to exploit the market-access opportunities that would allow the expansion of their trade-related sectors. Thus, advanced industrial countries have also provided bilateral assistance programs in order to assist capacity-building efforts in these areas.

These "special and differential treatments" and technical assistance do not mean that there exists essential disagreement between developed and developing countries about what constitutes a desirable economic system nor about the importance of the fundamental norms and principles of the international trade regime. In order to accomplish the primary function of global integration and harmonization of economic institutions and policies, the regime implicitly obliges advanced industrial countries to provide technical assistance and preferential treatment to developing and transitional countries so that they can manage market-oriented economic policies more effectively. Only through these efforts will policymakers be able to comply with, and make use of, WTO laws more properly, and increase confidence in the regime.[22] Without the assistance and differentiation, they would find it very hard to fulfill the same obligations as those of advanced industrial countries, which would likely lead to the breakdown of the regime. Therefore, the necessity of providing these additional measures can be regarded as an indispensable "complementary" function of the regime that aims to bring developing countries inside the regime. In this regard, the differential treatments provided by the WTO for developing and transitional countries are quite different in character and goals from those of the GATT. This represents vividly the "reversed" character of the dual functions of the WTO regime in contrast with the GATT.

Conclusion

The foregoing analysis examines the functional implications of the international trade regime. In reality, however, the way each state has liberalized its economic system varies significantly. Each country or region has its own historical background, political circumstances, comparative advantages and political-economic ties with other countries or regions. These characteristics have diversified the processes and outcomes of the liberalization process in each country. The international trade regime, on the one hand, offering the opportunities of multilateral negotiations and a common frame of reference, ensures the homogeneity of the otherwise infinitely diversified processes and outcomes of liberalization. On the other hand, the regime in some respects enables, or even encourages, the diversified, characteristic and path-dependent forms of policy reforms in each country or region. Here I briefly examine how and to what extent the regime contributes to such divergence.

Divergence among issue areas

The developing and transitional countries as a whole by no means share common interests on all issue areas on the negotiating table. The varying interests among these countries emerged during the process of the Uruguay Round. They have demonstrated a tendency to rely increasingly on regional positions or issue-area coalitions such as textiles and clothing or agriculture (Jara 1993: 11). A new range of bargaining options has emerged allowing a selection of partners on an issue-specific basis (Tussie 1993b: 183).

The problem of agricultural trade liberalization created the issue-specific coalition in the process of the Uruguay Round, namely the Cairns Group in which developed and developing countries crossed old boundaries and converged.[23] Agricultural products had been granted special treatments under the GATT; export subsidies and quantitative restrictions were permitted under Article XVI and Article XI, respectively. The net-exporting countries of agricultural products that were eager to liberalize the rules of the regime assembled to strengthen the bargaining positions. On the other hand, policymakers in other countries who are politically responsible for protecting their inefficient agricultural sectors desperately fought to avoid rapid (or any) liberalization. In this regard, since there were both exporting and importing countries of agricultural products within developing countries, they could not share common interests on the issue.

As for the "new issues" mentioned in the previous section, the East Asian Newly Industrializing Countries (NICs) welcomed the introduction of these issues into the GATT regime. Since the NICs had abandoned the import-substitution policies, they pursued export-led growth with both public and private foreign capitals. In order to attract foreign investments continuously, policymakers in the NICs had to liberalize and rationalize their economic regulations and policies as soon as possible. In addition, a multilateral process was desirable for countries that had been increasingly threatened by bilateral pressure from the United States over the new trade issues. On the other hand, those countries that clung to the traditional import-substitution policies and extensive market-controlling strategies (India and Brazil in particular), but also including socialist governments (Cuba, Yugoslavia, Nicaragua, Tanzania), contended that a number of Tokyo Round issues such as safeguards, textiles and agriculture were unfinished, and that negotiation on the new issues would be premature.[24] Many developing countries supported the NICs' approach.[25]

The heterogeneity of the issue-specific interests of developing and transitional states represents, in part, the divergence in past developmental strategies, variation in comparative advantage, or variation in relationships with advanced industrial countries, particularly with the United States. Trade liberalization did not necessarily mean a simple, homogeneous and mutually profitable process for all developing and transitional countries. How then, could the international trade regime and multilateral trade negotiations under its auspices manage the divergence among these countries? First, the comprehensiveness of the international trade regime allowed enormous issue areas to be incorporated into the multinational negotiations. Second, the "single undertaking" principle enabled the package-dealing negotiation, exchanging concessions across issue areas. Therefore, despite the heterogeneity of preferences among these countries, policymakers in each country could seek to obtain beneficial concessions at the expense of many other issue areas.

Divergence among regions

Regional agreements are often one of the most powerful driving forces for trade liberalization. As multilateral trade negotiations have become more and more difficult with the multiplied members and issues, policymakers feel more inclined toward regional cooperation, which can be negotiated by a limited number of countries and issues and greater similarity in historical experiences, geographical situations and economic systems. The international trade regime basically permits such regional cooperation so long as it does not preclude multilateral liberalization efforts. Article XXIV of the GATT provides rules for free trade zones and customs unions. However, the requirements under Article XXIV, such as the restriction on discriminatory and trade-diverting effects, have been unilaterally interpreted and seriously distorted (Jara 1993: 24). In fact, regional cooperation usually has intense discriminatory and trade-diverting effects against the rest of the world. Moreover, some regional regimes can influence the liberalizing processes of member countries, as seen in the EU-accession requirements on eastern and central European countries. Thus, variation in the location of developing and transitional countries promotes divergent liberalization paths. The international trade regime, having been tolerant toward various forms of regional integration, has contributed to the expansion of such regional uniqueness.

Variation in domestic political conditions

Domestic political circumstances and institutions naturally affect the decision-making processes and policy outcomes. In a country that is liberalizing its former market-controlling protectionist system, policymakers will be put into conflict with traditionally protected groups, such as subsidized industries or protected farmers. Some governments may have broad political latitude to pursue drastic liberalizing reforms, while other governments may have to give in to protectionist demands in order to remain in power, which will necessarily act as a continuing constraint on liberalization. The international trade regime, since its establishment, has enabled member countries to choose a "compromised" style of trade liberalization, particularly in the form of elaborate trade remedies that permit members to protect seriously endangered domestic industries from international competition. As a result, developing and transitional countries can launch trade liberalization reforms, while protecting, if necessary, some economically noncompetitive but politically powerful industries in a GATT-consistent or WTO-consistent manner. Increased use of antidumping measures[26] or safeguards by developing countries reflect such incremental political processes of "compromised" trade liberalization. Therefore, we can say the highly flexible character of the international trade regime has provided members with various methods to achieve trade liberalization, reflecting diverse political environments within which policymakers must make decisions.

In analyzing the contemporary development strategies adopted in developing and transitional countries, it is necessary to pay attention to the external influences, assistance and even pressure from international organizations, as well as to pay close attention to the domestic decision-making processes. This chapter illustrates how and to what extent the international trade regime has affected the formation and transformation of the development strategies in these countries by proposing that we view the trade regimes as characterized by different "dual functions." Recognizing these synchronic and diachronic functions of the regime is helpful for more integrated studies of the way these countries have managed development in the last half century. It also sheds light on what their strategies will be in the future. At the same time, the framework presented here has to be complemented by individual case studies that explore the different ways development has progressed in each country, region and specific political situation. Such analyses will improve understanding of the multiple roles that the international trade regime played in various stages of the development process.

Notes

1 An international "regime" in this chapter refers to a set of fundamental principles, norms and values in a particular issue area (international trade here), and some concrete agreements that spell out the rules and procedures necessary to achieve the goals expressed in those principles (Krasner 1983).
2 See Krueger (1998: 3). Frankel also notes these two characteristics as the main causes of "globalization," saying that "[t]he two major drivers of economic globalization are reduced costs to transportation and communication in the private sector and reduced policy barriers to trade and investment on the part of the public sector" (Frankel 2000: 45). On the other hand, Keohane and Milner identify reduced transaction costs as a cause of "internationalization" of trade, with lowered trade barriers as its "effect." They refer to internationalization as "the processes generated by underlying shifts in transaction costs that produce observable flows of goods, services, and capital," whereas "the liberalization of foreign trade and investment policies, the deregulation of domestic markets, shifts in fiscal and monetary policy, and changes in the institutions designed to affect these policies" are included in "possible changes" provoked by economic internationalization (Keohane and Milner 1996: 4). As for the developing and socialist countries, we can see not only declined costs of transportation and communication but also lowered government barriers in advanced industrial countries by virtue of the international trade regime as the given external environment, which then would induce the developing and socialist countries to change their economic policies and institutions.
3 According to Kindleberger, public goods for stabilizing the international economy are a market for distressed goods, a steady flow of capital, a management of the structure of foreign-exchange rates and so on (Kindleberger 1981: 247).
4 This assumption of hegemonic stability theory that the collective action problem surrounding the supply of public goods for an open international trade regime are impossible to overcome has been a target of intense assaults by critics. They contend that, as Thomas Schelling's notion of "k-group" suggests, it is possible for two or more secondary powers to produce international collective goods after hegemonic power have declined because they have an incentive to avoid the collapse of the regime and consequently become willing to participate in collective action (Snidal 1985: 597–612); (Lake 1993: 462–7). Certainly it may be possible for two or more states to act collectively, but specific conditions must be achieved before public goods are actually provided. Therefore, whether or not the secondary powers of the European states or Japan have succeeded in the role of providing public goods after the decline of American hegemony is yet to be examined and demonstrated.
5 Krasner, who also presented a variation on hegemonic stability theory, does not assume a hegemonic state is benevolent, but coercive. A hegemonic state

"can use its economic resources to create an open economy.... It can withhold foreign grants and engage in competition, potentially ruinous for the weaker states." Here the hegemonic power uses its superiority to force other, smaller states to contribute to maintaining the trading system that satisfies its self-interest (Krasner 1976). In this case, what matters will be the relative ability of the hegemonic state to pressure subordinate states rather than the absolute ability to provide public goods. Both coercive and benevolent nature, however, can coexist in a hegemonic state (Snidal 1985: 585–90; Lake 1993: 467–8).
6 Keohane 1984: Ch. 5. See also, Oye (1986); Axelrod and Keohane (1986).
7 This kind of "gains" problem can occur among advanced industrial countries, of course. Krasner argues that there can be many ways to achieve mutual gains, and some may give a larger share to one state, while others give a larger share to another. Since there are many points along the Pareto frontier, distributional conflicts can happen over which point along the frontier should be chosen (Krasner 1991; Powell 1994: 334–43).
8 With the enlargement of suffrage and the democratization in Western Europe since the late nineteenth century, governments came to assume much more direct responsibility for domestic social security and economic stability. They could not maintain the laissez-faire liberalism pervasive in the mid-nineteenth century any longer but, rather, had to manage international economic transactions carefully so that domestic industries and their employees might not be beaten by foreign competitors. This "welfare-state consensus" was shared by most states in Western Europe, and constituted an implicit, but fundamental, principle of the GATT (Ruggie 1982: 379–98; Ikenberry 1989).
9 In contrast, Article XII requires members to apply it only when they face "imminent threat" and "very low reserves." For a comparison of the provisions of Article XII and Article XVIII: B, see GATT 1994: 346.
10 Expressed all in capitals to signify the contracting parties acting jointly under the GATT agreement.
11 Furthermore, Article XXXVI: 8, contained in Part IV (Trade and Development) of the GATT added in 1966, states that "the developed contracting parties do not expect reciprocity for commitments made by them in trade negotiations to reduce or remove tariffs and other barriers to the trade of less-developed contracting parties." Although, from the viewpoint of legal terminology, Part IV did not create any new rights or obligations between developing and developed countries, it reveals how bitterly the fundamental GATT principles were deprived of their legitimacy by the assault from developing countries.
12 On international constraints on domestic policy choices of developing countries, see Stallings (1992). Others place emphasis on the domestic political distribution of interests for the sustainability of liberalizing reforms induced by external factors (Biersteker 1992; Kahler 1992).
13 The external debt of developing countries rose from $141 billion in 1974 to $313 billion in 1978, $546 billion in 1982, and $620 billion in 1983 (Krueger 1995: 31).
14 On the political function of reciprocity, see Krueger 1998: 5–6.
15 Abbott argued that, under the international trade regime, public officials can act to further their nation's interest as a whole, and can avoid destructive pressures from protectionism. See Abbott (1985). But when it comes to the function of the international trade regime in developing countries, the regime made it difficult for policymakers in these countries to reject protectionist demands, and even helped protectionist interest groups to justify the claim that trade barriers are necessary for economic development.
16 Frieden and Rogowski describe various types of "exogenous easing" of international exchange (Frieden and Rogowski 1996: 26–7).

17 The pro-liberalizing effects of "globalization," however, vary across countries due to different institutional as well as political-economic conditions in each state. This point will be explained in the concluding section.
18 Among developing economies, South Asian and East Asian countries agreed to large reductions, 16.5 percent and 9.4 percent, respectively. Furthermore, although only 22 percent of all sorts of tariffs in developing countries had been "bound" under the GATT before the Uruguay Round, the number rose to 72 percent under the Uruguay Round agreement (Krueger 1995: 50). Although the average tariff reduction of Latin American countries in the Uruguay Round was rather small (2.4 percent), they carried out significant unilateral tariff reductions in the 1980s and 1990s. For example, Mexico reduced the average tariff rate from 23.5 percent in 1985 to 11.0 percent in 1988, Costa Rica from 22.3 percent in 1986 to 15.9 percent in 1992, Argentina from 30 percent in 1988 to 9 percent in 1991, and Brazil from 32.2 percent in 1990 to 14.2 percent in 1994 (Schatan 1993: 83; Rodriguez 1993: 109; Tussie 1993a: 128; Abreu 1993: 151).
19 "Between January 1995 and March 2001, there were 228 complaints, with about one quarter of the notifications coming from developing countries. More recently, nearly one half of the 46 complaints received during the 15 months from January 2000 through March 2001 were notified by developing countries" (WTO 2001: 2).
20 WTO (2001: 23). See also, Krueger (1995: 54–5).
21 The IF originated in October 1997 under the auspices of six agencies, namely the ITC, IMF, UNCTAD, UNDP, World Bank and WTO. The major goals of the IF are to prepare a multi-year country program, to hold a Round Table meeting and to evaluate results regularly by the staff of the six agencies and officials of developing countries.
22 Cullet also argues that "differential treatment is mostly based on mutually accepted non-reciprocity" whose eventual aim is the "empowerment of weaker actors" (Cullet 1999: 553–8). In addition, he notes that "differential treatment ... is no longer linked to the call for an overhaul of the economic and legal system.... In practice, differential treatment has thus become the price to be paid to ensure universal participation in ... agreements concerned with global problems" (Ibid.: 570–1).
23 The group consisted of Argentina, Australia, Brazil, Canada, Chile, Colombia, Fiji, Hungary, Indonesia, Malaysia, New Zealand, the Philippines, Thailand and Uruguay.
24 About the history and implication of the activities of these countries (the G10), see Kumar (1993).
25 These countries were regarded as the G20. They played a major role in generating a negotiating text for the Punta del Este meeting of the GATT in September 1986 (Haggard 1995: 43).
26 As of 1999, the number of antidumping investigations by developing countries is no less than that of advanced industrial states. The European Union and India each reported the highest number of initiations, at 68. Canada and Australia initiated 18 and 23 investigations respectively, while Brazil and South Africa each initiated 16 investigations.

References

Abbott, K.W. (1985) "The Trading Nation's Dilemma: the Functions of the Law of International Trade," *Harvard International Law Journal*, 26: 501–32.
Abreu, M.P. (1993) "Trade Policies and Bargaining in a Heavily Indebted

Economy: Brazil," in D. Tussie and D. Glover (eds) *The Developing Countries in World Trade: Policies and Bargaining Strategies*, Boulder, CO: Lynne Rienner Publishers.

Axelrod, R. and Keohane, R.O. (1986) "Achieving Cooperation under Anarchy: Strategies and Institutions," in K.A. Oye (ed.) *Cooperation under Anarchy*, Princeton, NJ: Princeton University Press.

Biersteker, T.J. (1992) "The 'Triumph' of Neoclassical Economics in the Developing World: Policy Convergence and Bases of Governance in the International Economic Order," in J.N. Rosenau and E.-O. Czempiel (eds) *Governance without Government: Order and Change in World Politics*, Cambridge, UK; New York: Cambridge University Press.

Carreau, D. and Juillard, P. (1998) *Droit International Économique*, 4e édn, Paris: L.G.D.J.

Cullet, P. (1999) "Differential Treatment in International Law: Towards a New Paradigm of Inter-State Relations," *European Journal of International Law*, 10: 549–82.

Finger, J.M. and Winters, L.A. (1998) "What Can the WTO Do for Developing Countries?" in A.O. Krueger (ed.) *The WTO as an International Organization*, Chicago, IL: The University of Chicago Press.

Frankel, J. (2000) "Globalization of the Economy," in J.S. Nye Jr. and J.D. Donahue (eds) *Governance in a Globalizing World*, Washington, DC: Brookings Institution Press.

Frieden, J.A. and Rogowski, R. (1996) "The Impact of the International Economy on National Policies: An Analytical Overview," in R.O. Keohane and H.V. Milner (eds) *Internationalization and Domestic Politics*, Cambridge, UK: Cambridge University Press.

GATT (1994) *Analytical Index: Guide to GATT Law and Practice*, 6th edn, Geneva: GATT.

Haggard, S. (1995) *Developing Nations and the Politics of Global Integration*, Washington, DC: The Brookings Institution.

Hudec, R.E. (1987) *Developing Countries in the GATT Legal System*, Aldershot, UK; Brookfield, VT: Gower, for the Trade Policy Research Centre, London.

Ikenberry, G.J. (1989) "Rethinking the Origins of American Hegemony," *Political Studies Quarterly*, 104: 375–400.

Jara, A. (1993) "Bargaining Strategies of Developing Countries in the Uruguay Round," in D. Tussie and D. Glover (eds) *The Developing Countries in World Trade: Policies and Bargaining Strategies*, Boulder, CO: Lynne Rienner Publishers.

Kahler, M. (1992) "External Influence, Conditionality, and the Politics of Adjustment," in S. Haggard and R.R. Kaufman (eds) *The Politics of Economic Adjustment*, Princeton, NJ: Princeton University Press.

Keohane, R.O. (1984) *After Hegemony: Cooperation and discord in the World Political Economy*, Princeton, NJ: Princeton University Press.

Keohane, R.O. and Milner, H.V. (1996) "Internationalization and Domestic Politics: An Introduction," in R.O. Keohane and H.V. Milner (eds) *Internationalization and Domestic Politics*, Cambridge, UK: Cambridge University Press.

Kindleberger, C.P. (1981) "Dominance and Leadership in the International Economy," *International Studies Quarterly*, 25: 242–54.

Krasner, S.D. (1976) "State Power and the Structure of International Trade," *World Politics*, 28: 317–47.

—— (1983) "Structural Causes and Regime Consequences: Regimes as Interven-

ing Variables," in S.D. Krasner (ed.) *International Regimes*, Ithaca, NY: Cornell University Press.
—— (1991) "Global Communications and National Power: Life on the Pareto Frontier," *World Politics*, 43: 336–66.
Krueger, A.O. (1995) *Trade Policies and Developing Nations*, Washington, DC: The Brookings Institution.
—— (1998) "Introduction," in A.O. Krueger (ed.) *The WTO as an International Organization*, Chicago, IL: The University of Chicago Press.
Kumar, R. (1993) "Developing-Country Coalitions in International Trade Negotiations," in D. Tussie and D. Glover (eds) *The Developing Countries in World Trade: Policies and Bargaining Strategies*, Boulder, CO: Lynne Rienner Publishers.
Lake, D.A. (1993) "Leadership, Hegemony, and the International Economy: Naked Emperor or Tattered Monarch with Potential?" *International Studies Quarterly*, 37: 459–89.
Oye, K.A. (1986) "Explaining Cooperation under Anarchy: Hypotheses and Strategies," in K.A. Oye (ed.) *Cooperation under Anarchy*, Princeton, NJ: Princeton University Press.
Powell, R. (1994) "Anarchy in International Relations Theory: The Neorealist–Neoliberal Debate," *International Organization*, 48: 313–44.
Rodriguez, E. (1993) "The Multiple Tracks of a Small Open Economy: Costa Rica," in D. Tussie and D. Glover (eds) *The Developing Countries in World Trade: Policies and Bargaining Strategies*, Boulder, CO: Lynne Rienner Publishers.
Ruggie, J.G. (1982) "International Regimes, Transactions and Change: Embedded Liberalism in the Postwar Economic Order," *International Organization*, 31: 379–415.
Schatan, C. (1993) "Out of the Crisis: Mexico," in D. Tussie and D. Glover (eds) *The Developing Countries in World Trade: Policies and Bargaining Strategies*, Boulder, CO: Lynne Rienner Publishers.
Snidal, D. (1985) "The Limits of Hegemonic Stability Theory," *International Organization*, 39: 579–614.
Stallings, B. (1992) "International Influence on Economic Policy: Debt, Stabilization, and Structural Reform," in S. Haggard and R.R. Kaufman (eds) *The Politics of Economic Adjustment*, Princeton, NJ: Princeton University Press.
Tussie, D. (1993a) "Bargaining at a Crossroads: Argentina," in D. Tussie and D. Glover (eds) *The Developing Countries in World Trade: Policies and Bargaining Strategies*, Boulder, CO: Lynne Rienner Publishers.
—— (1993b) "Holding the Balance: the Cairns Group," in D. Tussie and D. Glover (eds) *The Developing Countries in World Trade: Policies and Bargaining Strategies*, Boulder, CO: Lynne Rienner Publishers.
WTO (2001) *Annual Report 2001*, Geneva: WTO.

4 The governance of global issues through regionalism
NAFTA as an interface between multilateral and North–South policies

Isidro Morales

Introduction

The core argument of this chapter is that the regionalization process formalized under the North American Free Trade Agreement (NAFTA) has become a major strategy of US trade diplomacy for advancing and expanding a new regulatory framework for dealing with the pressures of globalization. These pressures feature the re-organization of corporate competitive strategies, as well as a new disciplinary body for regulating market access in trade, investment and other related issues. The first part of this chapter suggests that regional clubs are called for to play a major role in better internalizing global rules at the bilateral level. I argue that regional regimes, such as NAFTA, are becoming the major locus upon which new governance mechanisms are being grounded, mainly in the trade and production domains. The second part is aimed at explaining how Washington conceived NAFTA as an interface between multilateral and bilateral policies, and between a North–South agenda. A third section attempts to calculate a balance sheet of regional experiences, at least in some key domains. Our goal is to explore the benefits of the trade regime as a policy tool for facilitating the governance of specific issue-areas. Lastly, the final part is devoted to the analysis of the potential deepening or widening of the regional mechanism.

Institutional regionalism as the foundation of global governance

Globalization and regional regimes

Globalization, understood as a reconfiguration of space, time and productive organization, has eroded the notions of state–state cooperation grounded on state-centered hegemonic architectures, mainly due to the transformation that states themselves are witnessing. One of these major transformations has been the fragmentation of state power and authority.

Today, state authority is not bound to a specific territory, as the classic concept of sovereignty was. State authority is now overlapped, in its own territory and beyond it, by multi-leveled layers of authoritative institutions that remain distinct in spite of being intertwined with the state. This explains why the term governance is becoming more accurate for explaining the new relationship that globalization is establishing between states, power, markets and non-government actors. We understand governance as the capacity for steering, shaping, managing and leading the impact of transnational flows and relations in a given issue-area, through the interconnectedness of different polities and their institutions in which power, authority and legitimacy are shared (see also Rosenau 1997).

A major trait of governance is that in most cases power and authority is exercised as a means for steering, shaping and inducing a certain behavior, or a certain approach, in order to deal with transnational problems, rather than imposing a coercive action. Governance means that institutional attributions and capabilities are distributed, although in an asymmetrical way, throughout a net of linkages. If global governance in certain issue areas is to be assured in the post Cold-War era, the regional club seems to be the most adequate device for dealing with it. Regional clubs, that is, principled-regimes or organizations grouping different states around common interests, reduce the political cost of building and maintaining a minimum threshold of governance on specific global issues, such as trade, finance, technology, monetary policies and so on. The major goal of the regional club is to make members become institutionally consistent with the structural transformations taking place in their external environment.

Economists have argued about the advantages and attractiveness of these policy regimes.[1] They stress mostly the supply of "public goods" these regimes normally provide, that is, goods that are in general terms non excludable and non-rival in their consumption (Kaul *et al.* 1999: 5). Most of these goods have intangible properties, like peace, security, macroeconomic or financial stability, trade openness and so on. Public goods could be offered at the national, regional and global level. The boundaries between these functional levels are not only defined by geographic considerations, but also by the positive externalities they may provide to the global system even if public goods are supplied locally. Lastly, the economic argument says that public goods have supply problems, because private agents cannot bear the cost if they cannot reap the benefits of providing such goods. There is a "market failure" problem that makes state intervention and cooperation highly desirable.

Various institutional economics approaches have also suggested that "global" public goods could be by-products of a pressing demand for institutional change. If we assume that markets are, above all, transactions governed by institutions under a polity, those institutions are doomed to change once major actors have realized that the costs of maintaining them are higher than the anticipated benefits of transforming them. For centuries, markets, either local or "international," were organized under national lines and priorities. Over the past three or four decades, financial markets began to be organized according to a cross-border rationale, which later was extended into the production and consumption domains. The digitalization of informational processes and the emergence of the virtual space as a territory of exchange moved banks and companies to restructure their corporate operations according to transnational guidelines. Hence, policies governing markets according to national calculations became inefficient and more costly to maintain in some areas. Market actors started to press for a redefinition of market polices at "minilateral" and regional levels, conforming to a so-called demand for regime creation (Lawrence 1996).

The role performed by regional regimes explains in many ways their impressive proliferation during the past years. During the last decade, more than 70 regional agreements on integration or trade cooperation were reported to the General Agreements on Tariffs and Trade (GATT) and its successor, the World Trade Organization (WTO) (*The Economist* 1998: 19). The bottom line on these different types of clubs has been to create, through different means, a minimum of policy convergence towards trade, investment and financial openness. Some of these agreements, such as the European Union (EU), NAFTA and MERCOSUR have formulated wider goals with more sophisticated mechanisms of enforcement. At the same time, these clubs have become an alternative option between unilateral and multilateral actions that provide more easily achieved gains than unilateral or multilateral agreements.

The nature of principled regimes

Regimes are important because of their direct impact on the exercise of relational power, that is, in the way regimes shape actors' policy options and behavior. As Keohane has stated, they create "patterned behavior" through which actors do not have to recalculate their options each time they take a decision (Keohane 1984). In this sense, regimes shape policy change both internationally and domestically. They facilitate policy convergence around shared values and rules that make sense to collective action, and they restrain local actors from undertaking policy options that undermine agreed upon rules.

Principled regimes are not politically neutral. Rather, they are the product of political bargaining that reflects both the interests of state-bureaucracies and the interests of domestic constituencies. A whole literature highlighting the double-edged diplomatic game, both international and domestic, suggests that any agreement facilitating cooperation is possible if a coalition of interests is at stake (Putnam 1988). This explains why all regimes encompass a set of "shelter" domains and devices, through which states or specific local actors escape to the governance of the regime (see Rugman and Verbeke 1994). These sheltered domains are the product of a political exchange that makes the regime feasible and sustainable. In the case of NAFTA, Canada sheltered its cultural industry, the US some high technology sectors and Mexico the oil and energy industries as part of their strategies to make NAFTA possible and sustainable.

If the regional club is not politically neutral, but the product of a political coalition, clustering interests that express themselves at international and domestic levels, regional clubs are thus nested on political asymmetries and bargaining capabilities. Nobody doubts that without US leadership and hegemony the foundations and functioning of the so-called Bretton Woods system would have been impossible. This very same leadership has been crucial in order to transform and adapt the new system once the impact of globalization became manifest. The US has played a major role in redefining both multilateral and "minilateral" rules on the economic front, as witnessed by the launching and conclusion of the Uruguay Round, the creation of the WTO, and the creation of NAFTA.

Although political asymmetries explain the creation and transformation of principled regimes, their adaptability and sustainability depend on the anticipated gains, both political and economic, that members can expect. These anticipated gains must be higher than those potentially obtained through unilateral or multilateral action. Nobody doubts that small countries have benefitted from their membership in the EU, regardless of whether or not France, Germany or Italy remain the major players. Canadians and Mexicans agree, although on different bases, that the two of them have benefitted from NAFTA, in spite of the dominant US role. As long as anticipated benefits are obtained and some asymmetries balanced, though not eliminated, regimes remain durable, sustainable and open to further transformations.

However, the effectiveness of governance through principled-regimes will depend not only upon the degree of interconnectedness among the different polities and institutions in a given issue area, but also on their capacity to construct and maintain a community of shared beliefs that gives consistency to the agreement. In fact, the legitimacy and maintenance of the whole club remain anchored, in the long run, to matters of interconnectedness and shared values. As Manuel Castells (1997: 171) has already suggested, the major attributes for making a network perform effectively are its connectedness (its ability to transmit noise-free communication among its members), and its consistency (the sharing of interests between the network goals and the goals of its components). If a regime could be compared to a network of shared authority and power, and of informational and other institutional resources, the strategic role they play in the construction of a new economic order lies in their ability to remain interconnected and consistent. How is this reflected in the case of NAFTA?

NAFTA as a US-led building block: promoting policy change and convergence

From free trade to fair trade: leveling the playing field

Though NAFTA was discussed and legitimized using an economic rationale (welfare gains from liberalizing trade and investment) in the US, Canada and Mexico, it was mainly nested as a major strategy of US trade diplomacy aimed at including new fields under GATT jurisdiction. Since the early 1980s, and during the past two decades, Washington has followed a three-tier approach on foreign trade issues: multilateral, unilateral and "minilateral" (Saborio 1992). At the multilateral level, the US made significant efforts to end the Tokyo Round and to initiate the Uruguay Round in order to negotiate a more ambitious global trade agenda. At the unilateral level, the US Congress activated old jurisdictions and initiated new ones in order to abate, though with a wider and enlarged meaning, unfair trade practices. And finally, at the "minilateral" or regional level the US first engaged in free trade talks with Canada, its main trade partner, and later included Mexico in what later became NAFTA. Both the Canada–US Free Trade Agreement (CUSFTA) and NAFTA had the role of widening the agenda on trade negotiations and abating unfair trade practices.

This three-level approach to US trade diplomacy made trade negotiations and bargaining appear at times contradictory, at times complementary. However, in many respects Washington committed to a cross-cutting agenda, the common aim of which was to "level the playing field," as it was called. This concept was the rationale under which both multilateral talks under the Uruguay Round were pursued, and bilateral negotiations with both Mexico and Canada were undertaken. Though through different means, this was also the rationale under which Capitol Hill mandated and/or activated unilateral relief vis-à-vis unfair trade practices.

By framing key policy initiatives under the major goal of "leveling the playing field," Washington sent the message to its major partners that non-compliance with old principles (such as non-discrimination or Most-Favored-Nation treatment) (MFN), or with new ones (such as "barring structural impediments" to trade), will be punished either at the multilateral or unilateral levels. In other words, with the notion of leveling the playing field US trade diplomacy aimed at obtaining symmetrical treatment from its trade partners; that is, a similar treatment to that given by the US. The quest for "symmetry" of treatment is deeply rooted in the policy debates of the 1970s and 1980s, under which key economic problems and transformations were perceived as the costs of supporting "free riders" in the international economic arena.

The very best example of this new trend inaugurated at the unilateral level was the Trade Act of 1974 and its Section 301, through which Washington enlarged the notion of "unfair trade" practices. This section defined two types of targeted practices: those that violate agreements that the US has with any of its partners, and those that are "unjustifiable, unreasonable, or discriminatory and burdens or restricts United States commerce" (Grier 1993). In order to restrain the proliferation of these newly defined unfair trade practices, Congress gave the President the ability to apply trade sanctions in order to make offending parties abide by them. These sanctions could consist of denying or modifying any trade concessions or increasing any tariff or non-tariff barrier.

The use of economic sanctions for making states respect agreements is not new in US foreign trade diplomacy. What became new in this legislation was the power given to the US President for imposing sanctions even in those cases when no violation exists, that is, when foreign practices are being judged as "unjustified, unreasonable and discriminatory." Discriminatory practices were already proscribed under the GATT, but the first two practices were not. Washington understood as unjustifiable those policies or practices that are inconsistent with international agreements; that is, practices that are not illegal – according to bilateral or multilateral agreements – but that play against the rules of the game as understood by the US. "Unreasonable" was defined as any act, policy or practice that, although not violating the international legal rights of the US, is otherwise unfair or inequitable (Grier 1993). Through such a broad and vague definition, almost any economic practice against US interests could be targeted by unilateral sanctions (see also Goldstein 1993: 195).

Section 301 and its later refinement by the Omnibus Trade and Competitiveness Act of 1988 (the so-called Super 301) have never been perceived as protectionist in the US. By prosecuting practices that either violate legal rights or discriminate against the US, or that are just simply "inconsistent" or "inequitable" to US practices, the US Congress sent the message to the world that it was not targeting the entry of imports, but rather the enhancement of exports by inducing partners to play by the rules. Congress was, however, cautious and granted to the President the discretionary power for using sanctions. If the Executive judged that national security concerns were at stake, or that the use of sanctions would imply political costs, sanctions could be waived.

This explains why petitions under this section have been rather few (Goldstein 1993: 216–17), compared, for example, to other "classical" unfair trade remedy practices such as antidumping (AD) and countervailing duties (CVD). However, the importance of Section 301, Super 301, and other similar legislation was that they enlarged the conceptual scope through which "unfair trade practices" were portrayed in the US. "Unfair" meant not only a violation of an agreement or a discrimination against a partner, but also practices that were inconsistent, unjustifiable, unreasonable and inequitable to US commerce. By using the "threat" of imposing trade sanctions for abating "unfair" practices, Washington aimed to expand market access by "leveling the playing field" with the rest of its trade partners. Traditional tools such as AD and CVD were preferred instead as a mechanism for dealing with unfair practices. Unlike the authority stemming from Section 301, procedures for imposing AD and CVD levies are quasi-adjudicative and therefore not entirely subordinated to political or strategic consideration by the White House. The Department of Commerce (DOC) and the International Trade Commission (ITC) make final decisions on these procedures, with no interference by the US Trade Representative (USTR). AD petitions became a major tool for American producers seeking relief from "unfair" practices. CVD petitions increased as well, though the rate of acceptance was less than that of AD (Goldstein 1993: 217–19). The flexibility introduced by Congress for activating these mechanisms made them a major sign of US "neo-protectionism." These trade strategies were portrayed by critics as the proliferation of "managed-trade" deals across different industry sectors.

The activation of AD and CVD, combined with other relief mechanisms and the enactment of Super 301 in 1988, increased the uncertainty over access to the US market. By increasing the uncertainty, and consequently the costliness of accessing its own market, the US increased the incentive for its trade partners to join trade negotiations either at multilateral or bilateral level. Incentives to address US complaints increased once trade partners realized that market access was not the only issue. By legitimizing the use of unilateral retaliation as a means for enhancing exports, the US also increased the costs for their trading partners of keeping the status quo in their respective trade policies. This explains why the US could simultaneously pursue multilateral and "minilateral" trade negotiations while maintaining an aggressive unilateral trade agenda.

The road to NAFTA

The opening of the "minilateral" track in US trade diplomacy was nested, so to speak, in the midst of mounting unilateral trade actions propelled by Congress since the first half of the 1970s, followed by the new profile of the multilateral agenda the White House tried to advance since the mid-1980s under the GATT. The first step was to reach a Free Trade Agreement (FTA) with Canada. For the US, to strike a whole trade package with Canada, at a time in which American unilateralism was increasingly criticized by many countries, was a way to curb domestic protectionist pressures at home and demonstrate renewed commitment toward a liberal and open trade agenda. At the same time, it was a way to advance what Washington understood as leveling the playing field with its major partners at bilateral, regional or multilateral levels.

As for Canada, going into trade talks with its powerful neighbor and most important partner had both domestic and foreign policy implications. The Canadians entered into bilateral negotiations once the

Trudeau years were over and the Conservative Party won the elections in the fall of 1984. The Conservative Party, with Brian Mulroney as Prime Minister, came into power with a new policy agenda, which in many ways announced the end of the "inward oriented" option that prevailed during the 1970s.

Mulroney's Conservative administration made clear the end of an economic policy based on natural resource exploitation. The new policy goal was to increase Canadian competitiveness in manufacturing and services, and for that, elimination of domestic non-tariff barriers was necessary in order to attract foreign investment. Thus, for Mulroney, entering into bilateral trade negotiations with the US had the dual aim of locking in domestic policy changes that signaled the end of the Trudeau era, and negotiating a whole package for guaranteeing market access to its major trading partner.

In parallel to the progressive dismantling of the remaining tariffs between the two countries within a span of ten years, the importance of the CUSFTA was that it revealed that the core of what Washington was negotiating at the multilateral level could be obtained more rapidly and effectively at the bilateral level. Canada and the US agreed, for example, to eliminate most tariffs on agriculture, an opening that both Europe and Japan had been very reluctant to accept under GATT rules (see Hart 1989: 131). On the sectoral level, ad hoc agreements were reached in the fields of the automotive, wine and spirits and energy industries. The latter became fully deregulated, ending the state-led energy policy followed in previous years. In relation to government procurement, a reduction of the threshold established in the GATT was obtained,[2] although this threshold only included federal government purchases, not state and local ones.

In relation to unfair trade practices, a mixed balance was achieved. Although Canada wanted to negotiate a common code regulating subsidies and dumping, no common jurisdiction could thereafter be obtained in this agreement, or under NAFTA. What was obtained, by contrast, was the introduction of an alternative dispute settlement mechanism under which arbitration panels could substitute for domestic courts in reviewing administrative decisions related to dumping or subsidies. As previously stated, it was in the area of unfair trade legislation that the US Congress and trade agencies did not have the counterbalancing authority of the White House. Hence, much of the so-called "neo-protectionism" of the late 1970s and 1980s was the by-product of a flexible interpretation and implementation of the rules regulating dumping and subsidies. Although no better definition of subsidy could be obtained under the CUSFTA, what Canadians obtained from this agreement was the right to challenge American administrative agencies under bilateral panels whose power was precisely defined by the two countries. All this was stipulated under Chapter 19, considered by some Canadians as the jewel of the agreement. By substituting domestic courts with arbitrated panels for challenging administrative decisions, it was anticipated that the "overzealous" use of American legislation for masking protectionist interests could eventually be reduced. The way Chapter 19 was designed, in fact, made possible that the panelist's awards could be expedited, be decided on an adjudicative basis and be binding to both parties. Such an effective and expeditious dispute settlement mechanism had not been possible to reach at the multilateral level.

The CUSFTA also included a more flexible dispute settlement mechanism embodied in Chapter 18 addressing any action that could violate, impair or nullify the agreement. In this case, a so-called "Free Trade Commission" (composed of cabinet-level representatives of the two governments) mediates for the disputing parties in order to facilitate consultations and reach a possible mutually satisfactory solution. If a solution is not reached, the conflict can be addressed by a panel whose goal is to draft an "action plan" under which the disputing parties can negotiate a solution. If this does not occur, the plaintiff has the right to impose economic sanctions equivalent to the damage infringed upon it. In so doing, the CUSFTA legitimized the use of trade sanctions as a means of compensating the breach or the impairment of what was agreed upon. Until then, the use of trade sanctions for compelling partners to comply with the rules remained a unilateral decision, mainly by the US, as long as the decisions taken under the GATT panels remained declaratory, due to the rule of the "positive consensus."

Finally, the CUSFTA made what Michael Hart considers a "cautious start" on what was defined at the time on the "new issues" such as services, business travel, investment, intellectual property rights and financial services (Hart 1989: 75).

Mexico and NAFTA

Two years after CUSFTA came into force, Mexico and the US initiated negotiations for a rather similar agreement. Once Canada joined the negotiations, under the condition that nothing that was agreed upon in CUSFTA would be revised, Washington confirmed its "minilateral" approach not only to its major two trading partners, but also to the rest of the Western Hemisphere. In fact, parallel to the opening of the NAFTA talks, President George Bush launched in Miami his so-called Enterprise for the Americas Initiative (EAI), aiming at the creation of a whole free trade area with the rest of the continent. The fact that Mexico accepted negotiating an integration package with Washington earmarked the beginning of a new era of Inter-American cooperation, ending traditional Mexican suspicion vis-à-vis US foreign policy towards Latin America that prevailed during the Cold War. Thus, NAFTA became not only an interface between US unilateral and multilateral trade policies, but also a bridge between a North and South agenda. Through NAFTA and the EAI

Washington initiated a building bloc in order to internalize and make more acceptable its trade agenda to developing countries.

Mexico joined NAFTA for similar reasons to those that explained Canada's signature of the CUSFTA. Although less industrialized and developed than Canada, for Mexico the US has become its major export market and source of investment, as is true of Canada. The surge of "contingent protectionism" in the US from the mid-1970s increased bilateral commercial tensions. Similar to what happened with Canadian exports, Mexico was suddenly threatened by dumping and countervailing duties in the US. As with Canada, the decision in Mexico to negotiate came from a new political administration that made economic liberalization its major political banner. Entering into trade negotiations with the US had the intention of locking in the domestic economic reforms the Mexican government initiated in 1986, but that gained decisive momentum during the Salinas de Gortari years (1988–94). At that time, the government decided to negotiate a CUSFTA-like package in order to obtain major concessions that otherwise could not be won.

Although the content of NAFTA as well as the organization of negotiations were highly influenced by the US–Canada deal, the scope of the negotiations widened. The liberalization of tariff barriers to trade in goods was designed and decided upon following the CUSFTA model. Sectoral provisions were better specified, for example, in the agriculture, textile, automotive and energy industries. Similar to Canada with respect to its cultural industries, Mexico refused to open its energy sector.

As for additions, NAFTA explicitly deregulated service sectors, including finance, over which Mexico was originally reluctant to negotiate. Whole new chapters were drafted on property rights and investment measures. A great innovation introduced by NAFTA was in fact its Chapter 11, through which private corporations could directly challenge government decisions concerning expropriation and investment regulations against international tribunals. Another innovation was the negotiation of two side agreements dealing with labor and environmental issues. These two agreements were nested in the original NAFTA agreement once Bill Clinton became US President, and were intended to obtain the support of the US Congress in passing the agreement. Through these two side agreements, Mexico accepted the use of sanctions, in the form of fines, if there was a "persistent failure" to comply with its domestic environmental legislation. A similar situation was accepted if there was a "persistent failure" to comply with labor legislation regulating minimum wages, safety and security standards at work and child labor. Canada refused to accept sanctions from another country and agreed that any claim regarding a failure to comply with its environment and labor standards would be handled by their domestic courts.

Notwithstanding, NAFTA became the first trade agreement legitimizing the use of sanctions in order to induce a country to comply with its respective labor and environmental legislation.

The governance of economic openness at the regional level

Market access: outcomes and problems

Although the goal of this chapter is not to assess the economic impact of NAFTA at the regional level, Figures 4.1 to 4.4 suggest that the agreement has been successful at least in fueling trade exchange between Canada and Mexico and their common major trading partner. Mexico has benefitted the most from the deal. Mexican exports to the US have grown at higher rates than in pre-NAFTA years, notwithstanding that export expansion started when Mexico joined the GATT (Figure 4.3); US exports to Mexico have also grown considerably, though this growth seems to have been steady since Mexico joined the GATT. As for Canada, CUSFTA and NAFTA have not modified previous commercial trends (see Figures 4.1 and 4.2), probably because tariffs between the two countries were already low (at least lower than tariffs prevailing between the US and Mexico), and their economies were already integrated in terms of production chains. We should also consider that Canada and Mexico's trade with the US is mainly intra-industry as multinational corporations have internalized cross-border markets through intra-firm transactions. This may also explain why, from 2001 to 2003, two-way trade from these two countries to the US slowed down as a consequence of the recession witnessed in the latter country at the turn of the century. Furthermore, monetary and exchange-rate policies have had a bigger impact on trade flows than the sole phase-out of tariffs. Mexico's booming exports after NAFTA could be

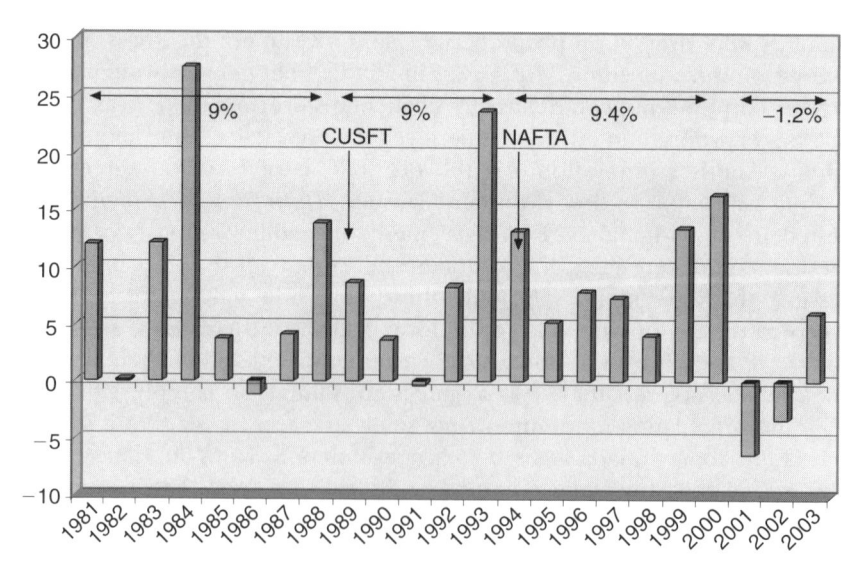

Figure 4.1 US imports from Canada 1981–2003 annual rate of growth (source: US Department of Commerce).

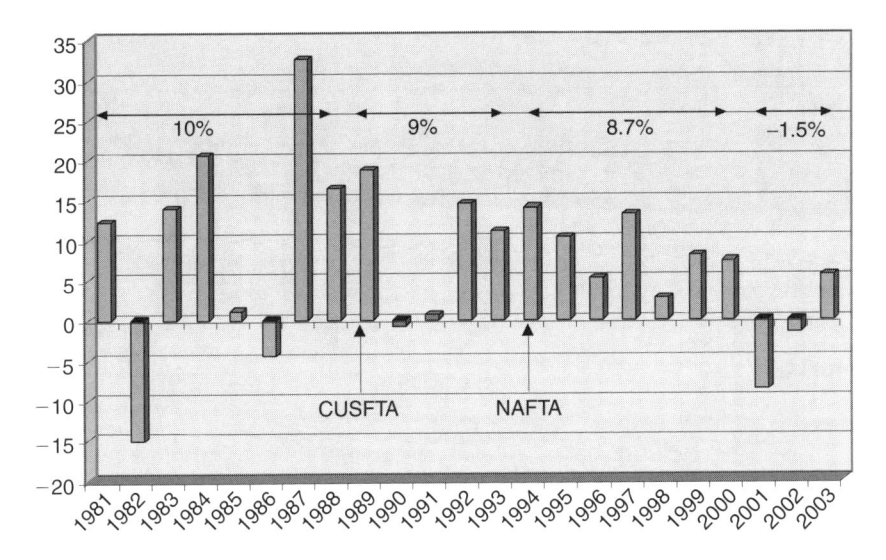

Figure 4.2 US exports to Canada 1981–2003 annual rate of growth (source: US Department of Commerce).

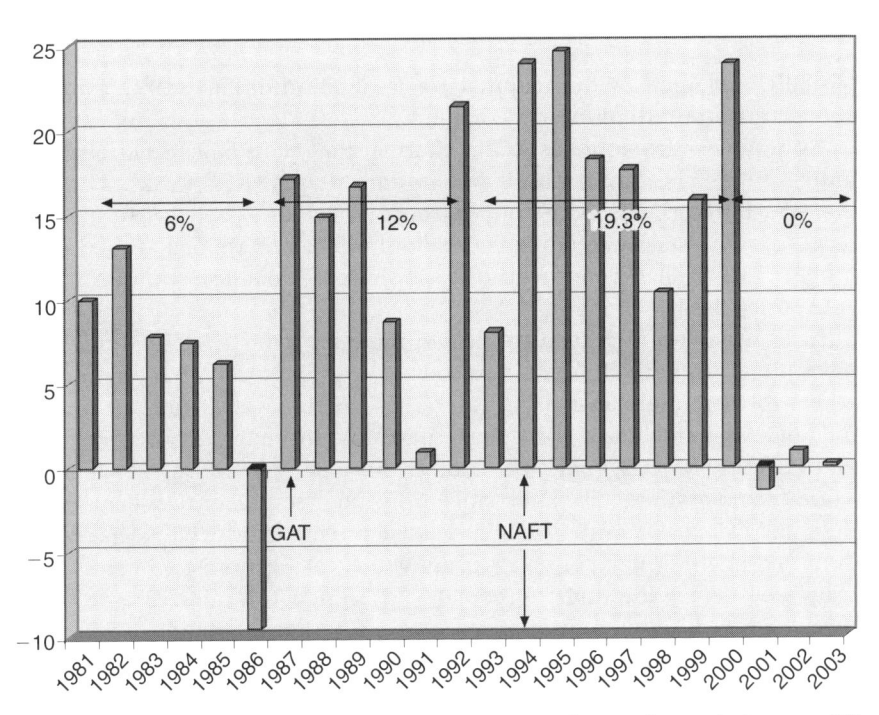

Figure 4.3 US imports from Mexico 1981–2003 annual rate of growth (source: US Department of Commerce).

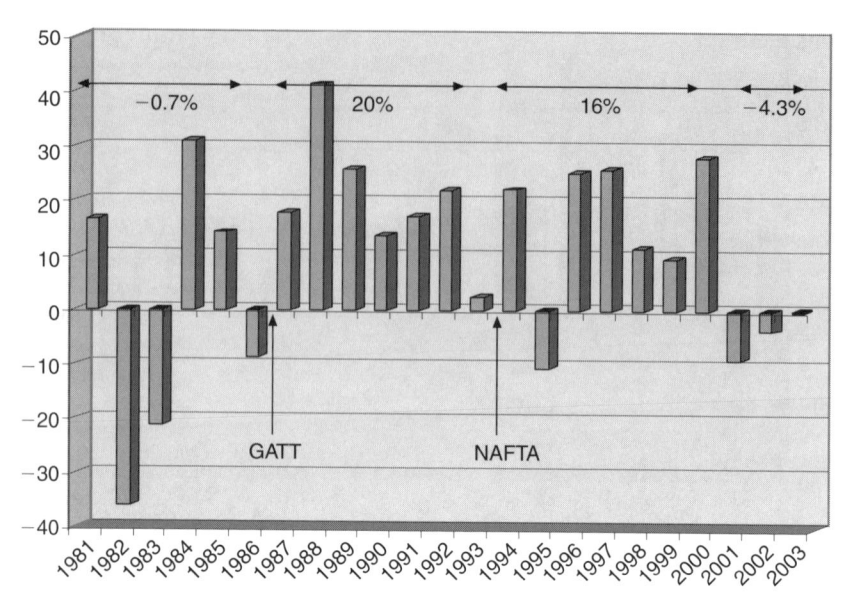

Figure 4.4 US exports to Mexico 1981–2003 annual rate of growth (source: US Department of Commerce).

partially explained by the major peso devaluation of early 1995, and the concurrent strength of the US economy.

Nonetheless, as long as trade among the economies keeps up its momentum, there are grounds for arguing that NAFTA works. The fact that Washington has nominally agreed to act as "paymaster" for this venture, witnessed by the financial bailout offered to Mexico at the beginning of 1995, has reinforced the supportive coalitions under which NAFTA was built.

In terms of an architecture for the regional governance of trade and investment flows, we should ask ourselves whether NAFTA has guaranteed access to the American market for both Canada and Mexico; or leveled the "playing-field" among the three partners. In general terms we could say that NAFTA has made US protectionist policies more manageable. The incorporation of alternative dispute settlement mechanisms, designed to operate either on adjudicative or conciliatory bases, has modified the institutional context within which protectionist policies were processed before the trade agreement was signed (Morales 1999). Of the three cases arbitrated and finalized under Chapter 20, panel awards confirmed the complaints of Canadians (one complaint) and Mexicans (two) against the US. Arbitration panels under Chapter 19, that is those reviewing the imposition of AD and CVDs by national administrative agencies, have been more popular. As of December 2004, 97 cases have been submitted, out of these 37 have been finalized, 31 have been suspended or the claiming Party has dropped its complaint, and the remaining cases are still waiting for a decision or remain active. Most of the disputes under this chapter are related to dumping procedures, rather than subsidies, and most of the reviews target US agencies.

Though panel procedures concerning dumping and subsidies have not been as speedy as anticipated, panelists have proved to be professional and balanced. Six out of 16 cases reviewing US agencies decisions have been completely remanded by panel awards, and four partially remanded. The rest have been fully confirmed. That is, more than 50 percent of all awarded cases reviewing administrative decisions of US authorities have been judged as inconsistent with US legislation. This rate of "success" benefitting either Canada or Mexico was much more elusive before NAFTA, according to the empirical record (Goldstein 1996). We could even say that, at least in the field of unfair trade practices, the playing field has been leveled vis-à-vis the other NAFTA partners. One out of 14 final awards reviewing Canadian agencies has been fully remanded, four have been remanded in part, and the rest of them fully affirmed. One out of seven cases involving Mexico has been fully confirmed, and the rest of them fully remanded or remanded in part. (See: http://www.nafta-sec-alena.org/.) In other words, Mexico is still on the learning curve in managing its unfair trade legislation.

NAFTA has indeed corrected some protectionist biases of the administrative agencies of all three partners; however, it has failed to eliminate strongly rooted protectionist interests in the region, mainly those coming from the US. The saga of the softwood lumber dispute between Canada and the US epitomizes the nature of conflict involving trade disputes among the partners. As is well known, US lumber producers have claimed since 1981 that Canadian imports of lumber are subsidized and causing damage to their production.[3] The controversy reached its climax when it was handled under the rules of the CUSFTA. Panels reviewed and remanded both the DOC's decision on subsidies and the ITA's decision on material injury. In the case of subsidies, panelists did not find that Canadian stumpage fees were provided on a specific basis, nor that the ban on exports of logs from British Columbia had specific benefits that made it necessary to consider a countervailing duty. However, US agencies held firm in their position, which led to a second remand from the panelists. The second remand confirmed the panel's original position, but this time panelists split along national lines.[4] The US finally activated the Extraordinary Challenge Committee (ECC) agreed under the CUSFTA (and passed into NAFTA) and the judges confirmed the panel's decision although not by unanimity.

As for the test of injury, the panel determined that there was no evidence, according to US laws, that Canadian lumber imports were damaging the US industry. This decision had to be remanded two more times before US agencies finally accepted it, without any split in the members of the panel. These two awards provided evidence, as Gilbert Gagné asserted, that the definitions of "subsidy" and "injury" in US law and practice had become so flexible as to accommodate almost any petition for a trade relief (Gagné 1999: 85). Canada had joined CUSFTA precisely to make more transparent both the interpretation and implementation of US trade legislation. In this sense, the work of the panel groups and Chapter 19's mechanisms (i.e. the role of the ECC) were successful.

However, the role of the CUSFTA panels could not avoid the politicization of what had already become the most sensitive trade dispute between the two countries. The US government invoked Section 301 of the 1974 Trade Act in order to force a deal with the Canadians. Once the dispute was handled under the CUSFTA mechanism, proceedings were initiated in order to challenge the constitutionality of the panel's decision in US courts. Once panels finalized the case, the US government delayed the reimbursement of duties collected, and the CFLI threatened to reopen the case as soon as possible. All these political pressures ended up with the signing, in 1996, of a new ad hoc agreement through which lumber exchange between the two countries became subjected to a tariff-rate quota.[5] The agreement created its own dispute settlement mechanism, which permitted contending parties to circumvent the dispute mechanisms of the CUSFTA and NAFTA.

The five-year peace agreement expired on 31 March 2001, and in early 2002 the DOC announced, yet again, an affirmative determination of dumping and subsidies against softwood lumber coming from Canada. In April 2002, the Canadian government requested a panel review under NAFTA of the US final subsidy and antidumping determinations. In January 2003, the WTO established another panel at Canada's request to resolve on the methodology used by the DOC to determine the margin of dumping. All panels have remanded in part US final decisions and methodology. A NAFTA panel found, for instance, that US ITC determination was unsupported by "substantial evidence and inconsistent with US law" (cf. http://www.international.gc.ca/). As of December 2004, the US has resisted the panel awards, either by using appellate mechanisms or by simply inducing panelists to remand previous remands (see Anderson 2004 and Inside US Trade 2004). All these pressures and legal fights will probably lead to a revised version of the agreement reached in 1996.

Many other trade-related disputes have emerged among NAFTA partners without being resolved under the formal dispute settlement mechanisms. Take for example the tomato and avocado disputes between Mexico and the US, or the Helms Burton Act that involved both Canada and Mexico against the US. In the first case price and quota undertakings – to some extent similar to those established under the softwood lumber case – were negotiated. In the second, consultations were activated under Chapter 20, and the White House eventually declined to enforce the extra-territorial consequences of the Law.

A recent case, involving cross-border trucking services between Mexico and the US, shows how domestic protectionist pressures could compromise US principled-obligations to its partners. In line with NAFTA requirements, the US should have permitted cross-border trucking services and related investment for Mexicans in border states at the end of 1995, and subsequently throughout the US as of 1 January 2000. Until recently, the US government denied access to any carrier or investor coming from Mexico, while entry barriers have already been removed to Canadians. The denial by US agencies was grounded on an overinterpretation of Articles 1202 and 1203 of the NAFTA, by which parties grant National and MFN treatment to trucking services. Through these articles, a Party commits itself to grant a no less favorable treatment, "in like circumstances," to services provided by nationals or by other parties. US agencies alleged that the inclusion of the phrase "in like circumstances," limits the national treatment and MFN obligations

> to circumstances with regard to trucking operations which are like, and that because "adequate procedures are not yet in Mexico to ensure U.S. highway safety," NAFTA permits Parties to accord differential, and even less favorable, treatment where appropriate to meet legitimate regulatory objectives.
> (NAFTA Arbitral Panel Established Pursuant to Chapter Twenty 2001: 3)

Mexico rejected this questionable interpretation of Articles 1202 and 1203 of the NAFTA, because it would have meant that Mexicans had to adopt the same standards in its regulatory trucking system to those prevailing in the US, an issue that was neither raised nor discussed during the NAFTA negotiations. The Mexicans argued that the US inaction was motivated not by safety concerns but by protectionist pressures coming from organized labor in the US. The panel rejected the way US authorities abusively interpreted clear principles such as national treatment and "MFN" for masking protectionist interests. Very recently, the US government has accepted the panel ruling, which does not delete the obligation of Mexican trucking services to comply with US safety standards.

These disputes suggest that leveling the playing field among partners is far from achieved. This is not because Canada and Mexico are not as market-oriented as the US wishes they were. Rather, the US remains a protectionist country pressing for unilateral arrangements when sensitive trade issues are at stake. Does this mean that both CUSFTA and NAFTA have failed to deliver on the promises they originally made? After years of US-led free trade diplomacy, Canada and Mexico are still learning to cope with the two fronts opened by this venture. NAFTA not only promotes US foreign trade interests abroad, but also attempts to work as an institutional constraint to deter protectionist pressures at home. The first goal has been successful so far, as witnessed by trade performance and the institutional changes it has provoked in Canada's and Mexico's economic organization. As for the second goal, NAFTA is still far from leveling the playing field among partners, this time vis-à-vis US practices. US protectionism has become more manageable under NAFTA, but it is still far from being policed by commonly agreed-upon rules. However, managed-trade solutions have become the second best solution by which market access is not necessarily guaranteed, but it is at least negotiated. For avocado and tomato growers, lumber producers and suppliers of cross-border trucking, these managed-trade solutions become less costly than making the US play by the rules. That is, when dealing with US-sensitive issues, NAFTA institutional obligations and enforcement mechanisms have helped to defuse the problems and facilitated compromise.

Investment access: outcomes and problems

A second goal of NAFTA was to empower market actors vis-à-vis governments. For Washington, this goal was still framed in the wider principles of its trade policy, aimed at leveling the playing field with its trade partners. If partners should be as open as the US economy, this openness should include the financial and service sectors. This was achieved when NAFTA partners accepted extending the principles of national treatment and MFN to investors, investments and services operating in the region. As for Canada and Mexico, the empowerment of market actors came from two fronts. By signing CUSFTA and later NAFTA, both countries engaged and/or deepened market-oriented reforms in their own economies. The most dramatic case was Mexico's, where economic reforms initiated and accelerated by then-President Salinas, became irreversible thanks to the new agreement, which according to Mexican legislative tradition, became part of its own Constitution.

The empowerment of private actors was also done at the judicial and governance level. Chapter 11 of the Agreement defines rules of thumb for dealing with foreign investors. Apart from granting national treatment and MFN status, under this chapter performance requirements are prohibited, nationality constraints are banned for the selection of CEOs and administrative boards of firms, free monetary transfers are guaranteed and expropriations or measures tantamount to expropriations are also proscribed, except under very specific circumstances. Chapter 11 also enables firms and investors to activate a panel dispute against a state, without having to go through their own governments if any of the above rules are breached. No other arbitration mechanism within NAFTA makes such an empowerment of private actors as this. Final awards of arbitrated panels activated under Chapter 11 are binding and, in case governments neglect them, the complaining party has the option to activate a panel mechanism under Chapter 20.

Chapter 11 did not exist under CUSFTA, so in many ways it was envisioned as a device for deterring Mexico's discretionary policies concerning nationalization and foreign investment. In many ways, this chapter has meant a challenge to Mexico's and in some way Latin America's state-centered law paradigm regarding the treatment of foreign investments. It does substitute national tribunals for international arbitration when corporate property rights are at stake, and it overlaps with other legal systems still prevailing for national investors.

But the most controversial issue generated by this chapter has been its unanticipated, "perverse" effects. Conceived as a mechanism for making state policies concerning investments and investors more accountable, the current record shows that these same investors have changed the defensive mechanisms of the chapter into an offensive tool. One of the most controversial cases, the so-called Ethyl Corp. v. Canada, showed that by skillfully interpreting the ambiguities of the agreement, private firms can overrule government policies aimed at the protection of the environment, a goal that ironically NAFTA is also promoting. NAFTA ambiguities stem from a broad definition of investment and the absence of a narrowly framed definition of expropriation.

There is indeed very little limit to the scope of what Chapter 11 defines as an investment. The latter could be understood as a business, shares in a business, a loan to a business, real estate bought for business purposes and the broad concept of "interest" arising from the commitment of financial or human resources to economic activity. In the case of S.D. Mayers v. Canada, for instance, a Tribunal ruled the scope of investment as including such assets as market share and access to markets in the host state, suggesting that almost any kind of business activity can constitute an investment that is subject to protection (IISD 2001: 23).

Chapter 11 prohibits three types of expropriations: direct expropriation, indirect expropriation and measures tantamount to expropriation. The record of cases under this chapter suggests that the latter two definitions have become the same. The Ethyl Corp. v. Canada becomes relevant. When the Canadian government banned the importation of a chemical component (methylcycloentadienyl manganese tricarbonyl: MMT), as well as its inter-provincial trade, alleging environmental reasons, Ethyl Corp., a subsidiary of an American firm, sued the Canadian government alleging that the ban amounted to an expropriation of its business in Canada, for which it should be fully compensated. Although the Canadian government justified the ban by its concern over the potential toxic properties of magnesium, a component of MMT, the Tribunal ruled for the compensation of the firm and the Canadian government overruled the ban.

The argument that environmental legislation could be interpreted as tantamount to expropriation is new, and has raised concerns that any foreign-owned corporation could use similar arguments to attack new environmental regulations that have a potential impact on its profits. In fact, Chapter 11 has been used by firms as a two-edged sword: for protecting their rights, and for constraining governments from enacting policies addressing public concerns. The fact that disputes under this chapter are settled in a secret manner, with no obligation of governments to distribute information, and with important effects on public policies, has led some environmental organizations to talk of a "democratic deficit" in the field of the deregulation of investment.

The use of sanctions for complying with domestic legislation: the case of labor and environment

NAFTA has provoked numerous competing or alternative agendas coming from domestic political actors, interest groups and non-state actors. It seems as if the pace towards "continentalization" of the economy could also be occurring even as debates among interests are working on agendas that are sometimes complementary to, and sometimes alternatives to, NAFTA. A major characteristic of these agendas is that they are still rooted in national-based discussions. A further "continentalization" of production, exchange and capital mobility in North America under the principles of open regionalism will probably reinforce reactive strategies to the externalities provoked by cross-border regionalism. A divide between proactive and reactive policies vis-à-vis US-market-driven integration has already become the source of domestic and cross-border tensions within North America. However, this divide mainly reflects the interests and political calculations of US-based organizations, which coalesce as supporting or blocking any trade-related initiative coming from the government.

In the US, labor unions, principled organizations and other grass-roots movements have traditionally opposed NAFTA and a further opening of the US economy. They argue that giving preferential access to the US market has led to the loss of jobs in the US, and the degradation of environmental and social conditions. The arguments and votes of these organizations were so powerful that President Clinton in 1993 had to negotiate two side agreements, one for labor rights protection and another for environmental protection, in order to get NAFTA accepted by the US Congress.

In spite of the good record on trade performance of these three countries, these same advocate groups have criticized NAFTA and pressed Congress to impede the granting of fast track authority to the President. The refusal to concede for some years the so-called Trade Promotion Authority (TPA) was translated into a "vote of confidence" on NAFTA.[6] Though some of the claims of these groups do not pass the economic and historical record, they have proved to be politically efficient for shaping the perception of the average US citizen in relation to NAFTA and other outward-looking initiatives. According to polls performed in mid-1997, 66 percent of Americans believed that free trade agreements between the US and other countries cost jobs to the US, 58 percent agreed that foreign trade has had a negative impact on the US economy because cheap imports have cost wages and jobs; and 81 percent said that Congress should not accept trade agreements that give other countries a leverage to overturn US laws (School of Real-Life Results 1998).

The weakness of the labor-environment reactive coalition lies in the job-creation/job-loss debate. Growing and competitive imports coming to the US will always imply the export of non-competitive jobs abroad, with or without trade agreements. Furthermore, job losses are not only a consequence of trade; macroeconomic and monetary policies could become more decisive for shaping the job market. By contrast, the strong argument for this inward-looking coalition lies in environmental protection, further reinforced by the "perverse" effects that were revealed by some Chapter 11 awards.

Grass-roots movements have, however, become empowered by trade integration, but these movements still reflect the interests of civil society groups that have a say in US politics. Some groups existing either in Canada or Mexico, striving for the defense of the welfare state or of collective indigenous rights, are still peripheral to the debate about the governance of externalities provoked by the integration process.

Challenges and opportunities for the future

Though the drive towards integration in North America does not follow the European model, the evolving scenarios for the coming decades seem to reveal trends similar to those prevailing in Europe. Like the communitarian project, North America seems to be split between critical choices: to maintain the status quo or to head towards a deepening and/or widening dilemma.

Although keeping the status quo seems to be the favored option of NAFTA critics and detractors, this scenario seems difficult to maintain. A major point of this essay is that NAFTA, like any other regional economic regime, must be seen as a compromise forged between current policy options. As long as this linkage role is perceived as desired and necessary, regional regimes will remain attractive vis-à-vis other governance devices. Conversely, if new governance architectures become more attractive and preferable in terms of policy opportunities, regionalism will lose its appeal. Thus the so-called "demand" for regionalism will remain linked to the attractiveness and effectiveness of alternative governance mechanisms.

In the case of NAFTA, I have argued that this works as a compromise between unilateral and multilateral US policies, and as an intersection between North and South relationships. In other words, NAFTA is closer to a policy functional regime than to a real organization promoting and governing integration. It remains a major device of US trade diplomacy, through which Mexican and Canadian interests became accommodated. In this sense, keeping NAFTA as it is, that is, betting on the status quo, will depend on how trade and investment issues are handled at the trilateral

128 *Isidro Morales*

level and how related and exogenous issues, affecting NAFTA, could be handled using alternative governance mechanisms.

Understanding that NAFTA is mainly US-driven, the future of regionalism in North America raises the following questions:

1   What changes are in US interests? That is, how likely is it that Washington political elites will perceive the need to move from a regional economic regime toward a more integrative model, in which shared-authority mechanisms are put in place?
2   How might domestic and international constraints facilitate or restrain a push for change by American political elites? Here, the role of Congress becomes crucial. Just think about the difficulties the Clinton administration had obtaining the TPA in order to provide decisive momentum to a panoply of multi-level negotiations, either within the WTO, NAFTA or bilaterally.
3   How will Mexican and Canadian interests be articulated and accommodated vis-à-vis US policy preferences?

US priorities will remain a decisive factor in the future of North American regionalism. After 11 September, for instance, security and the struggle against terrorism became the priority in US foreign policy. A major consequence has been the redefinition of "secure borders," in which the expansion of the so-called "security perimeter" has included Canada and soon will include Mexico. Canada is currently talking about "intelligent borders" in order to justify the American presence of customs and security officials within its own territory. How Mexico will be integrated in this expanding trilateral architecture is not yet clear. This suggests, however, that when US interests are at stake and Washington attempts to redefine the rules of the game, trans-border initiatives are being set up and internalized at the regional and hemispheric level.

In another completely different move, Mexico attempted to launch "NAFTA-plus" talks, when President Fox came to power and pushed the migration and development agenda at the bilateral level. Although migration also became a priority in the US agenda, September 11 subordinated any policy initiative coming from Mexico to the imperatives of Washington-framed security policy. Nonetheless, Mexico and Washington could strike a deal on development policies under the so-called Alliance for Prosperity which was launched at the Monterrey Summit in March 2002. This initiative established four pillars (See Sojo *et al.* 2002):

1   It calls for better access to private investment for small and medium size enterprises. A major goal of the program is to reduce the cost of transferring remittances from Mexicans living in the US. According to this plan, Mexican migrants can now help to finance private construction projects, mainly private dwellings, for their families living in

Mexico. Projects for which credit is obtained in the US and disbursed in Mexico are also being considered. Efforts to fund the selling of US franchises and tourist-oriented development projects are also envisaged.

2   Technology transfer projects are being discussed such as having American universities offer courses on finance and administration, among other topics, for small and medium size businesses in Mexico. The promotion of Mexican handicrafts in the US, through institutional mechanisms, is also being considered. The goal is to improve entrepreneurial skills in Mexico.

3   Investment in infrastructure, targeting transport, power transmission and telecommunications is another objective. The promotion of US scholarships in order to enhance human capital in the US is being considered.

4   Improved institutional interconnectedness, through linkages between federal government institutions and regional and multilateral organizations, such as the Inter-American Development Bank (IDB), the Eximbank, the World Bank and other organisms, is desired.

A development approach like this remains loyal to the Washington Consensus policy options that were framed during the 1980s and have inspired structural reforms in Latin America and various trade associations, including NAFTA. That is, they bet on a corporate-led agenda in which entrepreneurial skills and market mechanisms are the backbone of development policies. In contrast with the European model of integration, under this scheme there is no room for discussing the need for, say, structural funds for the most deprived regions within North America, nor targeted policies for maintaining social cohesion and regional balances. Furthermore, this is not a trilateral initiative, but a bilateral one. In this sense, sensitive key issues for Mexico, like migration or income and welfare disparities, will continue to be dealt with according to the priorities of the US. For Washington, there is no need to raise these issues at the trilateral level, as it was for its policy aimed at leveling the playing field with its partners.

These two examples suggest that keeping the status quo within North America will remain difficult. There are areas, such as security, in which a trilateral move is already in the making, and there are other ones, like migration and economic equalization, in which bilateral relations will remain more important. This does not mean that discussions already opened in terms of creating a Trade and Investment Tribunal, a Customs Union, and even a Monetary Union will keep going, and will eventually gain momentum (see Pastor 2001). However, to "deepen" NAFTA solely in the trade and investment arena will further imbalance the representation of interests of societal groups. As it works now, NAFTA remains a corporate-led device fueling economic growth regardless of the social, political and cultural unbalances this may provoke.

The representation of corporate interests is already unbalanced in North America. Take for example the over-representation of corporate rights under Chapter 11 through which the governance of investment flows is privatized by granting firms the right and power to directly sue governments when their corporate rights are at stake. Under the experience of NAFTA, firms have been able to stop and renege on environmental policies enacted by states that play against their interests. In some cases, public interests have been subordinated to the primacy of private corporate interests thanks to this over-representation of corporate rights. Thus, a corporate-led, deeper level of market integration risks deepening both integrative and fragmentation trends in North America. Take the case of Mexico, in which preliminary data demonstrate that people in northern Mexico and in urban centers located in the central plateau are benefitting from export-oriented industries. Income gaps are widening between northern Mexico and the South. But this is occurring at the regional level as well. Some studies identify the creation of a dynamic continental region within North America, located from the Great Lakes area up to New York (Paelinck and Polèse 1999). This continental area encompasses key US states like Michigan and Illinois, and two key Canadian provinces, Toronto and Quebec. This is a kind of hub, with major spokes to California and Texas, where most Mexican and American exchanges take place. In other words, corporate-led integration is not evenly integrating the three countries but, rather, linking different productive spaces across the continent. How this reconfiguration of the productive space will impact social and political organization in North America remains to be seen.

Last but not least, there remains the issue of expanding NAFTA. As a potential starting point for a North and South agenda, NAFTA has become a blueprint for the creation of a Free Trade Area of the Americas (FTAA). Launched in parallel with the NAFTA negotiations by former President Bush in 1990, former President Clinton and current President George W. Bush have made of this initiative a major policy goal for the hemisphere. Once President George W. Bush obtained the TPA from Congress, in 2002, the Doha Round and FTAA negotiations gained momentum. The US agenda for the FTAA negotiations appears to be very similar, both in content and strategy, to the agenda pursued more than ten years ago when NAFTA negotiations were begun. Similar to those years, "minilateral" negotiations became intertwined with US multilateral positions within the WTO and bilateral approaches, as witnessed by the US–Chile negotiations. Similar to past negotiations, "minilateralism" pretends to promote an agenda more ambitious than what can be negotiated within the multilateral forum. In this sense, the optimal goal for the US is to get a "Doha-plus" agreement at the regional level. Similar to the NAFTA negotiations, the US, and more concretely, the US Congress is, once again, setting the timing and the coverage of the negotiations. A deal must be struck in June 2005 at the latest if Congress is to renew the TPA for two more years.

Both FTAA and the Doha Round pretend to deepen disciplines and commitments reached on the Uruguay Round. Apart from phasing out remaining tariffs in manufacturing, further liberalization is sought in areas such as investments, services, property rights, government procurement and agricultural products. Regarding agriculture, market access should be widened and the sensitive issue of regulating or suppressing export subsidies and domestic supports should be addressed. Finally, the mechanisms for surveillance and enforcement of agreed-upon rules, mainly regarding investment and property rights, remains another sensitive issue to be resolved.

Since trade negotiations are commanded by the principle of the "single undertaking" and consensus norms, the common denominator that can be reached within multilateral forums is normally lower than what can be obtained in "minilateral" ones, let alone within bilateral deals. This explains why Washington still maintains the three-tier approach to trade negotiations (multi, mini, bilateral). In each of them, Washington pretends to optimize the minimum it can get. After years of thorough negotiations, it is already clear that what Washington anticipates obtaining from the Latin American and Caribbean countries (LAC) increases in relation to the forum where negotiations take place. Within bilateral negotiations Washington increases its leverage to obtain the most it can from its partner, but at the same time the negotiating party has the opportunity, in accordance with its bargaining capabilities, to "customize" an agreement to its own preferences. In multilateral negotiations Washington obtains less as relatively weaker countries can increase their leverage by creating building blocks (as for example the G 20), for defending their interests. "Minilateral" negotiations, such as those for a FTAA, remain in an ambiguous middle ground.

The proliferation of integration mechanisms has provoked the emergence of different trade and policy "hubs" across the region. By signing bilateral agreements and participating in different regional schemes, Mexico and to some extent Canada, have become hubs themselves. Doubtlessly, Brazil has become another one with respect to MERCOSUR. Venezuela and Colombia attempt to play their own sub-regional roles. In June 2003 Washington signed an agreement with Chile that came into force in January of 2004. In many respects, the deal remains close to what was negotiated within NAFTA.

The US–Chile Free Trade Agreement (FTA) has become Washington's "NAFTA-plus" approach for other bilateral and "minilateral" negotiations, both within the western hemisphere and outside. In June 2004 USTR reached another FTA with five Central American (CA) countries, the coverage of which was extended to the Dominican Republic in August of that year. The agreements are a replica of the US–Chile FTA, customized, of course, to the particularities of CA and Caribbean economies. Though 61 percent of CA goods enter the US duty-free under the Caribbean Basin Initiative (CBI), CA countries were interested in signing an agreement with the US in order to widen and make permanent their access to the US market.[7] The deal aims to lock in domestic economic reform in the region as well as improving the institutional environment for attracting investments.[8]

The reasons Washington signed a Central America Free Trade Agreement (CAFTA) were politically and strategically motivated. US sales to this region represent only 1 percent of overall exports. Washington clearly sends the message that "NAFTA-plus" deals can still be struck in the region, replacing protracted negotiations pursued either in Geneva or in Puebla.[9] In fact, in spite of the reactivation of the Doha negotiations during the summer of 2004, it is clear that it will take years to negotiate the suppression of export subsidies and the reduction of domestic supports in developed countries, a hot issue at the WTO negotiations. As for the FTAA, during the ministerial hemispheric meeting held in Miami in November 2003, the final communiqué of that meeting called for a two-tier FTAA: one encompassing a common set of rights and obligations accepted by the 34 members, and another one negotiated, "à la carte," amongst interested members. From then on, FTAA negotiations have legitimized the "hub and spoke" approach followed by the US and Mercosur's preferences for negotiating trade and disciplinary rules in the WTO to the detriment of the FTAA. The US–Chile FTA and CAFTA represent a de facto enlargement of the NAFTA area. They constitute the general framework under which the second tier of the FTAA will be constructed. It is clear that NAFTA countries, Chile, Central America and probably Caribbean countries as well – excluding Cuba – will join a US-led initiative along these lines.

Conclusion

Globalization and regionalism seem to be two faces of the same coin. The first invokes a technological revolution that is transforming our notions of space, territory and time, and the second refers to the policy mechanisms, rules and paradigms through which global issues are being governed by a cluster of countries. In this sense, NAFTA has been successful as a device for changing the rules of the game in trade and investment matters and for inducing participating partners to adapt their own economic regulatory mechanisms to a benchmark defined by Washington at the multi-, mini- and unilateral levels. As long as the US economy keeps innovating and growing, North American integration defined according to US standards will remain legitimate and a blueprint for future negotiations, at both WTO and FTAA talks.

As it stands, the future of North American integration will remain rooted in the primacy of market-oriented mechanisms and corporate rights protection. Regional imbalances in income, health and education gaps (mainly between Mexico and its two partners), welfare policies, and differences in administrative organization within each country that affect cross-border issues, will be dealt with on an ad hoc basis. "Continentalism" will remain subordinated to American interests, as demonstrated by the magnification of the security agenda after the September 11 attacks. Thus, the challenge for "followers" will be to devise the institutional mechanisms for accommodating their own priorities within the continental agenda. To balance against the corporate-led integration scheme currently prevailing in North America, social, labor and welfare-led agendas remain important for future integrative efforts in the region. The integration path is accelerating fragmentation trends, similar to what globalization is provoking in other parts of the world. Thus, bridging gaps, increasing social opportunities and maintaining social cohesion remain challenges to be handled in the future, either at the local, federal, regional or multilateral levels. The European experiment has shown that this governance challenge can be addressed with great success. Though the North American experience is grounded on different circumstances, its success and achievements should not be that different.

Notes

1 As we know, these policy mechanisms are institutional arrangements normally bound by agreements or organizations through which consultation, negotiation, monitoring treaty compliance and other types of information are facilitated among members. As Stephen Krasner in a classical definition conceived them, regimes embody a set of principles, rules and decision-making procedures, both formal and informal, around which expectations of participants converge in a given issue-area (Krasner 1983: 186).
2 The GATT required that government purchases above US$225,000 be subject to competitive bidding. The CUSFTA reduced the threshold to US$25,000.
3 There are differences in the regimes of land ownership between the two countries and in the political organization of Canadian provinces vis-à-vis US federal states. Although US trade agencies decided in 1983 that timber allocation and stumpage rights were not countervailable, in 1986, once the powerful Coalition for Fair Lumber Imports (CFLI) was created, a renewed file submitted to the Department of Commerce (DOC) found that both the allocation of timber and stumpage fees were provided on a discretionary and specific basis, and were hence countervailable. Canada has since alleged that stumpage fees are a matter of public development policies, and that US agencies cannot decide how provincial governments must manage their natural resources. Anticipating the final decision of the Department of Commerce, the Canadian government decided to sign a Memorandum of Understanding (MOU) under which a tax of 15 percent was imposed on Canadian softwood lumber exports. That tariff was terminated in late 1991 at which point the DOC initiated its third countervailing investigation, which, as expected, was affirmative. This time Canada decided to challenge the US decision under Chapter 19 of the CUSFTA (see Ek 2001 and Gagné 1999).

4 The dissident vote came from the two American panelists. For further information on this issue, see Davey 1996: 172–82.
5 Above that quota (which was fixed as 14.7 billion board feet per year with no tax), a progressive taxation was imposed on lumber imports suggesting that the aim of the US government was to restrain Canadian exports, regardless of whether they were subsidized or not.
6 In July 2002, the TPA was finally voted on by Congress.
7 CBI is a Washington-led trade architecture of unilateral concessions to CA and Caribbean countries. These concessions are fragile because the US Congress may widen or narrow, unilaterally, their scope and duration.
8 For a general review of what is at stake in CAFTA, see Salazar-Xirinachs and Granados (2004).
9 The current city, in Mexico, where FTAA negotiations take place.

References

Anderson, G. (2004) "The Canada–United States Softwood Lumber Dispute: Where Politics and Theory Meet," *Journal of World Trade*, 38(4): 661–99.
Castells, M. (1997) *The Rise of the Network Society*, Malden, MA: Blackwell.
Davey, W. (1996) *Pine and Swine: Canada and the Dispute Trade Settlement: The FTA Experience and the NAFTA Prospects*, Ottawa: Carleton University, Centre for Trade Policy and Law.
The Economist (1998) "Where Next? A Survey of World Trade," *The Economist*, 3 October: 38.
Ek, C. (Coord.) (2001) "Canada–U.S. Relations," *CRS Report for Congress*, Washington, DC: Congressional Research Service.
Gagné, G. (1999) "The Canada–US Softwood Lumber Dispute: An Assessment after 15 Years," *Journal of World Trade*, 33(1): 67–86.
Goldstein, J. (1993) *Ideas, Interests, and American Trade Policy*, Ithaca, NY: Cornell University Press.
—— (1996) "International Law and Domestic Institutions: Reconciling North American 'Unfair' Trade Laws," *International Organization*, 50(4): 541–64.
Grier, J.H. (1993) "Section 301 'Unilateral' Responses to Violations of Trade Agreements and Unfair Foreign Trading Practices," drawn from National Trade Data Bank (NTDB), online: http://www.stat-usa.gov/tradtest.nsf (accessed 15/08/1996).
Hart, M. (1989) "The Future on the Table: The Continuing Negotiating Agenda under the Canada–United States Free Trade Agreement," in R.G. Dearden, M.M. Hart and D.P. Steger (eds) *Living with Free Trade: Canada, the Free Trade Agreement and the GATT*, Ottawa: Centre for Trade Policy and Law.
International Institute for Sustainable Development (IISD) (2001) *Private Rights, Public Problems: A guide to NAFTA's Controversial Chapter on Investor Right*, Canada: IISD.
Inside US Trade (2004) *Inside US Trade*, 15 October, 22 October, 12 November, 19 November.
Kaul, I., Gunberg, I. and Stern, M. (1999) "Defining Public Goods," in I. Kaul *et al.* (eds) *Global Public Goods: International Cooperation in the 21st Century*, New York: Oxford University Press.
Keohane, R. (1984) *After Hegemony: Cooperation and Discord in the World Political Economy*, Princeton, NJ: Princeton University Press.

Krasner, S. (1983) "Structural Causes and Regime Consequences: Regimes as Intervening Variables," in S. Krasner (ed.) *International Regimes*, Ithaca, NY: Cornell University Press.

Lawrence, R.Z. (1996) *Regionalism, Multilateralism, and Deeper Integration*, Washington, DC: The Brookings Institution.

Morales, I. (1999) "NAFTA: The Governance of Economic Openness," *The ANNALS of the American Political and Social Science (AAPSS)*, 565: 35–65.

North American Free Trade Agreement Arbitral Panel Established Pursuant to Chapter Twenty (2001) In the Matter of Cross-Border Trucking Services. *Final Report of the Panel*, Secretariat File No. USA-MEX-98-2008-01.

Paelinck, J. and Polèse, M. (1999) "Modelling the Regional Impact of Continental Economic Integration: Lessons from the European Union for NAFTA," *Regional Studies*, 33: 727–38.

Pastor, R. (2001) *Toward a North American Community*, Washington, DC: Institute for International Economics.

Putnam, R.S. (1988) "Diplomacy and Domestic Politics: the Logic of Two-Level Games," *International Organization*, 42(3): 427–60.

Rosenau, J. (1997) *Along the Domestic-Foreign Frontier: Exploring Governance in a Turbulent World*, Cambridge: Cambridge University Press.

Rugman, A. and Verbeke, A. (1994) "Foreign Direct Investment and NAFTA: A Conceptual Framework," in A. Rugman (ed.) *Foreign Investment and NAFTA*, Columbia: University of South Carolina Press.

Saborio, S. (1992) "The Long and Winding Road from Anchorage to Patagonia," in S. Saborio *et al.* (eds) *The Premise and the Promise: Free Trade in the Americas*, New Brunswick, NJ: Transaction.

Salazar-Xirinachs, J. and Granados, J. (2004) "The US–Central America Free Trade Agreement: Opportunities and Challenges," in J.J. Schott (ed.) *Free Trade Agreements. US Strategies and Priorities*, Washington, DC: Institute for International Economics.

"School of Real-Life Results" (1998) Public Citizens Global Trade Watch, online: http://www.citizen.org/ (accessed 18/07/1999).

Sojo, E. *et al.* (2002) "Sociedad para la Prosperidad. Reporte a los Presidentes Vicente Fox y George W. Bush," Monterrey, Mexico, 22 March. Electronic copy.

Part II
Financial crises and restructuring

5 Financial sector development in Latin America and East Asia

A comparison of Chile and South Korea

Barbara Stallings

Introduction

The financial crises in Mexico (1994–5) and several East Asian countries (1997–8) focused attention on the role played by the financial sector in economic development.[1] While the crises themselves provide dramatic evidence of the negative link between finance and development, the positive relationship is also of growing interest to both researchers and policymakers. The increased interest in finance contrasts with the approach in the earlier postwar period, when development economists concentrated on topics such as industrialization, technology transfer and international trade – the so-called real sector of the economy. Finance was generally assumed to accommodate the needs of production.

The burgeoning new literature that has emerged since the crises deals with many aspects of the financial sector in developing economies (for recent reviews, see World Bank 2001a; Levine 2004). Three of them are of particular relevance for our discussion in this chapter. The first involves the structure of the financial sector. Do banks continue to dominate financial transactions, or has diversification toward capital markets begun to take place? A second topic concerns ownership of the banking sector. Do public banks still play a major role, or has there been a shift toward private ownership? If private banks have become more important, what is the new balance between domestic and foreign institutions? A third topic focuses on access to finance. Is access limited to governments and large firms, or are small and medium-sized enterprises (SMEs) also able to obtain credit?

Debates on the structure of the financial sector began with respect to the industrial world. Contrasts were drawn between countries where capital markets played a dominant role (the United States and the United Kingdom) and those where banks were the main source of finance (most of continental Europe and Japan). While the political science literature found significant differences between market- and bank-based systems in terms of the implications for government policy (Zysman 1983), the economics literature tended to argue that both systems could work equally well (Allen and Gale 2000). Following the crises, these debates were translated into the developing-country context through a large World Bank project (Demirgüç-Kunt and Levine 2001). Again, the conclusion was that both banks and capital markets could provide needed finance; the important point was how well any given system functioned.

Despite these conclusions at the academic level, policymakers became concerned about financial diversification. International organizations – including the World Bank and International Monetary Fund (Litan et al. 2003), the Bank for International Settlements (BIS 2002), and the regional development banks (Kim 2001) – began to analyze the advantages of domestic bond markets. Several were stressed: establishing a market-determined interest rate to help investors calculate opportunity costs; increasing investment choices and thus raising the volume of savings; and avoiding the need to borrow abroad and thus assume excessive foreign exchange risks. Other experts concentrated on more specific institutional needs. From the government's perspective, a bond market is useful to finance fiscal deficits without increasing inflation and for running monetary policy. Private borrowers, both firms and households, need access to bond markets to obtain long-term finance for investment or mortgages. East Asian government officials argued that the crises in their region would have been less severe if domestic bond markets had provided an important source of credit. They followed up with action plans to stimulate regional markets and arrangements of various types (Yoshitomo and Shirai 2001; Ito and Park 2004). In Latin America, the reaction was slower, but calls to stimulate capital markets have also begun to appear there (Dowers and Masci 2003; World Bank 2004).

A second set of debates that assumed a prominent place in academic and policy circles after the financial crises of the 1990s focused specifically on the banking sector and asked about ownership characteristics. The traditional view among developing countries in the nineteenth and early twentieth centuries had been that state-owned development banks were necessary for at least two reasons. First, private banks would not be willing to finance the long-term, high-cost projects necessary for industrialization. Second, private banks would not provide financial services for small firms or poor households. At the same time, foreign banks were seen as likely to take resources out of developing countries rather than bring them in (Cárdenas et al. 2000; Bulmer-Thomas 2003).

The post-crisis literature has a very different perspective. It argues that public banks are the main source of the problems in the banking sector and that foreign banks can help resolve these problems. In particular, it claims that public banks operate on the basis of political criteria rather than being concerned with developmental or even social objectives. Given such motives, credit is considered likely to fund inefficient projects, which – even if they are actually carried out – will have low rates of return at the microeconomic level and undermine productivity and growth at the macroeconomic level. Empirical studies have found high state ownership of banks to be correlated with low growth rates, low efficiency, low profits, high volumes of non-performing loans and corruption (La Porta *et al.* 2002; Caprio *et al.* 2004). The literature on foreign banks makes claims that are nearly the mirror opposite. Foreign banks are said to be more efficient, more profitable, less corrupt and with fewer non-performing loans (Litan *et al.* 2001).

A third debate of interest addresses the question of access to finance. Again the focus is mainly on banks, since it is generally agreed that only large borrowers – whether from the public or private sector – have access to the capital markets. The issues are closely related to those on ownership; that is, how do public, private-domestic and foreign banks compare in the allocation of credit to poor households and SMEs? While we saw that one of the traditional justifications for public banks was providing credit to vulnerable groups, the new literature calls traditional claims into question. On the one hand, it questions whether public banks actually prioritize low-income households or small businesses as opposed to political supporters. On the other hand, it attempts to qualify the criticisms of foreign banks with respect to access. The empirical evidence on this topic is less voluminous than that on the other two topics. One study that is frequently cited agrees that foreign banks are more likely to finance large firms than small ones, but that the latter nonetheless are getting more credit than they would otherwise have had. Other researchers suggest that if foreign banks concentrate on large firms, this may encourage other banks to seek out smaller clients (Clarke *et al.* 2001).

This chapter analyzes the financial sector in general, and these three topics in particular, in the context of a comparison between Latin America and East Asia. Overall, significant differences have characterized the development strategies and outcomes in the two regions. The most obvious difference is that East Asian economies have grown far more rapidly than those in Latin America. Given the positive relationship between finance and growth, it would be expected that East Asian countries would have more credit available than their Latin American counterparts. In most instances, this expectation is borne out, and the financial sectors in Latin America and East Asia look quite different, as we will see.

Interestingly, however, our comparison of the two most successful countries in the two regions – Chile and South Korea – finds a different relationship. Since Chile and Korea are often viewed as the paradigmatic cases of market-oriented development strategies in Latin America and state-led strategies in East Asia, we were surprised to find important and growing similarities between the two in recent years. We explore this puzzle in the following pages. The chapter begins with a broad overview of the financial sector in the two regions. We then focus on the Chile–Korea comparison. Here we examine financial crisis and governmental response in the two cases. Then we turn to the financial sector per se and look first at the development of the banking, bond and equity markets. This is followed by an examination of the differences in ownership and in performance. Finally, we address the issue of access to credit for households and SMEs. The concluding section returns to the topic of convergence and suggests some reasons why this process might be occurring.

Historical evolution of the financial sector in Latin America and East Asia

Since the mid-1980s, there has been an interest in comparing Latin America and East Asia. Initially the comparisons centered on broad issues of development strategy and concentrated on what were then four highly successful "newly industrializing economies" in the two regions – Brazil and Mexico, Korea and Taiwan.[2] Later, more specific comparisons were introduced. The course of the 1980s, which represented a major setback for Latin America through a decade-long debt crisis while East Asia continued to surge ahead, meant that the comparisons were of primary interest to Latin America. How could they catch up with East Asia? What policy lessons could be learned? The Asian crisis of the late 1990s redressed this imbalance somewhat in that the Latin American countries had more experience with crisis management. The financial sector was one area, in particular, where East Asia seemed to have something to learn – both in positive and in negative terms.

In both regions, economists described the financial system during most of the postwar period as "repressed," which implied heavy government control of the banking sector. First, the authorities set interest rates on both deposits and loans. The real rates were often negative, at least *ex post*, as inflation exceeded nominal rates. Second, reserve requirements were high, so the commercial banks had little freedom to expand their portfolios. Third, governments issued administrative directives for the allocation of a substantial share of commercial bank credit. Fourth, government-owned banks were responsible for a large amount of the lending that took place. Fifth, complicated capital controls placed strict limits on the interactions between local borrowers or lenders and the international economy.

One by one, Latin American countries began moving away from this pattern in an attempt to increase the size and efficiency of the banking sector. The main changes were to free interest rates to be set by market forces, to lower reserve requirements, to limit or end directed credit and to privatize or close government-owned banks. A related institutional reform was the tendency toward making central banks autonomous of finance ministries. In addition, the capital account was opened, so that foreigners had easy access to the local financial systems, and local individuals and firms could make their own decisions on seeking funds abroad. Chile was the first country to move in this direction. Shortly after the military coup in 1973, the government began an overall liberalization program of which financial reform was a key element. Other countries followed in the 1980s and early 1990s. It was this early reform experience that made the Latin American financial sector of interest to East Asia.[3]

In East Asia, the financial sector was an important part of the economic model that produced the "East Asian Miracle." The banks served as the main channel between governments that decided which industries to promote and firms that implemented the strategies. In many cases, government-owned banks held a large share of deposits, which obviously facilitated control of credit, but in addition governments engaged in "administrative guidance" to steer private-sector credit to priority projects. Three types of targeting have been identified: targeting firms or industries, targeting types of firms (especially exporters or SMEs) and targeting social objectives. While subsidies of various kinds were provided as part of the credit arrangements, these may have been more carefully allocated according to performance than in other regions (World Bank 1993; see also Amsden 1994; Fishlow *et al.* 1994; Stiglitz and Yusuf 2001).

Some steps toward liberalization were taken in East Asia in the late 1980s and early 1990s, but many elements of the old domestic controls remained. Where more change came about was in external liberalization, so that banks and firms alike could access the international capital markets. In other words, international financial liberalization often preceded domestic liberalization, resulting in banks and firms taking on large amounts of foreign-currency debt without necessarily understanding the implications. Many experts attribute a large share of the blame for the crisis to this sequencing.

Despite the commonalities of the repressed financial systems in the two regions, an important difference divided them. For a variety of reasons that are beyond the scope of this chapter, East Asians traditionally had savings rates that were nearly double those of Latin Americans as a percentage of GDP. The average for the 1990s, for example, was 34 percent for East Asian and Pacific countries but only 20 percent for Latin America (World Bank 2001b: Appendix Table 13). All else equal, the higher savings rates meant that East Asia would have deeper financial markets than Latin America, and this was indeed the case.[4]

Table 5.1 shows financial depth (measured as the sum of bank loans and bonds outstanding plus stock market capitalization, as share of GDP) for a sample of Latin American and East Asian countries in 1990 and 2003. It indicates that financial depth in 1990 was 76 percent of GDP in Latin America compared to 137 percent in East Asia, or 80 percent higher in the latter. By 2003, the gap had exceeded 100 percent as financial depth increased to 226 percent of GDP in Asia compared to only 108 percent in Latin America.

Focusing on individual countries, an important contrast appears. With the exception of Indonesia and the Philippines (the only low-income

Table 5.1 Latin America and East Asia: financial depth,* 1990 and 2003

Region/country	1990	2003	% change
Latin America**	76	108	42
Argentina	42	98	133
Brazil	111	170	53
Chile	155	247	59
Colombia	40	76	90
Mexico	108	82	−24
Peru	23	55	139
Venezuela	54	26	−52
East Asia**	137	226	65
Indonesia	53	82	55
Korea	148	234	58
Malaysia	261	412	58
Philippines	60	119	98
Taiwan	172	270	57
Thailand	130	237	82

Sources: World Bank, *World Development Indicators*, online version (for bank claims and stock market capitalization); BIS website for bonds outstanding.

Notes
* Financial depth is the sum of bank loans, bonds outstanding and stock market capitalization as a share of GDP.
** Unweighted average for regional totals.

countries in the Asian sample), financial depth in all the Asian countries exceeds the Latin American average. Although there are differences among them, all are making progress toward strong financial sectors that can help support economic growth. In the Latin American sample, by contrast, two groups stand out. Brazil and Chile have financial sectors that are at a similar level to those found in the Asian countries. The others – Argentina,[5] Colombia, Mexico, Peru and Venezuela – trail far behind; two even slid backwards over the period. Since this second group of Latin American countries is a fairly heterogeneous one, more in-depth analysis is needed to understand the reasons for the low level of development of their financial markets.

The greater average financial depth in East Asia is reflected in several recent surveys of entrepreneurs in the two regions. The World Bank's "Investment Climate around the World" survey asks businesspeople in all regions about the principal obstacles they face. In Latin America, lack of finance was listed as the third most important problem, behind taxes and regulations and political instability. In developing Asian countries, with their deeper financial sector, finance was much lower on the list of obstacles (Batra *et al.* 2003). A survey by the Inter-American Development Bank (IDB) reinforced the World Bank result. The IADB study showed that in 18 of 20 Latin American countries, access to credit was reported by businesspeople as their most serious problem (IADB 2001: Part II).

Finally, another IADB project compared the development of new firms in Latin America and East Asia. Again, the finding was that lack of finance was much greater for Latin American start-ups than for those in East Asia (Kantis *et al.* 2001).

Financial crisis and government response: Chile and South Korea

Moving from a broad regional overview to our two main countries of interest, we begin the comparison with a brief analysis of the financial crises that Chile and Korea suffered and the response of the two governments; these processes set the stage for the rest of the analysis. While many of the elements are surprisingly similar, a significant difference is the time period in which the two crises took place. The Chilean crisis occurred in 1981–3, while Korea's crisis was not until 1997–8. During the intervening 15 years, important changes took place in the international environment, both in terms of the greater sophistication of the financial markets and the willingness of the IFIs to provide assistance. Although the Chilean economy in the early 1980s was far less sophisticated than its Korean counterpart in the late 1990s, and Chile's record of economic growth prior to the crisis was quite poor in comparison with Korea's, the problems they suffered and the way the two governments tackled the crises had much in common.

Both crises resulted from a mismanaged financial liberalization process, both internal and external. On the internal front, the freeing of interest rates, the end of directed credit and the privatization of state-owned banks were accompanied by a disregard for prudential regulation and supervision and sometimes by outright illegal activities. The combination resulted in inordinately rapid increases in credit, large loans to "related" clients and inadequate provisioning for potential losses. Eventually, these elements set the stage for a crisis. The situation was made worse by a simultaneous external financial liberalization, which was also mismanaged. A fixed exchange rate was maintained, which led to massive capital inflows and exchange rate misalignment, and improper sequencing favored short-term over long-term inflows. The rapid pace of liberalization exacerbated both problems. In addition, domestic firms (financial and non-financial) were allowed to enter the international markets to seek finance, creating currency mismatches, over-leveraging themselves, and endangering their future if/when the exchange rate had to be devalued.

Following major crises, even the most laissez-faire oriented governments had to step in to stop the hemorrhaging. In both cases, similar steps were taken. A first set included the takeover of non-performing loans, the recapitalization of the banks, and liquidations or mergers, bringing in foreign institutions. Later, in an attempt to prevent future crises, regulation and supervision were stepped up, greater information and transparency were required and better corporate governance was introduced.

The Chilean crisis erupted in 1981, the result of the most extreme kind of financial mismanagement, when the military government set out to eliminate virtually all regulations. The year after the banking crisis began, the situation was complicated by a balance-of-payments crisis, and the fixed exchange rate was devalued. The financial crisis was marked by the insolvency of the majority of the private national banks and finance houses, which were taken over or liquidated by the Banking Superintendent. By mid-1982, the crisis had become a systemic one, extending to many of the largest corporations, which also ended up in government hands.

Resolution of the crisis involved various measures to assist banks and debtors as well as the reprivatization of the institutions that the government had intervened. The overall operation is estimated to have cost more than 35 percent of GDP. In the aftermath of the crisis a new attitude emerged with respect to regulation and supervision of the banking sector. The Banking Law of 1986, which became an example for the region, reinforced the powers of the Superintendent. It required that portfolios be ranked by risk categories and that provisioning be made for higher risk credits. It also increased the transparency of the process. It tightened policies with respect to credits to "related" parties, defining the term more strictly and limiting such loans. Capital adequacy requirements were left at the previous levels, but definitions were tightened. Deposit insurance was eliminated for term deposits, so as to make depositors more vigilant, but all sight deposits were covered, as were accounts of small depositors.

In 1997, the Banking Law was modified to bring it up to date with international and domestic trends that had emerged over the preceding decade. At this time, Chile adhered to the 8 percent capital adequacy ratio advocated by the Bank for International Settlements (BIS); BIS risk categories were also adopted. Banks were permitted to increase their international activities: setting up subsidiaries abroad as well as engaging in new activities such as administering mutual funds, leasing, factoring and financial advising. They were also allowed to provide guarantees to clients in the international market. Finally, conditions were created for more banks, both national and foreign, to enter the Chilean market after a decade of closure.

As a consequence of the thorough cleanup of the banking industry and the improved system of regulation and supervision, the Chilean financial system functioned well in the 1990s. It is essential to point out, however, that this good performance also depended on the context in which it took place. On the one hand, macroeconomic policy contributed to a stable and growing economy, which had a strong positive interaction with the financial sector. On the other hand, the capital account of the balance of payments was managed so as to limit volatility from the international economy. All of these were necessary elements for the positive outcome.[6]

The Korean crisis was more unexpected. Indeed, Korea appeared to be an unlikely candidate for a financial crisis, as it had been one of the world's most successful economies in the postwar period. Until the late 1980s, however, the bank-dominated financial sector had had little autonomy, since the country's economic authorities often used the banks in the pursuit of their overall policy goals. An important shift occurred in 1993, with the deepening of the financial liberalization begun the previous decade. Although the government had intended to move slowly, the process accelerated, partially in response to Korea's application to join the Organization of Economic Cooperation and Development (OECD). In that context, both external and internal debt grew very rapidly, and insufficient attention was paid to the sequencing of reforms, leading to a shift toward short-term debt.

After the Thai crisis of July 1997, foreign creditors reconsidered their loans to Korean entities and began to withdraw. At the same time, many of the corporate conglomerates (chaebol) also failed, resulting in a systemic crisis. The government initially tried to handle the situation on its own, announcing deposit guarantees and providing liquidity to financial institutions. The size and speed of the crisis, however, drove it to an agreement with the IMF, which influenced but did not totally determine later steps. In a first phase of restructuring, in early 1998, public monies were used to close or reorganize troubled banks and dispose of non-performing loans through the asset management company, KAMCO. This process had to be repeated in late 2000 as a result of the worsening of corporate problems. In addition, banks were encouraged to recapitalize themselves, and foreign investment laws were changed to allow foreign participation. The number of banks and other financial institutions was reduced.

Another set of reforms involved strengthening prudential regulations, including accounting, auditing and disclosure requirements. The definition of NPLs was tightened, coming closer to international standards, and capital adequacy ratios were brought up to BIS levels. Corporate governance was also improved, with outside directors as well as checks and balances between management and board members. It is interesting to note that a number of the reforms had been presented to the Korean legislature before the crisis, but not approved. It was only in the aftermath of the crisis that support could be mobilized.[7]

The outcome of the restructuring process was positive from the point of view of economic growth and of traditional financial performance indicators. Profitability returned, capital adequacy ratios increased and NPLs were reduced. In addition, as will be discussed later, there was a significant shift in bank portfolios toward more consumer lending and fewer corporate loans. This latter trend, however, was carried to an extreme and resulted in a classic boom (2001–2) and bust (2003–4) cycle. The most active lenders were credit card companies, often owned by the major commercial banks. One of the credit card companies itself had to be rescued, but these recent problems in no way reached the significance of the 1997–8 events.

Structure of financial markets: Chile and Korea

The financial crises centered on the banking sector in Chile and Korea, but there is another important part of the financial sector that must also be taken into account. Indeed, both countries have been trying to promote development of the capital markets (bonds and equity) as a complement to the banks, and there has been an expansion of the capital markets in many emerging markets.[8]

Experts cite a variety of reasons to justify efforts to promote capital markets.[9] First, domestic capital markets reduce the need to borrow from abroad, thus limiting exchange rate risk and vulnerability to shifting market sentiment. Second, they offer savers new instruments, potentially attracting new savers, both domestic and foreign. Third, they match the need of investors (including institutional investors as well as the productive sector) for longer maturities. Fourth, they increase transparency in the financial markets and provide a source of information on risk and yield. And, finally, for the particular case of government bonds, they aid in carrying out fiscal and monetary policy.

Nonetheless, despite the advantages they offer, there are also stringent requirements for establishing and maintaining strong capital markets, which many developing countries have difficulty meeting. To do so, a country needs a strong legal system, a good financial infrastructure and substantial transparency and good corporate governance. In addition, if the markets are to operate properly, a large and liquid secondary market is needed for bonds and equity to make investors comfortable about making long-term investments.[10]

Both Chile and Korea have been promoting capital markets for many years. Table 5.2 shows the extent to which capital markets in the two countries have developed in comparison to banking. At the beginning of the 1990s, bank loans outstanding in Chile represented 73 percent of GDP, or a little less than half of the total financial markets (155 percent of GDP). Bonds outstanding were 37 percent of GDP, and stock market capitalization was 45 percent. The Korean pattern was very similar, although bank loans represented a slightly smaller share of GDP; overall, the markets in Korea in 1990 represented 148 percent of GDP. By the beginning of the new decade, things had changed in some ways. Chile's banking sector had not grown, but its bond and especially its equity markets had, so the overall total for the three markets reached 247 percent of GDP. The increase in Korea was of about the same magnitude, but the composition was quite different. Bonds were the leading growth sector, followed by bank loans, with equity markets trailing far behind. The overall market size for Korea in 2003 was 234 percent of GDP. It is interesting to note that most of the growth came after the financial crisis, as part of the government's attempt to strengthen the financial sector.

Both governments undertook special efforts to promote capital

Table 5.2 Chile and Korea: financial development, 1990 and 2003 (% of GDP)

Financial market	Chile			Korea		
	1990	2003	% change	1990	2003	% change
Bank loans	73	71	−3	66	106	61
Bonds outstanding	37	57	54	38	74	95
Stock market capitalization	45	119	164	44	54	23
Total	155	247	59	148	234	58

Sources: Same as Table 5.1.

markets, although they focused on different mechanisms. Chile worked indirectly through the creation of a set of institutional investors, deriving from the privatization of its pension system in the early 1980s. These investors demanded long-term assets and are generally credited with providing a strong boost for both the stock and bond markets. In addition, several laws passed during the 1990s aimed at improving corporate governance and providing tax incentives for investors. Recently, Chile has followed Korea in setting up a special stock exchange for small and medium-sized firms (Cifuentes et al. 2002; Walker and Lefort 2002).

Korea has also taken steps to promote its capital markets. While it had markets of significant size before the crisis, it has advanced since then as part of the overall recovery strategy. A first step was the full opening of domestic financial markets to foreign investors, who now account for over 40 percent of stock market capitalization (New York Times, 21 May 2004). Second was the modernization and expansion of the government bond market in order to finance the restructuring of the economy. Third, new institutions were created, including the Kosdaq market (for new firms) as well as derivatives markets. Fourth, corporate governance and transparency were improved substantially. In addition, more as an autonomous movement than a policy, corporate bonds have expanded to provide resources to deal with the crisis (Kim and Park 2002; Shin 2002). Finally, Korea joined its neighbors in policies to promote regional markets and greater financial integration.

As already indicated, an important prerequisite for proper capital market functioning is an active secondary market. Without liquidity, investors hesitate to risk their money since they will have difficulty exiting if they want to do so. In this area, Chile and Korea are quite different, as the latter has a much higher turnover in its capital markets. One reason may be related to the role of institutional investors in Chile. Given their need for long-term assets, they tend to buy and hold rather than trade. So, while they have been an important stimulus to the growth of the primary markets, they are less helpful with respect to the secondary markets.[11]

150 *Barbara Stallings*

Ownership in the banking sector: Chile and Korea

One of the most important consequences of the financial crises in both Latin America and East Asia was temporary and permanent changes in the ownership structure of the banking industry. The temporary changes were in the direction of greater government ownership, as the authorities saw no alternative but to assume control of many banks in order to prevent a meltdown of the financial system as a whole. In general, these changes were not meant to be permanent, only a way to stabilize the situation and clean up the banks before returning them to the private sector. The more permanent change was toward greater foreign control. This came about because the domestic private sector was generally incapable of providing the needed resources to recapitalize the banks. In recent cases of financial crisis, there was also pressure from the IFIs to change legislation to permit greater foreign ownership.

The ownership structure of banking is important for several reasons. One is that foreign banks are believed to be more efficient and to bring deeper pockets and more modern technology. At the same time, there is fear that they will cream off the most profitable clients and leave others without access to credit. Public-sector banks, by contrast, are said to be driven more by political than business motives and are perhaps less efficient as well. Some of the motives attributed to public-sector banks were mentioned earlier: promoting key industries, increasing exports and providing access to groups that would not otherwise have been able to obtain credit. Local private owners, then, are in the middle between the other two. They are more interested in making profits than in furthering social objectives, but they are often considered to be less efficient than their foreign competitors.[12]

Table 5.3 displays some rough estimates of the changes of ownership in the banking sectors of Chile and Korea from the mid-1990s to 2003. In looking at the table, it is important to keep in mind the timing difference. That is, for Chile, the period covered is well beyond the financial crisis, and the banks that had been taken over by the government as part of the rescue efforts had long since been reprivatized. Thus, the dominant change during the period shown was the move toward greater foreign control at the expense of the domestic private sector, while the single government-owned commercial bank more or less maintained its share of the market. In Korea, by contrast, the period runs from the pre-crisis through the middle of the reprivatization. The years in between included a substantial increase in government ownership during the crisis, which has been declining in the last few years, together with a burgeoning of foreign ownership.

In the mid-1990s, by best estimate, local businesspeople dominated the Chilean banking sector. Nearly 70 percent of the sector was under private domestic control, with the remainder more or less evenly split between

Table 5.3 Chile and Korea: ownership of assets in banking sector, 1994 and 2003 (%)

Owner	Chile		Korea*	
	1994	2003	1994	2003
Public sector	15	11	32	31
Private domestic	69	32	62	24
Foreign	16	57	6	44
Total	100	100	100	100

Sources: Author's estimates, based on country data, Fitch Rating reports, Montgomery (2003).

Note
* Includes national and regional commercial banks, foreign bank branches and specialized banks.

the public sector and foreign owners. By 2003, this picture had changed substantially. While the public-sector bank share fell slightly to about 11 percent of total assets, the more significant transfer occurred from local private owners to foreign banks. Foreign ownership rose from 16 percent to 57 percent, while private domestic ownership fell from 69 percent to 32 percent.

This shift was part of a larger process by which foreign capital – especially from Spain – entered Chilean (and other Latin American) markets. Other sectors where similar trends can be found include telecommunications, transportation, electricity, other utilities and some parts of the industrial sector (ECLAC 2000). In banking, the biggest players were the two main Spanish banks: Santander and BBVA. After a series of mergers and takeovers, Santander now owns the biggest bank in Chile, while BBVA owns the fifth largest. Together, they account for nearly one third of the market, and they also participate in other financial services such as pension fund administration. Two US banks (Citibank and FleetBoston, the former Bank of Boston) are the oldest foreign institutions in Chile, whose presence dates back nearly a century.[13] Other foreign banks in the Chilean market are from Canada (Scotia Bank), Holland (ABN Amro), Germany (Deutsche and Dresdner), Britain (HSBC) and Japan (Bank of Tokyo-Mitsubishi) (ECLAC 2003).

The pattern shown for Korea, as mentioned above, is influenced by the fact that the government is still in the process of reprivatizing the banks it acquired during the crisis. The government share was nearly constant between 1994 and 2003, at slightly more than 30 percent. In addition to its (falling) stake in the commercial banks, the government share both before and after the crisis includes the so-called specialized banks: Korean Development Bank, Korean Export-Import Bank, Industrial Bank of Korea. Although not defined as commercial banks by Korean regulations, they nevertheless meet the normal criteria, as they take deposits and make loans. The major change was in foreign ownership, which rose from 6 percent to 44 percent.[14] Thus, as in Chile, the private domestic sector was squeezed, falling in Korea from 62 percent in 1994 to only 24 percent in 2003. While the ownership pattern in the two countries still looks different, if current trends continue, those differences may be substantially reduced within a few years.

One of the interesting points about foreign investment in Korean banks is the type of institutions involved. While we have already seen that foreign owners in Chile are major international commercial banks from various parts of the world, few of these players were initially present in Korea. Rather the foreigners included private equity companies (e.g. the Carlyle Group, Lone Star and Newbridge), investment banks (Goldman Sachs), other financial institutions (the German insurance giant, Allianz) and a group of Korean expatriates who live in Japan. The only major international commercial banks with a Korean presence in 2003 were JP Morgan Chase, BNP, Standard Chartered and Commerzbank. Since then, however, two of the private equity companies have sold their shares to commercial banks, and a third is expected to do so soon.[15]

Financial market performance: Chile and Korea

Up till now, we have been looking at the structure of the financial markets, both in terms of the division between banks and capital markets and in terms of the ownership structure of the former. Now we continue looking at the banks and ask about their performance on various standard indicators. Here we find significant – but, again, decreasing – differences between the two countries.

Table 5.4 presents data on five indicators. In order to capture the impact of the crisis and the recovery in Korea, we show three time points: 1995–6, 1997–8 and 2004. The five indicators include: (1) the capital adequacy ratio set by the Bank for International Settlements (the minimum level for countries adhering to the 1988 BIS agreement is 8 percent capital as a share of risk-adjusted assets); (2) the level of non-performing loans (NPLs) as a share of total loans; (3) and (4) two measures of profitability including the return on total assets (ROA) and the return on equity (ROE); and (5) an indicator of the extent to which banks are extending credit, and thus contributing to economic growth, as measured by loans as a share of total bank assets.

As seen in the table, Chile's performance record consistently exceeded that of Korea before – and especially during – the crisis. Since then Korea has made a very strong recovery and now matches Chile on many indicators. In 1996, Chilean banks were much more profitable than their Korean counterparts, and their NPLs were much lower. (The BIS ratio was not available, since Chile did not adhere to the BIS agreement till 1997.)

Table 5.4 Chile and Korea: financial performance of banking sector, 1995/6–2004 (%)

Indicator	Chile			Korea*		
	1996	1997–8	2004**	1995–6	1997–8	2004**
BIS ratio	n.a.	13.0	13.5	9.2	7.6	10.8
NPLs	1.0	1.2	1.7	4.7	6.7	2.7
ROA	1.1	1.0	1.5	0.3	−2.1	0.8
ROE	15.5	10.5	16.4	4.0	−33.4	16.2
Loans/assets	73.4	74.7	69.9	52.6	45.3	69.2

Sources: IMF country reports and Fitch Rating reports.

Notes
* National commercial banks only.
** Data are for the first half of 2004.

In addition, the higher loan/asset ratio in Chile indicates that the banks were fulfilling their major role of providing credit rather than following the less risky strategy of investing in securities.

As would be expected, Korean performance fell dramatically in 1997–8 on all of the indicators. The BIS ratio fell below the international standard, and NPLs surged (at their peak in annual terms, NPLs were nearly 14 percent in 1999). Moreover, both measures of profitability became negative. Chile, in the meantime, was only mildly affected by the Asian crisis, seeing its performance deteriorate in small measure, but not so as to cause concern. As a new member of the BIS agreement, Chile's capital adequacy ratio was well above the minimum 8 percent.

By 2004, which was a good year for both countries, the indicators had become very similar. Korea had made a substantial recovery, thanks to the government's decisive steps to bring the crisis under control. The BIS ratio again exceeded the minimum, NPLs had fallen below 3 percent of loans, and profitability had surged. Chile more or less maintained its previous good performance, with profitability rising a bit, while the NPL ratio deteriorated by a small amount. The loan/asset ratio in the two cases was now just about the same, at nearly 70 percent.

Access to finance: Chile and Korea

Studying access to finance is a more difficult task than the topics addressed heretofore. The data are much harder to compile, and comparison across countries is more complex because of differing definitions of target groups. This section makes a preliminary attempt to compare the Chilean and Korean records in this area by looking at the types of loans provided by the banking sector (the share to businesses versus households) and the degree to which small and medium-sized firms have been

154   *Barbara Stallings*

able to obtain access to credit. Both of these topics focus on the banking sector, since the capital markets serve only the largest and most creditworthy clients (including governments). Thus, banks are the institutions to which individuals and small firms must look.

The first panel in Table 5.5 examines the distribution of total bank loans among businesses, consumers and mortgages. (It excludes loans for other purposes, such as trade credit and inter-bank loans.) Beginning with the pre-crisis period, we find a fairly similar pattern between the two countries: 71 percent of loans went to businesses in Chile compared to 65 percent in Korea. The biggest difference concerned consumer lending, where 20 percent of Korea's loan book involved this activity, while Chile's only included 12 percent. Mortgage lending, another form of lending to households, provided some compensation as mortgage lending accounted for 17 percent of bank loans in Chile versus 14 percent in Korea. Perhaps the biggest surprise in these data is that a lower share of credit went to business firms in Korea than in Chile, given the stereotype of Asian economies as more oriented to producers than consumers. This latter point is dramatically reinforced in the post-crisis data. By mid-2002, corporate loans in Korea had fallen to less than 48 percent, while consumer credit had risen to 41 percent. Mortgage lending fell slightly, to 12 percent. In Chile, over the same period, lending patterns changed only marginally, with a small shift from consumer credit to mortgages.

The abrupt change in credit patterns in Korea is a major effect of the bank and corporate restructuring process that has been going on since 1998. Several trends have all pushed in the same direction. First, the government has tried to discourage the traditional link between the banks

Table 5.5 Chile and Korea: access to finance, 1997 and 2000–1 (%)

Loans	Chile		Korea	
	1997	*2000–1*	*1997*	*2000–1*
(a) Distribution of total loans				
Business loans	71.3	70.7	65.4	47.6
Consumer loans	12.1	10.0	20.5	40.9
Mortgage loans	16.6	19.3	14.1	11.6
Total	100.0	100.0	100.0	100.0
(b) Distribution of business loans				
Large firms	61.7	63.6	32	29
SMEs	38.3	36.4	68	71
Total	100.0	100.0	100	100

Sources: Cho (2002) for Korea; Chilean Banking Superintendency and Román (2003) for Chile.

and the conglomerates (chaebol). Second, the chaebol themselves have not been investing much, so there is less demand for credit on the corporate side. Third, the banks have become more concerned with profitability and risk management than they had been in the pre-crisis period, and lending to households helps with both. On the one hand, higher interest rates can be charged;[16] on the other hand, aggregating the large number of households enables simple calculations of default probability.

While providing more credit to households and individual consumers stimulated demand and (probably) contributed to increased equity, it moved so fast that a classic bubble developed, especially among credit card companies, frequently owned by commercial banks. Between 1999 and 2002, the issue of new credit cards grew at an annual compound rate of 75 percent (*The Economist*, 8 February 2003). As is typical with credit booms, serious problems emerged as borrowers fell behind on payments; unpaid balances in March 2003 were $2.3 billion, up 27.5 percent from a year earlier (*New York Times*, 5 April 2003). Government regulators organized a rescue operation by requesting financial institutions to cover debts falling due on bonds issued by the nine credit card companies so as to avoid a new crisis, but the overall growth rate of the economy fell significantly as a result.

The second panel in Table 5.5 further disaggregates loans to businesses, showing the share going to large firms compared to small and medium-sized ones. Here again we find a dramatic difference between the two countries, both in levels and in trends. In the pre-crisis period, 62 percent of bank credit in Chile went to large firms and the remainder to small and medium-sized ones. In Korea, the numbers were reversed: 32 percent of loans to large firms and 68 percent to SMEs. The changes between the pre- and post-crisis measurements were not large, but the interesting point is that they went in opposite directions. In Chile, the share to large firms rose (to 64 percent), while in Korea it fell (to 29 percent). The latter data are for the year 2000, and there are some indications that the trend toward a greater share for SMEs accelerated afterwards. That is, the share of bank credit going to the chaebol was 25 percent in 2000, but less than 14 percent in mid-2002 (IMF 2003: 10).

These data must be regarded as extremely preliminary, since there are many potential problems with them.[17] Nonetheless, even assuming that the real differences are not as stark as these figures suggest, they are in line with other evidence. First is the government priority in Korea to promote SMEs as an alternative to the chaebol; several policies provide subsidies to the banks to move in this direction (Nugent and Yhee 2001). Second, as was the case with consumer loans, the banks have a market incentive to provide more loans to SMEs because they can charge higher interest rates. Third, as the chaebol are not investing heavily, demand for credit has diminished. And, fourth, when large firms do invest, insofar as they seek external finance, they are increasingly likely to tap the capital markets as they can get cheaper access in this way. In the Chilean case, the government has designed a number of programs to help SMEs obtain access to finance, and the commercial banks have also seen business opportunities in the sector. But they have yet to make a serious dent in the problem.[18]

Conclusions

This paper has analyzed differences and similarities between Chile and Korea, which arguably have the most successful financial sectors in their respective regions. The evidence shows a number of interesting points:

- Both economies suffered systemic crises, involving banks and corporations; although the timing was different, many of the symptoms were similar. More important, both governments responded energetically to clean up the problems and to prevent recurrences.
- Both countries have diversified and relatively deep financial systems; moreover, diversification and depth rose during the 1990s and early 2000s. Nonetheless, Korea has much more active secondary markets than does Chile.
- Chile has a larger foreign presence in the banking sector, constituted by major international commercial banks. Foreign investment in Korea's financial sector has increased substantially as a result of the crisis, although the actors tend to be investment companies rather than banks. On the other hand, Korea has a larger government presence, some of it a result of measures to deal with the crisis. If current trends toward privatization continue, however, these differences will be much reduced.
- Chile's performance on standard international indicators of asset quality, profitability and contributions to growth was stronger than Korea's before the crisis. Not surprisingly, Korea's indicators plummeted during the crisis, but they have improved substantially and are now approaching the Chilean level.
- Finally – perhaps the most important difference encountered – Korea has a much better record than Chile with respect to access to credit. On the one hand, a greater share of available credit goes to households rather than firms. On the other hand, a greater share of business loans goes to SMEs. Both trends have accelerated since the crisis in Korea, while not much change has taken place in Chile.

The most interesting point to emerge from this brief comparison of Chile and Korea is the increasing convergence between the financial systems in the two economies. Such convergence would not have been expected a decade ago, since we are talking about the Latin American country that has gone furthest in the market-oriented reform process (Chile) and the paradigmatic case of state-led growth in Asia (Korea). Moreover, we saw at the beginning of the paper that the broader Latin American and East Asian financial systems continue to present quite different profiles.

What is happening here? We seem to be witnessing an important phenomenon that appears precisely among the leading economies – a move in the direction of more market-oriented, "arm's length" practices established earlier in the Anglo-Saxon countries as a way of promoting efficiency and depth in the financial markets. Evidence of this change is appearing in both Europe and, to a lesser extent, in Japan. Chile shifted in this direction in the 1970s and then revalidated the move after the financial crisis of the early 1980s. Korea has now taken the lead in Asia of moving in the same direction. Others have been following. Even China has taken significant steps to liberalize its financial system (García Herrero and Santabárbara 2004).

Two sets of factors – short-term and longer-term – help explain the change in Korea. The short-term factors focus on the financial crisis of 1997–8. The crisis and the government's determination to stem the hemorrhaging rapidly and take steps to prevent future occurrences led to some of the similarities we have found. The most obvious one is the increased foreign ownership in Korea. At the same time, the crisis also accounted for the temporary increase in state control of the financial system, since the government intervened in a number of financial institutions to prevent their bankruptcy. (The Chilean government went even further in this direction in 1981–3.) The improvement in performance indicators is also due to the restructuring process.

But the crisis cannot account for all of the convergence, since it dates from the 1980s when Korea began to liberalize its domestic financial sector and open it to greater international integration. Interest rates were deregulated, barriers to entry were lowered, policy-based lending was phased out, and the capital market was partially opened. Pressures to move in this direction came from internal forces (especially the business sector) as well as external ones (foreign competitors, especially after Korea's application to join the OECD) in the context of financial globalization. All of these processes accelerated after the crisis and as part of the IMF rescue package.

Thus, both Korea's successes and its failures pushed in the direction of creating a financial sector that looks more and more like that of Chile, its Latin American counterpart. An important remaining difference involves the question of access, especially credit for SMEs. At first glance, it appears that the large share of funds for these firms is attributable to the continuation of government controls in Korea. Special provisions at the Bank of Korea, together with lending from the government-owned banks, are surely part of the answer. The commercial banks' new focus on profitability is another factor. Since finance for SMEs is a topic of great interest for most Latin American countries, Korea's experience in this area might provide some insights for that region. Likewise, Chile's successful management of a market-based financial sector over two decades could offer useful lessons for Asia.

Notes

1 This chapter is part of a larger project on "The Role of the Financial Sector in Latin America and East Asia," financed by the Ford Foundation. The author appreciates this support as well as comments received at a presentation of an earlier version of the chapter at the XI Congress of the International Federation for Latin American and Caribbean Studies (FIEALC) in Osaka, Japan.
2 See, for example, Gereffi and Wyman (1990), one of the earliest and most influential examples of this new literature.
3 On the Latin American reforms, see Stallings and Peres (2000).
4 Of course, the relationship is complicated since the financial system is one of the determinants of the savings rate.
5 The recent Argentine crisis greatly undermined the financial sector; data are not yet available to evaluate the extent of the damage.
6 On the Chilean financial crisis and the aftermath, see Arellano and Cortázar (1982); Sanhueza (1999, 2001); Budnevich (2000); Ffrench-Davis and Tapia (2001); Held and Jiménez (2001); Stallings and Studart (2003).
7 On the Korean financial crisis and the aftermath, see Hahm (1999); Kim *et al.* (2000); Cho (2002); Coe and Kim (2002); Park and Lee (2002); Ahn and Cha (2004).
8 On recent trends in capital markets in Latin America and East Asia, see Stallings (2003).
9 Many have feared that development of the capital markets would displace banks. In reality, the two are generally complementary; see Hawkins (2002).
10 On the advantages of, and requirements for, capital markets, see various articles in BIS (2002) and Litan *et al.* (2003).
11 For example, the average turnover ratio over the 1996–2000 period on the Korean stock market was 290, while that in Chile was only ten (see Standard and Poor's 2002).
12 On public-sector banks, see Yeyati *et al.* (2004); on foreign banks, see Litan *et al.* (2001).
13 During 2004, FleetBoston was taken over by Bank of America. Policy with respect to the Latin American subsidiaries remains to be determined.
14 This share is higher than shown by some other sources. One reason is that the data above are more recent than others have used, but different definitions of "foreign ownership" also are important.
15 In 2004, Citibank expanded in the Korean market by buying a medium-sized bank, KorAm, from Carlyle, JP Morgan Chase, Standard Chartered and individual investors. In January 2005, Standard Chartered announced a deal to buy Newbridge's share in Korea First Bank, and it is expected that HSBC will purchase Lone Star's share in Korea Exchange Bank as soon as this is legally possible.
16 According to one estimate, the risk-adjusted return on consumer loans can be 5 percent or higher, compared to 0.2 percent for loans to large firms (*The Economist*, "Survey of Asian Finance," 8 February 2003).
17 Among other problems, the source used for Korea (Cho 2002) does not provide a definition of SME, so the cut-off may be quite different in the two cases. The definition in Chile is any firm with sales up to $2.5 million, which includes 99 percent of all firms. Of this percentage, micro firms represent 82.5

percent, small firms 14.5 percent, and medium-sized firms 2 percent; see Román (2003).
18 Interestingly, the Chilean programs seem to have been more effective with credit to micro firms; see Román (2003).

References

Ahn, C.Y. and Cha, B. (2004) "Financial Sector Restructuring in South Korea: Accomplishments and Unfinished Agenda," *Asian Economic Papers*, 3(1): 1–21.
Allen, F. and Gale, D. (2000) *Comparing Economic Systems*, Cambridge, MA: MIT Press.
Amsden, A. (ed.) (1994) "The World Bank's 'East Asian Miracle: Economic Growth and Public Policy,'" *World Development*, 22(4) (special section): 615–70.
Arellano, J.P. and Cortázar, R. (1982) "Del milagro a la crisis: algunas reflexiones sobre el momento económico," *Colección Estudios CIEPLAN* 8.
Batra, G., Kaufmann, D. and Stone, A. (2003) *Investment Climate around the World: Voices of Firms from the World Business Environmental Survey*, Washington, DC: World Bank.
BIS (Bank for International Settlements) (2002) *The Development of Bond Markets in Emerging Economies*, BIS Papers No. 11, Basle.
Budnevich, C. (2000) "El sistema financiero chileno y su institucionalidad regulatoria: las políticas bancarias en los noventa," in O. Muñoz (ed.) *El estado y el sector privado: construyendo una nueva economía en los años 90*, Santiago: FLACSO/Dolmen.
Bulmer-Thomas, V. (2003) *The Economic History of Latin America since Independence*, 2nd edition, Cambridge: Cambridge University Press.
Caprio, G. *et al.* (eds) (2004) *The Future of State-Owned Financial Institutions*, Washington, DC: Brookings Institution Press.
Cárdenas, E., Ocampo, J.A. and Thorp, R. (eds) (2000) *An Economic History of Twentieth-Century Latin America, Volume 3. Industrialization and the State in Latin America: The Postwar Years*, London: Palgrave.
Cho, Y.J. (2002) "Financial Repression, Liberalization, Crisis, and Restructuring: Lessons from Korea's Financial Sector Policies," ADBI Research Paper 47, Tokyo.
Cifuentes, R. *et al.* (2002) "Capital Markets in Chile: From Financial Repression to Financial Deepening," Working Paper No. 154, Santiago: Central Bank of Chile.
Claessens, S., Demirigüç-Kunt, A. and Huizinga, H. (2001) "How Does Foreign Entry Affect Domestic Banking Markets?" *Journal of Banking and Finance* 25(5): 891–911.
Clarke, G., Cull, R. and Martínez Peria, M.S. (2001) "Does Foreign Bank Penetration Reduce Access to Credit in Developing Countries? Evidence from Asking Borrowers," World Bank Policy Research Working Paper 2716, Washington, DC.
Coe, D. and Kim, S. (eds) (2002) *Korean Crisis and Recovery*, Seoul: IMF/KIEP.
Demirgüç-Kunt, A. and Levine, R. (eds) (2001) *Financial Structure and Economic Growth*, Cambridge, MA: MIT Press.
Dowers, K. and Masci, P. (eds) (2003) *Focus on Capital: New Approaches to Developing Latin American Capital Markets*, Washington, DC: IADB.
ECLAC (Economic Commission for Latin America and the Caribbean) (2000) *Foreign Investment in Latin America and the Caribbean, 1999 Report*, Santiago: ECLAC.

—— (2003) *Foreign Investment in Latin America and the Caribbean, 2002 Report*, Santiago: ECLAC.
The Economist (2003) "Survey of Asian Finance," *The Economist*, 8 February 2003.
Ffrench-Davis, R. and Griffith-Jones, S. (eds) (2003) *From Capital Surges to Drought: Seeking Stability for Emerging Economies*, London: Macmillan/Palgrave.
Ffrench-Davis, R. and Tapia, H. (2001) "Three Varieties of Capital Surge Management in Chile," in R. Ffrench-Davis (ed.) *Financial Crises in "Successful" Emerging Economies*, Washington, DC: Brookings Institution Press.
Fishlow, A. et al. (1994) *Miracle or Design? Lessons from the East Asian Experience*, Washington, DC: Overseas Development Council.
García-Herrero, A. and Santabárbara, D. (2004) "Where is the Chinese Banking System Going with the Ongoing Reform?" Banco de España, Documentos Ocasionales No. 0406, Madrid.
Gereffi, G. and Wyman, D. (eds) (1990) *Manufacturing Miracles: Paths of Industrialization in Latin American and East Asia*, Princeton, NJ: Princeton University Press.
Hahm, J.H. (1999) "Financial System Restructuring in Korea: The Crisis and its Resolution," in S. Masuyama, D. Vanderbrink and S.Y. Chia (eds) *East Asia's Financial System: Evolution and Crisis*, Tokyo: Nomura/ISEAS.
Hawkins, J. (2002) "Bond Markets and Banks in Emerging Economies," BIS Paper No. 11, Basle.
Held, G. and Jiménez, L.F. (2001) "Liberalización financiera, crisis, y reforma del sistema bancario chileno: 1974–1999," in R. Ffrench-Davis and B. Stallings (eds) *Reformas, crecimiento y políticas sociales en Chile desde 1973*, Santiago: CEPAL/LOM.
IADB (Inter-American Development Bank) (2001) *Economic and Social Progress in Latin America, 2001 Report*, Washington, DC: IADB.
IMF (International Monetary Fund) (2003) *Republic of Korea: Financial System Stability Assessment*, Country Report No. 03/81, Washington, DC.
Ito, T. and Park, Y.C. (eds) (2004) *Developing Asian Bond Markets: Challenges and Strategies*, Canberra: Australian National University Asia Pacific Press.
Kantis, H. et al. (2001) *Entrepreneurship in Emerging Economies: The Creation and Development of New Firms in Latin America and East Asia*, Washington, DC: IADB.
Kim, E.M., Kim, J.K. and Kim, J.I. (2000) "Reconstruction of the Chaebols and Financial Sector in Korea: Progress and Assessment since the Financial Crisis," ICSEAD Working Paper Series 2000-23, Kitakyushu, Japan.
Kim, S. and Park, J. (2002) "Structural Change in the Corporate Bond Market in Korea after the Currency Crisis," BIS Paper No. 11, Basle.
Kim, Y.H. (ed.) (2001) *Government Bond Market Development in Asia*, Manila: Asian Development Bank.
La Porta, R., López-de-Silanes, F. and Shleifer, A. (2002) "Government Ownership of Banks," *Journal of Finance* 57(1): 265–301.
Levine, R. (2004) "Finance and Growth: Theory and Evidence," NBER Working Paper 10766, Cambridge, MA.
Litan, R., Masson, P. and Pomerleano, M. (eds) (2001) *Open Doors: Foreign Participation in Financial Systems in Developing Countries*, Washington, DC: Brookings Institution Press.
Litan, R., Pomerleano, M. and Sundararajan, V. (eds) (2003) *The Future of Domestic Capital Markets in Developing Countries*, Washington, DC: Brookings Institution Press.

Montgomery, H. (2003) "The Role of Foreign Banks in Post-Crisis Asia: The Importance of Method of Entry," ADBI Research Paper No. 51.

Nugent, J. and Yhee, S.G. (2001) "Small and Medium Enterprises in Korea: Achievements, Constraints, and Policy Issues," Washington, DC: World Bank Institute.

Park, Y.C. and Lee, J.W. (2002) "Financial Crisis and Recovery: Patterns of Adjustment in East Asia," ADBI Research Paper No. 45, Tokyo.

Román, E. (2003) "Acceso al crédito bancario de las microempresas chilenas: lecciones de la década de los noventa," Serie Financiamiento del Desarrollo, ECLAC, Santiago.

Sanhueza, G. (1999) "La crisis financiera en los años ochenta en Chile: análisis de sus soluciones y sus costos," *Economía Chilena* 2(1): 43–68.

—— (2001) "Chilean Banking Crisis of the 1980s: Solutions and Estimations of the Costs," Working Paper No. 104, Central Bank of Chile.

Shin, I. (2002) "Evolution of the KOSDAQ Stock Market: Evaluation and Policy Issues," paper presented at AT10 Researchers Meeting, Tokyo.

Stallings, B. (2003) "Domestic Capital Markets in Latin America and East Asia: An Alternative to Foreign Capital?" paper prepared for ADBI Conference on Economic Development and Integration in Asia and Latin America, Tokyo.

Stallings, B. and Peres, W. (2000) *Growth, Employment, and Equity: The Impact of the Economic Reforms in Latin America and the Caribbean*, Washington, DC: Brookings Institution Press.

Stallings, B. and Studart, R. (2003) "Financial Regulation and Supervision in Emerging Markets: The Experience of Latin America since the Tequila Crisis," in R. Ffrench-Davis and S. Griffith-Jones (eds) *From Capital Surges to Drought: Seeking Stability for Emerging Economies*, London: Macmillan/Palgrave.

Standard and Poor's (2002) *Emerging Stock Markets Factbook, 2001*, New York: Standard and Poor's.

Stiglitz, J. and Yusuf, S. (eds) (2001) *Rethinking the East Asian Miracle*, New York: Oxford University Press.

Walker, E. and Lefort, F. (2002) "Pension Reform and Capital Markets: Are There Any (Hard) Links?" Social Protection Discussion Paper Series No. 0201, Washington, DC: World Bank.

World Bank (1993) *The East Asian Miracle: Economic Growth and Public Policy*, New York: Oxford University Press for the World Bank.

—— (2001a) *Finance for Growth: Policy Choices in a Volatile World*, New York: Oxford University Press for the World Bank.

—— (2001b) *World Development Report, 2000/2001*, New York: Oxford University Press for the World Bank.

—— (2004) *Whither Latin American Capital Markets?* Washington: World Bank, Office of the Chief Economist, Latin American and Caribbean Region.

Yoshitomi, M. and Shirai, S. (2001) "Designing a Financial Market Structure in Post-Crisis Asia: How to Develop Corporate Bond Markets," ADBI Working Paper No. 15, Tokyo.

Zysman, J. (1983) *Governments, Markets, and Growth: Financial Systems and the Politics of Industrial Change*, Ithaca, NY: Cornell University Press.

6 Restructuring the financial and corporate sector
The South Korean experience

Choong Yong Ahn

Introduction

In the wake of the Asian Financial Crisis, South Korea (hereafter Korea) sought the largest-ever emergency financial assistance package, amounting to US$57 billion, from the IMF in early December 1997 to avoid a moratorium on its foreign debt. The financial assistance was provided to Korea on the condition that it would undertake far-reaching structural reforms in almost every segment of its economy. In compliance with that condition, Korea has been simultaneously overhauling its inefficiency-ridden financial, corporate, public and labor sectors, sometimes beyond the IMF mandate.

Bad debts in both the financial and corporate sectors were at the core of Korea's financial crisis, which was triggered by contagion and currency speculation in July 1997. In order to break a vicious circle between a banking crisis and a corporate crisis, Korea has undertaken a series of restructuring programs in the banking sector, while non-bank financial institutions (NBFIs) have also undertaken their own restructuring.

In the process of restructuring, it was proven that both the breadth and the depth of corporate and financial distress in Korea was unprecedented. The level and structure of corporate debt, the number of debtors and creditors involved, and the weak legal environment presented large obstacles in the restructuring of the financial and corporate sectors.

While carrying out the Korea–IMF reform program, Korea experienced the worst economic setback in 1998 since its adoption of the export-oriented development strategy in the early 1960s. After the outbreak of the crisis, the unemployment rate increased continuously, peaking at 8.6 percent, more than three percentage points higher than its pre-crisis level, with 1.8 million people out of work.

However and surprisingly, Korea's economy in 1999 bounced back to positive 10.7 percent growth from its lowest growth rate of negative 6.7 percent in 1998. Thanks to signs of recovery in 1999, which was astonishingly faster than expected, mainly due to comprehensive economic reforms as mandated by the IMF conditionality, a rapidly rising trade surplus and foreign exchange reserves, as well as a bullish stock market trend, Korea obtained an upgrade in sovereign ratings. Moody's Investor Services had lowered Korea's sovereign rating from A1 before the crisis to Ba1 on February 1999, but this rating was raised again to A3 on 28 March 2002.

However, recent economic indicators since the fourth quarter of 2000, including the GDP growth rate, unemployment rate and managerial indexes of both finance and banking sectors, appear to demonstrate that the restructuring of both financial and corporate sectors is still incomplete. By the end of 2000, Korea's economy began to show some "reform fatigue," making the remaining items on the reform agenda still serious. Despite some important remaining reforms, on 23 August 2001 Korea was able to repay IMF loans of US$19.5 billion, two years and eight months earlier than the original schedule, making it the first among Asian countries which received the IMF bailout funds to complete its repayments.

The purpose of this chapter is first to describe what Korea has accomplished in terms of restructuring its financial and corporate sectors over the past three and a half years, and then to address the unfinished restructuring agenda and a newly emerging development paradigm with some policy implications. Attention is given to how Korea has cleaned up its bad debts accumulated in the financial sector. Because of the intertwined nature of the financial and corporate sectors, the chapter also addresses some important restructuring issues of still highly leveraged corporations, which are so critically linked to the creation of sound and healthy financial institutions.

The next section describes a "compressed growth" process and rising non-performing loans (NPLs), viewed from both the financial sector and corporate sector. The third discusses various phases of restructuring in the financial sector that have been accomplished up to date, while the fourth discusses the restructuring of the corporate sector. The fifth section presents various disposition methods of NPLs by the financial community. The sixth presents a post-crisis development model in addition to reviewing the continuing agenda for financial and corporate sector restructuring in the years to come. The chapter concludes with some overall remarks and some policy implications.

"Compressed growth," accumulated inefficiency and rising NPLs

Intertwined NPLs

During the high growth period, and especially in the early 1990s, Korean chaebols, large conglomerates, undertook ambitious expansion and diversification drives including numerous overseas investment projects. Furthermore, the Korean government supported this expansion and often directed chaebols into specific lines of business. The chaebols' expansion drives were mainly funded with aggressive borrowings, often short term, from Korean commercial and merchant banks, and quite frequently from foreign financial institutions for overseas projects (Ahn 2001b). Banks relied primarily on collateral in the allocation of credit, and paid relatively little attention to earnings performance and cash flow generation, or the corporations' ability to repay. In addition, chaebols generally supplied guarantees to their affiliates and subsidiaries to secure loans. Although most of the major subsidiaries of chaebols are publicly listed, they have traditionally raised little in new equity in Korea's poorly developed capital market (Classens et al. 1998).

A vicious chain of inefficiency between the financial and the corporate sectors has grown since the second stage of the heavy chemical industrial drive in the early 1980s (Ahn 2001b). Chaebols have been promoted by means of government administered credit allocation to achieve the government's industrial targeting in order to take advantage of economies of scale.[1] Both administered credit allocation, which often resulted in excessive lending without prudential financial rules, while chaebols' focus on increasing market share and pursuing diversification through debt financing with little attention to profitability caused an inefficiency syndrome in Korea's economy. Consequently, the demise of the financial and corporate sectors was intertwined. As corporate bankruptcies rose, financial institutions became burdened with bad debts and were no longer able to roll over their domestic or foreign liabilities.

As Lieberman and Mako (1998) noted, this "compressed growth" policy via aggressive, leveraged expansion through debt financing worked well as long as the economy and exports expanded vigorously and the returns on new investment exceeded the cost of capital. Within this environment, high debt/equity ratios were a risky but winning strategy for Korea (Stiglitz 1999). High leverage allowed Korean firms to grow more rapidly than if they had had to rely on retained earnings.

In recent years, however, business group financial performance among the top 30 chaebols worsened in terms of free cash flow, return on equity, profit margin and interest coverage ratio, while their debt/equity ratios recorded their highest levels by international standards (Table 6.1). Rapid wage increases, a result of a highly unionized and strong labor force in the wake of the democratization process in the late 1980s and onward often outstripped productivity growth (Ahn and Kim 1997). Declining demand and falling prices for Korea's major export items such as semiconductors, chemicals, shipbuilding and steel products further weakened profitability in recent years. For example, in 1997, profitability declined substantially, with the ordinary income/sales ratio falling to −0.3 percent and remaining at a similar level, while some substantially higher positive profitability levels were evident in the US, Japan and Taiwan (Table 6.2).

Table 6.1 Debt/equity ratio in the manufacturing industry (%)

	US	Japan	Taiwan	Korea		
	1997	1997	1995	1997	1998	2001
Debt/Equity ratio	153.5	193.2	85.7	396.3	303.0	182.2
Total borrowings and bonds payable to total assets	25.6	33.1	26.2	54.2	50.8	39.8

Sources: The Bank of Korea, *Financial Statement Analysis for 1999* (1999: 16); The Bank of Korea, *Monthly Bulletin* (May 2002: 55–77).

Table 6.2 International comparisons of manufacturing firm's profitability (%)

	US	Japan	Taiwan	Korea		
	1997	1997	1995	1997	1998	2001
Ordinary income/Sales	8.3	3.4	5.1	−0.3	−1.8	0.4
Operating income/Sales	7.6	3.5	7.3	8.3	6.1	5.5

Sources: The Bank of Korea, *Analysis of Corporate Management*, 1998, and *Financial Statement Analysis for 1999* (1999: 19); The Bank of Korea, *Monthly Bulletin* (May 2002: 55–77).

Expanding NPLs and forward looking criteria

A crucial aspect of Korea's financial restructuring efforts is related to the size and disposal of NPLs. Obviously, NPLs are the result of widespread insolvency problems in its corporate sector as well as its financial sector. The figure for non-performing loans of banks provided by the FSC (Financial Supervisory Commission) stood at 87.26 trillion won (US$63 billion) as of the end of March 1998. This accounted for 16.89 percent of total bank loans, or 20.72 percent of Korea's GDP in 1997 (Table 6.3).[2] According to the data provided by the FSC, the total combined debt of the top 30 chaebols amounted to 342 trillion won at the end of 1998.

Any attempt to restructure only the financial sector is likely to fail. For example, over-extended firms in the corporate sector also need to restructure their balance sheets, and to increase both equity and the maturity

Table 6.3 Non-performing loans (ending March 1998) (trillion won)

	Total loans	Non-performing loans (% of total)
Banks	516.6062	87.2645 (16.89)
Other Fin. Institutions	256.9355	24.7611 (9.64)
Total	773.5779	112.0256 (14.48)

Source: Financial Supervisory Commission.

profiles of their debt loads, in order to become viable corporations. The longer-term process of real restructuring will need to include improved corporate governance, product line rationalization, increases in productivity and a fundamental change in corporate strategies and culture, focusing on profitability and liquidity versus aggressive expansion at virtually any cost (Lieberman and Mako 1998).

Indeed, the disposal of NPLs is at the heart of Korea's financial reform as well as corporate sector restructuring. It serves to gauge how vigorously the sector has undergone the restructuring process, and how much healthier both sectors have become. Accordingly, the size of NPLs will point toward the feasibility and effectiveness of present and future reform measures, and will predict mid- and long-term financial stability.

In July 1998, there was a major strengthening of provision requirements and loan classification standards based on forward-looking criteria regarding future cash flows. In accordance with international practices, loans in arrears of three months or more are now classified as substandard or below, and loans in arrears of one to three months are considered precautionary loans, as shown in Table 6.4. As a consequence, most of the emergency loans made to technically bankrupt companies are now reclassified as substandard loans, instead of precautionary loans. This reclassification has caused another serious problem for recapitalization in Korea's banking sector.

What appears sound and solid from the first round of restructuring can go wrong, unless continued restructuring of the financial sector takes place in a timely manner. Korea's own restructuring story can be a case in point. As the NPLs of the financial sector rose again after introducing stricter asset classification rules based on forward-looking criteria, Korea's financial sector needed another injection of public funds in order to meet the IMF's mandate.

During the first half of 1999, major Korean commercial banks, after restructuring with an injection of public funds equivalent to more than 50 trillion won, obtained Bank of International Settlements (BIS) capital adequacy status. However, stricter capital adequacy standards and additional loan loss provisions, due to the adopted forward-looking criteria, sharply affected the profitability of banks that had already been exposed to Daewoo's huge debts, amounting to 23 trillion won.

On the corporate side, 80 corporations, including those from 15 chae-

Table 6.4 Changes in loan classification standards

Period of overdue payment	Old	New
1 month to 3 months	Normal	Precautionary
3 months to 6 months	Precautionary	Substandard or doubtful
Longer than 6 months	Substandard or doubtful	Substandard or doubtful

bols, underwent corporate restructuring. Their aggregate debt at the end of March 1999 exceeded 30 trillion won, the bulk of which had already been classified as either "precautionary" or "non-performing." Furthermore, the forward-looking loan criteria caused a substantial part of the precautionary category of loans to be reclassified as non-performing.

Based on the International Monetary Fund (IMF) policy recommendations, the forward-looking criteria for NPLs became effective in January 2000. In addition, the provision requirement for precautionary loans was raised from 1 percent to 2 percent. The new provision requirements were introduced for commercial papers (CP), guaranteed bills and privately placed bonds belonging to trust accounts.

In order to capture the problematic loans given to Korea's corporate sector, including chaebols, it is important to see the changes that have occurred in the size of NPLs following the instruction of forward-looking criteria as recommended by the BIS and IMF. Despite Korea's proactive restructuring effort, many critics argue that the 64 trillion won fiscal support package is not sufficient to restore the health of the financial system – at least for banks. The size of NPLs is likely to continue to rise while corporate restructuring is being undertaken under a global asset quality standard.

Kwon and Nam (1999) investigated the nature of loans and the impact of NPLs on corporate restructuring based on forward-looking criteria, in which they considered the corporate sector's debt levels and its debt-servicing capability, while focusing on the future size of NPLs. They used the interest coverage ratio (computed as operating income divided by interest expenses, hereafter referred to as ICR) as a scale to determine whether the loans and credits to the sample corporations would be performing or not, a method employed by Goldman Sachs (1998), Credit Swiss First Boston (1998) and others.[3] NPLs in their study were defined as loans and credits extended to corporations with ICRs[4] of less than 100 percent. This is a standard way of assessing the debt-servicing capability of a corporate borrower. When a corporate borrower is incapable of generating enough earnings to cover interest expenses, loans and credits extended to the borrowers are regarded as "problematic." Furthermore, the recent dismantling of Korea's second largest chaebol, Daewoo, in early 2000 aggravated the rising trend of NPLs.

According to Kwon and Nam's study, NPLs, newly defined, applied to the 1995–8 period sharply increased for two consecutive years prior to the financial crisis. NPLs held by listed companies amounted to 32.1 percent of their total debts in 1998. Furthermore, the number of companies whose ICR did not reach 100 percent accounted for 37.5 percent of the total number of listed companies (Table 6.5). Their investigation shows that the NPL ratio of unlisted companies appears higher than that of listed companies. Moreover, the unlisted companies' NPL ratios had already exceeded the 30 percent level in 1996, and substantially increased to 37.8

168 Choong Yong Ahn

Table 6.5 Sample estimates on NPL ratio and NPL company (listed) ratio with interest coverage ratio less than 100%

Year	NPL ratio of sample firms (%)	Ratio of sample companies with ICR less than 100%
1995	12.1	16.5
1996	20.1	24.2
1997	31.2	35.3
1998	32.1	37.5

Source: Kwon and Nam (1999).

percent in 1997, as they faced the economy-wide crisis. Such a large magnitude of NPLs of listed and unlisted companies is convincing evidence that the financial crisis was mainly attributable to mounting debts and low profits in the corporate sector.

By comparing the sample estimates of NPLs based on forward-looking criteria for the year 1998, based on the borrowers' debt-servicing capability, Kwon and Nam (1999) estimated that the total distressed debts of the entire corporate sector could easily reach 260 trillion won. This is equivalent to 32.1 percent of the 820 trillion won worth of total credit extended to the corporate sector in 1998. Given that the speculated NPL size is much higher than the government's current estimation of 118 trillion won in 2000, Kwon and Nam's estimation results suggest that there should be a second phase in the financial restructuring program.

Another critical issue is related to whether banks are capable of properly assessing the future cash flows of borrowing firms. One of the many reasons for the rise of NPLs in Korea may be the downturn in corporate profitability, high interest rates, high tax rates and high inflation rates.[5]

A drastic drop in the ICR can be made through asset sales or debt restructuring by creditor financial institutions. Debt restructuring includes a variety of options such as debt-equity swaps, debt forgiveness, debt relief and others. The choice and related prices are, of course, negotiable between debtor and creditor. Debt-equity swaps and debt reduction will alleviate the debt burden of corporate borrowers, thereby improving their ICRs. However, the stock of corporate debt is so large that sustainable debt-equity ratios cannot be achieved over a reasonable time frame, but only through the flow of new equity, asset sales and retirement of debt (Classens *et al.* 1998).

Phases of financial sector restructuring

Macroeconomic background

Financial sector restructuring could be addressed more properly by looking at changes of key macroeconomic indicators during the reform

Table 6.6 Major economic indicators (1996–2001)

	1996	1997	1998	1999	2000	2001
GDP growth rate (%)	7.1	5.5	−5.8	10.7	8.8	3.0
• Private consumption	96.9	3.1	−9.6	10.3	7.1	−1.7
• Facility investment	8.2	−11.3	−38.5	38.0	34.3	−9.8
• Construction	3.0	2.7	−10.2	−9.2	−3.7	5.8
• Commodity exports	14.5	5.0	15.6	16.3	21.6	−12.7
• Commodity imports	13.9	−3.8	−24.6	28.9	20.0	−12.1
Current account balance (in $100m)	−230.0	−81.7	403.6	244.8	103	86.2
Trade account balance (in $100m)	−149.6	−31.8	413.3	283.7	167	133.9
• Exports* (in $100m)	1,299.7	1,386.2	1,321.3	1,451.6	1,767.0	1,513.7
• Imports* (in $100m)	1,449.3	1,418.0	904.9	1,167.9	1,600.0	1,379.8
Consumer price (%)	5.0	3.2	7.5	0.8	2.3	4.1

Source: The Bank of Korea, *Monthly Bulletin* (March and April 2001).

Note
* Customs clearance base.

Table 6.7 Changes in foreign exchange reserves (US$ million)

	End of 1997	End of 1999	End of 2000	End of 2001
Foreign exchange reserves	20,405.5	74,054.5	96,198.1	102,821.4
Gold	36.9	67.1	67.6	68.3
SDRs	58.9	0.7	3.5	3.3
Reserve position in IMF	599.3	286.5	271.8	262.2
Foreign exchange	19,710.4	73.700.3	95,855.1	102,487.5

Source: The Bank of Korea, *Monthly Economic Bulletin* (Various Issues 2001).

period. A swift economic recovery in 1999 and 2000, from the worst economic setback in the past four decades, appeared to be evident as shown in Table 6.6. However, 2001 witnessed a slowdown caused by the declining information technology sector and related downturn of the US economy.

During almost four years of reform, the most positive development occurred in Korea's foreign exchange reserve, as shown in Table 6.7. Overall, foreign exchange reserves swelled from US$20.4 billion at the end of 1997 to greater than US$112 billion in June 2002. The won/dollar exchange rate also stabilized at about 1,100 won in 1999, from an average rate of US$1,700 in December 1997, as a completely free exchange rate policy was adopted under the IMF conditionality. The interest rate, denoted by yields on three-year corporate bonds, also declined from 18.3 percent in March 1998, to 8.98 in August 2000. More importantly, Korea's composite stock index rose more than 300 percent by the end of 1999, compared to the level at the end of 1997.

However, beginning in the third quarter of 2000, Korea's economy started to show serious symptoms of recession, making the financial sector's restructuring more difficult than originally thought. Some structural warning signals in the Korean economy were not seriously addressed prior to the outbreak of the Asian Financial Crisis. In this regard, intertwined bad debts between the financial and corporate sectors proved to be the most serious one.

Resolution of non-viable financial institutions

Resolution of non-viable banks

The first measure to initiate the IMF mandated structural reform, which also took into account the mounting debts accumulated during the high growth period, was the resolution of non-viable financial institutions. The restructuring of the financial sector was carried out in the following manner during the first round of restructuring. First of all, the Korea Deposit Insurance Corporation (KDIC) recapitalized Korea First Bank and Seoul Bank, which had been in the worst trouble, in January 1998. Next, the Financial Supervisory Commission (FSC) had accounting firms inspect the assets and liabilities of 12 banks that had failed to meet BIS's 8 percent capital adequacy ratios by the end of 1997, and required them to present management rehabilitation plans.

Upon examination of these plans, the FSC decided to order the exit of five non-viable banks. These exits were achieved through a Purchase and Assumption (P&A) formula, whereby each acquiring bank would purchase the sound assets and assume the liabilities of the acquired banks. The five acquiring banks were chosen on the basis of their BIS capital adequacy ratios, which stood at more than 8 percent at the end of 1997. Meanwhile, among the remaining seven banks that had their management rehabilitation plans conditionally approved, five banks merged into two banks, while the other two banks were not involved in merger or takeover activity.[6]

By injecting public funds into severely undercapitalized but viable banks, Korea had implemented almost 100 percent of the public support package, completing the first round of its financial restructuring, primarily in the banking sector, by the end of 1999. During the first round of restructuring, a total of 64 trillion won of public funds were injected to resolve the problem of non-performing loans in the financial sector, in order to clean financial institutions through recapitalization.

During the second round of restructuring, the government again ordered six larger commercial banks (Hanvit, Chohung, Korea Exchange, Peace, Kwangju and Cheju), which had been recapitalized by public funds during the first round of restructuring or whose capital adequacy ratios were again below the BIS 8 percent guideline as of June 2000, plus Kyungnam Bank, whose financial status was expected to worsen due to the realization of potential bad loans, to submit their management rehabilitation plans.

After appraising their normalization plans, the government took other comprehensive restructuring actions for these banks in 2000. First, it allowed Chohung Bank and Korea Exchange Bank to pursue their management improvement plans independently, including recapitalization and resolution of NPLs. Recognizing that it would be difficult for the Hanvit, Peace, Kwangju and Kyungnam Banks to improve their financial status independently, the government extended public funds to them to improve their financial positions. The government also decided to bring them under a financial holding company, to be established by the Korea Deposit Insurance Corporation (KDIC).

As the government imposed harsh financial reforms during the first phase of restructuring, the banking sector should be prepared to undergo further restructuring spurred by newly emerging market forces. Stricter asset quality standards, and a virtual elimination of the depositor protection policy[7] implemented in 2001, may force less competitive banks to fall prey to mergers and acquisitions. Hybrid financial services will appear to tear down the walls which separate different financial activities. The government must therefore address the external framework in which voluntary restructuring can take place, especially during the second round of financial reform.

The government also pursued some global strategic alliances with foreign banking institutions. In this regard, Korea sold Korea First Bank to New Bridge Capital at the end of 1999. The foreign management of Korea First Bank was expected to introduce a new credit culture to the Korean banking community. The transfer of bank management of the leading Seoul-based commercial banks to foreign authorities appears to be another tangible result of the government's restructuring drive.

Restructuring of non-bank financial institutions (NBFIs)

In the second phase of restructuring the financial sector, it may be necessary to overhaul the non-bank financial institutions (NBFIs), specifically the investment trust corporations. In this regard, Stiglitz (1999) pointed out:

> The NBFIs make up nearly half of the financial sector in Korea – quite a large share by international standards. This means any approach to restructure the financial sector that focuses only on commercial banks is, at best, "half-baked." The assets of the Investment Trust Corporations (ITCs) have tripled in just the past two years, as corporations – especially the top 5 chaebols – used the trusts as a way around the tightening of the bank credit. Use of the ITC escape hatch postponed

the reckoning for Daewoo, allowing the chaebol to become even more heavily indebted as it sought to grow out of its problems.

Stiglitz (1999)

The second round of restructuring followed to achieve the overall objectives of financial sector restructuring, including that of NBFIs. During the year 2000, 175 financial institutions, most of them mutual savings and finance companies and credit unions, either exited the market or merged with other institutions. The government supported those ailing NBFIs with public funds of 35 trillion won through recapitalization, repayments of deposits and purchase of their NPLs.

Thus, another critical agenda item for implementing the second round of financial restructuring should be related to the other half of Korea's financial sector. The NBFIs must become more transparent and should be subject to enhanced supervision. Also, several critical measures must be introduced without delay. First, a new governance system, similar to the one already in existence in the banking sector, needs to be institutionalized to ensure a checks-and-balances system. Second, the NBFIs should be required to report their assets at market value. By and large, they should be covered by many of the same prudential regulations as the banking sector. Third, it is critical that non-financial corporations' holdings of shares in NBFIs be regulated as their shareholdings in commercial banks are. Fourth, ownership of the NBFIs should be regulated.[8]

In the past and even now, although the NBFI sector has not been covered by explicit insurance, the Korean government has offered implicit insurance. With the extension of the Bond Stabilization Fund by 30 trillion won at the urging of the FSC to rescue ailing NBFIs, the "clean" commercial banks are likely to become "unclean." As a result, the remaining reform drive in the financial sector must address the inefficiency chain that penetrates the banking and NBFI sectors.

On the NBFI side, the government suspended a number of merchant banking corporations, which were suffering from a flight of deposits, due to their reduced credibility in the wake of the dismantling of the Daewoo Group. As a result, the number of merchant banking corporations in normal operations decreased from 30 before the financial crisis to just five at the end of 2000.

In dealing with investment trust companies, the government split two such companies, whose normal operation had been impossible due to Daewoo's financial problems, into two units: a securities company and an investment trust management company. While extending public funds to improve the financial positions of the securities companies, the government concluded Memoranda of Understanding (MOUs) concerning management normalization, and required self-rescue efforts such as disposal of assets and rationalization of their staff and branch networks.

After evaluating the financial status of eight life and six non-life insurance companies whose payment reserve requirement ratios were below 100 percent, the government ordered three life insurers and two non-life insurers to implement prompt corrective actions to attain 100 percent ratios. In 2001, 41 mutual savings and finance companies and 125 credit unions with little possibility of normalization, as a result of accumulated bad loans and unauthorized operations, either exited the market or merged with other financial institutions.

A rapid development of financial engineering techniques appears to play an important role in the NBFI sector. For example, cyber trading commissions at some brokerages that offer online stock trading have already fallen from 0.5 percent to 0.1 percent. The advent of cyber stockbrokers will lead to further drops in commission fees. Within this new environment, small and medium sized securities companies without much capital or specialty will either be closed or will have to find a means of survival.

Table 6.8 summarizes changes in the number of financial institutions as a result of two rounds of comprehensive financial sector restructuring during 1998–2001. The exit of non-viable financial institutions continued in 1999, 2000 and 2001 through mergers, debt-equity swaps and liquidations. As shown in Table 6.8, a total of 446 financial institutions exited the market over the four-year period 1998–2001.

Corporate sector restructuring

Another aspect of Korea's major restructuring efforts is related to the widespread insolvency problem in its corporate sector, especially during the restructuring period. According to statistics released by the Bank of Korea, 17,168 firms failed in 1997, a 52.53 percent increase over failures in 1994. From January through April 1999, an average of 3,000 firms failed each month, bringing annual bankruptcy cases to nearly 23,000 (Table 6.9). This in turn exerted great pressure on financial institutions. A total of 188 have been either closed down or merged on their own initiative. The corporate debt of the top 28 chaebols reached 247 trillion won at the end of 1997, with the average debt-equity ratio reaching 449 percent per firm.[9]

Given the level of corporate debt, it is evident that overcoming the financial crisis is directly related to industrial and corporate restructuring, the success of which, in turn, hinges upon the orderly exit of ailing firms. A competitive market with free entry and exit would ensure that the assets of failed firms are efficiently utilized through liquidation via cash auctions. However, the Korean capital market is largely underdeveloped and imperfect. For example, there may not be a market for the insolvent firm's assets, or these assets may be undervalued, while a firm that is fundamentally sound but only temporarily without liquidity may not be saved. While liquidation of truly distressed firms releases resources for other,

Table 6.8 Changes in the number of financial institutions[a] during 1998–2001

	No. of institutions at end 1997	1998–2000 Exit[b]	1998–2000 Merger[c]	1998–2000 Newly established	2001 Exit[b]	2001 Merger[c]	2001 Newly established	No. of institutions at end 2001
Banks	33	5	6	–	–	2[d]	–	20
Merchant banking corporations	30	18	3	1	4	3[e]	–	3
Securities companies	36	6	1	14	–	–	3	46
Investment trust (management) companies	31	6	1	3	–	–	3	30
Life insurance companies[f]	31	5	5	–	2	–	–	19
Non-life insurance companies	14	–	1	–	–	–	1	14
Mutual savings & finance companies	231	72	25	12	23	1	–	122
Credit unions	1,666	257	101	9	48	1	–	1,268
Total	2,072	369	143	39	77	7	7	1,522

Source: The Bank of Korea (2001 *Annual Report*: 50).

Notes
a Excluding bridge financial institutions and branches of foreign institutions.
b Including revocation of license (application), bankruptcy and liquidation.
c The number of financial institutions that ceased to exist following mergers.
d Kookmin Bank and Housing and Commercial Bank merged as Kookmin Bank; Peace Bank converted into a credit card company.
e Hyundai-Ulsan Merchant Banking Corporation and Tongyang Merchant Banking Corporation merged to form Tongyang-Hyundai Merchant Banking Corporation. This subsequently absorbed Regent Merchant Banking Corporation but was in turn absorbed by Tongyang Securities Company. As a result, the three merchant banking corporations ceased to exist following the mergers.
f Excluding Postal Insurance.

Table 6.9 Number of bankruptcies: 1994–2002

	1994	1995	1996	1997	1998	1999	2000	Year Total	2001 Sep.	Oct.	Nov.	Dec.	2002 Jan.	Feb.
Total	11,255	13,922	11,589	17,168	22,828	6,718	6,693	5,277	373	414	409	447	384	285
Incorporated firms	4,503	6,031	5,157	8,226	10,536	3,371	3,840	3,220	246	242	274	286	250	194
(%)	40	43.3	44.5	47.9	46.2	50.2	57.4	61	66	58.5	67	64	65.1	68.1
Large firms	5	5	7	58	39	7	33	11	3	1	0	1	1	0

Source: The Bank of Korea.

Note
Percentage of total bankrupted firms.

more productive activities, saving firms that are temporarily insolvent but fundamentally sound can increase social welfare.

One way to save such a firm is for debtors and creditors to renegotiate the terms of the debt by means of a debt-workout program.[10] However, private workouts are often difficult to achieve due to collective action problems on the part of creditors as well as the high cost of renegotiating the debt structure every time a debtor defaults. Due to problems related to private workouts, most countries have developed standard legal mechanisms within which financially distressed firms are protected from their creditors, and are given the chance to reorganize.

Throughout the decades of government-induced growth, chaebols became closely entwined with politicians. The government provided the top 30 chaebols with a host of implicit guarantees. As a result, company managers were more concerned with garnering outside influence than they were with making their companies profitable, and their boards of directors or minority shareholders had little power to curb the managers' misbehavior. Moral hazards were prevalent, and conglomerates that were "too big to fail" consequently wielded considerable power in society.

Corporate restructuring has been a major goal of post-crisis reforms in Korea. Even before his inauguration on 25 February 1998, both President-elect Kim Dae-Jung and business leaders agreed upon the five principles of corporate restructuring listed in Table 6.10. Since then, Korea's corporate sector restructuring has been carried on with a clear timetable on the basis of these guidelines, despite short-term difficulties.

Among the concrete measures adopted so far is the requirement for the top 30 chaebols to submit consolidated financial statements, which link all affiliates from 1999. These financial statements will provide a more accurate picture of chaebol management by clarifying intra-chaebol transactions, publicizing shares held between affiliates and highlighting cross-payment guarantees and credit trading. Out of 30 chaebols, the top five account for about half of Korea's total debt, equivalent to US$500 billion (150 percent of GDP), and more than a third of manufacturing output.[11]

Following the complete dismantling of the Daewoo Group, Korea's second largest chaebol in terms of asset size, in November 1999, Korea's

Table 6.10 Five major principles of corporate restructuring

1 Transparency of corporate management.
2 Dismantling cross-debt guarantees.
3 Significantly improving capital structure.
4 Identifying core businesses and strengthening cooperative relationships with small and medium-sized companies.
5 Enhancing accountability of controlling shareholders and enhancing their management accountability.

corporate restructuring performance could best be measured by determining the extent to which the five major principles of corporate restructuring were implemented by the remaining top four chaebols. As shown in Table 6.11, these top four chaebols by-and-large succeeded in keeping their promises as agreed upon in the restructuring MOU with the government by the end of 1999.

Indeed, the exit of the Daewoo Group was one of the most dramatic examples in Korea's industrial development history. Daewoo was loaded with an excessive debt burden totaling 60 trillion won, including nearly US$10 billion in foreign debt, half of which would have fallen due within 1999. However, the government, after a thorough review of the group's financial situation, allowed an exit strategy for non-viable firms. It also permitted, through market forces, the Mergers and Acquisitions (M&As) of viable firms, as well as workout programs by creditor banks for those remaining viable firms that could not be successfully merged.

The Daewoo story clearly demonstrated that the traditional belief of "too big to fail" in Korea no longer holds. Analysts viewed the restructuring program for Daewoo as a manifestation of the government's determination to reform the nation's family-controlled chaebols under a "convoy management" practice.

Since the domestic macroeconomic situation has greatly improved since the first quarter of 1999, with 10.7 percent growth prospects, and a more than 300 percent rise in Korea's composite stock index compared to the level at the end of 1997, Korea's economy is well positioned to provide a sufficient cushion to deal with some adverse side effects of vigorous corporate restructuring. Taking advantage of Korea's bullish stock market in 1999, most chaebols were able to meet the debt–equity ratio of 200 percent largely through new equity issues and asset revaluation schemes, without having to make serious efforts to sell off their subsidiaries or assets.

Finally, the government has adopted a special program for small and medium enterprises (SMEs) troubled in the wake of the financial crisis. Realizing that it could not address the corporate restructuring needs of large groups and concurrently assess the needs of SMEs, the government decided to roll over the debts of the SMEs by extending working capital maturities. The scope of corporate workout programs is now also being expanded to include SMEs. Creditor banks evaluated the financial status of approximately 22,000 SMEs with outstanding loans of 1 billion won or more, and classified about 13,000 of these as viable. These viable SMEs were then selected as candidate firms for workout programs.

Table 6.11 Implementation of restructuring MOU as agreed between the top four chaebols and creditor banks

	Plan		Implemented	Execution ratio (%)	
	1999 (A)	(1Q–3Q) 1999 (B)	(1Q–3Q) 1999 (C)	C/B	C/A
Self-rescue efforts (in million won)	33.6	22.2	26.8	120.6	79.8
• Asset sales	13.7	8.8	10.9	124.7	80.0
• Recapitalization	19.9	13.4	15.9	117.9	79.7
Inducement of foreign capital (100 million $)	71.9	50.9	61.6	121.0	85.6
Elimination of cross-debt guarantee (in trillion won)	2.7	1.6	2.7	166.2	99.2
Spinoffs (cases)	173	131	427	326.0	246.8
Introduction of new governance system (cases)	136	136	143	105.1	105.1
Reduction of subsidiary (cases)	84	55	61	110.9	72.6

Source: Financial Supervisory Commission website (November 1999).

Disposition methods of NPLs

Injection of public funds

Because of the rise in the number of NPLs on the part of the banks that already received public funds during the first round of restructuring, the government needs to inject further public funds amounting to 50 trillion won. The government requested that five banks submit rehabilitation proposals to determine whether each bank could be viable through its own self-rescue efforts. Those banks that are regarded as non-viable are subject to regrouping or M&As. To this end, the government encouraged the establishment of financial holding companies to ensure more efficient and easier M&As in the financial sector.[12] This might allow financial institutions to grow bigger and engage in various financial businesses with reduced risk. A critical issue is related to what extent chaebols can participate in the financial holding companies.

Cleaning up of bad debts accumulated in the financial sector required a substantial amount of public funds. The total amount of public funds injected by the end of May 2002 is presented by the sub-sector of the financial community and support type in Table 6.12. The public funds continue to support financial sector restructuring. Table 6.13 shows the amount of public funds mobilized by source and support type during the period November 1997 to May 2002. Over the same period, the Korean government poured in a total of about 156.3 trillion won.

Rehabilitation actions

Of course, the injection of public funds into troubled banks was provided on the condition that the banks downsize their employees and operational units. Table 6.14 shows that more than 40 percent of bank employees have been released, and 20.2 percent of local branches have been closed down over the four-year period. Indeed, the financial restructuring was

Table 6.12 Injection of public funds by end May 2002 (billion won)

	Recapitalization	Contribution	Deposit payment	Purchase of asset	Purchase of NPLs	Total
Banks	33.9	13.6	–	14.0	24.5	86.0
Non-banks	26.3	2.8	26.1	0.9	11.9	68.0
Overseas financial subsidiaries	–	–	–	–	2.3	2.3
Total	60.2	16.4	26.1	14.9	38.7	156.3

Source: The Ministry of Finance and Economy, *"Public Fund White Paper"* (2001) and *Public Release* (25 June 2002).

Table 6.13 Use of public funds for financial sector by source and support type (November 1997–May 2002) (billion won)

	Recapitalization	Contribution	Deposit payment	Purchase of asset	Purchase of NPLs	Total
KDIC	47.5	16.4	26.1	8.6	–	98.6
KAMCO	–	–	–	–	38.7	38.7
Fiscal resources	11.8	–	–	6.3	–	18.1
Bank of Korea	0.9	–	–	–	–	0.9
Total	60.2	16.4	26.1	14.9	38.7	156.3

Source: The Ministry of Finance and Economy, *"Public Fund White Paper"* (2001) and *Public Release* (25 June 2002).

Table 6.14 Change in number of employees at domestic financial institutions

	End–97 (A)	End–2001 (B)	Difference (A–B)	(A–B)/A
No. of employees	113,994	68.360	45.634	40.0%
No. of local branches	5,987	4,776	1,211	20.2%

Source: Financial Supervisory Service, *Monthly Financial Statistics Bulletin*.

accompanied by the painful action of laying off large numbers of employees for the first time in Korea's modern development history.

Restructuring tools

Institutions involved

An immediate focus of restructuring efforts in the corporate sector has been on troubled large conglomerates. Various financial restructuring methods include debt/equity conversions, asset sales, inducement of foreign investment and new equity infusions.

The government has relied heavily on bank-led voluntary corporate debt workouts for chaebols. Hence restructuring and recapitalization of banks is a central element in the strategy for corporate and financial restructuring. Eight major creditor banks, identified as leading banks, took responsibility for negotiating workouts with 64 major corporate groups. Each of the banks has formed its respective workout unit.

In order to facilitate the restructuring process of the corporate sector, regulations governing foreign ownership in listed stocks have been changed to allow 100 percent foreign ownership. The M&A regime has been liberalized to allow hostile takeovers by foreigners; tax incentives (e.g. on asset sales) have been introduced; the real estate market has been opened to foreigners; financial disclosure and reporting have been strengthened; and insolvency procedures have been improved. Changes have also been made to the labor law, which now allows layoffs, and measures have been taken to improve labor market flexibility.

A bridge bank has assumed distressed assets from merchant banks, and the Korea Asset Management Corporation (KAMCO) has bought non-performing loans from commercial banks. By the end of September 1998, 37 trillion won of such loans had been purchased by KAMCO, at a cost of 17.2 trillion won. KAMCO will have to restructure these loans and has a number of tools at its disposal, including asset-backed securities, loan portfolio sales, asset sales, and M&As or direct investment. By May 2002, KAMCO had bought NPLs amounting to 38.7 trillion won. KAMCO should therefore be viewed as an important actor in the corporate restructuring process.

Introduction of corporate restructuring vehicles (CRVs) and debt/equity swaps

To facilitate the resolution of bad loans held by financial institutions, the Corporate Restructuring Vehicle Act (effective from 23 October 2000) and its associated Enforcement Decree (effective from 31 October 2000) were promulgated. A corporate restructuring vehicle (CRV) is a paper company, which generates profits through asset operations and distributes them to its shareholders. The operation of its assets is done by making investments in companies which have signed a corporate improvement planning agreement with creditor financial institutions, or by purchasing bad loans from the financial institutions which have concluded such agreements. To establish a CRV, more than three promoters, including at least two creditor financial institutions, must register it with the FSC. The minimum capital of a CRV is 500 million won and its maximum life is five years. Creditor financial institutions may hold stocks of the CRV in excess of the investment limit stipulated in business-related legislation, including the General Banking Act.

The goal of the CRV is to manage insolvent firms put under debt workout programs in place of creditor banks, but in a more efficient and effective manner by using specialists and investment techniques.[13] Under the present system, the role of creditor banks is limited to external supervision due to the lack of management expertise, while the management of the workout firms is left to the firm's officials, who caused the mismanagement in the first place. Some benefits of a CRV are: a) to facilitate disposal of assets by creditor banks; b) to facilitate effective management and governance on companies undertaking a workout process; c) to encourage foreign capital investment; and d) to stimulate capital markets. In other countries, asset management companies (AMCs) have played the role of absorbing distressed banks' assets and restructuring financially troubled enterprises.

In Korea, debt–equity swaps have proved to be one of the most effective methods in restructuring highly leveraged corporations and creditor banks. As debt–equity swaps are employed as a method of corporate restructuring, the government controls companies via state-run banks.

As a result, the overall economy might be influenced by government policy, not by market principles. Nevertheless, in practice, debt–equity swaps are frequently used in Korea to resolve potential bad loans and to raise capital adequacy ratios. In order to prevent moral hazards like this, it is necessary to build a responsible management system in the financial sector, which might lead to corporate restructuring.

Capital market development

Given the huge size of the overall debt of corporate firms in Korea, a key strategy for corporate restructuring will have to be achieved by a substantial conversion of debt to equity, which will bring a change in the domestic capital market and also a shift in household savings patterns. Improvements have to be made in the corporate financial market structure in order for corporations to directly raise their necessary funds. Therefore, serious efforts have to be made to expand the equity market in Korea by encouraging collective investment vehicles, including mutual funds and investment and trust business. Deeper capital markets will help shift corporate finances away from debt and associated risks hitherto carried by the banking system.

Improvement of corporate performance

As a result of a series of corporate restructuring efforts, Korea's corporate debt–equity ratio has been substantially reduced over the period 1995–2001, as shown in Table 6.15. The lower debt–equity ratio has also been accompanied by a significant improvement in corporate profitability.

Continuing agenda

From "administered restructuring" to "market induced restructuring"

In the future round of restructuring, both the institutional and the regulatory frameworks must be firmly established so that "market induced

Table 6.15 Corporate performances (1995–2001) (%)

	1995	1996	1997	1998	1999	2000	2001
Debt equity ratio	286.8	317.1	396.3	303.0	214.7	210.6	182.2
Ordinary income to sales	3.6	1.0	−0.3	−1.9	1.7	1.3	0.4
Operating income to sales	8.3	6.5	8.3	6.1	6.6	7.4	5.5
Interest coverage ratio	149.6	112.1	129.1	68.3	96.1	157.2	132.6

Source: The Bank of Korea, Financial Statement Analysis, each year.

restructuring" can replace the "administered restructuring" that was inevitable during the crisis period. In this regard, the sequence and schedule of privatizing "nationalized banks" must be clearly spelled-out in advance.

Once both screening and exit of non-viable financial institutions are determined by the government, a policy focus can be placed on stimulating the economy by lowering interest rates in order to facilitate the restructuring process. It should be noted that the timely exit of non-viable firms out of the market should be accelerated to restore more confidence in the market. The Corporate Reorganization Law, the Composition Law and the Bankruptcy laws were amended in 1998 to achieve this objective.

Facilitation of corporate restructuring

To facilitate the prompt disposal of financial institutions' non-performing loans and to avoid additional bad loans, the Corporate Restructuring Promotion Act was passed. A system was put in place to allow the setup of real estate investment companies for corporate restructuring and the period of corporate reorganization proceedings was shortened.

The Corporate Restructuring Promotion Act (which came into effect on 15 September 2001; subsequent dates in parentheses are dates of implementation) is to remain in effect as a temporary measure until the end of 2005, together with its associated Enforcement Decree (15 September 2001). It empowers creditor financial institutions to initiate prompt restructuring measures against companies displaying symptoms of insolvency and establishes a system for the adjustment of outstanding credit among financial institutions. The Act calls for creditor banks to regularly appraise the credit risk of companies that have obtained credit from financial institutions of at least 50 billion won and take appropriate measures for post hoc management.

In particular, if a company exhibits symptoms of insolvency on evaluation of its credit risks, the main creditor bank may consider its turnaround feasible after appraising the company's business plan. Then it may have that company adopt measures for corporate restructuring. These may include joint management by creditor financial institutions, joint management by creditor banks, management by the main creditor bank and composition of its debts or corporate reorganization. If there appears no possibility of a turnaround, however, the main creditor bank is obliged to submit an application to the court for the company to be declared bankrupt or have the company file for dissolution, liquidation or bankruptcy.

In the case of a main creditor bank pursuing the restructuring of a company exhibiting symptoms of insolvency through joint management by creditor financial institutions or creditor banks, the Corporate Restructuring Co-ordination Committee should consist of creditor financial institutions or creditor banks. The committee makes decisions on the designation of the company as exhibiting symptoms of insolvency, the joint management by creditor financial institutions, the period for deferment of claims, plans for the readjustment of claims or new credit extension and the conclusion of an agreement to implement a management turnaround plan. The committee's decisions should be made with the approval of creditor financial institutions holding at least 75 percent of gross credit outstanding to the company. Meanwhile, creditor financial institutions opposing the decision for joint management, the readjustment of claims, or new credit extension are allowed to request to the committee that the other creditor financial institutions purchase their loans. The main creditor bank should examine the performance of the company on a quarterly basis concerning its implementation of the turnaround plan after concluding an agreement with the company on its rehabilitation.

If on the basis of the findings of the quarterly examination, the committee considers that the execution of the management rehabilitation plan will be problematic, then the main credit bank must halt the joint management agreement.

Strengthening the management of public funds

To enhance the fairness and transparency of the management of public funds and push for their effective use, the Public Fund Management Act (effective from 20 December 2000) and its associated Enforcement Decree (effective from 14 February 2001) were passed into law. It provided for the establishment of a Public Fund Committee at the Ministry of Finance and Economy. They were entrusted with the comprehensive overseeing of the operation of public funds and screening and the coordination of their provision and collection. The Minister of Finance and Economy must submit a quarterly report on the use of public funds to the National Assembly, and the Public Fund Committee must publish a white paper on the management of public funds by the end of August every year.

As a means of preventing moral hazard on the part of financial institutions, those that receive public funds are obliged to conclude an MOU for the implementation of management normalization plans with the government or the Korea Deposit Insurance Corporation (KDIC). Management normalization plans should include details concerning the target capital adequacy ratios, the profit to assets ratio, the bad loan ratio, restructuring plans and the written consent of the in-house labor union for restructuring.

In a bid to promote recovery of public funds, a Sales Screening subcommittee is to be set up under the Public Fund Committee and given the task of screening the appropriateness of the sale of assets, including the financial institution stockholdings of the government, the KDIC and the Korea Asset Management Corporation (KAMCO). Should a financial institution which has received public funds become insolvent or be dissolved, the court is obliged to designate the KDIC or a member of its staff as a receiver or liquidator, other pertinent legislation notwithstanding.

At the same time, the Depositor Protection Act was revised, effective 1 January 2001. In the event of designating financial institutions as non-viable financial institutions or financial institutions showing signs of insolvency, the KDIC is also able to demand that the relevant financial institutions submit documents concerning their business and property status or to investigate them directly. In cases where the KDIC judges it necessary to suspend the repayment of deposits or cancel the license of financial institutions following an investigation of their business and property status, it may request the Financial Supervisory Commission (FSC) to take the appropriate actions to deal with the troubled financial institutions. The Act stipulates that defaulters on debt repayments to ailing financial institutions should be included among those bad-loan-related persons whose relevant business and property status can be investigated by the KDIC. The KDIC is also allowed to withhold the payment of deposit insurance claims to those responsible for bad loans and those having a special relationship with them.

In preparation for possible losses stemming from fraud or embezzlement by the staff of financial institutions, the KDIC is allowed to require that financial institutions buy compensation liability insurance. If financial institutions decline to buy such insurance, the KDIC is authorized to initiate an insurance contract with an insurance company on their behalf and at their own expense.

Facilitation of bad loan resolution

In order to facilitate the resolution of bad loans held by financial institutions, a CRV should operate over 50 percent of its total assets through the purchase of securities floated by companies that have concluded corporate improvement planning agreements, the purchase of credit for loans to such companies or the extension of loans and payment guarantees to them. A CRV may borrow funds up to twice its equity capital and float corporate bonds up to an amount ten times its capital and reserves.

In a parallel move, the government revised the Enforcement Decree of the Act Concerning the Efficient Disposal of Financial Institutions' Non-Performing Assets and Establishment of the Korea Asset Management Corporation (effective from 29 May 2000). This expanded those financial institutions from which KAMCO may acquire non-performing loans to subsidiaries that are established by financial institutions for the purchase and resolution of claims, and financial institutions established under the Depositor Protection Act to resolve claims.

By May 2002, 156.3 trillion won in public funds had been used to support financial sector restructuring. According to the report to the National Assembly by the government, the government had retrieved about 24.3 percent, or 32.8 trillion won of the public funds spent so far by early 2001.

By 19 November 2001, the government had retrieved some 32.8 trillion won, or 24.3 percent of the total public funds injected. Of the total, about 21.6 trillion won came from the resale of non-performing loans or their collateral while the remaining 11.2 trillion won was recovered through equity sales and other sources.

The low recovery ratio of public funds causes a supply and demand imbalance arising from the conversion of maturities. It also suggests that the delay of repayment of public funds is inevitable for at least over a generation. As a matter of fact, the Public Fund Overseeing Committee announced the delaying of repayment of public funds up to 20 years.[14] As public funds were raised mainly through the issue of state bonds repayable in five years and maturities for public funds converge in a short period, the government bonds need to be placed to repay and refinance maturing debts.

Protection of investors including minority shareholders

To strengthen the protection of stock investors, including minority shareholders, the government made it obligatory for registered corporations to include outside members on their boards of directors and eased conditions for cumulative voting requirements and the exercise of minority shareholders' rights in listed or registered corporations. It also made investment trust management companies responsible for compensating investors for damages.

Under the revised Securities and Exchange Act (1 April 2001) and its associated Enforcement Decree (7 July 2001), registered companies, excluding venture firms with total assets of less than 100 million won, must have at least one quarter of their board of directors consist of outside members. The number of outside directors for registered corporations with total assets of over two trillion won should be not less than three and they should make up at least half of the total membership of the board of directors. An audit committee should also be set up to oversee the execution of their duties.

In the election of directors of listed or registered corporations with total assets of over two trillion won, the minimum shareholding required for the exercise of cumulative voting rights was lowered from 3 percent to 1 percent. In relation to a vote to change the articles concerning cumulative voting, the voting rights of shareholders with a holding greater than 3 percent were limited to 3 percent.

When listed or registered companies give notice of a general meeting of shareholders, they must disclose details of transactions with the largest shareholders or those standing in a special relationship to them. In particular, when its transactions with the largest shareholders or those standing in a special relationship to them surpass a certain level, a listed or registered corporation with total assets of at least two trillion won must receive approval from the board of directors and report the details of the relevant transactions to the general meeting of shareholders.

Public sector and labor sector reforms

Under the IMF conditionality, Korea was also required to carry out reforms in both the public and labor sectors. Public corporations were to be privatized, and a new governance system was introduced to improve profitability. Korea's traditional labor-management relationship caused inflexibility in the labor market. Layoffs are now allowed when a company faces serious managerial difficulty. The government has provided a social safety net for those unemployed as a result of restructuring. However, Korea's achievement in reforming the two sectors has not been as satisfactory as the financial sector reforms. Privatization of public corporations must be accelerated, and the flexibility of the labor market has to be enhanced while seeking ways to neutralize the occasionally militant labor union activities.

Concluding remarks

In essence, Korea's restructuring of its financial sector has been a process of breaking away from the vicious chain of inefficiency that exists between the financial sector and the corporate sector. While following the IMF prescriptions, the predominant sequence of major restructuring has involved first the financial sector, and has then moved to the corporate sector, to ensure normalization of financial intermediation.

The Korean reform story following the Asian Financial Crisis clearly suggests that a serious financial sector restructuring is not a "once and for all" matter; it requires a never-ending drive in a consistent and transparent framework. Financial restructuring is also deeply linked to the restructuring of the corporate sector. After breaking up the chaebol system into a series of independent business units, Korea needs to design a new industrial structure for the coming digital economy. This calls for reinvigoration of the economy by encouraging a climate of innovation led by SMEs and venture start-ups in parallel with large enterprises. Product development and continual improvements in quality should be encouraged through sophisticated technology. Meanwhile, the industrial structure has to be transformed to create high value-added industries, such as knowledge-intensive industries.

As Pagano (1993) suggested, effective financial intermediation that ensures efficient allocation of scarce capital to where it has the highest payoff is a critical component in the search for a new development paradigm in Korea. In this context, as Stiglitz (1999: 15) pointed out, Korean banks must continue working to "learn how to be banks." They should break away from the embedded traditions and customs, such as implicit government guarantees as expressed in the belief that "banks should never fail," or tight and "friendly" long-term relationships with large borrowers. In addition to the changing credit culture, banks must develop modern management practices for risks such as liquidity risk, foreign exchange risk and interest rate risk.

In order to make the financial sector the "brain" of any well-functioning market economy,[15] Korea needs an injection of new managerial expertise into the financial sector, especially into the banking sector, which has been branded as a cradle of old, tradition-bound people who built their careers during the high growth period.

In the years to come, successful structural reforms for the financial sector could be achieved by completing the following key tasks: a) return of "nationalized banks" to the private sector; b) restructuring of non-banking sectors to include the introduction of a new governance system, and separation of ownership between industrial conglomerates and financial conglomerates; c) accelerated restructuring of heavily indebted corporations; d) further improvements in accounting, auditing and financial disclosure; e) gradual reduction of the budget deficit by tax reform and by issuing fewer bonds to keep the budget deficit below 2.5 percent of GDP; and f) modernization of the insolvency system.

During the period 1998 to 2002, Korea's conglomerates have undertaken a far-reaching restructuring program in terms of debt reductions, downsizing, elimination of inter-unit debt guarantees, asset sales, recapitalization and foreign capital attraction. These efforts clearly suggest that subsidiary companies of chaebols should become independent viable business units. An unexpected and exuberant KOSDAQ venture market during the reform period is signaling some important changes in the chaebol-dominated economic structure. The advent of e-commerce and the related knowledge-based economy is also making a clear impact. With a newly emerging financial sector as the "brain" of a well-functioning market economy, Korea should be able to search for a new growth engine from newly born and viable chaebols, SMEs and venture businesses and to succeed in establishing a sound knowledge-based economy.

Notes

1 For details on the background of the chaebol-led heavy and chemical industrial drive within the export-led development strategy, see Ahn and Kim (1997).
2 Korean GDP in 1997 was 420.986 trillion won. The proportion of bad loans in Korea is huge compared to that of the US during its Savings & Loans crisis; bad loans of FDIC member financial institutions almost reached 4 percent of total loans and 2.5 percent of US GDP in 1987.

3 They surveyed all non-financial listed companies numbering between 600 and 662, and over 5,000 unlisted companies over the period 1995–8, which were subject to external auditing. The sample companies accounted for about 79.5 percent of total corporate debt in Korea as of the end of 1997, or 644.9 trillion won. The Korea Development Institute (1998) estimated total debts in the corporate sector to be 810.7 trillion won as of the end of 1998.
4 ICR is commonly defined as the ratio of earnings before interest payment and taxes (EBIT) to interest expense.
5 The Bank of Korea's study (2002) demonstrated that there exists a very high correlation between corporate debt ratio and their variables, plus the level of autonomous management of the banking sector of the capital market.
6 The Commercial Bank of Korea and Hanil Bank merged into Hanvit Bank, while Chohung Bank took over Chungbuk Bank and Kangwon Bank. Korea Exchange Bank recapitalized with 350 billion won, which was contributed by the Commerzbank of Germany. Peace Bank chose to withdraw from international business. Among the banks whose BIS ratios exceeded 8 percent at the end of 1997, Hana Bank merged with Boram Bank, and Kookmin Bank with Korea Long-term Credit Bank.
7 As of early 2001, a bank deposit only up to half a million won, including principle and interest, is protected.
8 For example, chaebols with more than 50 percent of their own capital that is related to non-financial and real sector activities are not allowed to engage in financial businesses.
9 *Korea Economic Daily*, 30 March 1998. Corporate debt is approximately $177.57 billion, based on the exchange rate as of 3 June 1998 ($1 = 1,391 won).
10 The debt-workout, or workout program, is out-of-court settlements between creditors and debtors who have defaulted, utilizing the so-called London Rules. A Corporate Restructuring Accord (CRA) has been signed by 200 banks and non-bank financial institutions, which commits them to follow the agreed workout procedure. The Corporate Restructuring Co-ordination Committee (CRCC), an arbitration committee, was created to resolve the differences between financial institutions and a debtor in the event they cannot reach an agreement.
11 Sri-Ram Aiyer (1999: 3).
12 *The Korea Times* on 5 January 2000 reported the government's intention by quoting a New Year's speech by Finance-Economy Minister Kang Bong-Kyun to the Audience of Senior Banking Officials.
13 Creditor banks are currently required to oversee the management of these firms as well as schedule their debt.
14 See *The Korea Herald*, 19 November 2001, 11.
15 See Stiglitz (1999) on the "brain function" of the financial sector. He pointed out that long-term relationships between lenders and borrowers can be a conduit for crucial information that helps the brain function, but they can also atrophy the ability to judge creditworthiness.

Bibliography

Ahn, C.Y. (2001a) "A Search for Robust East Asian Development Models after the Financial Crisis: Mutual Learning from East Asian Experiences," *Journal of Asian Economics*, 12(3): 419–43.
—— (2001b) "Corporate and Financial Restructuring in South Korea: Accomplishments and Continuing Challenges," *Japanese Economic Review*, 52(4): 452–70.

Ahn, C.Y. and Kim, J.H. (1997) "The Outward-Looking Trade Policy and the Industrial Development of South Korea," in D.S. Cha *et al.* (eds) *The Korean Economy 1945–1995: Performance and Vision for the 21st Century*, Seoul: Korea Development Institute.

Aiyer, S. (1999) "Corporate Reform: Key to Consolidating Korea's Recovery," paper presented at the International Conference on Economic Crisis and Restructuring in Korea hosted by Korea Development Institute, 3 December.

Cha, B. (1999) "Financial Market Reform in Korea after the Asian Financial Crisis," paper presented at the SJE-KIF International Symposium on Structural Adjustment after the Asian Financial Crisis, organized by Seoul Journal of Economies, Seoul National University and Korea Institute of Finance, 27 August.

Cho, Y.J. and Rhee, C. (1999) "Macroeconomic Adjustments of the East Asian Economies after the Crisis: A Comparative Study," paper presented at the SJE-KIF International Symposium on Structural Adjustment after the Asian Financial Crisis, organized by Seoul Journal of Economies, Seoul National University and Korea Institute of Finance, 27 August.

Classens, S., Djankov, S. and Ferri, G. (1998) "Corporate Distress in East Asia: Assessing the Impact of Interest and Exchange Rates Shocks," Mimeo., World Bank.

Credit Suisse First Boston (1998) *Corporate Debt Monitor*, Equity Research Asia.

Davis, E.P. (1995) *Debt Financial Fragility and Systemic Risk*, New York: Oxford University Press.

Goldman Sachs (1998) *Asset Quality for Korean Banks: Bottom-Up Approach for Estimating NPL*.

Kim, S.J. (1999) "Restructuring of Ownership and Governance in the Non-Bank Financial Institutions in Korea," a policy survey report, 99-09, Korea Institute of Finance.

Korea Development Institute (1998) "Corporate Debts in Korea," Mimeo. (in Korean).

Kwon, J. and Nam, J. (1999) "'Distressed Corporate Debt in Korea,' Korea Institute for International Economic Policy," Working Paper 99-11.

Lieberman, I.W. and Mako, W. (1998) "Korea's Corporate Crisis: Its Origins and a Strategy for Financial Restructuring," proceedings on Korean Economic Restructuring: Evaluation and Prospects, organized by Korea Institute for International Economic Policy, 23 October.

Pagano, M. (1993) "Financial Markets and Growth," *European Economic Review*, 37(2): 613–22.

Stiglitz, J. (1999) "The Korean Miracle: Growth, Crisis, and Recovery Accomplishment of the Past, Challenges of the Future," a keynote speech at the International Conference on Economic Crisis and Restructuring in Korea hosted by Korea Development Institute, 3 December.

7 Economic performance, crisis and institutional reforms in East Asia and Latin America

Akira Suehiro

Introduction

As many as 109 financial crises occurred between 1980 and 1999, according to an original survey by the World Bank. This fact suggests that the world economy has entered a stage of instability and uncertainty following the 1980s (http://www.worldbank.org/html). Indeed, a debt crisis hit Latin America in the early 1980s, while East Asia – Northeast Asia plus Southeast Asia – also suffered a long-term economic recession due to the resulting worldwide recession. In the first half of the 1990s, an economic crisis affected Russia and Eastern Europe while they underwent institutional reforms aimed at transforming their economic systems from centrally planned economies to market-oriented ones. In the mid-1990s, a currency crisis again attacked Latin America, particularly Mexico. In 1997 a currency and financial crisis took place in East Asia, ending an economic boom that had continued since the end of the 1980s.

This chapter aims to find similarities and differences in economic performance, government expenditure patterns, the role of private firms, targets of economic reforms to overcome the crisis and institution building efforts in East Asia and Latin America. It pays special attention to the questions of who has contributed as an agent to national economic development, what were the major causes for economic crisis and which fields became targets for reforms in the two regions during the 1980s and the 1990s. By conducting a comparative study in the two regions, this chapter also focuses on the experience of Thailand to answer the question of how East Asian countries have tackled economic reforms and have changed their major targets from outward-looking institutional reforms based on the Anglo-American model to more inward-looking social policies. By examining these questions, the chapter hopes to identify the key elements to be studied when constructing a possible agenda to seek stable, sustainable growth in the future.

Economic performance: East Asia and Latin America

Table 7.1 summarizes major economic indicators for the past two decades (1980–99) in three major regions (East Asia, South Asia and Latin America).[1] So far as per capita GNP (or GNI) is concerned, East Asian countries have achieved a higher level (US$8,670 in 1999) than Latin American countries (US$4,210).[2] However, we also discover a great gap in per capita income among Asian countries themselves: between East Asia and South Asia; old NICs (South Korea, Taiwan, Hong Kong, Singapore) and new NICs (Malaysia and Thailand); and six old ASEAN members (Philippines, Thailand, Malaysia, Indonesia, Singapore and Brunei) and four new ASEAN members (Viet Nam, Laos, Cambodia and Myanmar). In contrast to Asian countries, there is a smaller gap in per capita income among Latin American countries, excluding Argentina which was US$11,324 per capita in 1999.

Regarding the annual GDP growth rate during the 1980s and 1990s, figures in East Asia (6.6 percent→5.9 percent) have decreased due to a depreciation of local currencies against the US dollar after the currency crisis in 1997 and the subsequent economic recession. By contrast, growth rates rose in both South Asia, from 4.2 percent to 6.4 percent, and Latin America, from 1.7 percent to 4.0 percent, remarkably during the 1990s owing to economic liberalization and economic restructuring at that time.

The most marked difference in the two regions is identified by export performance in terms of both export growth rate and the ratio of manufactured exports against total exports. East Asia achieved around 11 percent growth per annum during the 1980s and 1990s, and the ratio of manufactured exports to total exports increased to as high as 76 percent in 1999. On the other hand, Latin America quickly increased its annual export growth rate from 4.8 percent in the 1980s to 8.2 percent in the 1990s, but its level was still lower than that of East Asia. In particular, the ratio of manufactured exports (36 percent in 1999) is far lower compared to that of East Asia. As a result, the export ratio against nominal GDP in the two major regions reveals quite different levels and very different trends: increase from 50 percent in 1990 to 64 percent in 1999 in East Asia vs. a slight decrease from 20 percent to 19 percent in the corresponding year in Latin America.

How can we explain this significant difference in export performance? Possible answers may be connected to differences in government policies and the role of private firms following the end of the 1960s. During the 1970s, world trade enjoyed an annual growth rate of 19.6 percent, which was the highest sustained level ever over the past century, while the long-term interest rate for bank loans averaged a mere 1 percent. Due to the second oil crisis in 1979 and the collapse of the primary commodities market boom by the early 1980s, the annual growth rate of world trade drastically dropped to 4 percent in the 1980s, while long-term interest rates increased to 6 percent per annum on average (Suehiro 2000a: 17).

East Asia's old NICs took advantage of this opportunity in the 1970s, and every government made a switch in the major target industries from import substitution policies to export-oriented ones. This covered such labor-intensive industries as textiles, garments, sports shoes, processed food and electronic parts.[3] For instance, in South Korea, the export value of textile goods impressively increased from US$81 million in 1970 to US$2,937 million in 1980, while in Taiwan, the export value of electrical goods increased from US$182 million to US$3,599 million in the corresponding period. At the same time, local private firms actively moved into export-oriented industries in response to new government policies and in collaboration with foreign firms. They also quickly expanded their businesses to take advantage of the expansion in world trade and to secure overseas banking loans bearing the lowest interest rates.

East Asian companies began to export their manufactured goods to the United States and imported necessary intermediate and capital goods from Japan. According to the survey of Twu Jaw-yann on the "triangle trade clearing system," NICs exported US$62,249 million (trade surplus US$37,031 million) worth of goods to the United States in 1987, but they had to import US$39,455 million in goods (trade deficit US$20,643 million) from Japan. On the other hand, Japan exported US$83,580 million in goods (trade surplus US$52,090 million) to the United States in the same year (Twu 1990: 26). These figures suggest that the United States played an important role as a giant importer or an absorber for both NICs and Japan in this trade clearing system. At the same time, the American market was very attractive for East Asian exporters. This was because the US government extended the Generalized System of Preferences (GSP) to exportable goods from developing countries, including those in East Asia. Up to the end of the 1980s, when the United States lifted GSP for East Asia, they were no doubt the largest beneficiary group of the system (Hirakawa 1992).

In addition to this preferential treatment, the United States also served as a large absorber of manufactured goods, such as garments, electrical products and other consumer goods. The American market was principally characterized by a multilateral structure in its consumption pattern, which was determined by different consumer behavior accruing to varying life cycles and income disparity by ethnic group and occupation.

For instance, American markets of imported watches were divided into three groups: high quality mechanical watches from Europe; standardized quality mechanical and LCD watches from Japan; and lower priced mass-produced LCD watches from Hong Kong (Suehiro 2000a: 73). Likewise, it was not difficult for South Korean and Taiwanese black and white televisions with lower prices to find their own market among lower income classes. Furthermore, enhanced competition between Japanese and the other East Asian firms to expand their market shares in the United States contributed to an improved international competitiveness for East Asian

Table 7.1 Summary table of comparison of East Asia, South Asia and Latin America: 1980s and 1990s

Major items	Period coverage	East Asia including Southeast Asia.	South Asia	Latin America
I PERFORMANCE				
1 Macro performance				
1.1 Per Capita GDP	1999	High, but wide gap	Low	Fairly high, levelling
1.2 GDP growth rate	1980s, 90s	High 6.6% → 5.9%	Increase 4.2% → 6.4%	Increase 1.7% → 4.0%
1.3 Export growth rate	1980s, 90s	High 11.0% → 10.9%	Fairly 7.2% → 7.0%	Increase 4.8% → 8.2%
1.4 Manufactured exports	1990, 99	High 65% → 76%	High 75% → 80%	Low, increase 27% → 36%
1.5 Export ratio for GDP	1990, 99	High 50% → 64%	Low 12% → 13%	Low 20% → 19%
1.6 Investment ratio	1990, 99	High 33% → 27%	Low 22% → 20%	Low 19% → 20%
1.7 Saving ratio	1990, 99	High 35% → 34%	Low 17% → 16%	Low 24% → 20%
1.8 Inflation	1990s	Low	Low	Very high
2 Labor force				
2.1 Labor force growth rate	1980s, 90s	Decrease 2.6% → 2.2%	Increase 2.3% → 2.6%	Decrease 3.0% → 2.5%
2.2 Female ratio	1980, 99	High 38% → 41%	Low 29% → 30%	Low, increase 27% → 34%
2.3 Urbanization	1980, 99	Low, but widely varied	Very low	Very high
3 FDI and external Debt				
3.1 FDI	1990, 99	Large, and increasing	Small, but increasing	Fairly, and quick increase
3.2 External debt	1990, 99	Quickly increasing	Low	Moderate
3.3 External debt/GNI	1999	High 61%	Low 30%	Moderate 48%
3.4 Foreign banking loans	1990s	High, Europeans, Japanese	?	High, Americans
4 Social service expenditure				
4.1 Total expenditure	1990, 98	Low 24% → 27%	Very low 8% → 9%	High 43% → 57%
4.2 Expenditure on education	1998–2000	Moderate 3.7%	Low 2.5%	Relatively high 4.3%
4.3 Expenditure on health	2000	Moderate 1.7%	Very low 0.9%	High 3.4%
5 Poverty				
5.1 Poverty line, national	1990s	Decrease	High	Increase, urban area
5.2 Income gap	1990s	Moderate	High	High

6 Firms and stock market				
6.1 Listed companies	1999	Large number	Very large number	Small number
6.2 State enterprises	1980s, 90s	Still important in some countries	Dominant	Privatized
6.3 Multinationals	1980s, 90s	Joint ventures	Small	Large, 100% ownership American dominant
6.4 Local firms	1980s, 90s	Japanese dominant Zaibatsu-type family business	Zaibatsu-type family business	Family business
II POLITICS				
7 Ideology	1980s	Developmentalism	Democracy, fundamentalism	Populism
8 Political regime	1980s	Authoritarianism	Democracy	Authoritarianism
	1990s	→Democratization		→Post Authoritarinism
		→Neo Populism		→Neo populism
9 Cold War impact	1980s	Very strong	Strong	Weak
III ECONOMIC REFORMS				
10 Economic liberalization		late 80s to 90s	90s	early 80s to mid 80s
11 Privatization		mid 80s: Singapore, Korea, Taiwan	Slow	90s, quickly
12 IMF–World Bank		late 90s: Thailand, Malaysia, financial reforms corporate restructuring		liberalization structural adjustment
13 Corporate Governance		Strong initiative	Nil	Weak
IV REGIONALISM				
14 Regional integration, Regional cooperation		APEC (1989); ASEAN, AFTA (2003)	Since 2000, India became active in promoting India ASEAN FTA	NAFTA (1994); MERCOSUL (1993–6)
		ASEAN + Japan, Korea, China		

Note
Compiled by the author on the basis of World Bank, *World Development Report*, various issues.

exporters (Suehiro 2000a: 52–5). Similar development patterns can be seen in the case of the ICs industry in South Korea and in the case of the machine tool industry in Taiwan (Amsden 1977). In this sense, local firms in East Asia could enjoy the so-called "advantages of economic backwardness" (Gerschenkron) of late comers in the technological catching-up process, and provided a good case for upgrading their "competitive advantage" in the world market (Amsden 1989; Suehiro 2000a: Ch. 2).

In contrast to the East Asian experience, Latin American governments did not change their import substitution industrialization policies or inward-looking industrial development strategies during the 1970s. Domestic markets for import substitution industries were protected by high import tariffs and over-valued exchange rates. It was after the 1980s, when private firms were hit by the debt-crisis, that Latin America gradually shifted its economic structure from an inward-looking focus to an outward-looking one (Koike and Nishijima eds 1997). In addition to the conservativeness of government economic policies, local firms were challenged by strong competition from state and multinational enterprises in the domestic market. It was very difficult for entrepreneurial local firms to export their manufactured products directly to the United States because American firms with 100 percent ownership had already established strong stakes in every Latin American host country.

Therefore, the scope of the business bases and the types of exportable products were limited for local private firms in Latin America. According to an empirical study by Horisaka on the Brazilian economy in 1985, the business fields where local private firms were dominant in terms of annual turnover were confined to retail, supermarkets, construction, garment, paper and pulp and furniture, while *foreign firms* controlled automobile (100 percent: the share of annual turnover in the industry concerned), pharmaceuticals (86 percent), toiletry (73 percent), telecommunications (66 percent), plastic products (64 percent), beverages and tobacco (61 percent), electronics (48 percent) and so on. At the same time, state enterprises also dominated several important fields including mining (55 percent), iron and steel (67 percent) and petrochemicals (77 percent) as well as public services (100 percent) (Koike and Horisaka eds 1999: 35). Both government policies and limited competition combined to contribute to the underdevelopment of local private firms.[4] For these reasons, Latin American countries missed a good opportunity to promote their manufactured exports during the 1970s. Rather, an increasing external public debt contributed to serious crises in Latin America in the early 1980s.

Public social service expenditures: East Asia and Latin America

Another interesting fact that we observe in Table 7.1 is a wide gap in the proportion of social service expenditures against total public expenditures in the two regions in 1998: 27 percent in East Asia and 57 percent in Latin America. In addition, the proportion in Latin America increased from 43 percent in 1990 to 57 percent in 1998. Social service expenditures here include public expenditures in education, health, social insurance and social assistance. Such prominent differences in public expenditures seem closely related to differences in both the power structure and social welfare (social security) system to support people's lives.

For instance, governments based on populist regimes in Latin America were required to construct good alliances with class-based organizations such as trade unions and state enterprise employees associations, and hence they had to allocate a large part of their national budgets for these collaborators in the forms of social insurance or health assistance. A detailed study by Usami on the social security system in Argentina informs us well as to why and how the Peron government introduced a comprehensive scheme of social security for the people by carefully referring to the power structure at that time (Usami ed. 2001: Introduction and Ch. 9).

On the other hand, East Asian governments based on authoritarian and "developmentalist" regimes put much more priority on economic development or accelerated industrial development rather than on income redistribution and social development. In this area, economic growth and development have been the main engines of welfare, and welfarism has been shunned. More widely, "there is a shared but generally unspoken belief that responsibility for welfare is shared by the public and private sector. Community, firm and family are all expected to play a part" (Holliday and Wilding eds 2003: 166–7).[5] At the same time, the governments would look at their people as members of the nation-state who should contribute to the priority national target rather than members of class-based organizations who focus on their own economic interests. In addition to the difference in national targets, the governments attempted to oppress the activity of trade unions directly as we see in Thailand after the Sarit regime (1958), or to introduce an indirect control on workers through the establishment of the government-sponsored workers' organization such as the reorganization of the National Trade Union Council (NTUC: 1968) in Singapore and the Employers-Employees Consultative Council (1972) in South Korea (Suehiro 2000a: 118).

Differences in non-governmental social welfare (social security) systems also contributed to this gap in social service expenditures in the two regions. Generally speaking, a large firm in East Asian countries, like in Japan, is expected to play a significant role in supporting the social welfare of its employees as well as in sustaining their long-term employment. Based on this consensus, a private firm frequently provides company-sponsored hospital and social insurance benefits, family allowance and retirement fund. Firms also introduced a company pension fund scheme with the financial support of employers. In turn, employees depend on their company-based retirement fund and company pension fund rather than the national pension scheme for their source of income after retirement. It was after the 1990s that the governments in East Asian countries except Japan eventually started extending the objective of the well organized social security system from government officers and veterans to employees in the private sector and farmers: Korea in 1986 (revised in 1995); Taiwan in 1988 (revised in 1994); Hong Kong in 1993; Singapore in 1991; Thailand in 1990 (pension scheme in 1999); Malaysia in 1991 (revised in 1995); the Philippines in 1997 and China in 1996/97 (Ramesh and Asher 2000; Holliday and Wilding eds 2003; Kamimura and Suehiro eds 2003).

Why have the governments in East Asian countries not been so active in constructing the national social security system in the past? In order to answer this question, we must examine not only the special role of large private firms but also *quasi-economic development policies* undertaken by the governments under the "developmentalist" regime in favor of peasants and workers in the manufacturing sectors. Subsidies on agricultural products or price stabilization schemes of agricultural products (in South Korea, China, the Philippines, Indonesia, etc.), subsidies on public transportation services (in Thailand, the Philippines), supply of agricultural credit with lower interest rates (in Thailand), and supply of public housing service with special loans for workers and government officers (in Singapore, Thailand and Hong Kong) should be included in the category of public social services.[6]

Traditional custom and practices have also played an important role in supplementing the limited social security system in East Asian countries. For instance, in rural areas, aged parents often rent their farming land at a lower charge to their children, and the children in turn look after their parents before inheriting land. In this case, landlordship between parents and children supplements public social insurance for aged persons. Traditional mutual assistance practices among members of the community and the extended family system also served as an informal social safety net supplementing poor public social services in East Asia up to the 1990s.

On the other hand, in urban areas in Hong Kong and Thailand, traditional Chinese associations which were set up for the purposes of charities and social services have for a long time served as core institutions to help aged persons, handicapped persons and children with a single parent. It is reported that 672 out of 756 organizations which were registered as NGOs in Hong Kong (1998) belonged to this type of traditional association. More importantly, these associations are now providing social services to the people not only with their own budgets but also with financial support from the government (Sawada 2002). In contrast to a variety of social welfare systems in East Asia, non-governmental sources of social services in Latin America seem to be concentrated in the activities of religious associations.

Ironically, following economic liberalization, the governments in Latin America were required to privatize state enterprises or government-sponsored hospitals, and to drastically curtail public expenditure on social services. The comprehensive scheme of national social security system was collapsed, and its reorganization on the basis of free competition and effective operation became more important for the governments to respond to liberalized economy (Usami ed. 2001). However, privatization of state enterprises and the elimination of public expenditure will create instability in labor relations and bring about new income disparities for the poor. As a result, the governments are facing serious dilemmas between the reconstruction of social stability by increasing public expenditure and the privatization of social services through market forces to reduce fiscal deficits.

On the other hand, East Asian governments recently began to implement formal public social services, including national pension schemes. The deepening economic recession after the currency crisis made it difficult for private firms to fully sustain the social welfare of employees on their own. In the long run, since East Asian governments had to constantly increase public expenditure for social services and job creation, they are also facing the same dilemma as Latin America (Kamimura and Suehiro eds 2003). At any rate, construction of a sustainable social welfare system has now become one of the most essential elements in formulating sustainable economic growth under the pressure of economic globalization and liberalization.

Sequences of liberalization, economic crisis and structural adjustment

One interesting point here is a different pattern in the two regions in the inter-relationship among the introduction of liberalization policies, causes of economic crisis and the implementation of structural reforms. In the case of Latin America, economic crisis due to accumulated external public debt took place first, followed by intensive economic liberalization (deregulation) as part of structural reforms or structural adjustment programs initiated by international financial organizations (IMF, the World Bank and IDA). In this case, liberalization was conducted on the basis of the policy ideas of the so-called "Washington Consensus in the first generation," which mainly aimed to eliminate various obstacles hindering the sound development of a market economy and to reduce government regulations of economic activities (Williamson 1990; Williamson ed. 1994).

This type of Washington Consensus addresses four major economic purposes: 1) inflation constraint and improvement of economic fundamentals; 2) economic stabilization through an equilibrium in the balance of payments; 3) economic growth on the basis of a free market mechanism; and 4) improvement of income distribution. In order to achieve these economic purposes, new policies usually focused on lifting quantitative restrictions on imports, reducing import tariffs, lifting regulations on industrial investment and foreign direct investment (FDI), deregulating controls on foreign currency trade and foreign exchange rates, and so on (Edwards 1995; Suehiro and Nakagawa eds 2001: see Chronology for Chile, Mexico and Brazil). These policies are summarized as the classical approach of economic liberalization ("getting the price mechanism right"). What should not be overlooked here is that the World Bank ordered Latin American governments to privatize a large number of state enterprises. This was done because the economic crisis in the early 1980s was understood to be a direct result of quick increases in public external debt due mainly to heavy investments in and huge amounts of public expenditure on state enterprises.

Similar to the cases of Latin America, the Philippines, Thailand and Indonesia also started restructuring state enterprises in exchange for World Bank sponsored structural adjustment loans (SALs) between 1981 and 1983. These countries introduced more moderate or partial economic liberalization policies that focused on trade liberalization, deregulation of control on foreign exchange rates and reduction of government subsidies for the agricultural sector and public transportation services. However, the pace of policy implementation was not so fast as those taken in Latin America, nor was its coverage so comprehensive (Suehiro and Higashi eds 2000: Ch. 1). On the other hand, South Korea (1987), Taiwan (1985 and 1989) and Singapore (1986) started new policies of privatization and liberalization in selected fields without any pressure from international financial organizations. They introduced these policies rather independently for the sake of activating the private sector in order to overcome long-term economic recession after the end of the 1970s (Suehiro 2000a: 172–4).

Since the end of the 1980s, most East Asian countries have embraced liberalization in the financial sector, international capital trade, foreign currency trade and industrial investment including FDI. An important incentive for this switch in economic policies was not external pressure but autonomous decisions by the governments. In particular, they geared toward financial liberalization when they decided to change their country statuses from Article XIV Parties of the IMF (applied to developing countries) to Article VIII Parties, which meant they had to meet conditions of deregulation in both capital trade and foreign currency trade. At the same time, East Asian countries enjoyed an economic boom in that period, and they had to seek financial resources overseas (through FDI and overseas borrowings) to finance savings and investment gaps (the investment ratio accounted for between 35 percent and 45 percent, while the saving ratio was between 25 percent and 35 percent).[7] For this reason, it was an urgent task for the governments to liberalize their financial sectors and FDI policies to invite fresh money from abroad.

However, the quick financial liberalization with no actual development of domestic financial institutions, the rush of European and Japanese banking loans seeking wide profit margins because of divergent interest rates between the home country and East Asian countries, and the speculative movements of international hedge funds such as Robertson's Tiger Fund and Soros' Quantum Fund combined to lead East Asian countries into monetary instability and, later, serious currency crises. Therefore, economic liberalization in East Asia preceded the crisis and was a partial reason for the financial crisis. This was quite different from Latin America, where the governments were forced to introduce economic liberalization after the crisis in order to address poor macroeconomic fundamentals.

This sequential difference in liberalization and crisis naturally produced another difference with regard to the economic reform programs set forth by governments in East Asia and Latin America. In brief, economic reforms in East Asia no longer aimed at formulating liberalization and deregulation on the basis of the *first generation Washington Consensus*, as in the case of Latin America during the 1980s. Rather, East Asia now is targeting reforms to create various legal and institutional frameworks to help market forces function more effectively on the basis of the *second generation Washington Consensus*. Jeffrey Sachs characterized this new type of reform as the "getting the institutions right" approach, and distinguished it from the first generation reform target of "getting the price mechanism right" (Woo *et al.* eds 2000: 42). The World Bank also addressed the same idea, and used the title "Building Institutions for Markets" for its World Development Report 2002 (World Bank 2002).

Major targets of economic reforms: East Asia and Latin America

Since the East Asian currency crisis erupted in 1997, many scholars have argued over its primary causes. Some emphasized the role of fast-moving, short-term international capital, while others noted the decline of international competitiveness in labor-intensive industries in this area (World Bank 1998; Haggard 2000; Woo *et al.* 2000). Among them, the IMF and World Bank focused on structural weaknesses or institutional vulnerability, particularly in local financial institutions and corporate governance. This view is clearly presented in the 1998 World Bank Report:

> The main lesson from the East Asian crisis is that it is important to take an integrated approach to the issues of corporate governance and financing. The poor system of corporate governance contributed to the crisis by shielding the banks, financial companies, and corporations from market discipline. Rather than ensuring internal oversight and allowing external monitoring, corporate governance has been characterized by ineffective boards of directors, weak internal control, unreliable financial reporting, lack of adequate disclosure, lax enforcement to ensure compliance, and poor audits. These problems are evidenced by unreported losses and understated liabilities.
>
> (World Bank 1998: 57)

In this context, the World Bank naturally proposed to the governments of the crisis-hit East Asian countries two interconnected types of reform: the restructuring of financial institutions and corporate restructuring. The financial restructuring prescription included the introduction of the BIS capital adequacy standard (8 percent of total outstanding loans) and improving loan loss provisioning (standard/doubtful/loss) to global standards, strict monitoring by commercial banks on credit loans and the enactment of corporate bankruptcy laws to speedily resolve the non-performing loan (NPL) problem in favor of creditors. Meanwhile, corporate restructuring mainly aimed at developing *direct corporate finance* (equity and corporate bond markets), instead of *indirect corporate finance* (banking loans), to improve equity to debt ratios and reforming locally listed companies in line with the so-called Anglo-American model of good corporate governance. The establishment of good corporate governance in accordance with the global standard included appointment of independent directors, establishment of independent audit committees, information disclosure to investors and enforcement of minority shareholders' rights (World Bank 1998; World Bank 2000; Nabi and Shivakumar 2001).

Comparing these economic reforms in East Asia with those in Latin America, which mainly aimed to restructure *the public sector* by privatizing state enterprises and improving the central fiscal system, we find that the former stressed the importance of restructuring *the private sector* in general and local companies in particular. At the same time, the governments in East Asia are expected to play a significant role in economic activities. But their roles are no longer as *conductors* who directly intervene in the market, but as *coordinators* who facilitate institutional and legal frameworks for good corporate governance and sound market mechanisms. The World Bank report concluded that: "East Asia's development over the next ten years will rest on three strategic initiatives for institutions and growth: managing globalization, revitalizing business, and forcing a new social contract" (World Bank 2000: 146–7).

By contrast, governments in Latin America hardly touched on the reform of the private sector. They neither restructured local commercial banks nor touched on local stock markets reform. Rather, they tried to screen local firms by market forces through the promotion of free entry of foreign firms into privatized state enterprises and domestic industries. As a result, many state enterprises and large local firms were taken over by leading European and American multinational corporations (MNCs), while few local firms could survive in selected fields such as natural resources-based industry, agro-industry, food processing industry, electric power industry and so on (Ferraz 2002). For instance, a local group in the electric power industry based in Chile successfully integrated their business on the regional base by using an active mergers and acquisitions (M&A) strategy, but this company was finally taken over by a European conglomerate in 2000 (Hoshino ed. 2002: Ch. 4). Those that failed to adjust their corporate activities to the global economy were inevitably forced to leave the market.

A detailed study by Ferraz *et al.* on the changes in ownership of private firms in Latin America during the 1990s offers a surprising fact. According to the study, between 1990 and 2000, M&A in Latin America amounted to 3,085 cases and accounted for US$218 billion, which were mostly initiated not by local groups but by foreign firms. Consequently, the number of foreign firms in the largest 500 Latin American companies quickly increased from 149 (30 percent) in 1990–2 and 156 (31 percent) in 1994–6 to 231 (46 percent) in 1998–2000. While the proportion of combined sales of foreign firms against total sales of the largest 500 companies increased from 27 percent through 32 percent to 42 percent in the corresponding years. M&A took place in East Asia after the crisis, but its size in Latin America was far larger than that in East Asia.[8] Furthermore, M&A in East Asia were undertaken on the basis of friendly negotiation in such a way as a foreign partner (for instance, a Japanese firm) agreed to buy local shareholdings to help local partners, instead of through hostile takeovers.

In sum, unlike in Latin America, economic reforms in East Asia appeared to put the first priority on institutional development in which international financial institutions principally aimed at restructuring the economic systems and institutions including corporate law, corporate finance and auditing systems on the basis of the second generation Washington Consensus. But we cannot assume that each government has followed the policy recommendation of international financial institutions after the crisis. Then can we expect that institutional reforms adopted by the governments will work effectively in principle? Finally, can we assume that these reforms will lead East Asian economies to sustainable growth? In order to answer these questions, let's examine the case of economic reforms in Thailand.

Economic reforms in Thailand: 1997–2004

Thailand is known as a country that triggered, or was the first victim of, the region-wide crisis that struck East Asia in 1997. From 1988, Thailand enjoyed an unprecedented economic expansion owing to a foreign direct investment boom and an active strategy among local business groups to diversify business lines. For instance, net inflow of foreign direct investment in 1990 alone (64.7 billion baht, US$2.6 billion) achieved the same level of accumulated investment over a previous 15-year period between 1973 and 1987 (64.6 billion baht).[9] The liberalization policy of the government started at the end of the 1980s and accelerated the investment boom both in the real sector, such as the manufacturing and telecommunications industries, and in other sectors, such as land and equities. Such an active investment boom naturally resulted in an expanding gap between the investment ratio against nominal GDP (35–40 percent) and the savings ratio against nominal GDP (23–25 percent) in the early 1990s (Suehiro and Higashi eds 2000: 28–30).

This investment/savings gap was financed by international credit including off-shore loans. Indeed, the total amount of foreign debt Thailand took on quickly jumped from US$18,321 million in 1986 to US$90,536 million in 1996. Of this, the proportion of private sector debt to total foreign debt quickly increased from 34.0 percent to 81.4 percent over the same period. What was more important is the fact that short-term credit (within one year, mostly three-month and six-month loans), used mainly for investment in property and equities, increased its share from 15.8 percent to 41.5 percent in the corresponding period (Suehiro and Higashi eds 2000: 31). These figures imply that the Thai economy turned into a bubble economy, which is usually indicated by excess liquidity and rapid growth of the non-real sector.

On the other hand, the central bank did not touch on the foreign exchange system, which was principally linked to the US dollar. This was because they were afraid that a depreciation of the local currency (Thai baht) against the US dollar would directly damage the financial position of local firms whose investment sources heavily depended on US dollar denominated foreign loans. Then, groups of international hedge funds began to attack the Thai baht as they expected its value to decline. They took on significant US dollar holdings in exchange for Thai baht. The Bank of Thailand (BOT) in turn recouped the Thai baht by consuming foreign reserves from 1996 forward. In this process, the foreign reserves of Thailand quickly dropped from US$23,600 million in December 1996 to US$5,300 million in May 1997 and then to just US$1,100 million in July 1997 (Suehiro 2000a: 90). At last, the government was forced to give up the fixed exchange rate system and changed it into a managed floating system on 2 July 1997. The currency and financial crisis in Thailand immediately spread to other East Asian countries, and resulted in a region-wide economic crisis by the end of 1997 (World Bank: 1998; Jomo ed. 1998).

Immediately after the shift to a managed floating exchange system, the Thai government asked the IMF for standby credit to finance the shortage of foreign reserves, and the IMF, World Bank, Japan and other East Asian countries agreed to provide a total of US$17.2 billion credit in exchange for a "Letter of Intents" (LOIs) or the so-called "policy conditionality." This conditionality was principally based on a conventional approach to an "economic stabilization with total demand-side control," including three major policies: 1) stabilization of the foreign exchange rate by inputting a standby credit; 2) reduction of public expenditure and a tax increase in order to finance economic reforms; and 3) strict control on the money supply in order to constrain possible inflation and to prevent the outflow of foreign capital due to depreciation of local currency (See Figure 7.1).

Comparing the standby credit for Latin American and Southeast Asian countries in the early 1980s, however, we see a distinguishable difference

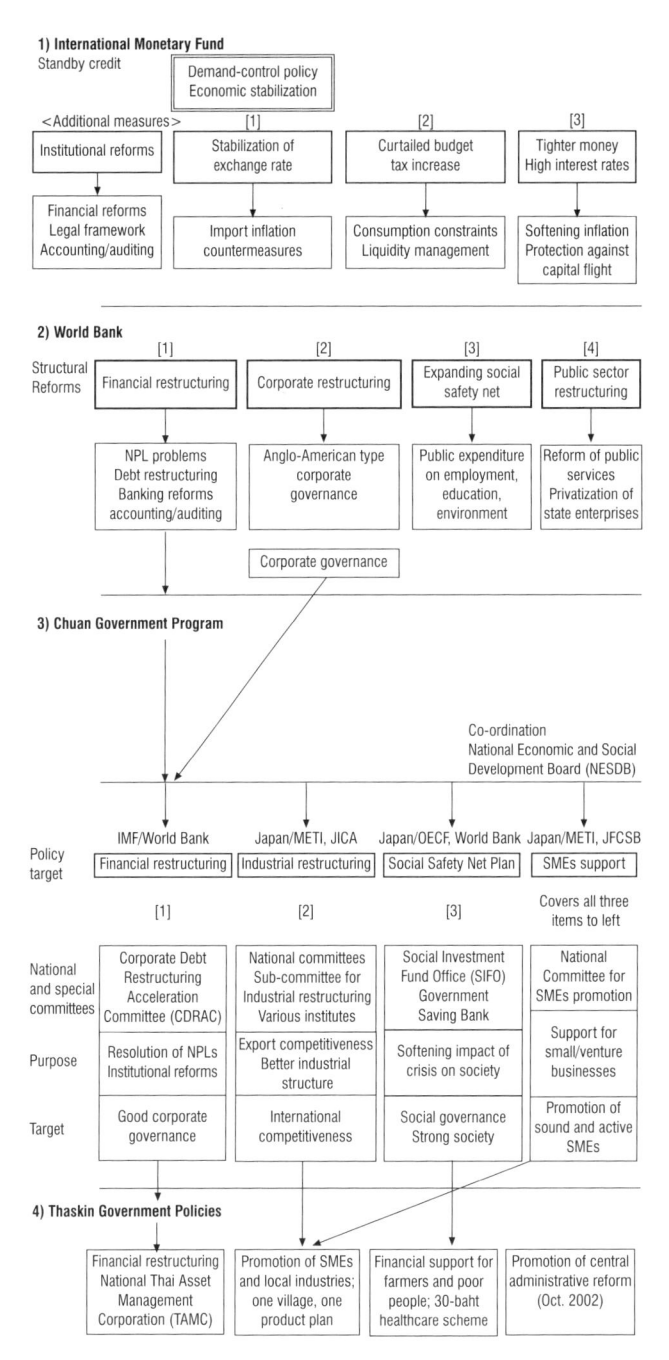

Figure 7.1 Economic and social restructuring programs in Thailand (1997–2001) (source: Drafted by the author).

Notes
METI: Ministry of Economic, Trade and Industry; OECF: Overseas Economic Cooperation Fund (now JBIC); JICA: Japan International Corporation Agency; JFCSB: Japan Finance Corporation for Small Business.

in the IMF approach to the East Asian crisis-hit countries. This was because the IMF forced the governments to not only implement economic stabilization policies but also to introduce *institutional reforms* including financial and corporate restructuring schemes. This new policy agenda was employed in South Korea and Indonesia as well. As was seen earlier, the IMF developed its policy recommendation in accordance with the Washington Consensus in the second generation. In order to complete the institutional reforms, the IMF changed the tenure of its credit from one to two years to three to four years (Extended Fund Facility scheme: EFF) (Suehiro 2000a: 98).

The new IMF policy toward East Asian crisis-hit countries was immediately followed and firmly supported by its close collaborator, the World Bank. When the World Bank provided its structural adjustment loans (SALs) to the Thai government, it proposed reforms similar to the IMF. These policies included: 1) *a financial restructuring scheme* aimed at resolution of NPL problems and reorganization of local commercial banks in accordance with the global standards on capital adequacy and loan loss provisioning; and 2) *a corporate restructuring scheme* which targeted the idea of "good corporate governance" which consisted of information disclosure, appointment of independent directors, the establishment of an independent audit committee and enhancement of minority shareholders' right (Nabi and Shivakumar 2001: 45–54).

In addition to these reforms that were required by the IMF, the World Bank tried to introduce social protection policies to alleviate the dislocations caused by the deepening economic recession (see Figure 7.1). Although the IMF's principal purpose was to stabilize the macro economy, strict control of the money supply and drastic curtailment of public expenditure inevitably resulted in a fierce credit crunch and sharp drop in domestic consumption. According to the World Bank evaluation, East Asian countries were experiencing an unprecedented crisis during 1998, comparable to the economic disaster in the United States and Germany under the Great Depression (World Bank 1999: 9). In order to overcome this serious situation, the World Bank proposed that governments would introduce a Keynesian type economic policy to create provisional jobs for unemployed persons through extra public expenditure. At the same time, the World Bank strongly recommended the restructuring of the public sector by promoting privatization of ineffective state enterprises and a 10 percent reduction in the number of government officers.

Prime Minister Chuan Leekpai strictly followed these IMF and World Bank policy recommendations after he established a coalition government in November 1997. For instance, his government ordered 56 of the existing 92 finance companies to close their operations in December 1997 under strong pressure from the IMF. From January to August 1998, his government also disbanded four of fourteen existing local commercial banks and reorganized them into the state-controlled ones. In August, they ordered all financial institutions to introduce the BIS capital adequacy standard and to introduce a loan loss provisioning fund to tackle increasing NPLs (Suehiro ed. 2002: Ch. 4). Concerning corporate restructuring, the Stock and Exchange Commission of Thailand (SEC) and the Stock Exchange of Thailand (SET) announced guidance on "good corporate governance" in January 1998, and obliged all the listed companies to appoint at least two independent directors and to establish an independent audit committee by the end of 1999 (Suehiro 2001c). In addition to these Anglo-American type reforms, the government also started revision of existing economic laws including the Company Bankruptcy Act, the Public Limited Company Act, the Accounting Act and the Auditing Act in line with the global standards or, to be more precise, in accordance with an "Anglo-American" model (Suehiro ed. 2002: Ch. 2).

Apart from these policies, the Chuan government started other reforms in collaboration with the Japanese government. These reforms consisted of two major parts: 1) an industrial restructuring plan (IRP) which aimed at improving the international competitiveness of export-oriented industries such as electronics and food processing and reorganizing heavy industries which suffered from excess production capacity; and 2) the promotion of small and medium-sized enterprises (SMEs) which suffered seriously from capital shortages after the crisis, but would be expected to play a significant role in supporting industry (Suehiro 2000b, see also Figure 7.1). The Japanese government agreed to provide US$340 million for these schemes together with a delegation of technical experts called the Mizutani mission. In brief, in contrast to the IMF and the World Bank-led reforms focusing on the financial and corporate sectors, the Japanese government-sponsored loans put top priority on the real sector, especially the manufacturing sector to which a large number of Japanese enterprises had committed substantial investment (Suehiro 2001b).[10]

Aside from these policies, the leadership of the Thai government began working out a social protection scheme. Although the World Bank and Japan's Overseas Economic Cooperation Fund (OECF, which was integrated into Japan's Bank for International Cooperation or JBIC in 2000) provided a sizable portion of the necessary funds, the scheme was mainly designed by the ad hoc National Committee on Social Policy which included leading figures of NGO groups such as Mo Prawet Wasi and Anek Nakhabut. This scheme was named a Social Investment Plan (SIP), and the government requested local people and local community-based organizations to propose grass-root projects on the basis of their own needs (Anek 2002). After screening proposed plans, the government granted funds through nation-wide branches of the Government Savings Bank. It was reported that as many as 70,000 projects were proposed. However, merely 450 projects were approved because most of the projects had no concrete plan.[11] After this poor result, SIP was transferred to the Ministry of the Interior in 1999, and was reorganized into a new scheme with the purpose of promoting a "community-based economy" (*setthakit chumchon*) closely connected to the decentralization policy that the new 1997 Constitution required the government to implement (Prawat 1998, 1999).[12]

After the Chuan government's tenure ended, Thailand held a general election in January 2001. The Democrat Party, core political party of the Chuan government, was completely defeated by Thai Rak Thai Party (TRT: Thai people love Thailand) due partly to the slow economic recovery and partly to its poor policy agenda. By contrast, TRT proposed a set of new policies to the people in a nation-wide campaign. Owing to this campaign, TRT successfully won 248 out of 500 total seats (50 percent) in the House of Representatives, while the Chuan-led Democrat Party won only 126 seats (25 percent). Given the result of the general election, Thaksin Shinawatra, the party leader of TRT, became the prime minister and eventually altered many of the institutional reforms that had been pushed by the Chuan government. He also launched unique policies (*Thaksinomics*), or the so-called *dual-track policies*, which aimed at enhancing international competitiveness in targeted industries on the one hand, and reducing poverty problems through the introduction of various schemes in favor of rural people on the other (Pasuk and Baker 2004: Chs 4 and 5).

For the financial restructuring scheme, the Chuan government had tackled the NPL problems by employing a self-help scheme. Namely, creditors and debtors directly negotiated with each other, while the Thai Bankers Association (TBA) and the Bank of Thailand (BOT) served as coordinators to promote debt restructuring. However, the Thaksin government altered this time-consuming self-help scheme, creating instead a more direct solution of the NPL problem for creditors by setting up the government-sponsored Thailand Assets Management Corporation (TAMC). As a result, most large-scale NPLs of commercial banks, especially those in the government-sponsored banks, were transferred to the TAMC. Thanks to the establishment of the TAMC, the percentage of NPLs held by local financial institutions, including state-owned banks, dramatically dropped from 47 percent in July 1999 to 10 percent in December 2001 (Suehiro ed. 2002: 11).

On the other hand, as far as stock market reform is concerned, the Chuan government planned to conduct a complete revision of the existing Public Limited Company Act in conjunction with the Anglo-American concept of corporate governance. According to the original plan, the new Act would introduce three major revisions: increase of the director's role in monitoring companies, enhancement of minority shareholders' rights and prohibition of mutual credit guarantees among companies belonging to the same business group. But the Thaksin government mutilated this plan and enacted a new Act with a minor revision. It stressed the activation of local stock markets by giving local firms tax incentives rather than introducing a legal framework to promote "good corporate governance" (Suehiro ed. 2002: Ch. 3). It also neglected the industrial restructuring plan that the Chuan government had introduced. This plan originally covered 13 industries, and would be carried out according to the action plan formulated in June 1998 (Suehiro 2000b: 46–9). But Thaksin shelved this plan, and instead he emphasized promotion of local industries and cottage industries in rural areas as can be seen in the program of "one village [tambon] one product" (OTOP). At the same time, he also introduced a new National Competitiveness Plan, in which five industries were strategically selected for promotion to aid Thailand's competitive advantage in international economic competition (NESDB 2003: 81–3).[13]

The policy agenda of the Thaksin government places priority on social protection policies that favor rural people, poor people and owners of SMEs (NESDB 2003, 2005. See Table 7.2). These policies include: 1) a

Table 7.2 Performance of the social protection policies under the Thaksin government of Thailand (as of September 2004)

Programs	Policy performance
1 Village fund	1.3 million farmers joined the program with a total investment amount of 22.4 billion baht. Out of this, farmers repaid 12.7 billion bahts.
2 People's Bank	Government provides financial supports for 850,000 cases (owners of small businesses), and outstanding loans amounted to 17,827 million baht by September 2004.
3 Debt moratorium for poor farmers	Government provides moratorium for 2 million cases, amounting to 75,500 million baht.
4 One tambon (village), one product (OTOP)	26,000 villages joined the programs. Total sales by the OTOP accounted for 42,000 million baht including exports (5,000 million baht).
5 SMEs finance	Financial support by the government for the SMEs amounted to 157 billion baht between 2001 and 2004.
6 30 Baht healthcare scheme	Patients can receive healthcare service from public hospitals and health centers so long as they pay 30 baht at each first visit. Amounted to 47,075,000 persons by the end of 2004.
7 Ban Nua Arthon Project (special housing project for low income groups)	Total of 48,000 households obtained houses through this project.

Source: Ministry of Finance, Thailand (2004) (in Thai).

village (*tambon*) fund scheme in which the government provides one million baht to all the villages (71,507 villages) and urban communities (4,040 communities) in a metropolitan area to create new projects; 2) the "one village one product" movement in which the government provides financial and technical support to the local community for the development of specific products such as natural silk fabric and traditional ceramics; 3) a three year moratorium on debt repayment for poor farmers; 4) the establishment of a People's Bank in which borrowers are not required to offer collateral and surety; 5) the reorganization of the Small Industries Finance Corporation (SIFO) into an SME Development Bank for the purpose of helping the owners of SMEs; 6) a 30 baht healthcare scheme in which all people who have not belonged to any social security scheme can receive health care in government-sponsored health centers or clinics.

It is surprising that all of these schemes came into existence within one year after the establishment of the Thaksin government. By February 2002, the government completed providing village funds to 70,439 villages in the whole country, while as many as 2,360,000 farmers applied for the debt moratorium scheme, which amounted to 75.5 billion baht (Prime Minister's Office 2002). Between October 2001 and August 2002, the government issued a certification card (gold card) for the 30 baht healthcare scheme to 45,900,000 individuals (the total population of Thailand was 62,800,000 in 2002), and it was reported that 35,000,000 people already had medical service in 4,200 health centers across the country (*Krunthep Thurakit*, 27 August 2002). The coverage of this scheme increased to 47,075,000 individuals by the end of 2004 (NESDB 2005: 6–8). According to the latest evaluation by the Ministry of Finance on the Thaksin government performance, the percentage of the population below the national poverty standard dropped from 15.9 percent in 1999 to 9.8 percent in 2002, while the ratio of unemployed persons also dropped from 4.19 percent to 2.24 percent in the same period (Ministry of Finance 2004). As for the social protection policies such as the village fund project, we can see noteworthy results under the leadership of Prime Minister Thaksin between 2001 and 2004 (see Table 7.2).

Carefully looking at the various policies of the governments to overcome the crisis, we see notable changes in reform targets from an outward-looking focus on globalization to an inward-looking focus on domestic matters.[14] The Thaksin government chose a different path from the East Asia economic model (a catch-up type industrialization through manufactured export promotion), which the Japanese government promoted in the industrial restructuring prescriptions it advised.[15]

What is the final target for economic reforms?

What should be noted here is the fact that such a counter-balancing movement against both the Anglo-American model and the East Asia economic model is not confined to the case of Thailand. Rather, this movement spread to other East Asian countries such as Malaysia and Indonesia. It is true that the East Asian crisis-hit countries strictly followed the policy recommendations of the IMF and the World Bank in the initial stage of the economic crisis. But each government began to recognize that the Anglo-American model and the East Asian economic model do not always contribute to economic recovery in a real sense, or to social stability. As a result, they are now turning their eyes from the economic sector to the social sector and from global standards to their own style of policy autonomy. We may say that such a movement consists of a part of the local response of East Asian countries to ongoing economic globalization and liberalization.

Another new movement may be seen in the political arena in East Asia. As is shown typically in Thailand, Prime Minister Thaksin has attempted to implement his policy ideas on the basis of his strong leadership and high national popularity. He prefers strategic meetings to public hearings when formulating concrete plans. He prefers direct dialogue with the people to time-consuming discussion in parliament to solve various problems. He also tries to introduce a "top-down" system into Thai politics against the "bottom-up" system that had steadily developed in line with the democratization movement during the 1990s (Pasuk and Baker 2004: 135–44).

In sum, he is going to introduce a "Thaksinocracy" instead of democracy. Thaksinocracy is principally derived from his own experience as the top manager of the largest business empire (SHIN Corporation group) in the Thai telecommunications industry. In a speech in 1997, Thaksin said that: "A country is a company. A company is a country. They are the same. The management is the same." In this context, he identified himself as a "CEO Prime Minister" (ibid. 101–2). Based on this unique political idea, Thaksin asks all the ministers and all the heads of departments in government offices to make their "vision, mission and goals" clear and he asks them to implement policies more quickly and efficiently, just as in the management of a private company.

At the same time, Thaksin puts the priority on his personal popularity. This is because he believes the national popularity of the prime minister is the best indicator of the quality of the government, just like the stock price is seen as the best tool of measuring the quality of a company. On this account, he prefers direct dialogue with the people to discussion in parliament due to its contribution to this popularity, and prefers a "top-down" system to a "bottom-up" system for the sake of speed and efficiency in policy implementation. It is true that the prime minister is selected through the general election on the basis of political parties, and a variety of institutions to promote democracy such as a Constitutional Court and an Election Committee have been introduced into Thai politics. But the Thaksin government is different to a textbook parliamentary democracy because its legitimacy is basically sustained by the prime minister's distinguished leadership, his unchallenged economic power and his widespread popularity.[16]

Conventional argument frequently presupposes that political democratization and economic liberalization will combine together to develop a country into a civil society-based state. But in the real world, East Asian countries since the crisis have moved in a different direction in terms of socio-political structure, away from a civil society model. Rather, they are moving toward a populist regime characterized by individual political leadership and inward-looking policies. Thailand provides a good case study, as its evolution follows, more or less, the same patterns as Malaysia, the Philippines and Indonesia. Nevertheless, it is likely that no one will be able to stop the long-term globalization, liberalization and democratization of the world. In this sense, both East Asian countries and Latin American countries are facing a fundamental problem of how to coordinate their internal needs with the given external conditions.

Notes

1 Since 2000, three major regions have shown different patterns of economic performance: strong recovery in East Asia in general and in South Korea and Thailand in particular; rapid increase of exports related to IT industries from India; and relatively lower growth in Latin America.
2 These figures are averages and so neglect population size. Taking population size into consideration, Latin America and the Caribbean have US$3,680 GNI per capita and US$7,030 PPP GNI per capita in 2000. This is larger than similar figures in East Asia and the Pacific where GNI per capita is US$1,060 and PPP GNI per capita is US$4,120 in the same years (World Bank 2002: 233).
3 Bela Balassa (1981), who was an economic advisor to the World Bank in the early 1980s, called this type of government policy an outward-looking industrial development strategy.
4 For an interesting account of the changing status of local big family businesses, state enterprises and multinational corporations in Latin America after the middle of the 1990s, see Hoshino ed. (2004).
5 Holliday and Wilding eds (2003: 173) characterized such development-oriented social policy as "productivist subordination of social policy to economic policy" and divided the four East Asian countries or regions into three major classifications: facilitative (Hong Kong), developmental-universalist (South Korea and Taiwan) and developmental-particularist (Singapore).
6 For more accounts for housing policies in East Asia, see Holliday and Wilding eds (2003: Ch. 5).
7 For the saving and investment ratio gap in East Asia and Latin America by the early 1990s, Hosono (1994) provides informative data and suggests a different pattern of investment financed by high domestic savings and FDI in East Asia and lower investment with low domestic savings in Latin America. See also Table 7.1 of this Chapter.
8 Looking at the extent of M&A activity in the three-year periods from 1995 to 1997 and from 1998 to 2000, we see, in Latin America, increases from US$10,115 million to US$35,080 million in Argentina, from US$29,361 million to US$61,750 million in Brazil and from US$5,188 million to US$12,855

million in Chile. Likewise, in crisis-hit East Asian countries, the increase was from US$1,592 million to US$20,489 million in South Korea, from US$1,671 million to US$2,666 million in Indonesia, and from US$1,058 million to US$7,789 million in Thailand (Ferraz and Hamaguchi 2002: 389).
9 Computed from Bank of Thailand, *Economic and Financial Statistics* (Quarterly), various issues.
10 Since the mid-1980s, the Ministry of International Trade and Industry (MITI) (which later changed its name to the Ministry of Economy, International Trade and Industry, or METI) proposed to ASEAN countries a package of technical assistance for industrial restructuring based on the Japanese experience. However, ASEAN countries showed hardly any interest to this proposal. It was only after the 1997 crisis that ASEAN countries requested such type of assistance.
11 Based on the author's interview with an official in Bangkok in March 1999.
12 Increased experience and various other information accumulated in the process of SIP were transferred to the National Economic and Social Development Board (NESDB). The NESDB started a new project for poverty reduction in collaboration with the World Bank in 2001.
13 These five industries include automobiles, food processing, fashion (garments-gems and jewelry-leather products), the tourist industry and software.
14 Such change in policy does not imply that Thaksin neglects the world-wide trend toward liberalization and globalization. Rather, Thailand is one of the most active countries in East Asia promoting region-based free trade agreements (FTA) as well as bilateral economic partnership agreements (EPA) as we see in the cases of the Thailand–China agreement on free trade of agricultural products in October of 2003 and the Thailand–India FTA agreement in July of 2004.
15 The Fortune Global Forum in Hong Kong portrayed "Mr. Thaksin as a maverick populist and nationalist who could steer Thailand away from an open economy, embracing international trade and capital to an inward looking development path." Likewise, a Morgan Stanley analyst characterized Thaksin's strategy as a first step in dismantling the East Asian economic model (Lian 2001: 2).
16 According to public opinion polls, Prime Minister Thaksin's approval rating was at its peak of 71.9 percent in May 2001. But it dropped down to 48.1 percent in September 2004 due to his political one-man show and problems with Islamic separatists in the south.

References

Amsden, A.H. (1977) "The Division of Labor Is Limited by the Type of Market: The Taiwanese Machine Tool Industry," *World Development*, 5(3): 217–33.
—— (1989) *Asia's Next Giant: South Korea and Late Industrialization*, New York: Oxford University Press.
Anek Nakhabut (2002) *Kop Ban Kun Muang duai Phalang Phaendin* [Protect a Home, Save a Country, and Country's Force], Bangkok: Government Saving Bank (in Thai).
Balassa, B. (1981) *The Newly Industrializing Countries in the World Economy*, New York: Pergamon Press.
Edwards, S. (1995) *Crisis and Reform in Latin America: From Despair to Hope*, World Bank Report, New York: Oxford University Press.
Ferraz, J.C. (2002) "Economic Liberalization, Ownership Change and Inward Internationalization in Latin America," paper submitted to an international

workshop on *Managing Development and Transition in a Globalizing World* at the Institute of Social Science, University of Tokyo on 24–5 July.

Ferraz, J.C. and Hamaguchi, N. (2002) "Introduction for Special Issue: M&A and Privatization in Developing Countries," *The Developing Economies*, 40(4): 383–99.

Haggard, S. (2000) *The Political Economy of the Asian Financial Crisis*, Washington, DC: Institute for International Economics.

Hirakawa, H. (1992) *NIES: Sekai Sisutemu to Kaihatsu* [NIES: the World System and Development], Tokyo: Dobunkan Shuppan (in Japanese).

Holliday, I. and Wilding, P. (eds) (2003) *Welfare Capitalism in East Asia: Social Policy in the Tiger Economies*, London: Palgrave Macmillan.

Hoshino, T. (ed.) (2002) *Hatten Tojyokoku no Kigyo to Gurobarizeshon* (Firms and Globalization in the Developing Countries), Chiba: Institute of Developing Economies (in Japanese).

—— (2004) *Famili Bijinesu no Keiei to Kakushin: Ajia to Raten Amerika* [Management and Innovation in Family Business: A Comparative Study of Asia and Latin America], Chiba: Institute of Developing Economies (in Japanese).

Hosono, A. (1994) "Higashi Ajia no Keizai Hatten to Ratenamerika [Economic Development in East Asia and Latin America]," Japan Bank for Export and Import, *Kaigai Tousi Kenkyushoho*, 20(5) (in Japanese).

Jomo, K.S. (ed.) (1998) *Tigers in Trouble: Financial Governance, Liberalization and Crises in East Asia*, London: Zed Books.

Kamimura, Y. and Suehiro A. (eds) (2003) *Higashi Ajia no Fukushi Sisutemu Kochiku* [Welfare System in East Asia], ISS Research Series No. 10, Tokyo: Institute of Social Science, University of Tokyo (in Japanese).

Koike, Y. and Horisaka K. (eds) (1999) *Raten Amerika Sin-seisan-shisutemu-ron: Posuto-yunyuu-daitai-kogyoka no Chosen* [New Production System in Latin America: An Alternative to Import Substitution Model], Tokyo: Institute of Developing Economies (in Japanese).

Koike, Y. and Nishijima, S. (eds) (1997) *Shijo to Seihu: Raten Amerika no Aratana Kaihatsu Wakugumi* (Market and State: A New Framework for Development in Latin America), Tokyo: Institute of Developing Economies (in Japanese).

Lian, D. (2001) "First Step in Dismantling the East Asia Economic Model," *Asia/Pacific Economics* (Morgan Stanley Dean Witter), 16 May.

Ministry of Finance (MOF, Thailand) (2004) *Phon-ngan Krasuwang Kan-khlang 4 Piraek lae Yutthasat Krasuwang Kan-khlang 2548–2551* (Performance of the MOF in the first four years and MOF's strategy during the years from 2005 to 2008), Bangkok: MOF (in Thai).

Nabi, I. and Shivakumar, J. (2001) *Back from the Brink: Thailand's Response to the 1997 Economic Crisis*, Bangkok: The World Bank Office Bangkok.

NESDB (National Economic and Social Development Board, Thailand) (2003) *Thailand in Brief 2003*, Bangkok: NESDB.

—— (2005) *Rai-gan Kan Tit-tam Pramoen-phon Kan Phattana Setthakit lae Sangkhom khong Prathet: 3 Pi khong Paen Phattana Chabap thi 9* (Evaluation Report on the Economic and Social Development of Thailand: Three Years of the Ninth Economic Plan), Bangkok: NESDB, July.

Pasuk, P. and Baker, C. (2004) *Thaksin: The Business of Politics in Thailand*, Chiang Mai: Silkworm Books.

Prawet Wasi, M. (1998) *Yutthasat Chart phua Khwam Khem-kheng thang Setthakit.*

Sangkhom lae Silatham [State Strategy to Strengthen Economy, Society and Moral], Bangkok: Samnakphim Mo Chaoban (in Thai).
—— (1999) *Setthakit Phophiang lae Prachasangkhom* [Sufficient Economy and Civil Society], Bangkok: Samnakphim Mo Chaoban (in Thai).
Prime Minister's Office, the Government of Thailand, (2002) *Summary Report on the Thaksin Government for the Year of 2001*, Bangkok: Prime Minister's Office (in Thai).
Ramesh, M. and Asher, M.G. (2000) *Welfare Capitalism in Southeast Asia: Social Security, Health and Education Policies*, New York: Palgrave.
Sawada, Y. (2002) "Hong Kong: Uneasiness among Administrative Agents," in S. Shigetomi (ed.) *The State and NGOs: Perspective from Asia*, Singapore: Institute of Southeast Asian Studies.
Suehiro, A. (2000a) *Kyacchiappugata Kougyouka-ron: Ajia Keizai no Kiseki to Tenbo* [Catch-up Industrialization: The Trajectory and Prospects of Asian Economies], Nagoya: Nagoya University Press (in Japanese).
—— (2000b) "Tai no Keizai Kaikaku: Sangyo Kozou Kaizen Jigyo to Chushokigyo Shien [Economic Reforms in Thailand: Industrial Restructuring Plan and Assistance to the SMEs]," *Shakai Kagaku Kenkyu* (Institute of Social Science, University of Tokyo), 51(4): 25–65 (in Japanese).
—— (2001a) *Family Business Gone Wrong: Ownership Pattern and Corporate Performance in Thailand*, Asian Development Bank Institute Working Paper 19, Tokyo: ADB Institute.
—— (2001b) "Nihon no Aratana Ajia Kanyo: Chiteki Shien wa Kanouka? [Japan's New Commitment to Asia: Is an Intellectual Cooperation for Economic Policies Possible or not?]," in A. Suehiro and S. Yamakage (eds) *Ajia Seiji Keizai-ron: Ajia no nakano Nihon wo mezasite* [The Political Economy of Asia: In Search of Japan in the Asian Region], Tokyo: NTT Shuppan (in Japanese).
—— (2001c) "Asian Corporate Governance: Disclosure-Based Screening System and Family Business Restructuring in Thailand," in *Shakai Kagaku Kenkyu*, 52(5): 55–97.
—— (ed.) (2002) *Tai no Seido Kaikaku to Kigyo no Saihen* [Institutional Reforms and Corporate Restructuring in Thailand], Chiba: Institute of Developing Economies (in Japanese).
Suehiro, A. and Higashi, S. (eds) (2000) *Tai no Keizai Seisaku: Seido, Soshiki, Akuta* [Economic Policy in Thailand: The Role of Institutions and Actors], Chiba: Institute of Developing Economies (in Japanese).
Suehiro, A. and Nakagawa J. (eds) (2001) *Liberalization, Economic Crisis and Social Restructuring in Asia, Latin America and Russia/Eastern Europe: Part II Chronology*, ISS Research Series No. 2, Tokyo: Institute of Social Science, University of Tokyo.
Twu, J. (1990) *Toyo Shihonshugi* [Oriental Capitalism], Tokyo: Kodansha Shinsho (in Japanese).
Usami, K. (ed.) (2001) *Raten-amerika Fukushi Kokka-ron Kenkyu Josetsu* [An Introductory Study of Social Welfare State in Latin America], Chiba: Institute of Developing Economies (in Japanese).
Williamson, J. (1990) *The Progress of Policy Reform in Latin America*, Washington, DC: Institute for International Economics.
Williamson, J. (ed.) (1994) *The Political Economy of Policy Reform*, Washington, DC: Institute for International Economics.

Woo, W.T., Sachs, J. and Schwab, K. (2000) *The Asian Financial Crisis: Lessons for a Resilient Asia*, Cambridge, Mass.: MIT Press.
World Bank (1998) *East Asia: The Road to Recovery*, New York: Oxford University Press.
—— (1999) *Global Economic Prospects and the Developing Countries 1998/99: Beyond Financial Crisis*, Washington, DC: World Bank.
—— (2000a) *East Asia: Recovery and Beyond*, New York: Oxford University Press.
—— (2000b) *World Development Report 2000/2001: Attacking Poverty*, Washington, DC: World Bank.
—— (2002) *World Development Report 2002: Building Institutions for Markets*, Washington, DC: World Bank.
Yusuf, S. and Evenett, S.J. (2002) *Can East Asia Compete? Innovation for Global Markets*, New York: Oxford University Press.

8 Business groups as an organizational device for economic catch-up

Keun Lee

Introduction

While Berle and Means (1932) discussed the rise of managerial capitalism a long time ago, a recent survey by La Porta *et al.* (1999) observes that the classical separation of ownership and control observed in it is rather an exception, and that it is more common around the world to have family-controlled firms often taking the form of business groups. Khanna (2000) and Granovetter (1995) provide good surveys of several issues regarding business groups, including the very essential question of how to define these groups. One of the issues is dynamic performance and the efficiency of the business group. Actually, the business groups, like Korean chaebols, have been subject to political scrutiny as the financial crises swept Asia, perceived as the home of "crony capitalism."

The concept of the controlling minority structure (CMS) firms proposed by Bebchuk *et al.* (2000) helps us understand why the business groups tend to fall into the serious agency problem which led to unjustifiable investment drives and the moral hazard problem. In the CMS firms, a shareholder exercises control while retaining only a small fraction of the equity claims on a company's cash flows. Such a radical separation of control and cash flow rights, which is the cause of the agency problem, can occur in three principal ways: through cross-ownership ties, a dual-class share structure and stock pyramids. These methods are used by business groups in many countries, including chaebols in Korea.

Then, two questions surface; first, why the business groups are developing in so many countries, and, second, what went wrong in many of them. This chapter tries to tackle these questions. Of course, the first question is not new, and there are old answers. That is, the business groups develop in the settings with market failures, like in emerging economies (Leff 1978; Goto 1982; Khanna and Palepu 1997). The fact that the business groups abound in such emerging and/or transition economies as Korea (Chang and Choi 1988; Steers *et al.* 1989), India (Ghemawat and Khanna 1998), Hong Kong (Au *et al.* 2000), Latin America (Khanna and Palepu 2000; Guillen 2000; Strachan 1976), China (Lee and Woo 2002; Peng

2000; Keister 1998) and in Russia (Freinkman 1995) should be evidence of their association with market failure or "institutional voids." However, if we see the business groups simply as an evolutionary response to the institutional environment of the economy, there is no interesting policy or strategic issue involved.

This chapter will look at the first question from a new perspective, namely the economic catch-up perspective. We will see the business groups as an organizational device for economic catch-up, and suggest that the business groups not only just emerge in response to market failure but also serve as a vehicle for economic catch-up. In this light, we call attention to the phenomenon that the business groups facilitate affiliate firms to enter new markets by providing cross-subsidy during their initial phase of business and that the business group firms, often enjoying lower than average profitability, tend to settle down with lower variation of profitability.

Regarding the second question, namely why they tend to fall into trouble, we argue that while business groups are effective in response to market failure and/or catch-up, the benefits come with long-term caveats in three dimensions. The following three potential dangers are discussed in sequence. First, the benefits of economic value creation by the business groups tend to decline over the long run as institutions evolve and markets become mature. Second, family-controlled business groups, taking the form of the CMS firm, tend to be subject to increasingly serious agency problems resulting in an value-destroying, inefficient investment drive. Third, the existence of the big players such as business groups in an economy might hamper the sound development of a competitive market economy by distorting or manipulating the course of liberalization, deregulation, or opening-up.

The two questions raised above will be dealt with, with primary reference to the Korean chaebols for which we have some new evidence and data, although examples from other countries will be used too. The following section discusses the first question, namely two alternative perspectives to the business groups, market failure and economic catch-up perspectives. The third section addresses the three long-term dangers with the business groups. The chapter concludes with a brief summary and remarks.

Fulfilling the institutional voids and the task of economic catch-up

Filling the institutional voids

It was since as early as works by Leff (1978) and Goto (1982) that the existence of business groups became associated with the underdeveloped nature of the market mechanism in developing countries. This "market failure" story regarding the emergence of business groups has further developed into the "institutional voids" argument by Khanna and Palepu (1997; 2000).

Their argument is that since many of the institutions that support business activities are absent in many parts of the world, the business groups emerge to fill the institutional voids. Below let me provide a brief summary of their argument. First, in product markets, given the lack of information about products and transaction-related claims-processing institutions, companies in emerging markets face much higher costs in building credible brands than their counterparts in advanced economies. Thus, a conglomerate with some reputation can use its group name to enter a new business and it can also spread the costs of maintaining brand names. In capital markets, without access to information, investors refrain from putting money into unfamiliar ventures. In such a context, established diversified groups have superior access to capital markets.

In labor markets, given the lack of well-trained business people and educational facilities, the groups can create value by developing promising managers within the group, and can spread the fixed costs of professional development over the businesses in the group. Also, when the labor market is rigid, running an internal labor market within a group can provide additional room for flexibility. Finally, given that the governments in emerging economies intervene much more extensively in business operations, diversified groups can create value by acting as intermediaries when their affiliate companies need to deal with the regulatory bureaucracy. The larger the group is, the easier it is to carry the costs of maintaining government relations.

The fact that so many emerging economies have seen and saw the development of various forms of business groups is evidence in support of this market or institutional failure argument. Also, there exists a large volume of empirical research that has confirmed the positive contribution of the business groups in terms of financial performance, internal capital market and so on in emerging markets, whereas the literature finds the opposite results with the American case (Berger and Ofek 1995; Lang and Stulz 1994).

Thus, the important matter to remember, as Khanna and Palepu (1997; 2000) observe, is that groups compensate for a variety of missing institutions in an environment, so that such benefits of group affiliation as do exist may manifest themselves in quite different ways in different contexts and at different times. To put it slightly differently, we should also note that the specific forms business groups take in each country vary depending upon the economic, political and legal condition of the country.

Actually, no single firm in the developing or transition economies has taken the form of the business group as an outcome of intentional strategic decision-making. The firms evolve to be a group or others. The famous story of the LG group in Korea, introduced in Milgrom and

Roberts (1992), well illustrates the evolutionary nature of the firm growing out of a single U-form firm into a business group. If we see the business groups as an evolutionary response to the institutional environment of the economy, there is no interesting policy or strategic issue involved. Fortunately, in the next subsection, we will argue that the business group is not simply a passive response to the environment but serves as an organizational device for economic catch-up.

Device for economic catch-up

Most catch-up economies face the problem of capital scarcity unless they have enough domestic savings even from the early stage of industrialization, like Taiwan and China. When Korea started on the course of industrialization in the early 1960s, it was evident that its growth potential was seriously constrained by savings available for investment. Given the limited size of the financial resources available, it was a reasonable solution to pool the capital into several big hands in the business. In other words, the government wanted to promote a small number of big businesses to expedite economic growth.

Since then, the rapid economic growth achieved in Korea has often been associated with the growth of big business groups, so-called chaebols, whose Chinese characters are the same as zaibatsu, namely the pre-war ancestor of keiretsu in Japan. Gerlach (1989) and Steers *et al.* (1989) take an active position such that Japanese keiretsu and Korean chaebols are the organizational basis for the rising strength of their economies, and that this form of industrial organization makes it more difficult for foreign firms to penetrate the Japanese or Korean markets. We call this view a catch-up device view of the business groups, and contrast this with the market failure view originated with Leff (1978) and Goto (1982). It is also interesting to see that in China, another catching-up economy, the government promoted the development of the big business groups, while there was also a very strong and bottom-up voluntary emergence of more small scale business groups, too (Chi 1996; Hahn 1997; Lee and Woo 2002).

If we see the business groups as a device for economic catch-up, the main function or benefits of such an organization should be something beyond merely filling the "institutional voids." We observe that the main strength of the business groups in catch-up is to facilitate entry into new markets or lines of business that were formerly monopolized by the fore-running companies. The business groups can facilitate market entry by mobilizing financial resources into new affiliates and helping them during the initial period of business by providing markets, capital, technology and brand names.

As a matter of fact, Lincoln *et al.* (1996) find that the keiretsu ties go beyond the main bank-based network, and that there is a redistribution effect reducing variability of the keiretsu firms. In other words, weak companies, like those in their starting period, benefit from group affiliation (they recover or grow faster), while strong ones do not (they are subsequently outperformed by independent firms).

In a similar context, Lee, Ryu and Yoon (2001) examine the variation in productive efficiency of chaebol and non-chaebol firms to investigate the observation that chaebols are constantly engaged in the launching of new ventures but that they try to maintain a certain level of efficiency at the group level. This observation translates into a hypothesis that there would be a higher "within-chaebol" variation in inefficiency but a lower "between-chaebol" variation. Actually, they found that the variation among the chaebol affiliates is 0.013, while that among the independent firms is only 0.0045 or even 0.0021.[1] In sorting out the "between-chaebol" efficiency, after assigning an inefficiency index for each chaebol group, they calculate the inefficiency variation among the top 22 chaebols. The variation in this case turns out to be only 0.0022, a value similar to that of the non-chaebol firms. So we confirm that the "between-chaebol" inefficiency variation is a lot smaller than its "within-chaebol" counterpart.

The group-level initiative to launch new business by setting up a new firm and covering its losses during the initial period was a well-known phenomena in Korea. A famous example would be Samsung's memory chip business. This business is now Samsung's biggest cash cow, although it made huge losses during the initial period. This kind of collective catch-up strategy is especially effective when the involved technology shows a rapid learning curve such that efficiency improves rapidly with the accumulation of production experience.

The finance literature also finds the so-called "socialism" in internal capital markets of the business groups such investment flows into loss-making or under-performing affiliates or division in the group or conglomerates (Shin and Park 1999). While the literature tends to interpret this as an inefficient behavior, an alternative interpretation would be that this is market entry strategy by the group level endeavor and it makes sense in dynamic context.

Long-term danger with the business group

Reduction of the group premium with institutional changes

As discussed above, value creation by unrelated group diversification is possible as there are diverse institutional voids that could be filled by the business groups. However, as market institutions evolve over time, such diversification premiums can decrease. Khanna and Palepu (2000) provide an empirical verification of such reasoning using the long-term data of Chilean firms. Evolution of institutions in general means maturing of market mechanisms characterized by a gradual emergence of intermediaries and a gradual reduction of ambient transaction costs. Therefore, it becomes increasingly difficult for the business group to create value through running internal (labor and capital) market across their diverse affiliates.

There is some literature trying to measure the diversification premium or discount by comparing group firms with non-group firms. Some of them use the "chop-shop" approach.[2] If a firm is composed of multi-industry segments/divisions, the value of the firm is assumed to be the sum of the several segments' values. Then, the excess value of the firm is defined by the difference between the firm's actual value and the imputed value. In US multi-segment firms, Berger and Ofek (1995) found negative value creation or diversification discount. The diversification discount of the US firms in Berger and Ofek (1995) was 13 percent to 15 percent during the 1986–91 period. However, Fauver et al. (1999) reported that the different diversification effects on firm value depends on the income level and legal systems, and found that no diversification discount or premium exists in low income countries and in countries whose legal system is of German origin.

G. Lee (1999) confirms the decline of diversification premium over the long run using the data of the Korean firms. He also uses the "chop-shop" approach. To calculate the imputed value, he uses two alternative variables: sales revenues and earnings-before-income taxes (hereafter EBIT). He first calculates the industry median of capital-to-sales ratio (capital to EBIT ratio) for the stand-alone companies in each industry. Here, capital is the sum of the market value of equity and the book value of debt.[3] Then, the imputed value of a group-affiliated company is obtained by multiplying this median (or mean) ratio to the actual sales revenues or EBIT. This way, the imputed value represents the hypothetical value of a group-affiliated company, assuming that it was operated as a stand-alone business.

G. Lee finds positive value creation by the group formation, but thinks that the value premium of the group-affiliated companies may be due to other firm-specific characteristics than the group-induced diversification. To check this possibility, he has also run the regression model for the two excess value measures, controlling for various firm characteristics, such as size, profitability and growth potentials. The regression results also confirm the positive value premium of group-affiliated companies as showing significantly positive coefficients of the group dummies. The premium using the sales multiplier is 6.3 percent and that using the EBIT multiplier is 7.5 percent.

To check the changes in the premium, he divides the sample period into four sub-periods, and runs the regressions. He finds that the diversification premium decreased over the years, finally turning to a negative value during the 1994–6 period. In 1984–7, the premium was about 10.5 percent. However it decreased to about 8.9 percent in 1988–90, 6.3 percent in 1991–3 and finally −4.7 percent in 1994–6.

With the continuing decrease of diversification premium in the 1990s, we finally had the financial crisis in 1997, which was triggered by the successive collapses of chaebols. Based on our framework, we think that the fundamental change in the nature of the institutional environment lay at the bottom of the crisis of the chaebols. As clues to the declining performance of chaebols, we note the following two important changes (Lee 2002).

First, the government has gradually stopped the explicit promotion of, or giving favor to, specific industries and firms. This does not mean that the government stopped intervention in the private sector, but it means that many kinds of once legal promotional policies of the government have disappeared. These policies included the so-called "policy loans" which were given to designated firms in the target industries at interest rates much lower than market rates, special export credits given at lower interest rates and arbitrary tax exemptions to the target industries.[4] Since the big business groups had been the main beneficiaries of such preferential treatment, these changes in the government attitude and its actions toward the private sector contributed to the lowering of the rents enjoyed by the chaebols.

Second, we should note the rising wave of globalization and the WTO spirit of free trade in the 1990s. The 1990s was the decade in which the Korean economy saw the fulfillment of most of its liberalization programs, including both trade and capital markets. Such liberalization measures caught further momentum following the Korean entry into the OECD in 1996. There had been a steady downward trend of effective protection rates over the 1963–90 period. Toward the end of the 1980s, the effective protection rates for manufacturing goods were reduced to less than 10 percent or even fell to negative levels. Furthermore, the tariff rates for imported goods decreased from more than 20 percent in the early 1980s to about 5 percent in the mid 1990s.

With the domestic market opened and liberalized, Korean firms, including chaebols, have faced increasing competition from foreign firms. In the world markets, on the one hand, Korean comparative advantages as a low wage country have disappeared with the rise of ASEAN and Chinese exporters, and, on the other hand, Korean products cannot afford to compete with the products from an advanced country, like Japan, in terms of quality and product differentiation. In general, this trend of globalization and liberalization has contributed to the lowering of the rents and decrease in profit rates enjoyed by the Korean chaebols. Since chaebols were the dominant players in the protected domestic markets and the main exporters of Korea under the government support, we can reason that chaebols were hit more badly than the small and medium-sized companies. As a matter of fact, according to Yoon's estimation (Yoon 1998) of the long-term trend of the profit rates (ROE: net income to stock holders' equity) over the 1980 to 1996 period, the profit rates for the large-sized firms, namely largely chaebol firms, tend to be consistently lower than the small or medium-sized firms since the mid-1980s when the trend of profitability passed its peak.[5]

What do these changes mean for the balance sheet of the costs and benefits of the chaebol-type firms and their diversification strategy? It is clear that the benefits side has lost. With lower benefits, balancing the costs and benefits of the chaebol has become difficult, and now the costs side has started to loom largely. In other words, the costs of over-diversification are suddenly felt much more strongly than before. As mentioned above, diversification was a somewhat rational response of the chaebols to the environment. But, now that the environment had changed, it was not easy to make money in many industries. Unfortunately, the chaebols did not command enough flexibility to meet the new challenge, or were too big to change quickly. The source of the inflexibility has to do with both the seemingly M-form like over-diversified organization with few exit possibilities and the unchanged mind of the top management.

The founder-managers of chaebols were succeeded by their sons, who often did not have verified managerial talents. The challenge to the inherited management was in general more demanding as the size of the firms had grown bigger and the entry into the global business environment was more complicated as well. In other words, the burden on the top management had become much heavier and the need for decentralization was evident. Decentralization was necessary as the member firms in the Korean chaebols enjoyed much less autonomy than the division in the M-form and because the necessary separation of the strategic and operational decision-making processes was not made. In short, the chaebols' problem was that they pursued a diversification strategy while their structure was a quite centralized one. In other words, the tension between "strategy and structure" had become serious as the institutional environment had changed.

In sum, the above discussion suggests that the business groups should try to find the optimum level of diversification as the external institutional environment changes, and that pursuit of the same level of diversification is value-destroying, rather than value-creating.

Inefficiency of investment drive in a leveraged CMS firm

The literature on corporate organization tends to perceive two kinds of firms. One is the firm of concentrated ownership where there is an owner of the firm with a controlling share of the firm, and the other is the firm of dispersed ownership where ownership is quite dispersed over a large number of shareholders, each with only a negligible share of the firm. The literature finds that the firm with concentrated ownership is free from agency costs of hired management while it is exposed to the danger of management entrenchment. In contrast, the firm with dispersed ownership could enjoy the benefits of professional management whereas it is potentially exposed to the agency costs of the hired management. It is not hard to notice that neither form of firm can command a priori dominance over the other, and so many empirical papers have ended up with conflicting results over the relative performance between the two types of the firms.

What, then about the business group? What kind of firm is this? Concentrated ownership or dispersed ownership? Of course, ownership of business groups can be concentrated or dispersed. But, we contend that there is great possibility that ownership of the business group can be in between the two extremes. Bebchuk *et al.* (2000) propose the controlling minority structure firms as the third kind of firm, and find that the firms of controlling minority structures are widespread around the world, especially in the form of business groups. In CMS firms, a shareholder exercises control while retaining only a small fraction of the equity claims on a company's cash flows. Such a radical separation of control and cash flow rights can occur in three principal ways: through cross-ownership ties, a dual-class share structure, and stock pyramids. All three of these methods are used by the business groups in many countries, including the Korean chaebols.

What, then is the problem with the CMS firm? The CMS structure resembles controlled structure insofar as it insulates the controller from the market for corporate control, but it resembles dispersed ownership insofar as it places corporate control in the hands of an insider who holds a small fraction of equity. Thus, the CMS threatens to combine the incentive problems associated with both the concentrated structure and the dispersed ownership in a single ownership structure.

Theoretical models in Bebchuk *et al.* (2000) explain why inefficient projects are chosen and unprofitable expansion is pursued under the CMS. Suppose that there are projects which can produce a value (V) that includes cash flow (S) available to all shareholders and private benefits of control (B). Then, between the two alternative projects that generate different cash flow and private benefits, the model shows that the probability that the project generating a bigger private benefit is chosen increase at a sharply increasing rate as α decreases (α is cash flow rights of the controlling minority shareholder). For example, with a value of α as 10 percent, which is roughly the average value in the top 30 chaebols, a controller will reject the efficient project unless the value gap between the two projects is more than 27 percent.

Another model in Bebchuk *et al.* (2000) also explains that given any distribution of opportunities to expand and contract, the likelihood that a CMS firm will make an inefficient decision – and thus the expected agency cost – grows larger as the controller's equity stake α becomes smaller. In their model, a controller will prefer to expand (or not to contract) a firm if $\alpha(V-B) + B > \alpha P$, where P is the buying or selling price of the asset. For example, with a value of α as 10 percent, the controller will refuse to sell the asset unless the firm receives a price 45 percent higher than the real value of the asset to the firm. Equivalently, the controller will acquire the asset unless the price is more than 45 percent higher than its real value to the firm.

In this model, too, the deciding factor is the magnitude of private benefits accruing to the controller when he keeps or acquires the asset, and private benefits tend to come from self-dealing or appropriation opportunities. In the Korean context, typical private benefits also took the form of arbitrary and preferential borrowing from the firms and many kinds of outright cash payments to the controlling shareholders. These models suggest that the unique agency costs structure of the chaebol as a CMS firm pushes chaebols to pursue more growth than otherwise.

Bebchuk *et al.* (2000) find that a similar kind of agency cost happens to the borrower-controller of the firms as the debt-equity ratio increases. In other words, the higher the debt-equity ratio, the more likely the controller is to take risky projects which provide more return upon success. This is the agency cost of the highly leveraged firm. Milgrom and Roberts (1992) also observe that an unjustifiable expansion drive can prevail when the controller of the firm expects that the costs of any failure would be shared or transferred to the lenders, whereas the benefits of any success are monopolized by the incumbent management.

Relative performance comparison between the business groups and stand-alone firms has been one of the important issues in both academia and practices. In the Korean context, the debate has been the comparison between the chaebols and non-chaebols. In this debate, chaebols are considered to be firms under concentrated ownership since researchers find a controlling family in each chaebol group. This chapter does not accept this perception of the chaebol and argues that it is misleading and cannot explain the observed behavior of chaebols. We observe that a chaebol is neither a dispersed ownership firm nor a concentrated ownership firm, and is rather a kind of CMS (controlling minority structure) firm. If we perceive chaebols as a kind of CMS firm, it becomes quite easy to explain several important features of chaebols, including aggressive expansion which is often unjustifiable in terms of the interests of the shareholders.

If we look at the growth of chaebols in terms of artificial rents associated with institutional voids or state intervention in terms of domestic market protection and preferential loans, it would be natural for chaebols to take advantage of these rents in pursuing growth with diversification. However, the existence of rents does not seem enough to explain the expansion tendency of chaebols, especially given the fact that there has been a substantial degree of market liberalization and reduction of subsidized loans since the 1980s. As a matter of fact, the chaebols were perceived to acquire, or enter into, businesses which were not justifiable in terms of rate of return of investment even in the 1990s. In other words, we need to look at the intrinsic mechanism leading to the unjustifiable investment drive which had contributed to the declining financial performance of the business groups. This is the reason we need to resort to the concept of CMS firms. According to this model, a CMS firm like a chaebol tends to pursue "unjustifiable" growth since the actual share of the controller is so small. Such an investment drive should lead to over-capacity and low productive efficiency as confirmed by the regression analysis of the production functions done in Lee *et al.* (2002). Joh (2003) also finds that the separation of control rights and cash flow rights in Korean chaebols led to lower profitability.

Lee *et al.* (2002) have examined the controller's share in the chaebol and non-chaebol firms to find that the owner-controller's shares are significantly higher in non-chaebol firms. It confirms that in the chaebol firms, the owners' share continued to decline over the sample period, which is confirmed by a simple regression using time-trend as an explanatory variable. We can thus infer that the decreasing share of the owner-controller aggravated the agency costs of the controlling-owner, and led to the inefficient investment drive in the chaebol firms.

To verify this argument, Lee *et al.* (2002) have run the regressions where the difference in the investment rate between chaebols and non-chaebols is specified as a function of cash flow of the firm, the difference between chaebols and non-chaebols in the share of owner-controller and a proxy for Tobin's Q measured by the market value divided by the book value of the firms. The model is similar to the model used in Sharfstein (1998) and Kim (2002). They find that the coefficient of the ownership difference variable was negative and significant in the 1990s, while it was negative and not significant in the 1980s. It shows that the investment rate difference between chaebol and non-chaebol firms in the 1990s can be explained by the difference in the shares held by the owner-controller, and that the smaller the owner-controller's shares is in each firm, as in chaebol firms, the more the firms invest. As a matter of fact, the chaebol firms started to invest much more in the 1990s, compared to non-chaebol firms.[6]

This result with long-term trend of controller's share and investment drive has important implications for the business group as a device for development and transition. We know that the controller's share tends to decrease with firm growth over time unless he/she has enormous personal financial resources to keep up his/her share at a certain level. Given the CMS structure in place, the continuing decrease of the share of the controlling family implies the aggravation of the agency costs and the increasing possibility of inefficient investment decision and firm expansion. What would be the final consequences of this dynamic process had already been shown by the sad story of the Korean chaebols. The strategic implication is then that the business groups should act to correct the CMS structure of the firm. Various things are to be done. The first is to reduce the private benefits of the controller by making the management more transparent and accountable since it is this private benefit that the controller is aiming at. Formation of stock pyramids itself might not be regulated. As long as there is active participation of non-controlling shareholders and high protection of their rights, for instance, by derivative suits and class actions, any expropriation of non-controlling shareholders in the CMS firm may be checked better. Enhanced checks and balance with better corporate governance would also help solve the problem of inefficient investment decisions by the controller.

The vested interests of the big business hampering liberalization

As explained above, while it was good to have big business groups for the purpose of a fast track approach to economic development, it might become a hurdle in further economic development in the long run. In other words, as Khanna (2000) and Kali (1999) point out, the mere existence of a group might hamper the development of the market. The explanation goes like this. Since groups rely on internal sources of financing, the demand for analyst services might be attenuated. Analysts might find it difficult to evaluate groups. In this context, we would like to illustrate the case of Korea where the existence of big players like chaebols distorted the course of financial liberalization.[7]

In the early phase of Korea's economic development, when the government was in a position to select chaebols for subsidized credit, the quasi-internal organization was efficient as it could economize on the cost of information gathering and policy implementation (C. Lee 1982). Thus, the role of its financial system was largely that of financing the growth of chaebols at the behest of the government. It was the state that made the decision in allocating subsidized credit, and the commercial banks, which were nationalized, served in effect as a channel of government-directed credit allocation.

The success of the quasi-internal organization, however, planted the seeds of its own demise as chaebols grew and became a dominant force in the national economy. This system encouraged chaebols to pursue a heavily indebted growth strategy, and as long as the state was in control of credit allocation and chaebols had no major alternative source of credit, the state was able to use them as an effective instrument for economic development. In time, however, chaebols grew and their power vis-à-vis the state increased as their place in the economy expanded. In consequence, the government could no longer unilaterally change its financial policy, freeing interest rates, as the resulting higher rates would have put a heavy debt burden on chaebols.

Thus, even after the big business grew beyond "small infants," the government tended to find it difficult to initiate policies that would affect the big business adversely. For example, in the early 1980s the government began undertaking several measures of financial liberalization under the influence of rising free-market ideology and pressures from abroad to open financial markets. Actually, throughout the 1980s the government undertook several measures of financial liberalization, but they did not change its basic stance of low interest rate policy. Rather, the government had to allow the chaebols to acquire and/or start several non-bank financial institutions (NBFIs) as they wanted to have alternative financial sources other than the commercial banks that were under government control.

Thus, one of the byproducts of the limited financial liberalization in the 1980s was the growth of NBFIs, many of which were owned by chaebols and were used by them as a source of external financing. This access to an alternative source of finance gave chaebols greater independence from the government, and this independence plus their importance in the national economy gave them the political power to influence government policies, especially various liberalization matters. Granted that free-market ideology and the increasing pressure from the outside world set the stage for financial liberalization in Korea, it was the interest politics of chaebols that shaped the final outcome of Korea's post-1993 financial liberalization.

Economic liberalization, if correctly carried out, is supposed to establish a competitive market in which many sellers of financial instruments compete in an open, rule-based manner. But, in an economy where there are a few dominant players with a strong stake in controlling their sources of finance, the course that economic liberalization takes may not be what many of its advocates had in mind. It will be manipulated to reflect the interests of big players, and its outcome is likely to be different from a competitive market.

We can point out at least two abnormalities in the course of economic liberalization in Korea. First, it is natural and desirable that liberalization and inducement of foreign direct investment should go first before the liberalization of portfolio investment is enacted. However, in the case of Korea, even until the late 1990s, the amount of FDI was very small. The multinational corporations (MNCs), that could pose a potential threat to chaebols playing in oligopolistic domestic markets, were not much either welcomed or encouraged by the dominant policy coalition between the government and chaebols.

Second, "inward" financial liberalization should go first, so as to allow foreign banks and financial institutions to come into Korea and compete against local financial institutions. However, in the case of Korea, it was done in reverse order; in other words, "outward" financial liberalization was carried out first so that chaebols and chaebol-owned banks and NBFI's may go abroad to borrow at much lower interest rates than the local rates. Actually, it was a kind of "give-and-take" between the government and the chaebols; the government wanted to initiate full-scale financial liberalization which was expected to increase interest rates, and, in return, had to give chaebols alternative and attractive sources for financial transactions, that is, offshore banking. But, neither the government nor the chaebols wanted to open fully the domestic financial markets for foreign financial players. The outcome was simply "asymmetric" financial liberalization.

Our analysis of the Korean experience clearly demonstrates that simply removing the state from financial markets in an economy dominated by a few large players will not necessarily lead to the establishment of a well-functioning financial system. In such an economy, as in Korea with its chaebols – a legacy of the earlier development strategy – a few dominant players will manipulate financial liberalization to achieve their parochial objectives that are not necessarily in the nation's interest. Thus, unless this structural problem of a few players dominating the economy is first resolved, deregulation – simply removing state intervention from markets – will not necessarily bring about an outcome beneficial to the nation. Worse, it may plant the seeds for a financial crisis at a later date.

Summary

There is a growing number of research papers on business groups as they are now found in numerous economies around the world. The majority of the literature looks at the business groups as a response to market failure or institutional voids in emerging economies. However, if we see business groups as an evolutionary response to the institutional environment of the economy, there is no interesting policy or strategic issue involved. This paper has argued that the business group is not simply a passive response to the environment but can serve as an organizational device for economic development and transition. We observe that the main strength of the business group in catch-up is to facilitate entry into new markets or lines of business that were formerly monopolized by the forerunning companies. The business group can facilitate market entry by mobilizing financial resources into new affiliates and helping them during the initial period of business by providing markets, capital, technology and brand names.

This paper also addresses the important question of why business groups tend to fall into trouble. In this regard, it is argued that while the business group is effective in response to market failure and/or catch-up, the benefits come with long-term caveats in three dimensions. The following three potential dangers are discussed in sequence. First, the benefits of economic value creation by the business groups tend to decline over the long run as institutions evolve and markets become mature. Second, family-controlled business groups, taking the form of the CMS firm, tend to be subject to increasingly serious agency problems resulting in value-destroying, inefficient investment drives. Third, the existence of the big players like business groups in an economy might hamper the sound development of a competitive market economy by distorting or manipulating the course of liberalization, deregulation or opening-up.

Notes

1 To see whether this difference arises from the fact that in the sample many of the Chaebol affiliates are not listed companies, while all of the non-chaebol firms are listed, they also tried the same method using the listed companies to get the same results.
2 For the "chop-shop" approach, see Lang and Stulz (1994).
3 To get the market value of equity, we multiply a total number of stocks by the year average of the stock price.
4 It was actually during the 1980s that the government itself first declared it was switching from the policies of selective intervention to those of functional intervention. Since then, this policy line has been basically maintained.
5 The estimated profit rates are the adjusted measures, which are different from the profit rates measured in terms of the book values; they are estimated using the market values of the assets of the firms. In general, they show a decreasing trend over the period concerned. For the large-sized firms which include most of the chaebol firms, the profit rates have changed from 0.3 percent during the 1980–4 period and 13.3 percent during the 1985–8 period to 0.2 percent during the 1990–6 period.
6 Lee, Lee and Yoo (2001) also find that chaebols' investment was inefficient compared to non-chaebols, and this has to do with the ownership problem.
7 For more details, see Lee *et al.* (2002).

References

Au, K., Peng, M.W. and Wang, D. (2000) "Interlocking Directorates, Firm Strategies, and Performance in Hong Kong: Towards a Research Agenda," *Asia Pacific Journal of Management*, 17(1): 29–47.
Bebchuk, L., Reinier, K. and Triantis, G. (2000) "Stock Pyramids, Cross-Ownership, and Dual Class Equity: The Creation and Agency Costs of Separating Control from Cash Flow Rights," in R. Morck (ed.) *Concentrated Corporate Ownership*, Chicago: University of Chicago Press.
Berger, P. and Ofek, E. (1995) "Diversification's Effect on Firm Value," *Journal of Financial Economics*, 37(1): 39–65.
Berle, A.A. Jr. and Means, G.C. (1932) *The Modern Corporation and Private Property*, New York: McMillan.
Chang, S.J. and Choi, U.H. (1988) "Strategy, Structure and Performance of Korean Business Groups: A Transaction Cost Approach," *The Journal of Industrial Economics*, 37(2): 141–58.
Chi, S. (1996) *Zhongguo Qiyejituan Yanjiu [Studies on the China Corporate Group]*, Jinan: Jinan Chubanshe (Jinan Publishing House) (in Chinese).
Fauver, L., Houston, J. and Naranjo, A. (1999) "Capital Market Development, Legal Systems and the Value of Corporate Diversification: A Cross Country Analysis," University of Florida Working Paper.
Freinkman L. (1995) "Financial-Industrial Groups in Russia," *Communist Economies and Economic Transformation*, 7(1): 51–66.
Gerlach, M. (1989) "Keiretsu Organization in the Japanese Economy," in C.

Johnson, L. Tyson and J. Zysman (eds) *Politics and Productivity*, New York: Harper Business.

Ghemawat, P. and Khanna, T. (1998) "The Nature of Diversified Business Groups: A Research Agenda and Two Case Studies," *Journal of Industrial Economics*, 46(1): 35–61.

Goto, A. (1982) "Business Groups in Market Economy," *European Economic Review*, 19(1): 53–70.

Granovetter, M. (1995) "Coase Revisited: Business Groups in the Modern Economy," *Industrial and Corporate Change*, 4(1): 93–130.

Guillen M. (2000) "Business Groups in Emerging Economies: A Resource-Based View," *Academy of Management Journal*, 43(3): 362–80.

Hahn, D. (1997) "Guanyu zhongguo qiye jituan yu guojia konggu qongsi de yanjiu" (A Study on Business Groups and the State Holding Companies in China), unpublished doctoral dissertation, Peking University (in Chinese).

Joh, S.W. (2003) "Corporate Governance and Firm Profitability: Evidence from Korea before the Economic Crisis," *Journal of Financial Economics*, 68(2): 287–322.

Kali, R. (1999) "Endogenous Business Networks," *Journal of Law, Economics and Organization*, 15(3): 615–36.

Keister, L. (1998) "Engineering Growth: Business Group Structure and Firm Performance in China's Transition Economy," *American Journal of Sociology*, 104(2): 404–40.

Khanna, T. (2000) "Business Groups and Social Welfare in Emerging Markets: Existing Evidence and Unanswered Questions," *European Economic Review*, 44(4–6): 748–61.

Khanna, T. and Palepu, K. (1997) "Why Focused Strategies May Be Wrong for Emerging Markets," *Harvard Business Review*, 75(4): 41–51.

——(2000) "Is Group Affiliation Profitable in Emerging Markets? An Analysis of Diversified Indian Business Groups," *Journal of Finance* 55 (April): 867–91.

Kim, C. (2002) "Is The Investment of Korean Conglomerates Inefficient?" *Korean Economic Review*, 18(1): 5–24.

La Porta, R., Lopes-de-Silanies, F. and Schleifer, A. (1999) "Corporate Ownership around the World," *Journal of Finance*, 54(2): 471–517.

Lang, L. and Stulz, R. (1994) "Tobin's Q, Corporate Diversification, and Firm Performance," *Journal of Political Economy*, 102(6): 1248–80.

Lee, C.H. (1982) "The Government Financial System, and Large Private Enterprise in the Economic Development of South Korea," *World Development*, 20(2): 187–97.

Lee, C., Lee, K. and Lee, K.K. (2002) "chaebols, Financial Liberalization and Economic Crisis: Transformation of Quasi-Internal Organization in Korea," *Asian Economic Journal*, 16(1): 17–35.

Lee, G.B. (1999) "Three Essays on Economic Growth and Income Distribution in Korea," Ph.D. Thesis, Seoul National University (in English).

Lee, J., Lee, Y. and Yoo, J. (2001) "Inefficiency in Investment Decisions of Korean Diversified Conglomerates," presented at the 2001 convention of the Korean Association for Financial Economics.

Lee, K. (2002) "Corporate Governance and Growth in Korean chaebols," in U. Haley and F. Richter (eds) *Asian Post-Crisis Management: Business and Governmental Strategies for Sustainable Competitive Advantages*, New York: Palgrave.

Lee, K., Ryu, K. and Yoon, J. (2001) "Productive Efficiency of chaebols and Non-

Chaebol Firms in Korea," Working Paper, Institute of Economic Research, Seoul National University.

—— (2002) "Long Term Performance of the Business Groups: The Case of chaebols in Korea," presented at the International Conference on Corporate Governance in Asia, organized by the Asian Institute for Corporate Governance, Korea University, May 2002.

Lee, K. and Woo, W. (2002) "Business Groups in China: Compared with Korean chaebols," in R. Hooley and J. Yoo (eds) *The Post-Financial Crisis Challenges for Asian Industrialization*, Amsterdam: Elsevier Sciences.

Leff, N. (1978) "Industrial Organization and Entrepreneurship in the Developing Countries; the Economic Groups," *Economic Development and Cultural Changes*, 26(4): 661–75.

Lincoln, J.R., Gerlach, M.L. and Takahashi, P. (1996) "Interfirm Networks and Corporate Performance in Japan," *American Sociological Review*, 61(1): 67–88.

Milgrom, P. and Roberts, J. (1992) *Economics, Organization & Management*, New York: Prentice Hall.

Peng, M.W. (2000) *Business Strategies in Transition Economies*, Thousand Oaks, CA: Sage Publications.

Sharfstein, D.S. (1998) "The Dark Side of Internal Capital Market: Evidence from Diversified Conglomerates," NBER Working Paper No. 6532.

Shin, H. and Park, Y.S. (1999) "Financing Constraints and Internal Capital Markets: Evidence from Korean chaebols," *Journal of Corporate Finance*, 5: 169–91.

Steers, R., Shin, Y.K. and Ungson, G. (1989) *The Chaebol: Korea's New Industrial Might*, New York: Harper and Row.

Strachan, H. (1976) *Family and Other Business Groups in Economic Development: The Case of Nicaragua*, New York: Praeger.

Yoon, J.I. (1998) "A Study on the Return on Stockholders' Equity in Korea," Ph.D. Thesis in Economics, Seoul National University (in Korean).

9 Will inward internationalization foster economic development in Latin America?

João Carlos Ferraz, Airton Valente Jr. and Mariana Iootty

Introduction

This chapter covers three related subjects, taking Latin America as the focus of analysis: the general and recent trend towards economic liberalization; the ongoing process of ownership change; and the policy challenges associated with a process of inward internationalization which is the outstanding structural feature of these economies. Following this introduction, where the primary questions of this article are posed, a stylized account of recent Latin American history is given, focusing on changes in the national regimes of incentives and regulations, in order to provide the framework of conditions facing the region. In the third section a comparative account (developed countries in Asia and Latin America) of the process of capital internationalization is made. Following from there, the process of ownership change in Latin America and in Brazil is analyzed. The sixth section discusses the nature of investments carried out by foreign firms in developing countries. In the last section policy challenges and implications are derived.

For the purposes of this chapter, departing from definitions found in Schlegel (1977), development is to be understood as a process of growth, with structural change and wealth distribution, intensive in learning. Conditioning factors and determinants of development are region/period specific and, looking back in history, few regularities prevail.

In terms of determinants of progress, innovation is the direct cause of structural change; the process of competition is an important innovation driver, and entrepreneurs are the relevant agents of competition (Dosi *et al.* 1990). Where progress was observed, corporations linked up with innovation networks composed of other firms, and research institutions were capable of increasing competences in order to explore expanding markets (Dosi and Fabiani 1994; OCDE 1999). In fact, as proposed by Boulding (1992), learning processes constitute a basic pillar of economic development. The State has had a proactive role in every process of national transformation even though its format, size and forms of intervention change among countries and over time. For analytical and normative purposes the relevant issue is not whether the State has a role to play in development, but how it is involved, and to what degree of success (Evans 1995).

Looking back in history and to the performance of nations, according to Maddison (1994), it is possible to observe a trend towards intra-leaders convergence and increasing distance between leaders and laggards. In this context, while only a few nations achieved productive catching-up, scientific and technological catching-up is an accomplishment for very few nations in very narrow areas of knowledge and expertise.

Given the increasing economic importance of innovation for development and the approximation between science, production and markets, are (dominant) economic agents in Latin America willing to develop local technological capabilities? This constitutes the core of the questions to be addressed in this article.

This is an exploratory analysis of ownership change and the main argument is as follows. In the recent past, through privatization and mergers and acquisitions, the ownership landscape of Latin American countries has been significantly internationalized, opening relevant questions in relation to the style of and possibilities for future development. It is argued that inward internationalization – an extensive process of one-way ownership change – is a very important recent phenomenon in the region, with long-lasting consequences. These new structural conditions pose important challenges. Within a context of liberalized economies, policy-makers of developing countries face the task of producing a new regime of incentives and regulations aimed at minimizing negative effects and maximizing benefits of internationalized economies.

Economic liberalization in Latin America

The most well known and relevant structural and framework conditions of Latin America are as follows:

- Rich natural resources and large potential markets, marked by strong regional and social inequalities;
- Insufficient and concentrated infrastructure conditions;
- Strong propensity towards generating low skilled jobs;
- Macroeconomic stabilization cum low investment rates as well as strong dependence on foreign resources;
- Economic liberalization as the main feature of national regimes with regard to incentives and regulation, meaning an increasing importance of private decision-making in the process of allocation of resources.

Given the importance of private competences for development, their main features are:

- Willingness to do business. There is a deep-rooted culture of negotiating and implementing contracts, within a capitalist framework. The vitality of the private sector is very remarkable;
- National and transnational companies occupy different spaces. Transnational companies (TNCs) are found in all areas/sectors/segments where the technical base is marked by wide opportunities and products are sensitive to income elasticity;
- Relative to international benchmarks, fragile competitiveness prevails; advantages are particularly noted in resource intensive industries;
- Companies are good at routines but weak in research activities. That is, local technological efforts are very low and firms extensively rely on external technologies.

Between 1930 and 1994 the region attained high growth but with a low contribution of technical progress (Abreu and Verner 1997). In the last 20 years macroeconomic instability and low rate of structural change prevailed in Latin America (Ferraz et al. 1999; Katz 1999). During the 1990s the main features associated with the productive sector were trade deficits, product and services updating and asymmetric modernization (CEPAL 1999).

During the 1980s Latin American economies were facing difficulties due to: (1) the debt crisis, which limited the access of local economies to growing international liquidity; (2) the disorganization of public finances, weakening the intervention capacity of the State and, (3) lack of economic dynamism, attendance to inflation, low growth and investment rates, increasing difficulties in accessing export markets and increasing obsolescence of productive systems.

These difficulties made clear the fragility of the so-called "inward oriented" or "import substitution" model: exports concentrated in the primary sector, protectionism for local economic activities, State presence in infrastructure and intermediate goods production and expansion of public expenditures.

External constraints, macroeconomic instability and low policy response capabilities proved to be a fertile ground for policy alternatives aimed at reverting the vicissitudes of the prevailing regime. Reforms were facilitated by the emergence, in international forums, of a new reference model, best summarized by what became known as the "Washington Consensus" (Williamson 1993).

Policy proposals were aimed at macroeconomic stabilization and economic liberalization and included: fiscal discipline, trade and financial liberalization, increasing reliance on market mechanisms, privatization and the heightened role of the private sector. Table 9.1 shows, in detail, the evolution of structural reforms in different countries of the region.

In terms of ownership regulations, the Latin American context is not different from international trends. Table 9.2 indicates that since 1991, an

Table 9.1 Evolution of structural reforms in Latin America 1970–95

	1976–9	1980–5	1986–90	1991–5
ARGENTINA				
Import liberalization	R	A	G	R
Export promotion		R	*	
Exchange liberalization	R	A		R
Deregulation of capital account	R	A	*	R
Deregulation for FDI	R			
Deregulation of exchange rate	R			
Privatization				R
BRAZIL				
Import liberalization			G	R
Export promotion				*
Exchange liberalization				R
Deregulation of capital account			G	
Deregulation for FDI				G
Deregulation of exchange rate				
Privatization				G&P
CHILE				
Import liberalization	R	*	*	R
Export promotion			P	
Exchange liberalization				R
Deregulation of capital account	P			
Deregulation for FDI	R			
Deregulation of exchange rate	R			
Privatization	R			P
MEXICO				
Import liberalization			P	
Export promotion	R		*	
Exchange liberalization		R		
Deregulation of capital account				R
Deregulation for FDI		R		
Deregulation of exchange rate		R		
Privatization		G&P		R

Source: CEPAL (1996).

Notes
R: radical reform; G: gradual reform; A: reversion of process; P: partial reform; *: suspension.

FDI-friendly trend has consistently increased. The number of countries that introduced changes in their investment regimes has increased from 35 in 1991 to 69 in 2000. This means that, in 2000, 147 countries all over the world were explicitly concerned with this issue, having adopted measures towards facilitating the entry and the operations of foreign firms on local grounds.

CEPAL (1996) suggests that differences in depth, breath and pattern of reforms are to be explained by countries' circumstances such as the following: economic conceptions of governmental technical teams, characteristics of local political systems and size of markets and the

Table 9.2 National regulatory changes, 1991–2003

	1991	1995	2000	2003
Number of countries that introduced changes in their investment regimes	35	64	69	82
Number of regulatory changes:	82	112	150	244
more favorable to FDI	80	106	147	220
less favorable to FDI	02	06	03	24

Source: UNCTAD, World Investment Report (2001, 2004).

Table 9.3 Latin America: evolution of consumer price index (December to December % variation)

	1991	1992	1993	1994	1995	1996	1997	1998	1999*
Latin America	199	414	877	333.1	25.8	18.2	10.4	10.3	8.6
Argentina	84.0	17.6	7.4	3.9	1.6	0.1	0.3	0.7	−1.3
Brazil	475.8	1,149.1	2,489.1	929.3	22.0	9.1	4.3	2.5	3.1
Chile	18.7	12.7	12.2	8.9	8.2	6.6	6.0	4.7	3.7
Mexico	18.9	11.9	8.0	7.1	52.1	27.7	15.7	18.6	17.4

Source: CEPAL (1999).

Note
*estimated.

existing productive and technological basis of countries. Argentina and Chile were already experimenting a first wave of liberal reforms during the 1970s, marking them as pioneers of a process that only later acquired a concerted format. Mexico inaugurated reforms during the first half of the 1980s, while in Brazil policy actions was undertaken during the 1991–5 period. During this last period most countries either entered a second wave of reforms or reinforced existing policy directions, showing a definite commitment to a regime of incentives and regulations favorable to economic liberalization. From the institutional perspective of globalization, the above evidence indicates a close approximation of the region to recommendations found in international organizations like the IMF and the World Bank or the liberal policy practices of most developed countries.

In these countries, with the exception of Chile, institutional changes were preceded by or introduced simultaneously with macroeconomic policies aiming at inflation control, through a combination of monetary or exchange anchors and import liberalization. Table 9.3 indicates that, in this area, all countries achieved significant success.

However, sustained economic growth was not attained and external vulnerability remained high. The regional current account remained negative throughout the 1990s, at around 2.6 percent (CEPAL 2002). The Argentinean crisis of 2001 onwards is an example; the expected negative growth rate for 2002 (between 15 and 20 percent) will be double that observed in the US during the 1929 Great Depression.

The analytical question to be addressed is as follows: if economic liberalization is becoming an important feature of national regimes with regard to incentive and regulation, what is the best way to aim at, simultaneously, (1) regulations capable of ensuring a pro-innovative competitive environment and (2) effective incentives to attract economic agents to invest in local technological capabilities?

The internationalization of capital

The increasing internationalization of the world economy can be seen in Table 9.4. Since 1982 FDI inflows have increased twenty times, reaching, in 2000, US$1.2 trillion. During these years, M&A, not greenfield investment, became the prevalent mode of expansion of foreign firms: from 26.7 percent of total FDI inflow in 1990 in Latin America, to 52.5 percent in 2000 (Table 9.5). This is a recent phenomenon, most probably associated with the worldwide liberalization of national economies. The specialized literature has always placed emphasis on the contribution of FDI investment to host economies, the most important being the opening up of new and modern operations. However, the panorama of the new millennium is very different from the past, as foreign firms are acquiring existing assets and market power in host countries. Although acquisitions imply organizational changes in acquired firms, and probably some degree of modernization, the net gains for local economies are smaller,

Table 9.4 Selected indicators of FDI and international production, 1982–2000 (US$ billion)

	1982	1990	2000	2003
World FDI inflows	57	202	1,271	559
Cross border M&A	n.a.	151	1,144	296
Sales of foreign affiliates	2,465	5,467	15,680	17,580
Employment of foreign affiliates (thousand employees)	17,454	23,721	45,587	54,170
Exports of foreign affiliates	637	1,166	3,572	3,077
Exports of goods and non-factor services (world)	2,124	4,381	7,036	9,228
Gross product of foreign affiliates	565	1,420	3,167	3,706
GDP at factor cost (world)	10,612	21,475	31,895	36,163*

Source: UNCTAD, *World Investment Report* (2001, 2004).

Note
*at current prices.

Table 9.5 M&A to FDI ratio (%)

Region	1995		2000	
	% asset sales to inward FDI	% asset acquisition to outward FDI	% asset sales to inward FDI	% asset acquisition to outward FDI
Developed Countries	80.9	56.1	105.2	104.6
Developing Counties	14.1	26.1	29.0	42.3
Latin America	26.7	54.1	52.5	138.5
Argentina	33.3	132.0	47.3	74.0
Brazil	31.4	170.6	15.7	22.6
Mexico	7.5	–	30.1	264.4
Asia	9.2	21.3	15.5	29.9

Source: Compiled from UNCTAD, *World Investment Report* (2001).

relative to greenfield investments. At the same time, as the market power of acquiring firms expands, consequences for the competitive environment and consumer welfare are still unclear. The meaning and implications of this process are still to open to interpretation.

With the expansion of investment there was a corresponding increase in sales of foreign affiliates, from US$2.4 trillion in 1982 to US$17.58 trillion in 2003. Total employment has also increased, but at a slower pace: from 17 million to 54 million since 1982. Export of foreign affiliates shows a similar trend, expanding at a higher rate in world exports. This means an increasing share of foreign affiliates in world exports: from 30 percent in 1982 to 51 percent in 2000. The net result of ownership internationalization is economically very relevant: the share of foreign affiliates of TNCs in world GDP increased from 5 to 10 percent between 1982 and 2003.

The internationalization of capital by means of FDI can be further examined in terms of investment flows and their contribution to capital formation in national economies and regions. As shown in Table 9.6, among developed countries between 1989 and 2000, FDI inflow and outflow have increased practically tenfold, from US$137 billion to US$1,046 billion. This means that investments by foreign companies in 2000 came to represent 19.4 percent of gross fixed capital formation of developed countries, up from 3.7 percent just ten years before. By all accounts, this expansion is phenomenal, with long lasting consequences, even taking into consideration that, after 2001, the rate of expansion apparently has been receding.

Among developed countries there are different FDI patterns: besides being the world leader in FDI, with 20 to 25 percent of total share, the USA showed a balanced pattern between inflow and outflow. Even though, in 2000, the capacity to attract investments was higher than the

Region	1989–94		1995		2000 (% GFCF 1999 data)		2003	
	Inflows	Outflows	Inflows	Outflows	Inflows	Outflows	Inflows	Outflows
Developed countries	**137,124**	**203,231**	**203,462**	**305,847**	**1,005,178**	**1,046,335**	**366,572**	**569,676**
% GFCF	**3.7**	**5.5**	**4.4**	**6.7**	**17**	**19.4**	**6.7**	**10.3**
USA	42,535	49,024	58,772	92,074	281,115	139,257	29,772	151,884
% GFCF	4.8	5.4	5.3	8.3	17.9	8.6	1.5	7.5
UK	19,236	24,249	24,435	43,562	130,428	249,794	14,514	55,093
% GFCF	10.7	14	10.9	23.7	32.5	80.6	5.0	19.0
Japan	969	29,576	39	22,508	8,187	32,886	6,324	28,800
% GFCF	–	2.9	–	1.5	1.1	1.9	0.6	2.6
Developing countries	**59,578**	**24,925**	**113,338**	**48,987**	**240,167**	**99,546**	**172,032**	**35,591**
% GFCF	**5.2**	**2.4**	**7.7**	**3.3**	**3.8**	**3.3**	**10.0**	**2.1**
L. America	17,506	3,698	32,311	7,306	86,172	13,442	49,721	10,665
% GFCF	**6.2**	1	**9.6**	**1.2**	**27.3**	**3.1**	**11.2**	**2.3**
Argentina	2,694	482	5,609	1,498	11,152	912	478	774
% GFCF	8.6	1.1	12.1	3.2	47.7	2.5	1.9	3.1
Brazil	1,498	595	5,475	1,163	33,547	2,984	10,143	249
% GFCF	1.7	0.7	3.8	0.8	31.3	1.4	11.4	0.3
Mexico	6,571	349	9,526	–263	13,162	1,600	10,783	1,390
% GFCF	10.1	0.5	20.6	–0.6	11.7	1.2	8.9	1.1
Asia	**37,659**	**20,335**	**75,293**	**41,149**	**143,479**	**85,204**	**107,119**	**23,608**
% GFCF	**4.9**	**3**	**7.2**	**4.1**	**9.6**	**3.5**	**9.3**	**2.1**
China	13,951	2,154	35,849	2,000	40,772	2,324	53,505	1,800
% GFCF	7.9	1.3	14.7	0.8	11.3	–	12.4	0.4
H. Kong	4,164	9,236	6,213	25,000	64,448	63,036	13,560	3,769
% GFCF	14.8	30.2	14.6	58.7	60.2	47.4	38.4	10.7
Korea	869	1,350	1,776	3,552	10,186	3,697	3,752	3,429
% GFCF	0.8	1.2	1	2	9.3	2.2	2.1	1.9
Malaysia	3,964	681	5,816	2,488	5,542	2,919	2,474	1,369
% GFCF	19.4	2.8	1.5	6.4	20.1	9.3	10.8	6.0

Source: Compiled from UNCTAD, *World Investment Report* (2001, 2004).

willingness to invest abroad, in 2003, the outflow surpassed the inflow. It is also notable that in the UK, in 2000 and 2003, the willingness to invest abroad was much higher than the capacity of that economy to attract FDI investment, reinforcing the previously established outward trend of that economy. In fact, the role of the UK is similar to that of Hong Kong in Asia; as a financial center to other economies, it captures resources and channels them worldwide. The Japanese case is very peculiar and opposite of the UK's. There, not only is the role of FDI in the economy much lower than that of other developed countries but also, most importantly, the willingness to invest abroad is much higher than the capacity to attract foreign firms. However, from 1995 onwards, there are important changes: outflow has stabilized while inflow has expanded.

For developing countries, as expected, the volume of FDI inflow is higher than FDI outflow; roughly a 2:1 ratio has persisted over the years. But, more recently, FDI inflow has expanded, coming to represent, in 2003, 10.0 percent of the region's capital formation. In that year US$172 billion was invested in developing regions while residents of these regions invested US$35 billion abroad. It is important to note that of this, US$3.7 billion of these investments originated solely from Hong Kong.

Latin America takes up one third of FDI inflows to developing regions, amounting, in 2003, to US$49 billion. This means that, during that year, 11.2 percent of the region's capital formation came from foreign companies while only 3.3 percent, or US$10.6 billion, was invested abroad. Capital inflow to the region increased in particular because of the role of Brazil; while in the period 1989–94 the country attracted only US$1.5 billion on average, inflow amounted to US$33 billion in 2000. As will be shown later in further detail, this sharp increase is associated with the return of price stabilization, economic liberalization and, most importantly, privatization. The interesting case in Latin America is that of Mexico; there FDI is relatively less important to capital formation (8.9 percent in 2003) despite the country's integration with the USA and Canada.

In Asia FDI has increased from an annual average of US$37 billion between 1989 and 1994 to US$107 billion in 2003. China and Hong Kong take up most of the resources: US$53 billion and US$13 billion respectively. FDI has increased substantially in Korea: from US$869 million on average, between 1989 and 1994, to US$10 billion in 2000. The pattern in Malaysia has not changed significantly over the years; it attracts between US$2.5 and US$5 billion of FDI annually. As stated above, the differing pattern is that of Hong Kong. In fact the region is the financial powerhouse of China and, perhaps, of other economies of the region.

As mentioned above, the new feature of the recent FDI upsurge is the increasing importance of M&A as the mode through which firms are investing abroad. Table 9.5 shows that the size of these operations is, in some cases, even greater than the amount of FDI inflow or outflow. In developed countries the ratio of asset acquisition to FDI outflow has increased from 56.1 percent to 104.6 percent, between 1995 and 2000. In developing regions, where capital inflow is more important, the absolute size and relative importance of inward M&A is lower than in developed regions, but it has increased from 14.1 percent of total inflow to 29 percent. In Latin America this trend is even more pronounced, as the ratio of M&A to FDI inflow increased from 26.7 percent to 52.5 percent. The exception is Brazil, because of the FDI upsurge in 2000. In Asia, however, although the trend is similar, the importance of M&A is less pronounced, reaching, in 2000, 15.5 percent of total FDI inflow.

The result of this recent expansion of internationalization is shown in Table 9.7. When the FDI stock data is taken into account, differences among regions and countries emerge more clearly. For developed countries internationalization is a dual carriageway, with prevalence of outward stocks over inward stocks, especially in the case of the UK. Presently the US shows a relatively balanced position, thanks to the increasing importance of inward investment. Japan demonstrates relatively low levels of asset internationalization in both directions.

For developing regions inward internationalization prevails; that is, the importance of inward FDI stocks is greater than outward stocks, representing 31.4 percent of 2003 GDP. But, even among developing regions, important differences exist: Latin America plays more of a host role than Asia. In the former, in 2003, inward stocks represented 36.8 percent of regional GDP while 10.7 percent of their assets were held elsewhere. Differences among the main countries of the region are not significant. In Asia, although the recipient position is higher than that of the investor (30.3 percent and 13.6 percent respectively), since 1980, the trend has been towards an increasing willingness of local firms to own assets elsewhere. Again, the explanation of this Asian pattern is to be found in the role Hong Kong has played in channeling increasing investment funds to the region, especially to China.

In short, this paper illustrates a relatively well-known economic fact. As shown in Table 9.8, developed countries do concentrate economic power over international transactions, being responsible for the majority of FDI inflow and outflow, exports, imports and technology payments. Developing countries perform better on exports and imports (27.5 percent and 26.2 percent of total) and as the recipient of FDI (21.4 percent of inflows and 31.3 percent of FDI stock). Latin America's share is higher on these last two items, while the Asian region performs better on exports and imports. Central and Eastern Europe are responsible for 4 percent of trade transactions and around 2 percent of FDI inflow. Africa is the region that shows least benefit from the internationalization of capital.

When the data for FDI inward stock is disaggregated into major economic activities, some interesting general and regional trends are revealed. As shown in Table 9.9, the relative importance of major economic sectors does not change: tertiary sectors are those into which FDI

Table 9.7 FDI outward/inward stock, selected years, countries and regions, in US$ million and as % of GDP

Region	1980 Inward stock	1980 Outward stock	1990 Inward stock	1990 Outward stock	2000 Inward stock	2000 Outward stock	2003 Inward stock	2003 Outward stock
Developed countries	**374,968**	**507,366**	**1,397,983**	**1,637,265**	**4,210,294**	**5,248,522**	**5,701,633**	**7,272,319**
% GDP	**4.7**	**6.4**	**8.4**	**9.8**	**14.5**	**19.0**	**20.7**	**26.4**
USA	83,046	220,178	394,911	430,521	1,238,627	1,244,654	1,553,955	20,169,013
% GDP	3.1	8.1	7.1	7.8	11.1	13.1	14.1	18.8
UK	63,014	80,434	203,894	229,294	482,798	901,769	672,014	1,128,584
% GDP	11.7	15	20.8	23.4	26.8	49.8	37.4	62.7
Japan	3,270	19,610	9,850	201,440	54,303	281,664	89,729	335,499
% GDP	0.3	1.9	0.3	6.8	1	5.7	2.1	7.8
Developing countries	**240,837**	**16,484**	**487,694**	**79,821**	**1,979,262**	**710,305**	**2,208,171**	**858,681**
% GDP	**10.2**	**0.9**	**13.4**	**2.6**	**28.0**	**10.1**	**31.4**	**12.2**
L. America	**49,960**	**9,119**	**116,678**	**19,476**	**606,907**	**111,051**	**647,678**	**183,843**
% GDP	**6.5**	**1.3**	**10.8**	**1.8**	**25.6**	**4.9**	**36.8**	**10.7**
Argentina	5,344	6,128	9,085	6,105	73,441	20,189	35,100	21,302
% GDP	6.9	8	6.4	4.3	22.1	6.8	27.1	16.4
Brazil	17,480	652	37,143	2,397	197,652	15,089	128,425	54,646
% GDP	7.4	0.3	8	0.5	21.6	1.6	25.8	11.0
Mexico	8,105	136	22,424	575	91,222	8,639	165,904	13,815
% GDP	3.6	–	8.5	0.2	16.4	1.5	26.5	2.2
Asia	**173,347**	**6,240**	**328,232**	**47,520**	**1,261,776**	**577,602**	**1,461,518**	**634,792**
% GDP	**14.2**	**0.7**	**15.4**	**2.7**	**30.2**	**13.6**	**30.3**	**13.6**
China	6,251	39	24,762	2,489	346,694	27,212	501,471	37,006
% GDP	3.1	–	7	0.7	30.9	2.5	35.6	2.6
H. Kong	138,767	148	162,665	11,920	469,776	384,732	375,048	336,098
% GDP	487	0.5	217.5	15.9	255.5	202.8	236.5	211.9
Korea	1,140	127	5,186	2,301	42,329	25,842	47,465	34,531
% GDP	1.8	0.2	2	0.9	7.9	5.5	7.8	5.7
Malaysia	5,169	197	10,318	2,671	54,315	19,799	58,978	29,685
% GDP	21.1	0.8	24.1	6.2	65.3	22.6	57.2	28.8

Source: Compiled from UNCTAD, *World Investment Report*, (2001, 2004).

Table 9.8 Geographical distribution of FDI flows, trade, domestic investment and technology payments, 1998–2000 (annual average, %)

Region	Inflows	Outflows	Exports	Imports	Investment	Tech. payment	FDI inward stock	FDI outward stock
Developed countries	76.3	92.9	68.4	69.7	74.5	85.6	66.7	87.8
Developing countries	21.4	6.8	27.5	26.2	23.3	13.1	31.3	11.9
Africa	0.8	0.1	1.6	1.5	1.4	0.8	1.5	0.3
Latin America	9.2	1.5	5.1	5.7	5.9	3.8	9.6	1.9
Asia & Pacific	11.2	5.2	20.4	18.5	15.8	0.1	20.0	9.7
Central & Eastern Europe	2.3	0.3	4.1	4.2	2.2	1.3	2.0	0.3
World	100	100	100	100	100	100	100	100

Source: UNCTAD, *World Investment Report* (2001).

mostly flows, followed by secondary and primary activities. However, between 1988 and 1999 these differences increase. By 1999 tertiary sectors had taken up 55.5 percent of total inward FDI stocks in developed countries, 52.2 percent in Latin America and 33.6 percent in Asia. Within tertiary activities, the financial sector is the outstanding internationalized economic activity.

The importance of FDI stocks in the primary sector decreased everywhere, with the exception of Latin America, where it increased from 9.6 percent in 1988 to 12.0 percent in 1999. In Asia emphasis is on manufacturing; it represented 68.9 percent and 60.2 percent of total FDI stock in 1988 and 1999 respectively. In Latin America and in developed regions, these activities took up approximately a third of total FDI stock, and changes are not pronounced. Chemical and electronic related sectors are the most internationalized; investments there are expanding, although their relative share decreased, especially in Asia.

There is an interesting contrast between Asia and Latin America in terms of size and rate of growth of investments in these two sectors, between 1988 and 1999. In Asia, FDI stocks in chemicals went up from US$8.3 to US$32.5 billion, a four-fold increase; in Latin America they increase two-fold, from US$6.7 to US$13.1 billion. In electrical and electronics, as expected, relatively to Latin America, Asia is ahead, but differences are very significant. While in Asia FDI stocks increased from US$9 to US$42.2 billion, in Latin America they remained stagnant, at US$3 billion, between 1988 and 1999. However, when tertiary activities are taken into account, the situation is reversed: FDI stocks are larger in Latin America. This data shows, clearly, that FDI in Asia is directed towards tradable goods and in Latin America towards non-tradable goods. Consequently trends in trade and current accounts of the two regions are diametrically opposite. Asia is a potential exporter of high-income elasticity of demand goods, while Latin America is a net importer.

As mentioned above, in the world, the financial sector is the leading internationalized economic activity. For this sector, in 1999, FDI stocks in developed countries amounted to US$518 billion, up from US$160 billion in 1988. In Latin America expansion is even greater, from US$3.1 to US$23.8 billion. In Asia there is also a sharp increase – from US$1.7 to US$14.0 billion, but the relative importance of FDI stocks is lower, around 2 percent of total stock.

For Latin America, Table 9.10 provides further detail on the general picture given above. When the 500 largest firms of the region are taken into account, the relative share of firms from the service sector increases from 34.4 percent in 1990–2 to 42.2 percent in 1998–2000. Correspondingly, there is a decrease in the number of firms belonging to the manufacturing industry. But, in economic terms, the picture is slightly different; the relative importance of firms from the primary sector decreased through the years, although they remained responsible for 22 percent of sales in 1998–2000. The contribution of firms from manufacturing

Table 9.9 FDI inward stock, by industry and region, 1988, 1999 (in US$ billion and %)

Industry	Developed countries				Asia				Latin America			
	1988		1999		1988		1999		1988		1999	
	Value	Share	Value	Share	Value	Share	Value	Share	Value	Share	Value	Share
Total	890.5	100.0	2,520.0	100.0	65.1	100.0	796.6	100.0	50.0	100.0	193.4	100.0
Primary	91.7	10.3	144.4	5.7	8.5	13.1	28.1	3.5	4.5	9.6	23.2	12.0
Secondary	350.8	39.4	916.3	36.4	44.9	68.9	479.4	60.2	30.9	65.8	63.4	32.8
Chemicals	42.9	4.8	190.7	7.6	8.3	12.7	32.5	4.1	6.7	14.3	13.1	6.8
E. Eletr*	36.9	4.1	81.8	3.2	9.0	13.9	42.2	5.3	3.0	6.5	3.0	1.6
Tertiary	418.0	46.9	1,399.3	55.5	11.1	17.1	267.5	33.6	11.5	24.6	101.0	52.2
Trade	128.3	14.4	322.8	12.8	1.0	1.6	32.7	4.1	2.1	4.4	12.0	6.2
Finance	160.0	18.0	518.8	20.6	1.7	2.6	14.0	1.8	3.1	6.7	23.8	12.3

Source: Compiled from UNCTAD, *World Investment Report* (2001).

Note
*E. Eletr: electro-electronic industries.

Table 9.10 The largest 500 Latin American companies, 1990–2000, by sector of origin (number, sales in US$ million and %)

	1990–2		1994–6		1998–2000	
	Value	%	Value	%	Value	%
Number	500	100.0	500	100.0	500	100.0
Primary	50	10.0	46	9.2	51	10.0
Manufacturing	278	55.6	264	52.8	239	47.8
Service	172	34.4	190	38.0	211	42.2
Sales	361.0	100.0	601.8	100.0	686.8	100.0
Primary	100.1	27.7	143.5	23.9	150.8	22.0
Manufacturing	153.0	42.4	259.9	43.2	277.9	40.5
Service	107.9	29.9	198.3	33.0	258.1	37.5

Source: CEPAL (2001, Cuadro I-A.4).

remained above 40 percent, and those from the tertiary sector increased their relative importance from 30 to 37.5 percent. During this same time period, firms from the primary sector increased sales by 50 percent, those from manufacturing by 80 percent, while those belonging to the service sector expanded sales from US$107 billion to US$258 billion.

Ownership change in Latin America

The 1990s was a period when Argentina, Brazil, Chile and Mexico liberalized their national regimes of incentives and regulation. Over the course of the decade, as microeconomic liberalization – including privatization – accompanied macroeconomic stabilization, confidence levels increased and, following international trends, there was a marked acceleration of capital inflows into the region, leading to significant ownership restructuring and changes in corporate control. Inward internationalization – a historical feature of the region – has been made even more pronounced.

Table 9.11 indicates the size of the privatization process in the largest Latin American countries between 1990 and 1999. To a great extent privatization programs are associated with the size of these economies; in Brazil, the largest country, privatizations in the 1990s amounted to US$61 billion, while in Argentina and Mexico they reached US$23 billion. The smaller amount in Chile is probably due to the fact that privatizations there occurred earlier on.

M&A operations were economically more significant, amounting to US$217 billion, during the 1990s. In fact the economic importance of M&A transactions is much higher, as not all transactions recorded in Table 9.12 registered information on values.

Figure 9.1 below confirms and gives an idea of the internationalization of ownership in Latin America. During the 1990s, in Argentina, Brazil and

Table 9.11 Privatizations in Latin America 1990–9 in numbers and US$ million

Country	Number of transactions	Number of transactions with declared values	Total value of transactions (US$ million)
Argentina	98	95	23,385
Brazil	113	113	61,568
Chile	17	15	2,070
Mexico	101	96	22,837
Total	329	319	109,860

Source: authors' elaboration based on IE-UFRJ Latin America M&A and Privatization Database.

Table 9.12 M&A in Latin America 1990–9 in numbers and US$ million

Country	Number of transactions	Value of transactions
Argentina	939	72,224
Brazil	1,055	67,892
Chile	366	25,832
Mexico	725	52,037
Total	3,085	217,987

Source: authors' elaboration on IE-UFRJ Latin America M&A and Privatization Database.

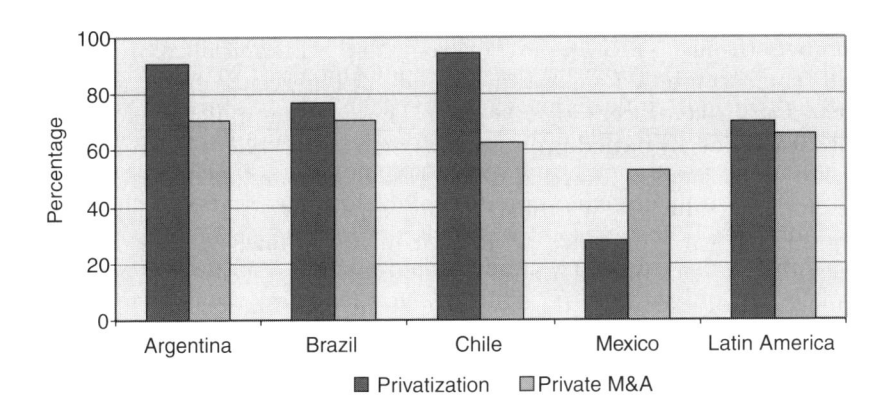

Figure 9.1 FDI in privatizations and M&A, percentage over value of transactions, 1990–9, by target country (source: IE-UFRJ Latin America M&A and Privatization Database).

Chile foreign capital had a dominant presence in privatizations and M&A transactions. The exception is Mexico, where the role of local capital was dominant.

Table 9.13 allows for further understanding of the internationalization process in Latin America. Among the elite of Latin American firms, it is

Table 9.13 The ownership of the largest 500 Latin American companies, 1990–2000 (number, sales in US$ million and %)

	1990–2		1994–6		1998–2000	
	Value	%	Value	%	Value	%
Number	500	100.0	500	100.0	500	100.0
Foreign	149	29.8	156	31.2	231	46.2
Local	264	52.8	280	56.0	231	46.2
State	87	17.4	64	12.8	38	7.6
Sales	361.009	100.0	601.794	100.0	686.776	100.0
Foreign	99.028	27.4	193.335	32.1	285.627	41.6
Local	142.250	39.4	246.700	41.0	259.784	37.8
State	119.731	33.2	161.759	26.9	141.365	20.6

Source: CEPAL (2001, Cuadro I-A.4).

possible through the years to observe a decrease in the relative importance of state owned companies, stability of local companies and an important expansion of foreign owned firms. In terms of sales, the gains in economic importance of foreign firms is even more pronounced as they expanded from US$99 billion in 1990–2 to US$285 billion in 1998–2000. Locally owned firms expanded sales by approximately 80 percent but their relative importance remained practically unchanged. State owned firms, however, while decreasing in relative importance in numbers (from 17.4 to 7.6 percent) remained economically more important. Their combined sales represented 33.2 percent of the group in 1990–2 and 20.6 percent in 1998–2000. These figures indicate that the relative size of locally owned firms is not as high as the other two groups.

The data suggests that Latin America is substantially different from developing countries in other regions, especially Asia. Although large diversified local groups are prominent in Latin America, they have not been able to block inward internationalization. On the contrary, emerging opportunities, especially those arising from privatization, were, by and large, exploited by foreign companies.

Table 9.14 provides evidence of the process of ownership change in chemical industries. The most interesting feature is the changing pattern of establishing business alliances, from joint ventures in the years preceding economic liberalization to asset acquisition afterwards.

Most importantly, though, when the origin of partners are taken into account in M&A operations in chemical industries in Argentina and Brazil (Table 9.15), it is possible to observe that transactions among foreign companies prevail. Taking into account the context of regional economic liberalization on one hand and the active process of international M&A on the other, ownership changes in Latin America are, to a certain extent, a reflex process of that occurring elsewhere.

Table 9.14 The role of M&A and joint ventures in chemical industries in the Mercosul

	1985–90		1991–9	
	M&A	Joint ventures	M&A	Joint ventures
Number of operations	121	107	462	116
%	53	47	80	20

Source: Sá (2002).

Table 9.15 Participants in M&A in chemical industries, by ownership (1985–99)

Country	Local/local (%)	Foreign/foreign (%)	Local/foreign (%)	Number of M&As
Brazil	30	57	13	346
Argentina	4	60	0	107

Source: Sá (2002).

Inward internationalization in Brazil

Foreign firms have historically played a key role in the industrialization of Brazil, and recent trends point out an increasing importance of such companies to the economy. A survey conducted by the Brazilian Central Bank in 2000 identified 11,404 companies with foreign ownership interests in excess of 10 percent of the voting capital, which indeed characterizes these firms as foreign corporations, many of them TNCs. Of these companies, 9,712 had over 50 percent of assets controlled by non-residents. In 1995, there were 6,322 companies with foreign ownership interests in excess of 10 percent of the voting capital, of which 4,902 had over 50 percent control by non-residents.

In 1995, these companies employed 1.3 million workers, 71.8 percent of which engaged in manufacturing activities. In 2000, foreign companies employed 1.7 million workers. Total assets expanded 67 percent in five years, from US$280 billion in 1995 to US$467 billion in 2000. In that year, total sales amounted to US$424 billion, or 39 percent of the GDP. As shown previously, this substantial increase in the importance of foreign firms to the Brazilian economy took place mainly through acquisitions of local firms.

Their presence in foreign trade is also quite significant. Even though the domestic market has been the primary focus of foreign companies in Brazil, exports increased from US$21.7 billion in 1995 to US$33.2 billion in 2000, or 46.7 percent and 60.4 percent of total Brazilian exports in

Table 9.16 Exports and imports of foreign firms – 1995, in US$ billion

Sector	Exports		Imports		Trade balance
	US$ billion	%	US$ billion	%	US$ billion
Basic Metals	2.7	12	0.9	5	1.8
Automotive	2.7	12	3.1	16	(−0.4)
Food/beverages	2.3	11	1.2	6	1.1
Chemicals	2.0	9	4.4	23	(−2.4)
Machinery	2.0	9	1.4	7	0.6
Pulp and paper	1.7	8	0.3	1.5	1.4
Tobacco	1.0	5	0.1	0.5	0.9
Electronics	0.2	1	1.6	8	(−1.4)
Other sectors	7.1	33	6.3	33	0.8
All sectors	21.7	100	19.3	100	2.4

Source: Central Bank (2002).

those years, respectively. Import coefficients of foreign firms are quite high, at US$19.3 billion in 1995 and US$31.5 billion in 2000, or 39.0 percent and 56.6 percent of total Brazilian imports in those years, respectively. As shown in Table 9.16, the trade balance of foreign firms reached US$2.4 billion in 1995. Companies in basic metals, pulp and paper and food and beverages were net exporters while those from automotive, electronics and chemicals were net importers.

As expected, intra-firm trade prevailed, being associated with 42 percent and 63 percent of exports in 1995 and 2000, respectively or US$9.1 and US$19.8 billion. On the import side, intra-firm trade amounted to US$8.5 billion and US$18.2 billion, in 1995 and 2000, respectively. Earnings and dividends received by investors in companies with foreign ownership in Brazil totaled US$6.1 billion in 1995 and US$6.6 billion in 2000, of which approximately 50 percent was remitted abroad.

The importance of foreign firms can also be examined in relation to the largest economic groups. In 2000, among the 500 largest private companies in Brazil, 232 were of foreign origin while 268 were locally owned national. The sales of these 500 companies amounted to US$283 billion; the sales of foreign firms reached US$129 billion in 2000. The share of sales of foreign firms among the 500 largest Brazilian companies remained around 30 percent up to 1995, increasing thereafter. During the period 1998–2000 their share reached 44.6 percent (Table 9.17).

Presently, the importance of TNCs in Brazil goes beyond the manufacturing production chains. A substantial amount of the "new wave" of FDI into Brazil in the 1990s has been channeled to the service sector. In the past, manufacturing was the favorite destination of FDI in Brazil but, as shown in Table 9.18, 76 percent of FDI inflows in 1996/2002 was directed

Table 9.17 Share of foreign companies in the sales of the largest companies of Brazil (%)

Year	Foreign	Private national	State
1990–2	31.1	42.3	26.6
1994–6	33.1	43.2	23.7
1998–2000	44.6	37.6	17.8

Source: *Exame Magazine*, various issues.

Table 9.18 FDI stock and inflows by sector

Sector	1995 FDI stock (US$ billion)	%	FDI inflows (1996–Feb. 2002) (US$ billion)	%
Total	42.2	100	126.5	100
Agriculture and Mining	0.7	1.7	3.4	2.7
Industry	23.3	55.1	26.1	20.7
Food	2.3	5.4	3.4	2.7
Automotive	2.9	6.9	6.5	5.1
Machinery	2.1	5.0	1.5	1.2
Chemical products	4.7	11.1	5.1	4.1
Others	11.3	26.7	9.6	7.6
Services	18.2	43.2	97.0	76.6
Commerce	2.9	6.7	10.8	8.5
Finance	1.2	3.0	18.1	14.3
Telecommunications	0.1	0.5	27.3	21.5
Business services	11.4	26.9	18.7	14.8
Public utilities	0	0	14.9	11.8
Others	2.6	6.3	7.2	5.7

Source: Central Bank (2002).

to service related activities. To the service sector an FDI inflow of US$97 billion was observed between 1996 and 2002, while FDI in industry and primary sectors amounted to US$26.1 and US$3.4 billion, respectively.

Within the service sector, telecommunications, business services, finance and public utilities have been the major FDI destinations. Indeed, these four activities have now a stock of US$91.7 billion, that is, over 50 percent of the entire Brazilian FDI stock. It is important to note that in 1995 the FDI stock of these four activities amounted to US$12.7 billion, of which US$11.4 billion in business services. At that time, finance and telecommunications had a meager FDI stock of US$1.3 billion, while public utilities had no FDI stock. The liberalization of policy instruments that supported the import substitution industrialization model, the launch of an extensive privatization program, the worldwide M&A trend and the expansion of the international integrated production were crucial factors propelling this "new wave" of foreign investments into the service sector.

Table 9.19 FDI stock by industry, 2002 (%)

Country/Region	Primary	Manufacturing	Services
Brazil*	2.4	29.0	68.6
Developed countries	10.0	40.8	49.2
Developing countries	6.7	45.5	47.7
World	9.4	41.6	48.9

Source: Compiled from UNCTAD, *World Investment Report* (2001, 2004).

Note
*Data from 1999.

As a result, by book value, presently the services sector has now the majority of FDI stock in the country. FDI stock in the service sector accounts for over 68 percent of total stock, industry 29 percent and the primary sector 2 percent. In contrast in 1989, before economic liberalization, over 70 percent of foreign investments was located in the industrial sector (Laplane 2000). Its present structure is similar in comparison to those of developed countries (Table 9.19).

A large number of foreign companies participating in the new FDI cycle are newcomers to the Brazilian economy, having origins in countries, like Spain and Portugal, that up to now were not major investors. The United States remains the most important source of FDI to Brazil, while Germany, Switzerland and Japan lost their relative positions, although they have continued to invest in the country.

As shown in Table 9.20, the United States accounts for barely 25 percent of total FDI stock. Other important investors – Germany, Switzerland and Japan – whose joint participation on the Brazilian FDI stock was over 25 percent until 1995, saw their joint share diminish to 12 percent recently. Spain and Portugal, whose investments were marginal in Brazil until 1995, increased their share to 10 and 4 percent, respectively, in the last years, through the privatization process. Netherlands and France are the third and fourth investors in Brazil. Canada, United Kingdom and Italy decreased their relative participation. Investments from Latin American countries have come mainly from Chile and Argentina taking advantage of the privatization program. This trend is not unusual considering that commercial flows within Latin America and within the MERCOSUR have increased in the last years.

The nature of investments by foreign firms

During the 1990s, direct investment aimed at privatization and mergers and acquisitions was instrumental in reorganizing public finances and to finance national current accounts. From a macroeconomic perspective, their contribution was quite relevant. But most privatization and M&A

Table 9.20 FDI stock in Brazil, by home country

Home country	FDI stock in 1995 US$ billion	%	FDI inflow 1996–Feb. 2002 US$ billion	%
United States	10.8	25.5	29.5	23.3
Spain	0.2	0.6	24.3	19.2
Netherlands	1.5	3.6	12.2	9.6
France	2.0	4.8	9.9	7.8
Portugal	0.1	0.3	9.3	7.3
Germany	5.8	13.7	2.8	2.2
United Kingdom	1.8	4.2	2.5	2.0
Japan	2.6	6.3	2.3	1.8
Italy	1.2	3.0	1.9	1.6
Belgium	0.6	1.3	1.7	1.4
Sweden	0.5	1.3	1.6	1.3
Canada	1.8	4.3	1.5	1.2
Switzerland	2.8	6.6	1.3	1.0
Argentina	0.3	0.9	0.0	0.0
Financial centers*	4.7	11.0	16.7	13.2
Others	5.4	12.7	8.5	6.7
Total	42.5	100.0	127.0	100.0

Source: Central Bank (2002).

Note
*Caribbean Financial centers: Cayman Island, Virgin Island, The Bahamas, Panama and the Bermudas.

were carried out in non-tradable sectors, with new actors buying positions into local markets. Given the extension of internationalization, an open macroeconomic issue for the future is the extent to which financial remittances to home bases are likely to affect national current accounts. To a great extent this depends on the nature of investments carried out by firms. The higher the commitment, the more likely they will be to remain in the country, regardless short-term disturbances.

In the region, the recent wave of ownership change has accentuated an important structural feature of the region: the co-existence of firms from diverse origins. The process of inward internationalization was already a feature of the Latin American region, and it was reinforced during the last decade. Thus foreign firms are relevant for the region's economic development in the future, especially because they tend to control positions in any market segment where high-income elasticity of demand and high technological opportunities prevail.

The recent wave of acquisitions and investment will be associated with the implementation of productive and technological strategies by new actors in specific markets. Whether these new actors are willing to consolidate and further expand their presence in the region, through new investment and implementation of pro-competitive strategies based on innovation and quality job creation, remains to be seen. Thus, the relevant questions the region is facing are as follows. What are the likely consequences of inward internationalization and ownership change? Will the region observe a (positive) local reproduction of international patterns of competition? Are firms likely to concentrate operations in specific regions/clusters? Will firms reinvest or remit profits? Will foreign firms carry out technology-related investments?

Although only time will reveal the nature of investments to be carried out, after this wide-raging process of ownership change, it is possible to speculate on the difficulties the region will be facing on the basis of the preliminary data presented below.

In terms of the nature of economic activities, Table 9.21 indicates that Japanese firms have different strategies according to host countries. In the USA decision-making activities are balanced with other functional activities of corporations, and there is a particular emphasis on operating R&D and design centers in that country. Mexico is clearly a production base from which to penetrate the North American markets, not as an R&D center. The Brazilian pattern is slightly different to the Mexican pattern: the ratio of decision-making offices to final production sites is higher, as well as the number of R&D centers. Taking into account that in Argentina and Chile the emphasis is basically on sales activities, this evidence may suggests that Brazil plays a role as a decision-making/design center for the South American region.

Table 9.22 provides further information upon which discussions on these subjects may be taken up.

The evidence is quite straightforward and expected. First, US parents concentrate value at home: the sales ratio of affiliates to parents is 38.5 percent, the investment ratio is 31.7 percent and the R&D ratio is 14.9 percent. The higher the strategic value of operations, the more likely firms are to implement them from home grounds. Second, other developed regions are the favorite destination of operations but, even

Table 9.21 Corporate networks of Japanese affiliates in selected American countries, 1999

Country	Regional headquarters and managerial officers	Sales offices	Final production sites	Parts and materials production	R&D and design centers
USA	897	877	887	446	580
Argentina	18	33	29	1	–
Brazil	53	94	77	10	40
Chile	1	8	1	–	–
Mexico	57	138	136	62	26

Source: UNCTAD, *World Investment Report* (2001).

Table 9.22 Sales, investment and R&D: US TNCs and affiliates in 1999 (US$ billion)

	Sales	Investment	Inv/sales	R&D	R&D/sales
US parents	5,709.5	357.8	6.3	123.5	2.2
All affiliates	2,195.3	113.4	5.2	18.4	0.8
Europe	1,201.5	53.9	4.5	12.4	1.0
UK	340.2	20.4	1.7	4.1	1.2
Japan	125.1	4.0	3.2	1.6	1.3
Latin America	245.6	18.6	7.6	0.6	0.2
Brazil	55.2	3.7	6.7	0.3	0.5
Asia	425.4	20.9	4.9	3.3	0.8

Source: Survey of Current Business: Operations of US MNCs companies – preliminary results from the 1999 Benchmark survey, R. Mataloni Jr. and D. Yorgason (2002: 24–54), mimeo.

there, R&D efforts are comparatively lower: while US parents spend 2.2 percent of sales in technological activities at home, in Europe these expenditures reach only 1.0 percent, in the UK 1.2 percent and in Japan 1.3 percent. Third, developing regions are considered as markets to be supplied from the home base, as far as strategic inputs are concerned. R&D to sales ratio in Latin America is 0.2 percent and, in Asia, 0.8 percent, nearly the same ratio as Europe.

Policy challenges

In Latin America, after decades of inward-oriented industrialization, the 1982 debt crisis and a long process of uncontrolled inflation, most countries went through structural and institutional reforms, oriented towards inflation control, liberalization, deregulation and privatization. But, even after such radical turnaround, sustained growth has not been attained in most countries.

Structural and macroeconomic instabilities are regularities in the region. Nature, direction and duration of economic and institutional instability define levels of uncertainty and confidence prevailing among economic agents, thus affecting their willingness to invest in exploring new business opportunities, in new plants, in innovation.

Structural change produces uncertainty and the need for adaptation. However, adaptive capabilities of agents and organizations differ. The recent evolution of Latin America has shown that this is a process generating winners and losers. More interestingly, though, since the Asian Financial Crisis, the recent process of change has not induced modifications in the relative position among different actors, organizations or countries. Those that were relatively stronger in the pre-crisis period have shown better adaptive capacity and vice versa.

As a result these economies are now even more internationalized than before, and this is a long-term and structural feature of Latin America. However, the region is facing a development paradox since history tells us that local capital and local innovation capabilities have been outstanding features of successful and sustained economic and social development. If ownership internationalization is to remain and local innovation capabilities must be pursued, then Latin American policy-makers are facing challenges associated with how to attract investments of this nature. To a great extent, this will mean an important departure from established policy practices, to new ways of regulating and inducing firms towards local value creation. So, it is very likely that public agencies will go through periods of intense transformation and adaptation, until the diffusion of a new set of practices – including methods of detecting, controlling and solving problems – take place.

Policy-wise, the challenges Latin American countries are facing is how to promote a national regime of incentives and regulations inductive to activities that generate qualifying jobs, in a context of open economies and ownership internationalization. Qualifying jobs mean the continuous creation of work opportunities that have the capacity to enhance the skill base of the labor force, thus potentially expanding the welfare of the population.

The region is facing a context marked by a higher degree of freedom of private decision-making in the process of resource allocation and an increasing power of international corporations in different markets. Thus, from a regulatory perspective, it is necessary to build up policy-making capabilities in specialized agencies oriented towards facilitating investment and restraining anti-competitive market structures and behavior. From the incentive perspective, the challenge is to promote national attractiveness for innovation. The proposition for discussion is to develop agencies and instruments oriented towards a double strategic movement. It is necessary to increase investments, aiming at, on one side, company efforts towards modernization and, on the other, expanding the local S&T infrastructure. For that policy-makers must identify and actively support those few companies and research institutes that implement innovation-based strategies.

Sustained increases in S&T financial resources aimed at these goals will increase the chances that in the future a specific region/country may attract economic agents (especially foreign firms/research institutes) to internalize technology-related activities. Taking Brazil as an example, if the country is to reach 2.5 percent of S&T expenditures in 2010, Table 9.23 below provides an idea of the extent of the necessary efforts.

Regardless of the extent of success in the above areas, a permanent challenge is to root innovation as one of the strategic and praised beliefs entrenched in any society. All economic, social and political actors must be convinced and have faith; must convince and convert others that S&T is beneficial to social and economic development. For that end, private

Table 9.23 Brazil: necessary efforts to advance in S&T

	GDP in real billion of 1999	S&T expenditure in real billion of 1999	S&T expenditure as % of GDP	Projected rate of annual increase (%)
1999	961	11.5	1.20	13.3

and public policy-makers must engage, with tenacity, in permanent mobilization aiming at objective and ambitious goals. But, beware: we all will be sailing against the wind!

References

Abreu, M. and Verner, D. (1997) *Long Term Brazilian Economic Growth*, Paris: OCDE Development Centre Studies.

Boulding, K. (1992) "Development, Equity and Liberation," in D.J. Savoie and I. Brecher (eds) *Equity and Efficiency in Economic Development*, Quebec/Ontario: McGill-Queen's University Press.

Central Bank (2002) Online. Available http://www.bacen.gov.br/?CENSO2000RES (accessed 10/02/2005).

CEPAL (1996) *Fortalecer el desarrollo: interacciones entre macro y microeconomia*, Santiago: United Nations Publication.

—— (1999) *Estudio Económico de América Latina Y El Caribe 1998–*, Santiago: United Nations Publication.

—— (2001) *La inversión estranjera en América Latina y el Caribe, 2000*, Santiago: United Nations Publications.

—— (2002) *Globalización y Desarrollo*, Santiago: United Nations Publication.

Dosi, G. and Fabiani, S. (1994) "Convergence and Divergence in the Long-term Growth of Open Economies," in G. Silverberg and L. Soete (eds) *The Economics of Growth and Technical Change*, Camberley: Edward Elgar.

Dosi, G., Pavitt, K. and Soete, L. (1990) *The Economics of Technical Change and International trade*, New York: New York University Press.

Evans, P. (1995) *Embedded Autonomy: States and Industrial Transformation*, Princeton: Princeton University Press.

Exame Magazine, various issues.

Ferraz, J.C., Kupfer, D. and Serrano, F. (1999) "Macro/Micro Interactions: Economic and Institutional Uncertainties and Structural Change in Brazilian Industry," *Oxford Development Studies*, 27(3): 279–304.

Katz, J. (1999) "Pasado y presente del comportamiento tecnologico de America Latina," unpublished paper, CEPAL, Santiago.

Laplane, M. (2000) "Empresas Transnacionais no Brasil nos Anos 90: Fatores de Atração, Estratégias e Impactos," unpublished paper, Universidade de Campinas.

Maddison, A. (1994) "Explaining the Economic Performance of Nations, 1820–1989," in W.J. Baumol, R. Nelson and E.N. Wolff (eds) *Convergence of Productivity: Cross-national Studies and Historical Evidence*, Oxford: Oxford University Press.

Mataloni Jr., R. and Yorgason, D. (2002) *Survey of Current Business: Operations of US MNCs Companies – Preliminary results from the 1999 Benchmark survey*, mimeo., Washington DC.

OCDE (1999) *Managing National Innovation Systems*, Paris: OCDE.
Sá, L.G. (2002) "Fusões e Aquisições na Indústria Química do Mercosul: Impacto das Desregulamentações e Estratégia de Crescimento," unpublished thesis, UFRJ.
Schlegel, J. (1977) *Towards a Redefinition of Development*, Paris: OCDE.
UNCTAD (2001) *World Investment Report*, New York: United Nations Publication.
—— (2004) *World Investment Report*, New York: United Nations Publication.
Williamson, J. (1993) "Democracy and the 'Washington Consensus,'" *World Development*, 21(8): 1329–36.

10 Determinants and effects of foreign direct investment in transition economies

Yuko Kinoshita and Nauro F. Campos[1]

Introduction

Foreign direct investment (FDI) has become one of the most prominent forms of private capital flows in many developing countries following the decline in official capital flows in the 1980s.

The sudden collapse of the socialist system in the late 1980s opened up numbers of opportunities for the Central and Eastern European and former Soviet Union countries. These economies were initially more industrialized and open than many other developing countries. They could also count on a relatively cheap and highly qualified workforce.

It is generally argued that FDI is an important catalyst of technology transfer for a recipient country. It would bring not only capital but also the technology and management know-how necessary for restructuring firms in the host economies.[2] Thus, one of the important policy questions is what the host government can do to attract FDI.

In this chapter, we examine the location determinants of FDI into 25 transition economies by utilizing the panel data between 1990 and 1998. In the empirical analyses, we take into account both host country characteristics and agglomeration economies as determinants of FDI location. In order to incorporate the past stock of FDI as a proxy for agglomeration economies, we use the standard generalized method of moments (GMM) in explaining a spatial distribution of FDI across these countries.

In the last part of the chapter, we examine whether or not FDI contributed to an increase in total factor productivity (TFP) growth by replicating the models in the past studies. Throughout different specifications, we find that FDI has a positive and robust effect on the productivity growth of these countries.

There is a vast literature on the locational determinants of FDI. Trade theory argues that the location choices by investing firms are influenced by the classical factors of comparative advantages specific to the country: market size, low wages, skilled labor force and infrastructure.[3] Another perspective suggests that the investment location choices can be explained by agglomeration economies (e.g. positive externalities by co-locating to others).[4]

Many policy makers in the transition countries are aware that FDI plays a key role in encouraging successful transition and many countries in the region offered various incentives to attract FDI in the country.[5] However, FDI inflows in the region have been disappointingly low despite the initial expectation compared to those into China, Mexico and some East Asian countries. In recent years, the increasing trend of FDI inflows was set in some transition economies. But the distribution of FDI stock across the transition countries remains uneven[6] with high concentration on three Central and East European (CEE) countries (Hungary, Poland and the Czech Republic).[7] The other countries are struggling to encourage the first wave of large investment to arrive.

The concentration of FDI in these three countries may be explained by initial differences prior to 1989. Three countries were different in some respects such as privatization process, the price level and the debt-GDP ratio. However, these three countries are relatively more open to trade than other transition economies. This favorable condition drew an initial rush of investment at the time of disintegration of the Council for Mutual Economic Assistance (CMEA) in 1991 and many more new investments followed the first investors, as their presence worked as the signaling of good local conditions to other investors, which magnified the differences in FDI flows even further.

Once agglomeration economies set in, there will be a snowballing effect of FDI inflows in successful countries. On the other hand, if classical factors of comparative advantages are more dominant than agglomeration economies as locational determinants, it is still possible for the remaining countries to reverse the trend.

In light of the above framework, the close look at the role of agglomeration economies in relation to classical factors of comparative advantages is all the more important in understanding the drivers of FDI flows into these countries. Despite its importance, the empirical analyses on FDI in transition economies[8] has been limited to a set of Central and Eastern European Countries (CEEC) countries due to paucity of data. This study attempts to fill this gap by utilizing data on a full sample of 25 transition economies.

This chapter is organized as follows. In the next section, we review the classical theoretical framework on the location determinants of FDI. In the third, we discuss the variables to be tested as the determinants of FDI in our empirical setting, the estimation method and data we use. The fourth reports regression results on the locational determinants of FDI and the fifth sheds light on the effects of FDI on economic growth. The last section concludes the chapter and outlines directions for future research.

Conceptual framework

A firm becomes multinational mainly for three reasons. The so-called OLI paradigm proposed by Dunning summarizes them as Ownership advantages, Location-specific advantages and Internalization. Firms endowed with ownership advantages or intangible assets expand operations abroad to internalize the benefits arising from ownership advantages and to match their strengths with location-specific comparative advantages.

In this study, we focus on the location-specific advantages of the host country as determinants of FDI in order to account for the geographical distribution of FDI inflows across transition economies. Large market size, proximity to home market, low-cost labor and favorable tax treatment in the host country are all considered as location advantages. At the same time, we also address transition-specific issues such as changes in macroeconomic and institutional environments.

Location-specific advantages are further classified by three types of motives of FDI. First, market-seeking investment is undertaken to sustain existing markets or to exploit new markets. For example, due to tariffs and other forms of barriers, the firm has to relocate production to the host country where it had previously served by exporting. Because the reason for this type of investment is to better serve a local market by local production, market size and market growth of the host economy are the main factors that encourage market-seeking FDI. The impediments in serving the market such as tariffs and transport costs also encourage this type of FDI.[9] Japanese FDI in automobiles in the US in the late 1980s is an example of this type of FDI.

Second, when firms invest abroad to acquire resources not available in the home country, the investment is called resource- or asset-seeking. Resources may be natural resources, raw materials or low-cost inputs such as labor. An example is investment made by the US and Japan in export assembly in electronics in Asia in search of cheap labor.[10] Unlike market-seeking FDI, this type of FDI is intended to serve not only the local market but also the home and third country markets. Availability of resources, cheap and skilled labor and physical infrastructure are the main attractors of resource-seeking FDI.

Third, the investment is rationalized or efficiency-seeking when the firm can gain from the common governance of geographically dispersed activities in the presence of economies of scale and scope. In this respect, prospective membership of the European Union conducive to the establishment of regional corporate networks and the presence of high transport and communication costs will encourage more of efficiency-seeking FDI.

There are also other factors that could influence the choice of investment locations in the region. Favorable macroeconomic conditions of the host country such as stable prices, low national debt and sustainable budget deficit are attractive to foreign investors. Social and political stability also encourage FDI inflows. The progress of economic reform is particularly important in the transition economy context. Other non-economic factors are the degree of corruption, legal enforcement and administrative efficiency, all of which facilitate business operating conditions.

The above framework of FDI gives guidance in identifying the set of economic, political and institutional variables to be tested as determinants of investment locations, which is discussed in detail in the next section.

There is much empirical evidence that FDI is spatially clustered. Agglomeration of FDI may be explained by differences in classical comparative advantages such as factor endowment and market size. Also, agglomeration is induced by the investors' tendency to herd. Especially when investors have insufficient information about the host country conditions, the existing stock of foreign investment made by others may work as a signal of favorable investment environments.[11] Alternatively, agglomeration economies emerge when there are positive externalities by co-locating near others due to the presence of knowledge spillovers, specialized labor markets and supplier network.[12] In our analysis, we include the agglomeration effect as a determinant of location choice together with the above economic and policy variables.

Data and methodology

There are typically two approaches to analyzing the location determinants of FDI. The first class of studies[13] explains the location choice made by investing firms by investors' perceptions or ratings of location-specific factors such as labor cost, corporate tax rates and market size. Namely, they regress the probability of locating in a certain location on various location-specific factors. In other studies,[14] the dependent variable is the actual amount of FDI flow or stock. The choice between the two approaches depends on what type of data is available for the analysis. If firm-level data is available, then the first approach will be employed. If investment data is available only at the aggregate level, then the second approach is viable.

The data we use in this study covers the period 1990–8 for 25 transition countries. The number of observations in the panel is 225 (=25 × 9). The definitions and summary statistics of the variables are found in appendices.

The panel data is meaningful for our study for several reasons. First, the agglomeration or self-reinforcing effects of FDI at the aggregate level can be addressed only if there is a time-series of FDI. Due to positive externalities by localization of industry, FDI in the past will lead to more FDI today. Second, during the time period covered in our data, transition economies had undertaken and completed economic reforms. Cross-sectional data would not allow us to assess changes of the reform variables.

Transition from planned to market economy started in the early 1990s in many of these countries but foreign investors were cautious in the beginning, with a few exceptions in Hungary and Poland. Due to the difficulty of obtaining FDI data sufficiently long enough, the past studies on FDI in transition economies are confined to the set of CEEC countries that are the major recipients of substantial FDI in the region. A recent study by Resmini (2000) examines the location determinants of FDI into ten CEEC countries. Bevan and Estrin (2000) use the data on FDI flows from 18 investing countries to 11 transition economies in explaining the determinants of FDI from both home and host country viewpoints.

In this study, we expand to the set of 25 transition economies. With additional countries in the data, we are hoping to introduce more heterogeneity as well as to incorporate different motives of investment in order to provide a more complete and detailed picture of the reasons for locating FDI in transition countries. The countries excluded in the past studies are Commonwealth of Independent States (CIS) countries. These are the countries that receive FDI mainly in non-manufacturing such as service and oil industries. A picture for the complete set of countries may differ from the ones obtained for the subset of the countries in the past studies because of differences in the areas in which they receive FDI.

Classical sources of comparative advantages

Investors choose a location of investment according to the expected profitability associated with each location. Profitability of investment is in turn affected by various country-specific factors as well as a type of investment motive. For example, market-seeking investors will be attracted to a country with a large local market and fast-growing market. Resource-seeking investors will look for a country with abundant natural resources. Efficiency-seeking investors will give more weight to geographical proximity to the home country to minimize the transportation cost.[15]

Thus, the location of FDI is closely tied with the comparative advantages of the country, which in turn affects the expected profitability of investment. The classical sources of comparative advantages are input prices, market size, growth of the market and relative abundance of natural resources.

For market-seeking FDI, the determining factor is the size of the host country market. We use GDP per capita as a measure of market size (YPC).[16]

Availability of cheap labor is crucial for vertical FDI. To exploit low cost of labor input, firms can justify relocating a part of the production process in foreign countries. We use nominal wage rate WAGEN as a proxy for labor cost. If vertical FDI is dominant, we expect a negative sign on the coefficient (e.g. the host country with lower labor cost attracts more FDI).

Investing firms should be concerned not only with the cost of labor but also the quality of labor. A more educated labor force can learn and adopt new technology faster and the cost of training local workers is less for investing firms. Labor quality is introduced as general secondary school enrollment rate (SS3).

Some CIS countries such as Azerbaijan, Kazakhstan and Russia have been receiving FDI mostly in resource-based industries as they are rich in oil and natural gas. This is considered to be an example of resource-seeking FDI. Natural resource-rich countries may attract foreign investment in those industries while they may divert investment from the manufacturing sector.[17] The variable we use is NATRES that indicates if the host country is "poor" (=0), "moderate" (=1) or "rich" (=2) in natural resources.[18]

Proximity to the home country is empirically an important factor for explaining the volume of trade flows between countries. The gravity model predicts that the closer the country is to the home country, the more trade flows between the two countries will be observed. The analogous argument may apply for FDI as FDI flows are closely related to trade flows. The sign of proximity to the home country can go either way depending on the type of FDI undertaken. In the case of market-seeking FDI, a further distance between the home and host country markets implies a higher transportation cost. A fixed cost of transporting goods would encourage production in a foreign market to exploit economies of scale. On the other hand, if goods produced abroad are shipped back to the home or the third country markets, then the closer the production site is to the home or the third country, the more efficient it is for Multinational Corporations (MNCs).

It would be best if we could measure the distance between the home and host country for this purpose. However, the data we use only contains the information on the host country of FDI flows and we use a proxy for geographical distance to the major investor in the region, say, Germany. The variable we use is DIST that measures the distance between Düsseldorf and the capital city of each country in kilometers. Also, Germany has historically close ties with transition economies in the region.[19] In particular, efficiency-seeking FDI in light of EU enlargement to the region will be encouraged if the country is closer to the major Western markets as proximity reduces communication and coordination costs.

Availability of good infrastructure is a necessary and sufficient condition for foreign investors to operate business locally regardless of the type of FDI. There are several candidates for the infrastructure variable. One is a percentage of paved roads in the country and the other is a number of main telephone lines. The first figure may be misleading. For instance, if there is one main road in the country and it is paved, then it is reported as 100. This is indeed the case in many countries in the sample. Thus, we use the number of main telephone lines (TELEPHON) as the infrastructure variable.

Other things being equal, we expect that the more FDI will be made in the countries with larger market size, lower labor cost, better educated labor force, abundant natural resources, and better infrastructure.

Policy variables

Investment decisions in emerging markets are also influenced by economic and political risks. Successful implementation of economic reform by the host government is a good signal to investors as stable macroeconomic performance implies less investment risk.

A record of price stability is a good indicator for sound macroeconomic management by the host government. For example, a history of low inflation and manageable fiscal deficits signals to investors how committed and credible the government is. For this, we use the average inflation rate (INFAV). At the onset of transition, as the countries liberalized prices and underwent structural changes in economic activities, all countries experienced the increase in the price level. As the countries proceeded with structural reforms and stabilization policies, the price level also subsided. The sustainability of moderate or low inflation tells investors how successful the host government is and thus the prospect of further growth. Thus, the lower the average inflation rate is in the host country, the more foreign investment will be attracted to the country.

Another indicator of economic reform is external liberalization index. We use the variable CLIE for a removal of trade controls and quotas, moderation of tariff rates and foreign exchange rate restrictions.[20] The more liberalized regime means the more successful reform and the more foreign investment flows.[21] In other cases, the more restrictive external regime may also induce FDI. If FDI is for tariff-jumping, FDI flows may negatively correlate with the external liberalization index.

Business operating conditions

Non-economic factors also influence returns to investment. The cost of investment consists of not only the actual costs of inputs but also non-economic costs such as bribery and time lost in dealing with local authorities.

To assess the business operation conditions of the host country for investing firms, we use two institutional variables, "rule of law" (RULELAW) and "quality of bureaucracy" (BUROQUAL).[22] The rule of law is a composite of three indicators: (i) sound political institutions and a strong court system,[23] (ii) the fairness of the judicial system over property rights, and (iii) the substance of the law itself.[24] The higher score in the rule of law implies the more sound and the better enforced the legal system is in the host country.

The quality of the bureaucracy is based on two indicators: (i) the extent to which the national bureaucracy enjoys autonomy from political pressure in a stable manner and whether or not it has an effective mechanism for recruiting and training, and (ii) the ease of regulations concerning licensing requirements and labor, environmental, consumer safety, and worker health. If this score is high, then the investors perceive less cost in dealing with the local bureaucracy.

Agglomeration economies

Agglomeration economies emerge when there are some positive externalities by co-locating near other economic units due to the presence of knowledge spillovers, specialized labor markets and supplier network.[25]

Various empirical studies present evidence on the presence and importance of such a self-reinforcing effect of foreign investment. Interestingly, FDI is found to agglomerate more often than mere financial investment partly because FDI is a long-term capital investment that is irreversible in a short run. For instance, Head, Ries and Swenson (1995) find industry-level agglomeration benefits play an important role in the location choice of Japanese manufacturing plants in the US. Wheeler and Mody (1992) confirm the importance of agglomeration for investors' location decisions using qualitative data on US firms. More recently, Chen and Kwan (2000) in the study of the determinants of FDI in Chinese regions also report the positive feedback effect of FDI. If there is a positive feedback effect, once the initial flow of FDI sets in, it should perpetuate itself and attract further FDI.

In this study, we use one-year lagged stock of FDI in the country as an independent variable to capture these agglomeration effects. A positive and significant coefficient of lagged stock of FDI means the presence of agglomeration economies. The inclusion of the lagged dependent variable on the right hand side of the Ordinary Least Squares (OLS) regression introduces the endogeneity problem. We address this issue in detail in the next section.

Estimation method

In order to test the presence of agglomeration effects, we have to relate current FDI to past FDI along with other explanatory variables. We follow the model proposed by Cheng and Kwan (2000) in which they formulate the role of past FDI values as the process of partial stock adjustment. They assume that it takes time for FDI to adjust to equilibrium or desired level.

Our empirical specification is based on the assumption of the presence of such an adjustment cost. We postulate a reduced form of the following equation:

$$Y_{it} = \alpha Y_{it-1} + \beta X_{it} + v_{it}$$
$$v_{it} = \eta_i + u_{it}$$

where Y_{it} is the stock of FDI in country i in year t, X_{it} is a vector of other explanatory variables such as market size, labor cost, labor quality, resource abundance, distance from Düsseldorf, infrastructure, policy variables and business operating conditions, and v_{it} is an error term that includes the unobservable country-specific attribute, η_i. If there is any agglomeration effect or a positive feedback effect, then α is expected to be positive. When there is a country-specific effect that is time invariant and unobservable as in the above specification, then the lagged dependent variable will be correlated with the error term and OLS will lead to asymptotically biased estimates. To get consistent estimates, we choose to use the generalized method of moments (GMM) technique proposed by Arellano and Bond (1991). In this approach, we first remove the country-specific effect by first-differencing equation set out above and estimate the following equation by using instrumental variables:

$$\Delta Y_{it} = \alpha \Delta Y_{it-1} + \beta \Delta X_{it} + \Delta u_{it}$$

where $\Delta Y_{it} = Y_{it} - Y_{it-1}$. In the above equation, ΔY_{it-1} is correlated with Δu_{it}. Valid instruments in this case are lagged levels of dependent variables, Y_{it-s} where $s \geq 2$ and $t = 3, 4, \ldots, T$. As the length of panel progresses, the number of valid instruments increases. If X_{it} is predetermined, then ΔX_{it-s} (for all s) can be used as additional instruments to increase the efficiency of the estimates. The validity of instruments is checked by the Sargan test. The second-order correlation of the error term in the first-differenced equation is checked by Arellano-Bond statistics for autocorrelation, which is distributed as N (0,1) asymptotically.

For a small number of samples relative to a number of parameter estimates, however, we are concerned with a possible bias introduced in the GMM estimation. Because the data set we employ may suffer from such a bias, we also estimate in fixed-effects model and compare with those obtained from GMM where appropriate.

The dependent variable Y_{it} is per capita FDI stock in constant million USD in year t. We constructed the series by using figures on FDI inflows taken from World Development Indicators (WDI).

Determinants of FDI inflows

Host country characteristics

Table 10.1 reports OLS regressions with fixed effects.[26] First, we look at the roles of host country characteristics without agglomeration effects. How much of variations of FDI inflows across transition economies are explained by classical factors? Column I in Table 10.1 answers this question. With no policy and risk variables and agglomeration economies being taken into account, most classical sources of comparative advantage

Table 10.1 Determinants of FDI: fixed effects (dependent variable = per capita FDI stock)

	I	II	III	IV
FDI stock (t − 1)	–	–	–	0.93***
				(0.04)
ypc	0.08***	0.05**	0.04	0.01
	(0.02)	(0.02)	(0.02)	(0.01)
wagen	−0.05	−0.08	−0.03	−0.05
	(0.15)	(0.14)	(0.14)	(0.06)
ss3	20.33***	15.02***	18.33***	2.84
	(4.43)	(4.43)	(4.52)	(2.16)
natres	−8.30	−2.78	−2.55	−0.44
	(7.13)	(6.88)	(6.71)	(3.25)
dist	0.02***	0.02***	0.02***	0.002
	(0.006)	(0.006)	(0.006)	(0.003)
telephon	5.25***	5.09***	5.57***	0.36
	(0.59)	(0.56)	(0.59)	(0.37)
infav	–	−0.006	−0.003	0.001
		(0.007)	(0.007)	(0.003)
clie	–	123.34***	102.44***	21.77
		(31.71)	(31.88)	(15.73)
rulelaw	–	–	26.27*	1.74
			(13.91)	(6.56)
buroqual	–	–	49.47*	28.29**
			(25.42)	(13.33)
N	148	148	148	140
R-squared	0.82	0.84	0.85	0.96

Notes
a Parentheses are standard errors. ***, ** and * indicate 1, 5, and 10% significance level, respectively.
b Time dummies included in all regressions.

bear statistical significance. Column I indicates that FDI into transition economies is mainly driven by the host country's market size, availability of skilled workers (or the level of human capital) and sufficient infrastructure. All regressions include time dummies.

Since natural resources and distance from Düsseldorf are both invariant over time in the data set, after taking first-differences, they both drop out. In order to recover the estimates of these variables, we transform them by multiplying by a time trend.

The positive and significant coefficient of DIST indicates that the further away the country is from Germany the more FDI it attracts. In other words, FDI is not gravitated towards Germany. There are a few possible explanations for this result. Horizontal FDI or intra-industry FDI is induced by the presence of transportation cost. If the motive for FDI is to serve the export (local) market, then the greater distance from the home country justifies more FDI flows. The other possibility is a bias in a coefficient due to omitted variables such as the agglomeration effect.

Labor cost is found to have a negative but insignificant effect on FDI inflows. Note that, without adjusting for labor productivity, low wage rate alone is not a good indicator for labor cost advantage. In fact, investors are attracted to the site with more educated workers than low cost labor as SS3 shows.

Abundance of natural resources is another rejected variable as a determinant of FDI. Richness in natural resources is not a main reason for FDI flows. Total cumulative FDI stock in CIS countries is greatest in resource-based industries. (e.g. Russia is in the third place in total FDI stock in the region.) However, once we take into account a scale effect by using per capita FDI stock, natural resources become no longer important.

In sum, column I indicates that FDI in these transition economies is seeking to sell in the local market rather than exploiting cheap inputs and factor endowments. Availability of skilled workers and sufficient infrastructure are a plus while abundance of natural resources and cheap labor do not help attract more FDI. In particular, the increasing importance of human capital as an attractor of FDI is also confirmed in a broader set of developing countries in Noorbakhsh and Youssef (2001) as more FDI is tilted towards the manufacturing sector than in the primary sector.

In column II, we add two policy variables. One is the average inflation rate to control for the success of macroeconomic reform. The other is the external liberalization index to measure how open the country is. The results are quantitatively very similar to column I. The explanatory power of the model is strengthened somewhat by the inclusion of an external liberalization index (CLIE). A positive and large coefficient of CLIE says that the progress of external liberalization is valued much by foreign investors. Inflation rate is negatively related to FDI flows but not statistically significant. This should not undermine the importance of price stabilization in the transition period. Rather, as the price stabilization is typically introduced in the initial stage of transition and external liberalization in the latter stage, investors may distinguish the winner of economic reform by looking at the outcome of external liberalization.

Similar results are found in column III after adding the institutional factors that facilitate business operations. Both the rule of law and quality of bureaucracy are positive and significant: the better perceived the judicial system is and the less corrupted is the local bureaucracy, the more FDI the country can attract. In Russia and CIS countries, corruptions and red tapes are often quoted as impediments to new foreign investment. The result here is consistent with this anecdotal evidence.

The results in columns I–III without the agglomeration effect consistently show that FDI in the region is driven by access to local market rather than by cheap labor. This observation is more relevant for the earlier comers of investment in the region when there is no prior investment made. Once a volume of investment reaches a critical mass, potential investors may simply follow the herd of other investors: more FDI today leads to more FDI tomorrow. Investors wondering whether to invest will flock to the countries that have already received much FDI because they believe that past FDI stock reflects favorable local conditions that are perceived by existing investors but not yet known to them.[27] Such agglomeration effects are proxied as a one-year lagged FDI stock per capita in this study.

Once we include the agglomeration effect (Column IV), there is a large increase in R square. Interestingly, the importance of the lagged dependent variable replaces the significance of other variables. One exception is the quality of bureaucracy. This implies that there is a strong tendency for foreign investors to agglomerate in certain locations. Attributes of other location-specific factors such as market size, labor cost and even policy variables become relatively less important for the choice of investment locations once the agglomeration effect sets in. The quality of bureaucracy yet remains.

However, it is well known that OLS often yields biased estimates in the presence of a lagged dependent variable on the right-hand side of the regression since the lagged dependent variable is endogenous by construction. This endogeneity problem has to be dealt with in the next subsection.

Agglomeration of foreign investors

Lagged dependent variable is not only non-random but also endogenous in the presence of an unobservable fixed effect and OLS estimates will be biased and inconsistent. Following Anderson and Hsiao (1981), we use the Generalized Method of Moments (GMM) Instrumental Variable estimator for dynamic panels that yields consistent estimates.[28]

Table 10.2 compares the result from OLS and that of GMM. All regressions include year dummies to control for time variation due to changes in external economic environment common across countries. The sizes of coefficients are similar in both regressions. The agglomeration effect and quality of bureaucracy remain significant in GMM. The main difference is observed in the external liberalization index. It becomes significant in GMM.

The p-value of the Sargan test is very small. Thus, we reject the null hypothesis at 1 percent level that there is no misspecification with the set of instruments we use in GMM. Second-order serial correlation is not detected according to the SOC test. However, as the Sargan test shows, the validity of instruments is questionable. Overall, a comparison between OLS and GMM results shows a bias in estimates in most variables is not great as seen in similar sizes of coefficients in both specifications. But the reform policy variable CLIE may have been biased in OLS.

Both results confirm the presence of agglomeration of FDI that over-

Table 10.2 Determinants of FDI (dependent variable = per capita FDI stock)

	OLS	GMM
FDI stock (t − 1)	0.93***	0.89***
	(0.04)	(0.06)
ypc	0.01	0.009
	(0.01)	(0.01)
wagen	−0.05	−0.08
	(0.06)	(0.06)
ss3	2.84	0.81
	(2.16)	(2.61)
natres	−0.44	−0.20
	(3.25)	(3.75)
dist	0.002	0.003
	(0.003)	(0.003)
telephon	0.36	0.32
	(0.37)	(0.42)
infav	0.001	0.002
	(0.003)	(0.003)
clie	21.77	38.18**
	(15.73)	(18.91)
rulelaw	1.74	−9.77
	(6.56)	(8.62)
buroqual	28.29**	33.96**
	(13.33)	(15.71)
N	140	116
Sargan test		0.000
SOC test		0.58

Notes
a Parentheses are standard errors. ***, ** and * indicate 1, 5, and 10% significance level, respectively.
b Time dummies included in all regressions.
c Sargan and SOC tests show the p-value for overidentifying restrictions and second-order serial correlation, respectively.

rides other location-specific factors such as market size and labor cost. The fact that both infrastructure and human capital variables are affected by an inclusion of agglomeration suggests that the agglomeration effect tends to be triggered by "created" comparative advantages (e.g. skilled labor force, availability of telephone lines) rather than indigenous ones (e.g. oil, gas and cheap labor).

After correcting for possible bias in OLS, we still see that the agglomeration effect plays a dominant role in guiding investors in choosing the investment location.

Is FDI into CIS countries driven by different factors?

We argue that different types of FDI are motivated by different factors. Market-seeking FDI goes to countries with large local market while resource-seeking FDI goes to countries with abundant natural resources. As Resmini (2000) reports, the locational determinants of FDI in transition economies vary greatly across different sectors. However, a sectoral breakdown of FDI is not available in the data we compiled. Generally, the sectors in which CIS countries[29] receive FDI are mainly in light manufacturing industries (e.g. food, tobacco) and resource-based industries by way of privatization whereas the sectoral distribution of FDI in other transition economies is more evenly spread with a slight skewness towards heavy manufacturing industries (e.g. automobile and machinery in the CEECs) and finance.

To introduce sectoral differences with the paucity of sectoral data, we divide the sample into non-CIS and CIS countries. As discussed before, sectoral differences in FDI inflows in non-CIS and CIS countries are large and we expect to see different factors driving FDI in these two groups.

Table 10.3 shows the estimates from GMM for these two groups. Some differences are observed in the results. First, the agglomeration effect is present in both but more pronounced in CIS countries. Second, another important determinant of FDI flows is availability of skilled labor for CIS countries and the external liberalization index for non-CIS countries.

Somewhat puzzling is the positive coefficient on distance from Germany. CIS countries are located further from the West than non-CIS countries. The main market they serve is Russia instead of Western Europe for historical and geographical reasons. In fact, when we replace DIST with distance from Moscow instead of Düsseldorf, the sign of the distance variable becomes negative and significant for CIS countries. This evidence shows that CIS countries gravitate towards Russia rather than the West.

For non-CIS countries, however, the Sargan test indicates the invalidity of the instruments. Due to small samples, GMM estimates may be asymptotically biased. In Table 10.4, we run fixed-effects model instead to compare with the results from Table 10.3.

In the first column in Table 10.4, non-CIS countries yield results similar to those obtained from GMM in Table 10.3. This implies that a bias in GMM for non-CIS countries is not so severe. For non-CIS countries, the agglomeration effect and human capital remain main drivers of FDI inflows. Note that DIST is no longer significant in OLS and that the rule of law becomes more crucial in explaining FDI inflows. In these variables, GMM in Table 10.3 might have introduced bias in that table.

Summarizing the results from Tables 10.3 and 10.4, we find that the agglomeration effect seems to be the most important variable in explaining FDI inflows. This is particularly so for CIS countries because there is less direct information about business operating conditions than in non-CIS countries. For investors, the signaling effect of other investors weighs more than classical economic factors of comparative advantages.

For non-CIS countries, the degree of external liberalization is a key

Table 10.3 Determinants of FDI: GMM (dependent variable = per capita FDI stock)

	Non CIS countries	CIS countries
FDI stock (t-1)	0.74***	0.89***
	(0.10)	(0.13)
ypc	0.008	0.005
	(0.028)	(0.016)
wagen	−0.12	0.23
	(0.08)	(0.29)
ss3	−2.24	2.27**
	(5.98)	(1.07)
natres	2.87	1.99
	(10.14)	(2.50)
dist	0.03	0.003**
	(0.02)	(0.001)
telephon	0.93	0.30
	(0.93)	(0.24)
infav	0.06	0.0004
	(0.05)	(0.001)
clie	309.33***	2.27
	(101.01)	(8.18)
rulelaw	−19.75	6.01
	(14.61)	(5.28)
buroqual	29.91	19.55
	(23.57)	(14.38)
N	67	49
Sargan test	0.06	0.98
SOC test	0.93	0.22

Notes
a Parentheses are standard errors. ***, ** and * indicate 1, 5 and 10% significance level, respectively.
b Time dummies included in all regressions.
c Sargan and SOC tests show the p-value for overidentifying restrictions and second-order serial correlation, respectively.

factor for promoting FDI. For CIS countries, favorable business operating conditions such as well-enforced rules and reasonable judicial systems encourage more FDI inflows. Availability of skilled labor force is another important determinant.

These differences stem from the fact that the two groups are in a different stage of economic development and that they attract FDI in different sectors. Non-CIS countries had a head-start in industrialization as they swiftly privatized nationally owned enterprises and they are more successful in accessing the global knowledge base via a relatively open trade regime. CIS countries are still lagging behind non-CIS countries in the level of industrial production and they are still shy of attracting substantial FDI flows. Our results suggest that the main impediments to FDI flows in CIS countries are a lack of skilled labor force and sound legal infrastructure.

Table 10.4 Determinants of FDI: FE model (dependent variable = per capita FDI stock)

	Non CIS countries	CIS countries
FDI stock (t − 1)	0.82***	1.08***
	(0.08)	(0.12)
ypc	0.006	0.00004
	(0.026)	(0.01)
wagen	−0.08	0.19
	(0.08)	(0.31)
ss3	−0.31	2.61**
	(4.87)	(1.18)
natres	2.96	0.64
	(8.97)	(2.55)
dist	0.02	0.001
	(0.01)	(0.001)
telephon	0.72	0.29
	(0.86)	(0.25)
infav	0.06	0.001
	(0.05)	(0.001)
clie	231.41***	−7.03
	(82.17)	(8.14)
rulelaw	−7.46	13.68***
	(12.60)	(4.63)
buroqual	31.54	14.66
	(20.76)	(12.47)
N	79	61
R-squared	0.97	0.95

Notes
a Parentheses are standard errors. ***, ** and * indicate 1, 5 and 10% significance level, respectively.
b Time dummies included in all regressions.

The effects of FDI on growth

In this section, we investigate whether or not the impact of FDI is positive as the theory predicts. We estimate five specifications that are standard in the growth and FDI literature.

We pay particular attention to endogenizing FDI. The specifications are aggregate production functions derived from the augmented Solow model (Mankiw et al. 1992), from the model developed by Borensztein et al. (1998) and that from Easterly (2001). Let us comment on each of these.

The model developed by Borensztein et al. (1998) yields the following basic specification (BGL1):

$$y = f (y0, hk, fdi, infl, govc, war, buroqual)$$

where y is real GDP growth, y0 is initial GDP, hk is human capital, fdi is foreign direct investment, infl is the inflation rate, govc is government consumption as a percentage of GDP, war is a dummy variable for war and buroqual is an institutional variable capturing the quality of the bureaucracy.[30] The model predicts that the effects of initial income, inflation, government consumption and war are negative, while those of human capital, FDI and institutions are positive.

We estimate two variants of the Borensztein *et al.* (1998) model. One is as follows (BGL2):

$$y = f \ (y0, hk, fdi, infl, govc, war, buroqual, inv)$$

where investment is included. This allows us to examine the relationship between foreign and domestic investment. As noted, these authors report that the coefficient on FDI itself is not statistically significant, even when an interaction term between FDI and human capital is introduced (the latter is statistically significant and forms the basis for their result). The second variant we report is the specification that includes this interaction term (BGL3).

The augmented Solow specification from Mankiw *et al.* (1992) will have the following form (MRW):

$$y = f \ (y0, inv, pop, hk, fdi)$$

where, for the variable not defined above, pop is population growth. Notice that because FDI is absent from the original formulation we have to modify it in the standard way by specifying technological change as a function of FDI.[31] The model predicts that the effects of initial income and of population growth are negative, while those of investment, human capital and FDI are positive.

The last econometric model we use in this paper is the outcome of a search for a specification that is able to highlight the main determinants of economic growth in the cross-country setup. The model postulated by Easterly (2001) is as follows (EAST):

$$y = f \ (y0, hk, fdi, infl, infra, oecdgrowth)$$

where, for the variables not defined above, infra is a proxy for the quality of the infrastructure in the host economy and oecdgrowth is a proxy for international activity.[32] The predictions are that the effects of initial income and inflation are negative while those of human capital, FDI and infrastructure and OECD growth are positive.

As noted, the determinants of FDI vary a great deal across transition. We thus proceed by estimating the specifications above using as instruments for FDI: the lagged stock of FDI (as a proxy for agglomeration effects), the quality of the bureaucracy, the number of telephone lines (as

Table 10.5 The impact of FDI on growth in transition economies, 1990–8 (FE model with instrumental variables) (dependent variable = GDP growth)

	BGL1	BGL2	BGL3	MRW	EAST
Constant	142.42***	80.96**	171.74***	234.51***	177.03***
	(54.62)	(41.35)	(55.11)	(52.19)	(44.21)
Initial income	−8.75***	−5.66**	−10.27***	−12.25***	−9.45***
	(2.82)	(2.22)	(2.85)	(2.98)	(2.69)
Human capital	−0.996**	−0.594	−1.27***	−1.83***	−1.34***
	(0.484)	(0.392)	(0.491)	(0.49)	(0.42)
Foreign direct investment	1.53***	0.862***	1.52***	1.79***	1.561***
	(0.4059)	(0.302)	(0.399)	(0.318)	(0.342)
Interaction term (FDI*HK)		−0.0001			
		(0.001)			
Inflation rate	−0.0009	−0.0009**	−0.0008		−0.0009**
	(0.0006)	(0.0005)	(0.0005)		(0.0005)
Government consumption	0.117	0.0009	0.067		
	(0.331)	(0.2939)	(0.328)		
Dummy for war	−19.17***	−21.31***	−18.62***		
	(6.265)	(5.38)	(6.208)		
Quality of the bureaucracy	0.501	3.61*	−0.143		
	(2.53)	(1.86)	(2.505)		
Investment			0.511**	0.552**	
			(0.225)	(0.253)	
Population growth				−0.052	
				(1.61)	
Telephone lines					0.0001
					(0.001)
Average growth in OECD					2.72***
					(1.04)
No. observations	157	157	156	156	164
R-squared	0.069	0.331	0.104	0.124	0.042

Notes:
a ***, ** and * indicate 1, 5 and 10% significance level, respectively.
b Standard errors in parenthesis. Dummy variables for countries and years are not reported. Instruments for FDI are: lagged stock of FDI, quality of the bureaucracy, telephone lines, external liberalization index and OECD growth.

a proxy for the quality of infrastructure), the external liberalization index and OECD growth.[33]

In Table 10.5 columns BGL1 and BGL2 show that the positive and statistically significant effect of FDI on real GDP growth obtain with or without the inclusion of the interaction term between FDI and human capital. The negative sign on the initial income coefficient supports the prediction of convergence from the neoclassical model. It can also be seen that stabilization policies (as proxied by the inflation rate) have played a role in generating faster rates of economic growth. We also find that political stability (as proxied by the dummy variable for armed conflict) has also contributed to higher growth rates during the transition period.

In column 3 (BGL3), the inclusion of domestic investment does not affect the positive impact of FDI on growth. As can be seen, the coefficient of FDI in BGL3 is very similar to that in BGL1 and domestic investment alone has a positive coefficient. This implies that a positive effect of FDI is independent of the presence of domestic investment and that FDI is complementary to domestic investment in increasing the growth rate.

The same pattern is detected in MRW. FDI remains an important determinant for faster economic growth and the size of the FDI coefficient is more pronounced in IV estimation. The remaining explanatory variables are the same as before. Low initial income level and high investment rate lead to higher rates of economic growth.

The last column of Table 10.5 shows the specification proposed by Easterly (2001). Again, the coefficient on FDI is positive and statistically significant at the 1 percent level. The results also show that the effects on the growth rates of transition economies of their initial income levels, inflation rates and of the level of economic activity in the OECD countries are all statistically significant and carry their expected signs. We find that the quality of the infrastructure does not seem to be an important determinant of growth rates in the transition economies.[34]

In summary, we find that for the transition economies FDI had a positive impact on economic growth. This finding remains robust after we instrument FDI in order to account for the variety of determinants in different transition economies. Regardless of the main determinants of FDI (e.g. good policies or favorable initial conditions), the positive effect of FDI on growth rates seems to prevail.

Conclusion

In this paper, we study the factors explaining the geographical distribution of FDI inflow across 25 transition economies by utilizing panel data between 1990 and 1998. The location determinants we test consist of three categories: the first country-specific advantages such as low-cost labor, large local market, skilled labor force, sufficient infrastructure and proximity to the West. The second group of variables tested is macroeconomic policy and policy that facilitates business-operating conditions. The third is the agglomeration effect of foreign investment. We explain FDI stock per capita in each country as a function of the above variables in the GMM estimation.

In regression results, we find the role of agglomeration economies the most significant determinant of foreign investment inflows in the transition economies. This result is robust throughout alternative specifications. The model without the agglomeration effect seems to show that FDI in the region is sought by market-seeking investors rather than resource-seeking investors. Once we introduce the agglomeration effect, however, market size becomes no longer an important location determinant.

Nevertheless, poor quality of bureaucracy in the host country is found to be a deterrent to foreign investment decisions even after controlling for the agglomeration effect. This suggests an interesting policy implication. Improving institutional governance such as bureaucratic quality is a strong signal of a favorable investment environment for many foreign investors. Economic and political stability is a necessary condition in order for a host country to attract foreign investment. Once it secures macroeconomic stability in the earlier stage of transition from a centrally planned to a market economy, the institutional dimension of the transition process becomes more important, particularly when a country tries to promote FDI.

The other determinant of FDI inflow is "openness" to trade measured as external liberalization index. Our results show that the more liberalized the country is towards external trade, the more FDI it will attract. This confirms the findings in earlier studies that trade and FDI are complementary to each other.

CIS and non-CIS countries (e.g. CEECs and the Baltic states) differ in the sector in which they attract FDI. The location determinants reflect such differences when we divide the samples into two groups. For CIS countries, there is a greater effect of agglomeration at work perhaps due to insufficient information about local conditions as a destination of investment. For these countries, securing the first wave of foreign investment flows is all the more important because this will lead to a cascading effect of investment in subsequent periods. Other factors that contribute to FDI inflows in CIS countries are availability of human capital and good rule of law, or a sound judicial system. For non-CIS countries, the agglomeration effect is present but to a lesser extent than in CIS countries. One determining factor in attracting FDI in these countries is a more liberalized trade regime.

We also investigate the effect of FDI on the economic growth rate of these countries during the same period and find that the impact of FDI on growth is positive and significant, which remains robust to various specifications.

Using a broader set of transition countries and a longer time span than in existing studies, we hope to introduce heterogeneity both in time and country in analyzing the location determinants of FDI. We confirm the presence of agglomeration economies as a dominant factor in explaining the pattern of geographical FDI distribution across these countries. Also important are the extent of trade liberalization and the quality of bureaucracy. An educated workforce is particularly important for CIS countries as it might reflect a change of direction in the areas of FDI they receive.

Appendix

A10.6 Definitions of variables

per capita FDI stock	Per capita cumulative FDI stock (constant million USD) [source: World Development Indicator]
lagged FDI stock	One-year lagged per capita FDI stock
ypc	GDP per capita (USD)
wagen	Gross nominal wage (USD) [source: UNECE "Economic Survey of Europeqa"]
ss3	General secondary school enrollment (%)
natres	Natural resource endowment: $=0$ if poor, $=1$ if moderate and $=2$ if rich [source: DDGT]
dist	Distance from Düsseldorf (km)
telephon	# of telephone mainlines per 1,000 people
infav	Average inflation rate (%)
clie	Cumulative external liberalization index, i.e. trade liberalization
rulelaw	Extent of law enforcement [source: Campos (2000)]
buroqual	Quality of bureaucracy [source: Campos (2000)]

A10.7 Summary statistics

	Obs	Mean	Std. Dev.	Min	Max
FDI stock	188	164	295	0	1,771
Lagged FDI stock	163	131	250	0	1,572
ypc	220	2,134	1,784	219	9,850
wagen	151	167	217	0.02	1,247
ss3	221	26	7.7	8.8	45.6
natres	225	0.52	0.75	0	2
dist	225	2,237	1,476	559	5,180
telephon	219	162	88	0	374
infav	225	434	1,304	−0.8	15,606
clie	225	2.74	2.45	0	9.5
rulelaw	225	6	2.46	2	10
buroqual	225	2.45	1.63	0.83	8.33

Notes

1 We thank Gordon Hanson, Boyan Jovanovic, James Levinsohn, Gérard Roland, John Sutton, Bernard Yeung and seminar participants at the University of Tokyo, MDT Meetings and CEPR/WDI Transition Conference for valuable comments. We also thank Aurelijus Dabušinskas, Anna Ratcheva, Evis Sinani and Dana Žlábková for excellent research assistance, and the William Davidson Institute at the University of Michigan for financial support and hospitality. The usual disclaimer applies.
2 See Estrin *et al.* (1997) and Lankes and Venables (1996).
3 Kravis and Lipsey (1982) find market size and openness to be important determinants for the location choices of US multinationals. Lucas (1993) finds

FDI inflows into seven Southeast Asian countries are sensitive to relative wage differentials.
4 See Wheeler and Mody (1992) and Kinoshita and Mody (2001).
5 See section 5 for further discussion on the benefits of FDI. Empirical evidence on the effectiveness of subsidies and tax holidays for foreign-owned firms is rather mixed. See Hanson (2000) for further discussions.
6 A standard neoclassical model of economic growth predicts that capital always flows from rich to poor countries, which is contradicted by empirical evidence. One way to reconcile them is to introduce the role of human capital in an input of production as in Lucas (1990).
7 The ranking of major recipients of FDI in terms of cumulative FDI inflows between 1989–99 is Poland, Hungary, the Czech Republic and Russia in descending order (see *Transition Report 2000*: 74 (EBRD 2000)).
8 Resmini (2000) and Bevan and Estrin (2000) study the determinants of FDI flows into 10 and 11 transition economies, respectively.
9 This is also called "horizontal FDI" as a firm duplicates the production process in foreign locations. See Markusen and Venables (1998).
10 This is "vertical FDI" as a firm relocates part of the vertical chain of production to a low-cost location.
11 See Kinoshita and Mody (2002).
12 The sources of externalities are identified differently in different models. Lucas (1988) argues that the accumulation of human capital generates positive spillovers while, in Krugman's (1991) model, transportation costs and fixed costs in production lead to the demand linkages of firms, which increases the incentives to agglomerate. See Fujita *et al.* (1999) for recent surveys of theories on agglomeration.
13 Coughlin *et al.* (1991), Wheeler and Mody (1992) and Head *et al.* (1995).
14 Lucas (1993), Singh and Jun (1996), Cheng and Kwan (2000), Resmini (2000) and Bevan and Estrin (2004).
15 See Dunning (1993) for further discussion.
16 Another variable to measure market potential is annual GDP growth.
17 Gylfason and Zoega (2001) find that abundant natural resources may crowd out physical capital and inhibit economic growth. See also Robinson *et al.* (2002).
18 This variable is constructed by De Melo *et al.* (1997).
19 We experimented with other distance variables such as distance from Brussels. But the results obtained are very similar.
20 The index is constructed by De Melo *et al.* (1997).
21 See Caves (1996) and Singh and Jun (1996), for example.
22 The variables are taken from Campos (2000).
23 It reflects the degree to which citizens are willing to accept the established institutions for making and implementing laws and adjudicating disputes.
24 This measures whether a post-communist constitution has been adopted, whether the constitution provides for property and human rights, whether the criminal code has been subject to reform, whether judges rule fairly and impartially and whether they were appointed during the communist era, whether the courts are free of political control, whether the state provides public defenders and whether ethnic minority rights are protected.
25 The sources of externalities are identified differently in different models. Lucas (1988) argues that the accumulation of human capital generates positive spillovers while, in Krugman's (1991) model, transportation costs and fixed costs in production lead to the demand linkages of firms to agglomerate further. See Fujita *et al.* (1999) for recent surveys of theories on agglomeration.
26 The Hausman test rejects random effects model.

27 See Kinoshita and Mody (2001) for further discussion.
28 The efficiency of estimates can be improved by adding more moment conditions. For the system GMM estimation, see Arellano and Bond (1991), Ahn and Schmidt (1995), Arellano and Bover (1995) and Blundell and Bond (1998).
29 Commonwealth of Independent States (CIS) are Armenia, Azerbaijan, Belarus, Georgia, Kazakhstan, Kyrgyzstan, Moldova, Russia, Tajikistan, Turkmenistan, Ukraine and Uzbekistan.
30 Due to data availability, there are some differences between the original specification and the one we use in this paper. There were dummy variables for Latin American and African countries that are not present in our specification. Originally, it also contained variables reflecting the number of assassinations per capita, the extent of political freedoms and the occurrence of civil wars. To substitute for these, we use a dummy variable for internal and external armed conflicts (war). The institutional variables in the original specification are not available, thus here we use a measure of the quality of the bureaucracy. We were not able to find panel data for the black market premium on the exchange rate for our sample of transition economies.
31 The same modification is done for the Easterly (2001) specification.
32 The Easterly specification also contains two variables, the black market premium on the exchange rate and the real exchange rate. We were unable to obtain these in the current data.
33 The results do not change after a dummy for the countries of the Commonwealth of Independent States is introduced. In particular, the coefficient on FDI remains positive and significant at the 1 percent level. These results are available from the authors upon request.
34 It should be mentioned that this latter result might be due to the poor quality of the data and the lack of alternative measures of infrastructure quality in these countries. We found data on another proxy for the quality of infrastructure, the percentage of roads paved, but quality was very poor.

References

Ahn, S.C. and Schmidt, P. (1995) "Efficient estimation models for dynamic panel data," *Journal of Econometrics*, 68(1): 5–28.

Anderson, T.W. and Hsiao, C. (1981) "Estimation of Dynamic Models with Error Components," *Journal of American Statistical Association*, 76: 598–606.

Arellano, M. and Bond, S. (1991) "Some Tests of Specification for Panel Data: Monte Carlo Evidence and an Application to Employment Equation," *Review of Economic Studies*, 58: 277–97.

Arellano, M. and Bover, O. (1995) "Another Look at Instrumental Variable Estimation of Error-Components Models," *Journal of Econometrics*, 68: 29–51.

Bevan, A. and Estrin, S. (2004) "The Determinants of Foreign Direct Investment into European Transition Economies," *Journal of Comparative Economics*, 32(4): 775–87.

Blundell, R. and Bond, S. (1998) "Initial Conditions and Moment Restrictions in Dynamic Panel Data Models," *Journal of Econometrics*, 87: 115–43.

Borensztein, E., DeGregorio, J. and Lee, J.-W. (1998) "How Does Foreign Direct Investment Affect Economic Growth?" *Journal of International Economics*, 45: 115–35.

Campos, N.F. (2000) "Context is Everything: Measuring Institutional Change in

Transition Economies," Washington, DC, World Bank Policy Research Paper No. 2269.

Caves, R. (1996) *Multinational Enterprise and Economic Analysis*, 2nd edn, Cambridge, New York: Cambridge University Press.

Cheng, L. and Kwan, Y. (2000) "What are the Determinants of the Location of Foreign Direct Investment? The Chinese Experience," *Journal of International Economics*, 51: 379–400.

Coughlin, C., Terza, J. and Arromdee, V. (1991) "State Characteristics and the Location of Foreign Direct Investment within the United States," *Review of Economics and Statistics*, 173(4): 675–83.

De Melo, M., Denizer, C., Gelb, A. and Tenev, S. (1997) "Circumstance and Choice: The Role of Initial Conditions Policies in Transition Economies," World Bank Policy Research Working Paper 1866.

Dunning, J. (1993) *Multinational Enterprises and the Global Economy*, Wokingham: Addison-Wesley.

Easterly, W. (2001) "The Lost Decades: Developing Countries' Stagnation in Spite of Policy Reform 1980–1998," *Journal of Economic Growth*, 6(2): 135–57.

Estrin, S., Hughes, K. and Todd, S. (1997) *Foreign Direct Investment in Central and Eastern Europe*, London, UK; Herdon, VA: Royal Institute of International Affairs.

Fujita, M., Krugman, P. and Venables, A. (1999) *The Spatial Economy: Cities, Regions, and International Trade*, Cambridge, MA: MIT Press.

Gylfason, T. and Zoega, G. (2001) "Natural Resources and Economic Growth: the Role of Investment," CEPR discussion paper No. 2743.

Hanson, G., (2000) "Should Countries Promote Foreign Direct Investment?" Mimeo., Department of Economics, University of Michigan.

Head, K., Ries, J. and Swenson, D. (1995) "Agglomeration Benefits and Location Choice: Evidence from Japanese Manufacturing Investments in the United States," *Journal of International Economics*, 38: 223–48.

Kinoshita, Y. and Mody, A. (2001) "Private Information for Foreign Investment Decisions in Emerging Markets," *Canadian Journal of Economics*, 34: 448–64.

Kravis, I.B. and Lipsey, R. (1982) "Location of Overseas Production and Production for Exports by US Manufacturing Firms," *Journal of International Economics*, 12: 201–23.

Krugman, P. (1991) "Increasing Returns and Economic Geography," *Journal of Political Economy*, 99: 483–99.

Lankes, P. and Venables, A. (1996) "Foreign Direct Investment in Economic Transition: The Changing Pattern of Investments," *Economics of Transition*, 4: 331–47.

Lucas, R.E. Jr. (1988) "The Mechanics of Economic Development," *Journal of Monetary Economics*, 22: 3–42.

—— (1990) "Why Doesn't Capital Flow from Rich to Poor Countries?" *American Economic Review Paper and Proceedings*, 80: 92–6.

Lucas, R. (1993) "On the Determinants of Direct Foreign Investment: Evidence from East and Southeast Asia," *World Development*, 21(3): 391–406.

Mankiw, G., Romer, D. and Weil, D. (1992) "A Contribution to the Empirics of Economic Growth," *Quarterly Journal of Economics*, 107(9): 1593–610.

Markusen, J. and Venables, A. (1998) "Multinational Firms and the New Trade Theory," *Journal of International Economics*, 46(2): 183–203.

Noorbakhsh, F. and Youssef, A. (2001) "Human Capital and FDI Inflows to Developing Countries: New Empirical Evidence," *World Development*, 29(9): 1593–610.

Resmini, L. (2000) "The Determinants of Foreign Direct Investment in the CEECs," *Economics of Transition*, 8(3): 665–89.

Robinson, J., Torvik, R. and Verdier, T. (2002) "Political Foundations of the Resource Curse," CEPR discussion paper No. 3422.

Singh, H. and Jun, K. (1996) "The Determinants of Foreign Direct Investment in Developing Countries," *Transnational Corporations*, 5(2): 67–105.

Wheeler, D. and Mody, A. (1992) "International Investment Location Decisions: The Case of U.S. Firms," *Journal of International Economics*, 33: 57–76.

Part III
Social policy in transition

11 Latin American social security reform in the 1990s

Koichi Usami

Introduction

Latin America's high levels of external debt were the cause of high inflation and negative economic growth in the 1980s, a period known as "The lost decade." As a solution to the crisis, many Latin American countries adopted a neoliberal policy which emphasized market mechanisms in the 1990s. The main elements of this policy program involved abolition of industrial protection, trade liberalization, deregulation and privatization of state-owned companies. With the implementation of these measures, import substitution industrialization (ISI), a model of economic growth before the 1980s, came to an end completely.

In this process, the contract of urban formal sector workers that were generally full-time and permanently employed was criticized for provoking a rise in labor costs, under keen market competition. The reduction of industrial sector protection and the hypertrophied public sector meant the abolition of guarantees of wages and employment conditions that urban formal sector workers had enjoyed institutionally. The social security system, implemented in Latin America during the period of import substitution industrialization and developed primarily for formal sector urban workers, was largely reformed in the context of economic liberalization and as a result of changes in industrial relations during the 1990s. This chapter gives an outline of social security reform achieved in the 1990s in Latin America, focusing on pension and health care systems, and mentions the primary factors leading to this reform. In the next section, I describe the characteristics of the social security system and the primary factors leading to its formation before the 1980s. In the third, the outline of the social security reform, implemented in the 1990s, is explained. In the fourth, the political and economic factors that promoted social security reform in the 1990s are discussed. The final section briefly synthesizes the findings.

The social security system before the 1980s

Diversity in social and economic situations among Latin American countries

Latin America consists of a diverse group of countries with regard to economic, political and social characteristics, from Brazil, with a population exceeding 160 million, to the Caribbean countries, each with a population of several tens of thousands. A great difference can be seen in the region with regard to economic development and social security expenditures. Table 11.1 shows a great diversity in the per capita GDP, from $9,070 in Argentina, to $431 in Nicaragua, in 1997. Examining public social expenditure, there is a great difference between Uruguay, where it represented 22.8 percent of the GDP, and El Salvador, where it represented 4.3 percent, in 1998–9. Wilensky indicates that there is a strong correlation between economic development and increase in social expenditure (Wilensky 1975). This theory is known as the "industrialization hypothesis." In Latin America, most countries with a low per capita GDP expend lower public social expenditure, while countries with a high per capita GDP exhibit a tendency for high public social expenditure. However, in the case of Mexico, with a per capita GDP reaching $4,265, public social expenditure represents only 9.1 percent of GDP. In contrast, in the case of Costa Rica, with a per capita GDP of $2,540, it reaches 16.8 percent of GDP. This shows that there is no absolute correlation between economic development and the level of public social expenditure. Moreover, the social security system differs from country to country, and, as Esping-Andersen and many other researchers point out, it is also necessary to take into consideration political factors affecting the social security system in Latin America (Esping-Andersen 1990).

In countries where public social expenditure represents a high percentage of GDP, such as Argentina, Brazil, Uruguay, Chile and Costa Rica, coverage of social insurance, mainly the pension system, is relatively extensive. In addition, social insurance services are improving, and the ratio of the population covered by the system is high. This paper examines countries with high public social expenditure, such as Argentina and Brazil, and also examines Mexico, the country with the largest Spanish-speaking population in the region. However, we must note that there is a comparatively large informal sector existing parallel to the formal sector in the region. This is also true of the "advanced countries" in the region, a point that cannot be overlooked. In contrast, though there are some exceptions, in countries with low levels of economic development and low public social expenditure, such as Honduras, Bolivia, and Nicaragua, the ratio of poor and indigent households is high, and the coverage of social insurance is low (see Table 11.1). It is commonly accepted among researchers that the adoption of policies to combat poverty is a priority for social

Table 11.1 Socio-economic indicators in Latin America

	Public social expenditure as % of GDP in 1998–9[a]	Ratio of urban pensioners as % of population in 1997[b]	Gini coefficient in 1999	Per capita GDP (US$) in 1997	Ratio of indigence (%)[c]
Argentina	20.05	77	0.542	9,070	4.30(1)
Bolivia	16.10	27	0.504	996	32.60
Brazil	21.10	68	0.625	4,930	9.60
Chile	16.00	70	0.553	5,271	4.70
Colombia	15.00	20	0.564	2,384	23.20
Costa Rica	16.80	42	0.454	2,540	7.50
El Salvador	4.30	19	0.462	1,935	18.30
Guatemala	6.20		0.543	1,691	28.00
Honduras	7.40	9	0.518	785	50.60
Mexico	9.10	26	0.507	4,265	13.20
Nicaragua	12.70	19	0.551	431	40.10
Panama	19.40	48	0.553	3,159	8.30
Paraguay	7.40	25	0.497	1,961	26.00
Peru	6.80		n.a.	2,674	n.a.
Dominica	6.60	18	0.509	1,841	12.80
Uruguay	22.80	89	0.440	6,026	0.90(2)
Venezuela	8.60	13	0.464	3,678	19.40

Source: CEPAL (2000b); CEPAL (2002); U.N. (1999).

Notes
a This includes education, health and nutrition, social security, employment and social assistance and sewage systems.
b Percentage of population aged 65 and over, receiving retirement and pension income in urban areas.
c Households below the indigence line in 1999. (1) and (2) cover those in urban areas only.

security systems in these countries. In Latin American countries the term "social security" is often used synonymously with "social insurance." In this paper, the term "social security" is used in its broad sense, including social insurance social assistance and health care.

Development of social security systems prior to the 1980s

The characteristics of social security systems in "advanced countries" in Latin America can be summarized as follows: 1) compared to East Asian newly industrialized countries, the implementation of the system started earlier, 2) the main beneficiaries of the social system were formal sector workers, 3) the social assistance policy available to informal sector workers who were not covered by social insurance was of a residual character, so that 4) there are differences in social insurance between the formal sector and the informal sector. There are also differences in social insurance benefits within the formal sector.

In "advanced countries" such as Argentina, Uruguay and Brazil, the pension system for government workers was established prior to World War II. After World War II, the expansion of the social insurance system continued so that in the period from the 1960s to the 1970s almost all categories of workers were covered by social insurance in these countries. However their real coverage was limited to formal sector workers.

Mesa-Lago considers Uruguay, Chile and Argentina as pioneers in the region in adopting a social insurance system. He observes that "The pioneers were the ones who first introduced social security systems (especially pensions), and these are the most developed countries in this sense; in other words, they have all the range of social insurances (pensions, diseases, maternity, labor and employment risks), as well as family allowance and social assistance covering almost the whole population, or at least the great majority of the population" (Mesa-Lago 2000: 19) (also see Table 11.2). He includes Cuba and Costa Rica among "advanced countries" of the region, but Brazil should be included within this group as well.

However, as shown in Table 11.1, even in the "advanced countries" of the region, the coverage rate of pensions varies from 89 percent in Uruguay to 42 percent in Costa Rica, and a considerable number of the elderly people are outside this coverage. Most of the elderly people without pensions belong to the informal sector, and it may be inferred that either they did not join the pension system or they did not pay contributions to the system. Moreover, in 1999, the rate of poor and indigent population in "advanced countries" cannot be considered low, with rates of 19.7 percent in Argentina and 37.5 percent in Brazil. Though this poor and indigent population was receiving social assistance such as food assistance, this could not meet their needs either from the viewpoint of quantity or quality. Grassi *et al.* take Argentina as an example to describe the characteristics of social security policy of these countries as "The wide and

Table 11.2 Comparison of social insurance systems in Latin America

	First program		Other social insurances			Coverage	
	Pension	Sickness	Work injury	Unemployment	Family	Total	Active
	1977					1989–98	
Argentina	1930s	X	X	X	X	80	82
Bolivia	1956	X	X		X	21	13
Chile	1924	X	X	X	X	93	80[a]
Colombia	1945	X	X		X	16	35
Costa Rica	1943	X	X		X	86	60[a]
Cuba	1920	X	X	X		100[b]	93[b]
El Salvador[c]	1953	X	X			16	26
Mexico	1941	X	X			58	44
Peru	1936	X	X			24	32
Uruguay	1919	X	X	X	X	88	80

Source: Mesa-Lago (2000: 55).

Notes

X: existence of some kind of system.
Pension includes old age, disability and death. Sickness includes sickness and maternity. Family means family allowances. Active means economically active population.
a Coverage increases highly if pension assistance is added.
b Legal coverage. Statistics are not available.
c There is a great age variation among multiple programs in 1979.

simultaneous development of worker category and his specific rights to protection favored at the same time the residual character of public assistance" (Grassi *et al.* 1994: 15).

Thus, it can be said that the characteristics of the social security system established before the 1980s in "advanced countries" of Latin America are: 1) the system centered on social insurance, 2) a great gap existed between the formal sector and informal sector and 3) in the social insurance system there was a difference in the conditions of contributions made and benefits received by workers depending on whether they belonged to the formal or informal sector. Figure 11.1 made by Londoño and Frenk shows the general health care system in Latin America, and indicates the difference in the structure of the health care system according to the social stratum. Poor people in the informal sector are users of public hospitals, and as a rule, they are not charged at all or they are charged a minimum amount for the service. The non-poor population is divided into two groups; workers in the formal sector are registered in the social insurance system, and covered by this system. On the other hand, the urban middle and upper classes are users of high quality private health care services/insurance. They are not covered by the social

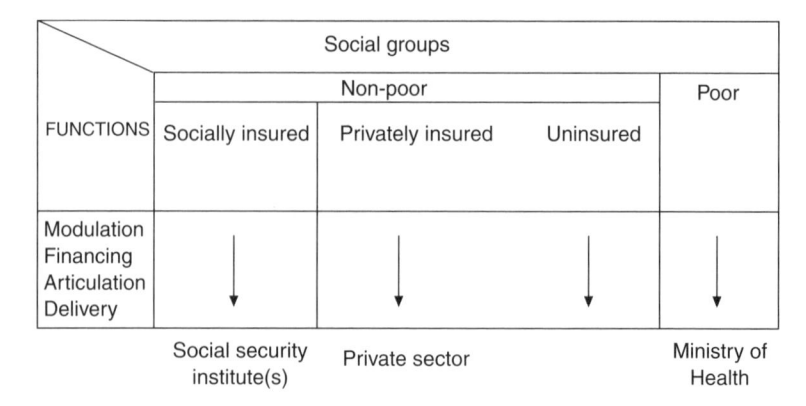

	Social groups			
	Non-poor			Poor
FUNCTIONS	Socially insured	Privately insured	Uninsured	
Modulation Financing Articulation Delivery	↓	↓	↓	↓
	Social security institute(s)	Private sector		Ministry of Health

Figure 11.1 Most common health model in Latin America (source: Londoño and Frenk (2000: 33)).

insurance system, or sometimes even if they are covered by the social insurance system, they prefer to use private health care services/insurance (Londoño and Frenk 2000: 33–4).

As we have seen above, the social security system in Latin America was, on the whole, social insurance centered, with a dual gap. In the case of Costa Rica, a social insurance model was implemented with a universal medical system. Moreover, in this country under the social democratic PLN administration, social assistance has been extended, including universalization of social security, creation of a national health plan, and introduction of family allowances (Wilson 1998: 102). Costa Rica, an "advanced country" in regard to social security in Latin America, has a relatively universal system, which makes the country an exception in the region, along with socialist Cuba.

Main factors contributing to the development of a Latin American social security model before the 1980s

The following factors can be identified as influencing the creation of the above mentioned social security system in Latin America before the 1980s: 1) the import substitution industrialization process started early and continued for a long period, 2) due to active intervention by the state in the economic sector, there was an expansion of the state sector, 3) as a result, there was an expansion of urban workers and the middle class, and labor unions came to have a certain political power, 4) the coming into power of populism, of which urban workers were the principal constituency and 5) even during military regimes, due to several reasons, there was an expansion of social insurance and so on.

Compared to East Asian countries, implementation of the import substitution industrialization model in Latin America started earlier, during the world economic crisis of the 1930s. Then, after World War II, the Latin American states started a full-scale promotion of import substitution industrialization policy, which continued for a long period, until the collapse of the model due to the economic crisis of the 1980s. In this process, the states protected the development of national industries by several measures, from imposing high tariff rates to establishing state-owned companies in the heavy and chemical industries and mineral resources sector. Expansion of the state sector was accompanied by the nationalization of the infrastructure sector, which had been owned by foreign capital, under the exaltation of economic nationalism of the post-World War II period. There was thus a strong participation of the state in economic development through import substitution industrialization in the post-World War II period.

As Huber asserts, "The development of social policy in Latin America has to be understood in the context of the political economy of import substitution industrialization" (Huber 1996: 144). Employment and salaries of urban workers in the formal sector were institutionally guaranteed by the import substitution industrialization protection measures and the large-scale employment favored by state expansion. Moreover, formal sector workers organized labor unions and held political influence.

Those countries with labor legislation favorable to formal sector workers and a social insurance system were under populist governments, as in the case of the Perón administration in Argentina, the Vargas administration in Brazil and the PRI (Partido Revolución Institucional) administration in Mexico. These governments, as was common to state corporatism, held workers of the urban formal sector as their principal constituency, and tried to exercise control over labor unions. (In the case of Mexico, farmers' unions were also part of the constituency.) Though there were differences from country to country in the provision of the social insurance system and unionized worker-oriented labor legislation, one characteristic was shared by these countries: the existence of governmental control over workers. However, it cannot be asserted that labor unions in these countries under populist administration were completely under state control. Because labor unions had a certain influence, social security policies were decided between the state corporatist oriented government and relatively influential labor unions. On the other hand, in the case of Chile, labor unions joined political parties such as the Communist, Socialist and Radical Parties, and became a strong pressure group (Mesa-Lago 1978: 28). In Costa Rica, even though the labor unions' power weakened after the civil war, the PLN (Partido Liberación Nacional), a newly organized social democrat party, came into power repeatedly and expanded the social security policy (Wilson 1998: 81–109).

Moreover, contrary to what may generally be expected, when military governments came into power after the collapse of populist administrations, there were cases in which social insurance was expanded in Latin America. Two groups of interpretation of this phenomenon are provided. The first refers to the emphasis upon the role performed by technocrats in the authoritarian regime. Malloy refers to Brazil as an example, and states "the orientation and goals of the military regime converged with those of social insurance technocrats to create an alliance willing and able to impose a systematic reform of the social insurance system" (Malloy 1979: 144). The second states that labor unions could preserve a certain influencing power against pressure from the military government, so that the military regime had to accept an expansion of social insurance as a concession. For example, in Argentina, during the Onganía administration in 1970, a compulsory social medical insurance law (ley de obras sociales) was approved, which covered all employed workers. In addition, labor unions could take over the administration of this medical insurance. This is considered the result of the 1969 large-scale riot led by labor unions and students in Córdoba. Pérez Irigoyen observes: "This concession made to labor unions was influenced by the political circumstances of the time" (Pérez Irigoyen 1989: 178).

Social security reform in the 1990s

Pension reform

After undergoing economic crisis in the 1980s, Latin American countries in the 1990s came to adopt a neoliberal economic policy, which emphasized market mechanisms. At the same time, social security reforms were implemented; for example social insurance reform, especially the pension system, became the central issue of reform. The former public system (a pay as you go system) was criticized for the deterioration of the pension system's liquidity, due to such factors as evasion of contribution, aging of the population, poorly defined payment conditions and the early retirement system. Thus, the pillar of the reform was the adoption of an individual capitalization system, which would contribute to the formation of the capital market and establish a close relationship between the contributions paid and benefits received. The first country to implement a drastic pension system reform was Chile, during the military administration in 1981. The pension reform in Chile constitutes the model of conversion to the capitalization system, as the new system was "the only one that includes a capitalization system with contributions made exclusively by workers and administrated by private entities" (Barreto de Oliveira 1994: 3).

However, among major countries in the region, Mexico has been the only one to implement a conversion to the capitalization system as a major part of its system. Other countries chose combinations of former systems with partial introduction of the capitalization system. Mesa-Lago classifies pension reforms implemented in Latin America during the 1990s into three types: a) Substitutive, a system that closed the public system and replaced it with a new system of fully funded individual accounts (FFI), as seen in Chile (1981), Bolivia (1987), México (1997) and El Salvador (1998); b) Compound, which did not close the old system but reformed the public system and integrated it as a basic-solidarity component with a new FFI component, as seen in Argentina (1994) and Uruguay (1996); c) Parallel, a system that did not close the public system but reformed it either partially or completely, and abolished a monopoly regime through the creation of a new FFI system that competes with the public system, seen in Perú (1993) and Colombia (1994) (Mesa-Lago 2000: 22).

Other social insurance reform

There was a trend towards incorporating the private sector in the reform of social security systems other than pension programs, especially health care services reform. However, similar to what happened in pension reforms, reforms implemented in health care systems varied from country to country, from the case of Brazil, where a universal health care system was adopted, to the case of Chile, where after urging the incorporation of the private sector into the health care system during the military administration, there was a trend toward strengthening the public sector with the onset of a democratic government (Barrientos 2000).

In Argentina, in addition to pension reform, an unemployment insurance plan was established for the first time in 1991, and significant reform was implemented in the medical insurance system in 1997. The adoption of unemployment insurance in 1991 was simultaneous with the enactment of an employment law which enabled flexible labor contracts, and constituted an answer to the increase in employment instability. In Argentina, the right to administer the medical insurance system "obras socials" was also granted to labor unions and, as a result, most "obras socials" are managed by labor unions. In this type of medical insurance system, workers automatically become enrolled in the medical insurance of their workplace. This procedure has been criticized for limiting competition among medical insurance and health care service providers and for producing excessive service and an increase in contributions paid (Panadeiros 1991: 13–27). In order to stimulate competition among providers of insurance and health care services, a new system allowing a free choice of insurers has been adopted. However, due to labor union opposition, it was decided not to include private medical insurance services in the range of options (Usami 2001). In addition, the public hospital system, which aids low-income individuals, has undergone a process of decentralization and is at present on its way to self-management (auto gestión).

In Brazil, social insurance relies heavily on the pension system; in fact, the expression "social insurance" is used to denote "pension." The pension system was divided into a system for private workers (a pay as you go system) and a non-contributory system for government workers. With regard to contributions and benefits, the pension system for government workers had been more favored than that of the private workers. Pension reform in Brazil was slow, and was limited to introducing restrictive conditions to the benefits of the private worker pension system (Koyasu 2001). After prolonged debates in Congress and Courthouse, pension reform for public employees, which includes levying contributions on public employees, was achieved by constitutional amendment in 2003.

Contrary to the slow progress in pension system reform, Brazil implemented a substantial reform in the health care system in 1990. This included the adoption of a completely universal system. The former system was divided into a social insurance system for the workers in the formal sector and a free health care service system for the workers in the informal sector. The latter failed to meet the needs from both quality and quantity perspectives. The new system, called "sistema único de salud" (sole medical system), consists of a free health care system offered in public health institutions to all citizens. However, problems still remain, as the middle and upper class populations, not satisfied with public health care facilities, turn to private health care institutions and insurance. Moreover, there are regions with no access to public medical institutions (Takagi 2001).

Health care reform in Chile experienced a parallel evolution with its pension reform. Medical insurance had been the main pillar of the former health care system, oriented to white-collar and blue-collar workers. As a result of the 1981 reform, those enrolled could choose between public medical insurance and private medical insurance. In addition, public hospitals are on their way to decentralization. However, since a democratic center-left administration came to power, there has been a tendency toward strengthening the public health care sector (Barrientos 2000).

Similarly, there has been a parallel evolution of pension and health care system reform in Mexico. The former Mexican system consisted of three components: 1) a medical insurance system for workers in the formal sector, 2) a public hospital system under the jurisdiction of the Ministry of Health oriented principally toward the informal sector not covered by insurance and 3) a private sector. The largest form of social insurance was the Instituto Mexicano de Seguro Social (IMSS) (Mexican Institute of Social Insurance) for private sector workers. When pension reform was implemented in 1995, the medical insurance system was separated from pension accounts, so that contributions to the medical insurance system from public funds increased, and the proportion of contribution funds decreased. Moreover, the IMSS created a new system oriented to non-participants, consisting of government assistance and contribution funds, and urged public enrollment in an IMSS medical insurance system. In addition, the public hospital system under the jurisdiction of the Ministry of Health is moving toward decentralization (Gómez-Dantés 2001; Tani 2001).

Background of the social security reform in the 1990s

Dismantling the ISI systems and its effects on social welfare

Neoliberal economic policies, which emphasized market principle and were adopted as a break away from the economic crisis of the 1980s and its aftermath, can be indicated as one of the circumstances in which social security reform was carried out in the 1990s. With the exception of Chile, where a military regime implemented a neoliberal economic reform and social insurance system reform, measures such as economic liberalization, deregulation and privatization of state-owned companies were carried out by democratic administrations. This was seen in the Menem administration in Argentina (1989–99), the Collor de Mello administration in Brazil (1990–2), the Salinas administration in Mexico (1988–94) and the Fujimori administration in Peru (1990–9). Implementation of these measures meant a complete replacement of the import substitution industrialization model by a market economy model. It can be pointed out that the globalization of the economy was taking place simultaneously with the implementation of a neoliberal economic policy in Latin America.

The shift to the market economy model meant the abolition of the protections given to wages and employment for formal sector workers by means of protectionist measures and the oversized state employment system implemented during the period of the import substitution industrialization. Moreover, economic liberalization and deregulation meant the intensification of domestic and foreign competition, and exerted pressure toward reduction of labor costs. Accordingly, full-day, permanent labor contracts were criticized as increasing labor costs. So industrial relations tend to be more flexible. Encouragement of market competition contributed to the improvement of competitiveness, but, on the other hand, it produced destabilization of employment (CEPAL 2000a: 20). In addition, there has been an increase in informal employment (those with no labor contract), and industrial relations in general have become unstable.

Social insurance system reform, mainly consisting of the change from a pay as you go pension system to a private capitalization system, is part of the conversion process to a market economy model. It was assumed that the inclusion of the private sector into the pension would allow the implementation of an efficient and high-quality service. Moreover, it was expected that the introduction of a private capitalization method in the pension system would produce the formation of capital markets and would contribute to economic development. Individual pension accounts in a private capitalization system clearly indicate the relationship between contributions and benefits, and it was believed that this would mitigate the contribution evasion problem. Moreover, it was asserted that individual accounts of the capitalization system were suitable to deal with the increase in job mutability that was considered the basis of flexible industrial relations.

However, during the economic growth of the 1990s, countries such as Argentina and Uruguay showed economic growth without an employment increase or a rise in unemployment. Unemployment rates in 2001 were 17.4 percent in Argentina, 15.4 percent in Uruguay, 16.9 percent in Panama and 18.5 percent in Colombia (CEPAL 2001a) (see Table 11.3). When high unemployment rates become constant and there is significant growth in informal employment, social insurance policies such as pension systems and medical insurance systems face the problem of decreasing enrollees and increasing contribution evasion.

Political factors of social security reform

The weakening of labor unions that received benefits from the former social security system can be seen as a political factor that allowed the implementation of a market oriented model of social security. In the past, labor unions feared that social security system reform would reduce their benefits. Thus, they would frequently stand against such reform. However, employment became unstable with economic liberalization, and thus, labor unions started to lose political influence due to decreasing membership. The trade union density in wage and salary earners decreased by 42.6 percent in Argentina (1986–95), by 28.2 percent in Mexico (1989–91) and by 42.6 percent in Venezuela (1988–95) (ILO 1997: 239). Thus corporatist political structures weakened under the market oriented economy model during the 1990s.

Latin American governments that implemented social security reform in parallel with neoliberal economic reform in the 1990s were all democratic governments. Some scholars ascribe the peculiarity of democracy in these governments as a factor allowing the implementation of large-scale reform. O'Donnell calls this type of democracy a "delegative democracy" ("democracia delegativa"). He states "delegative democracy consists in producing, through clean elections, a majority authorizing somebody to become an exclusive interpreter of the highest interests of the nation" (O'Donnell 1997: 294).

However, the results of market-oriented social security reform have not been uniform in the region. As shown above, the content of reforms implemented have been varied among the countries. It may be said that these differences reflect the differences in political situation and political system among them. Murillo takes the examples of Argentina, Mexico and Venezuela and explains "the interaction between labor unions and their allied parties on the road to market reforms based on labor competition

Table 11.3 Latin America and the Caribbean: urban unemployment (average annual rates)

		1992	1993	1994	1995	1996	1997	1998	1999	2000	2001	2002
L.A. & Caribbean		6.1	6.2	6.3	7.2	7.7	7.2	7.9	8.8	8.4	8.4	8.9
Argentina	Urban areas	7.0	9.6	11.5	17.5	17.2	14.9	12.9	14.3	15.1	17.4	19.7
Barbados	National total	24.3	21.9	19.7	15.6	14.5	12.3	10.4	9.2	9.2	9.9	10.3
Bolivia	Departmental capitals	5.4	5.8	3.1	3.6	3.8	4.4	6.1	8.0	7.5	8.5	10.3
Brazil	6 metropolitan areas	5.8	5.4	5.1	4.6	5.4	5.7	7.6	7.6	7.1	6.2	11.7
Chile	National total	6.7	6.5	7.8	7.4	6.4	6.1	6.4	9.8	9.2	9.1	9.0
Colombia	13 metropolitan areas	10.2	8.6	8.9	8.8	11.2	12.4	15.3	19.4	17.2	18.2	17.6
Costa Rica	Total urban areas	4.3	4.0	4.3	5.7	6.6	5.9	5.4	6.2	5.3	5.8	6.8
Cuba	National total	6.1	6.2	6.7	7.9	7.6	7.0	6.6	6.0	5.5	4.1	3.3
Dominican Rep.	National total	20.3	19.9	16.0	15.8	16.5	15.9	14.3	13.8	13.9	15.4	16.1
Ecuador	Total urban areas	8.9	8.9	7.8	7.7	10.4	9.3	11.5	14.4	14.1	10.4	8.6
El Salvador	Total urban areas	8.2	8.1	7.0	7.0	7.5	7.5	7.6	6.9	6.5	7.0	6.2
Guatemala	National total	1.6	2.6	3.5	3.9	5.2	5.1	3.8	n.a.	n.a.	n.a.	3.1
Honduras	National total	6.0	7.0	4.0	5.6	6.5	5.8	5.2	5.3	n.a.	5.9	6.1
Jamaica	National total	15.7	16.3	15.4	16.2	16.0	16.5	15.5	15.7	15.5	15.0	15.1
Mexico	Urban areas	2.8	3.4	3.7	6.2	5.5	3.7	3.2	2.5	2.2	2.5	2.7
Nicaragua	National total	14.4	17.8	17.1	16.9	16.0	14.3	13.2	10.7	9.8	10.7	12.9
Panama	Total urban areas	17.5	15.6	16.0	16.6	16.9	15.5	15.2	14.0	15.2	17.0	16.5
Paraguay	Total urban areas	5.3	5.1	4.4	5.3	8.2	7.1	6.6	9.4	10.0	10.8	14.7
Peru	Metropolitan Lima	9.4	9.9	8.8	8.2	8.0	9.2	8.5	9.2	8.5	9.3	9.4
Trinidad and Tobago	National total	19.6	19.8	18.4	17.2	16.2	15.0	14.2	13.2	12.2	10.8	10.4
Uruguay	Total urban areas	9.0	8.3	9.2	10.3	11.9	11.5	10.1	11.3	13.6	15.3	17.0
Venezuela	National total	7.8	6.6	8.7	10.3	11.8	11.4	11.3	15.0	13.9	13.3	15.8

Source: CEPAL (2001a and 2003).

and partisan coalitions" (Murillo 2001: 196). According to Murillo, differences in the reforms implemented are the results of these factors.

On the other hand, Takahashi (2001: 20–5) maintains that the political system is the reason why government worker pension system reform had not advanced in Brazil. She points out that "pensioner cum politicians trying to protect acquired benefits, functioned as potential veto players, and that Brazil's highly fragmented party system provided the RJU (Regime de Previdência do Serviço Público: Social Security Regime for Public Sector Workers) coalition with opportunities to veto policy change." In the case of Argentina, as medical insurance is closely related to labor union interests, labor unions have opposed its reform. This is why medical insurance reform has been slower than pension reform. In general, labor unions are losing their influence, but not entirely. In the Argentine political context, corporatism still maintains certain political viability. In these two countries, political legacies partially have constrained social security reform.

Meanwhile, governments which have a social democratic tendency came into power in South America, as in the case of Brazil in 1995, Argentina, with the de la Rua Alianza administration in 1999 and Chile, when Lagos from the socialist party became president in 1999. These administrations mitigated social problems caused by neoliberalism, and aim at economic and social models similar to the European social democrats' "Third Way," which aims at the coexistence of social equity and market mechanisms. Thus, their goal is to implement a more impartial and universal social security policy. Part of this has already been implemented. However, there exist a considerable number of public commitments that cannot be fulfilled due to financial limitations.

That is one of the reasons why the activities of civil society organizations were increasing in the 1990s. There are many reports of a rapid increase in the number of civil society organizations which advocated social assistance during the 1990s (e.g. Verduzco 2001). International financial organizations like the World Bank also supported this trend in improving the efficiency of social assistance. On the other hand, not a few scholars pointed out that social, political and economic transformation is part of the background of growth of civil society organizations. For example, Garretón stated that it is required for the third sectors to reconstruct the society in order to connect the political elites with the popular sector, when politics was oppressed by authoritarian regimes or society was atomized by neoliberal economic reform (Garretón 2001: 36).

Conclusion

Social security reform, especially pension reform implemented in Latin America in the 1990s, allowed the incorporation of the private sector into the former public social insurance system. The reform also tried to introduce market principles into social security policy. This process went in the same direction as the change of the economic model as it shifted from the import substitution industrialization model to the market-oriented model. Moreover, labor unions, weakened politically, lost their ability to sustain the former social insurance policies. At the same time, international financial institutions such as the IMF and World Bank recommended structural reforms to the countries of the region. Under these circumstances, social security reforms have been achieved by strong "delegative democracy" type governments.

However, there has not been a complete change in the Latin American social security system to a market model. In the case of pension systems, most countries adopted a combination system, which introduced a private capitalization system into a reformed public pay as you go system. Some authors (e.g. Pierson 1994) contend that preexisting political systems and institutions influenced the social security reform process and produced differences among them. Moreover, there are examples, as in the cases of medical insurance in Costa Rica and health care in Brazil, where policymakers maintained or introduced a universal system. It may be that this has been the product of differences in political circumstances and political systems among countries. Concerning health care reform, more research is required from a political science point of view, especially in the case of Brazil.

On the other hand, in the 1990s, industrial relations in some countries became unstable as unemployment rose, producing stagnation or a decrease in social insurance coverage. In this situation, social assistance policy increased in importance. Especially, as observed in Argentina's economic crisis in late 2001, implementation of urgent anti-crisis social assistance has been especially important. Similar to social insurance, urgent social assistance in the 1990s pursued efficiency and demanded strict targeting in most cases. In Argentina, there is a coexistence of targeting-oriented programs, such as implementation of a non-contributory pension system for elderly persons from a fixed age onwards, and universal characteristics programs such as food assistance for poor people. Moreover, NGOs have an active role in different fields, monitoring institutions responsible for the implementation of social assistance. The role of civil society as regards social assistance is on the rise.

References

Barreto de Oliveira, F.E. (ed.) (1994) *Social Security Systems in Latin America*, Washington, DC: IDB.
Barrientos, A. (2000) "Getting Better after Neoliberalism: Shift and Challenges of Health Policy in Chile," in P. Lloyd-Sherlock (ed.) *Health Care Reform and Poverty in Latin America*, London: University of London.
CEPAL (2000a) *El desafío de la equidad de género y de los derechos humanos en albores del siglo XXI?*, Santiago de Chile: CEPAL.

—— (2000b) *Social Panorama of Latin America 1999–2000*, Santiago de Chile: CEPAL.
—— (2001a) *Balance preliminar de las economías de América Latina y el Caribe 2001*, Santiago de Chile: CEPAL.
—— (2002) *Social Panorama of Latin America 2000–2001*, Santiago de Chile: CEPAL.
—— (2003) *Balance preliminar de las economías de América Latina y el Caribe 2003*, Santiago de Chile: CEPAL.
Esping-Andersen, G. (1990) *The Three Worlds of Welfare Capitalism*, Cambridge: Polity Press.
Garretón, M.A. (2001) *Cambios socials, actors y acción colectiva en América Latina*, Santiago de Chile: CEPAL.
Gómez-Dantés, O. (2000) "Health Reform and the Poor in Mexico," in P. Lloyd-Sherlock (ed.) *Health Care Reform and Poverty in Latin America*, London: University of London.
Grassi, E., Hintze, S. and Neufeld, M.R. (1994) *Política social, crisis y ajuste Estructural*, Buenos Aires: Espacio.
Huber, E. (1996) "Options for Social Policy in Latin America: Neoliberal versus Social Democratic Models," in G. Esping-Andersen (ed.) *Welfare State in Transition*, London: UNRISD.
ILO (1997) *World Labour Report 1997/98*, Geneva: ILO.
Koyasu, A. (2001) "The Brazilian Pension System: An Adverse Pressure on Cardozo Administration's Reform Agenda," in K. Usami (ed.) *The Welfare States in Latin America*, Chiba: IDE (in Japanese).
Londoño, J.L. and Frenk, F. (2000) "Structural Pluralism: Towards an Innovative Model for Health System Reform in Latin America," in P. Lloyd-Sherlock (ed.) *Health Care Reform and Poverty in Latin America*, London: University of London.
Malloy, J.M. (1979) *The Politics of Social Security*, Pittsburgh: University of Pittsburgh Press.
Mesa-Lago, C. (1978) *Social Security in Latin America*, Pittsburgh: University of Pittsburgh Press.
—— (2000) *Desarrollo social, reforma del estado y de la seguridad social. Al umbral del siglo XXI*, Santiago de Chile: CEPAL.
Murillo, M.V. (2001) *Labor Unions, Partisan Coalitions, and Market Reforms in Latin America*, Cambridge: Press Syndicate of the University of Cambridge.
O'Donnell, G. (1997) *Contrapuntos*, Buenos Aires: Paidós.
Panadeiros, M. (1991) *El Sistema de obras sociales en la Argentina: Diagnóstico y propuesta de reforma*, Buenos Aires: FIEL.
Pérez Irigoyen, C. (1989) "Política pública y salud," in E. Isuani *et al.* (eds) *Estado, democrático y política social*, Buenos Aires: EUDEBA.
Pierson, P. (1994) *Dismantling the Welfare State?*, Cambridge: Cambridge University press.
Takagi, K. (2001) "The Brazilian Health Care System: Does a Dream Come True?" *Latin America Report*, 18(2): 13–15 (in Japanese).
Takahashi, Y. (2001) "The Politics of Public Pension Reform in Brazil," *Anales de Estudios Latinoamericanos*, 21: 20–5.
Tani, H. (2001), "Reform to the Mexican IMSS Pension System," in K. Usami (ed.) *The Welfare States in Latin America*, Chiba: IDE (in Japanese).
U.N. (1999) *Statistical Yearbook 1997*, New York: UN.

Usami, K. (2001) "Health Insurance System and its Reform in Argentina," in K. Usami (ed.) *The Welfare States in Latin America*, Chiba: IDE (in Japanese).
Verduzco, G. (2001) "La evolución del tercer sector en México y el problema de su significado en la relación entre lo público y lo privado," *Estudios Sociológicos*, XIX(55): 36–40.
Wilensky, H.L. (1975) *The Welfare State and Equality: Structural and Ideological Roots of Public Expenditure*, Berkeley: University of California Press.
Wilson, B.M. (1998) *Costa Rica; Politics, Economics and Democracy*, Colorado: Lynne Rienner Publishers.

12 Welfare states in East Asia
Similar conditions, different past and divided future

Yasuhiro Kamimura

Why now?

An international debate on the welfare systems of East Asia was sparked by the 1997 economic crisis. Although domestic reforms had started in the early 1990s, what made them an international issue were the unprecedented economic crisis and the consequent social anxiety in the wake of the crisis. Because international agencies such as the IMF, the World Bank and the Asian Development Bank joined in the discussion, an arena has formed for debating welfare policy in the region, rather than country specific policy. These agencies have come to be influential in shaping the social policies of each country, not only by providing financial support, but also by offering knowledge and innovation.[1]

From emergency measures to long-term issues

It was the emergency measures that appeared first. The objective was mitigating the impact of mass unemployment and inflation brought about by the crisis. Gupta *et al.* (1998) produced an IMF working paper that summarized these measures. The measures discussed there, however, were limited to short-term policies such as provision of subsidies for food and fuel, distribution of medicine, job creation by expanding public works program and scholarship to minimize student dropouts. On the other hand, they did not examine such measures as the coverage expansion of social insurance, which might lead to long-run financial burdens.[2]

While the IMF took a short-term approach as above, the World Bank favored another approach. In recent years, the World Bank has come to recognize the importance of "social protection" and set up the Social Protection Unit in 1996. Professor Holzmann, who is the Sector Director of the Social Protection Unit, has proposed to reposition labor market intervention, social insurance and social safety nets within the framework of "social risk management." He suggested that the World Bank should cope not only with the emergency issues, but also with longer-term risk prevention (Holzmann and Jorgensen 1999; World Bank 2001). There is also a report titled "Towards an East Asian Social Protection Strategy," prepared for applying this framework to East Asia (World Bank 1999). Such "new" concepts from the World Bank have had a considerable effect upon the direction of the international debate on the welfare systems of East Asia.

Although the economy is recovering, the vulnerabilities of the East Asian welfare systems revealed by the crisis have not yet been overcome. Considering this situation, many international agencies have set up research projects for strengthening the welfare systems of East Asia, based on a long-term perspective.

The Asian Development Bank (ADB) has published *Social Protection in Asia and the Pacific* (Ortiz ed. 2001). According to Isabel Ortiz who organized the project, "social protection," a concept that includes labor market policies, social insurance, social assistance, area-based schemes and child protection, is essential for the ADB's mission to help the member countries achieve poverty reduction (ibid. 41). The document proposes guiding principles for each item of social protection.

On the other hand, the seminar titled "Lessons Towards a New Social Policy Agenda: Beyond the East Asia Socio-Economic Crisis," which was financed by the Asia–Europe Meeting (ASEM)[3] Trust Fund and coordinated by the World Bank, have published *New Social Policy Agendas for Europe and Asia* (Marshall and Butzbach eds 2003). In this document, many European researchers give suggestions for countries like Indonesia, Korea, Malaysia, the Philippines and Thailand, based on the knowledge of European welfare states. According to Katherine Marshall who organized the project, the seminar has discussed social policy issues that affect virtually every resident. These efforts go beyond the World Bank's traditional objectives like poverty alleviation and social development (ibid. 4).[4]

Needs for comparative welfare state studies

As sketched above, it became an international issue to strengthen the welfare systems of East Asia based on a long-term perspective. This region, however, has not been properly explored by comparative welfare state studies until recent years. There are many overgeneralizations about the whole region, on the one hand, as well as specific studies of particular countries, on the other. Our historical and comparative understanding of the issue remains very poor. Lacking a cohesive framework to understand the variety, the policy prescriptions of international agencies seem to split between the transcendental one-size-fits-all approach and the ad hoc country-specific approach. To find a way to overcome this shortcoming, comparative studies of East Asian welfare states are more seriously needed than ever before.[5]

What I would like here to accomplish is to present challenges and tentative visions, rather than to provide the full answers. I would like to organize the rest of this chapter in correspondence to the following three questions.

308 *Yasuhiro Kamimura*

1   Why have the social expenditures of East Asian countries been kept much lower than those of the advanced welfare states? Does it mean that the welfare systems of East Asia are "embryonic"? (next section)
2   While we often talk about the "East Asian model" of economic development, can we also identify a single trajectory of welfare development that can be labelled as the "East Asian welfare model"? (third section)
3   Which direction(s) are the welfare systems of East Asian countries marching in? How are they located in relation to the reform trajectories of the advanced welfare states? (fourth section)

Are they embryonic?

Why have the social expenditures of East Asian countries been kept much lower than those of the advanced welfare states? Does it mean the welfare systems of East Asia are "embryonic"? Let us start with a summary of available data.

Young population and modest expenditure

Figure 12.1 shows the trends of government expenditure on social security and welfare as a proportion of GDP in each country.[6] It illustrates three points. 1) As is often pointed out, the expenditures are generally lower than those of non-Asian advanced countries.[7] 2) Korea, Taiwan and Hong Kong are relatively generous. Taiwan has consistently been more generous than other countries. There is a marked increase in Korea from the late 1980s and in Hong Kong from the early 1990s. 3) Other countries (Singapore, Thailand, Malaysia, Indonesia and the Philippines) have not shown any substantial changes within this period.

Figure 12.2 indicates the trends of government expenditure on health

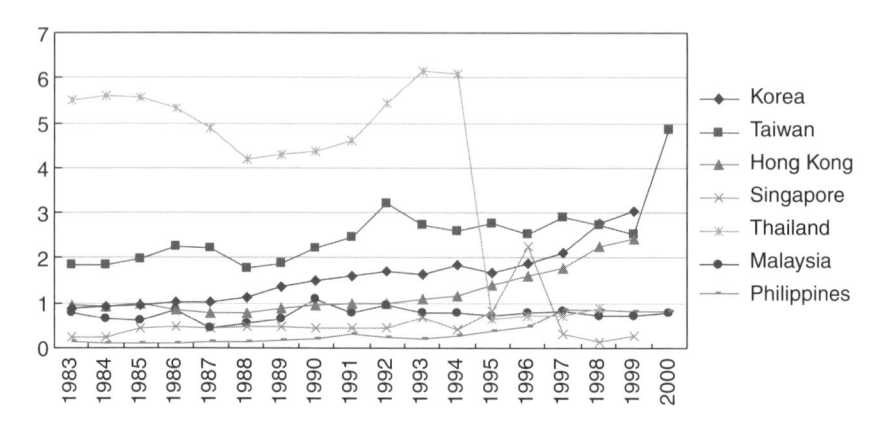

Figure 12.1 Government expenditure on social security and welfare (as % of GDP).

Welfare states in East Asia 309

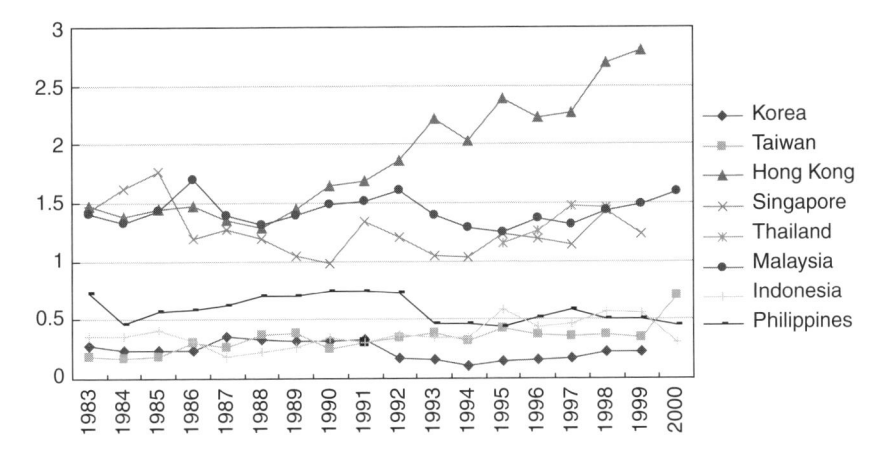

Figure 12.2 Government expenditure on health care (as % of GDP).

care. It presents three things. 1) Hong Kong, Singapore and Malaysia are relatively high. All of these countries share the legacy of British colonial rule. 2) There is a marked increase in Hong Kong from the early 1990s. 3) Again, these figures are lower than those of non-Asian advanced countries.

Figure 12.3 displays the trends of government expenditure on education.[8] We notice that: 1) Most countries spend more money on education than on social security and health. 2) Malaysia and Singapore are relatively high spenders.

We shall turn now to the correlation between expenditure and its predicted determinants. Figure 12.4 is a scatter diagram of economic level and social expenditure.[9] The two variables are roughly correlated. But

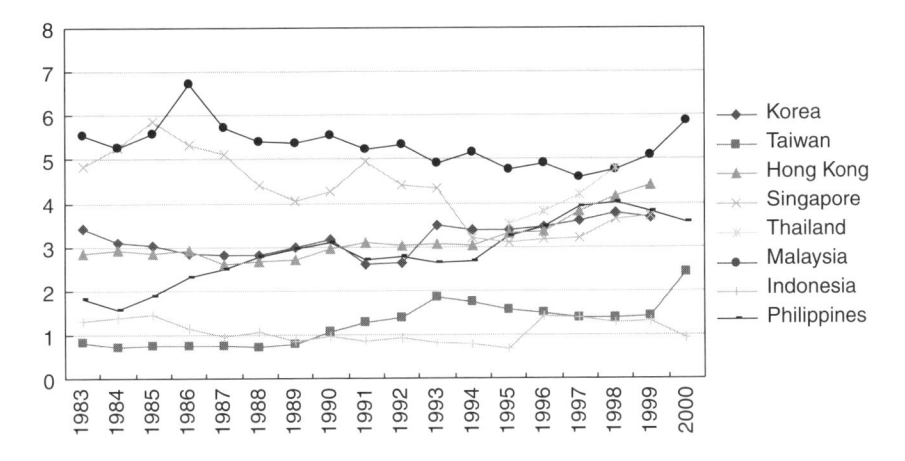

Figure 12.3 Government expenditure on education (as % of GDP).

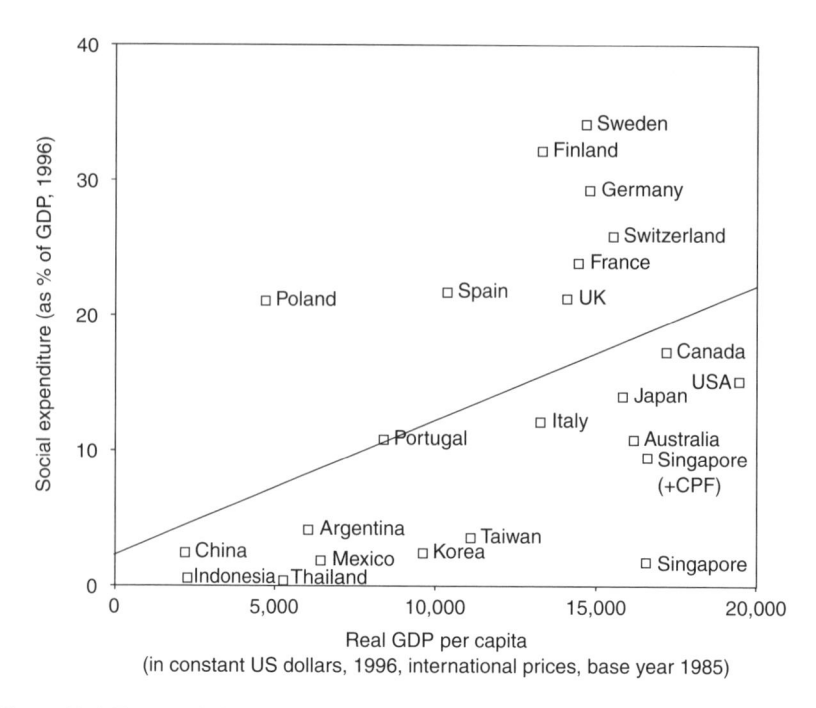

Figure 12.4 Economic level and social expenditure.

there are outlier countries like Singapore, where the level of social expenditure is not high given its economic level.[10] At the opposite end, there are also countries like Poland, where social expenditure is fairly high in relation to its economic level. It is also obvious that there is a considerable range of variation among the rich countries. Obviously it would be wrong to conclude that the GDP per capita is the only determinant of expenditure level.

Figure 12.5 and Figure 12.6 show the apparent correlation between expenditure and the ageing ratio.[11] Here we can find the tentative answer to the question of why social expenditures of East Asian countries are low. As Wilensky (1975) pointed out, we may tentatively say that the economic standard and ageing level of a country are still major factors that determine its efforts in the sphere of welfare.[12] In Figure 12.5, Taiwan seems to be situated at the takeoff point.

Initiation and coverage

But then, is it correct that the East Asian governments have not made any efforts in the field of social welfare? That is certainly not the case. As shown in Table 12.1, all ten countries examined here have introduced plans that manage old age, sickness and work injury. Four factors stand

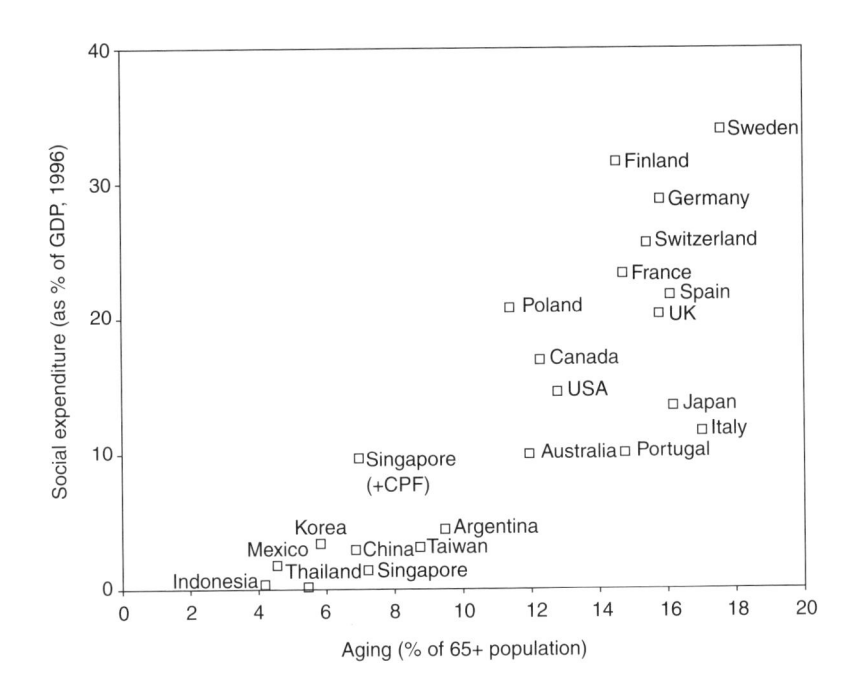

Figure 12.5 Aging and social expenditure.

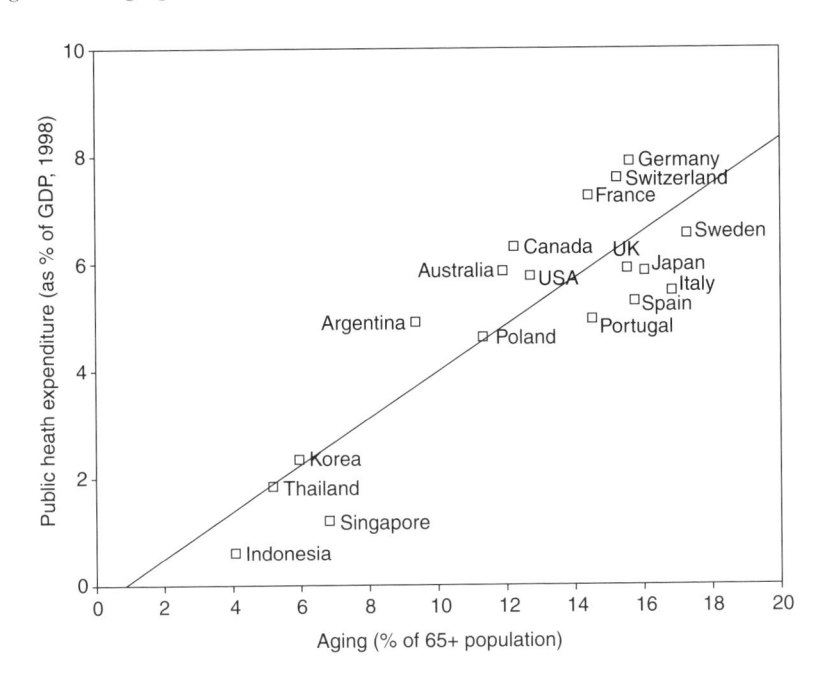

Figure 12.6 Aging and public health expenditure.

Table 12.1 Introduction of social security schemes in East Asian countries

	Japan	Korea	Taiwan	Hong Kong	Singapore
Old age	First law: 1941. Current laws: 1944 (employees' pension insurance); 1959 (national pension program); and 1985. Social insurance. *Contributors/ Labour force: 57.9%* (There is also the universal National Pension Scheme.)	First law: 1973 (not implemented until 1988). Current law: 1986, as amended 1989, 1993, 1995 and 1998. Social insurance. *Contributors/ Labour force: 46.5%*	First law: 1950. Current law: 1958, as amended 1988 and 1994. Social insurance (Lump-sum benefits only). *Contributors/ Labour force: 79.8%*	First law: 1971 (social assistance). Current law: 1993 (Comprehensive Social Security Assistance, CSSA). Social. assistance (There is also Mandatory Provident Fund, MPF, introduced in 2000.)	First law: 1953. Current law: 1985, as amended in 1991. Provident fund (Lump-sum benefits and annuity payments). *Contributors/ Labour force: 65.3%*
Sickness	First laws: 1922 (health insurance; implementation delayed until 1927) and 1938 (national health insurance). Current laws: 1958 and 1998 (national health insurance); and 1994 and 1997 (health insurance). Social insurance. *Public expenditure ratio: 78.7%*	First law: 1963 (Medical Insurance Law Implemented in 1977) and 1997 (National Medical Insurance Law). Current law: 1998 (Medical Insurance Law) and 1998 (National Medical Insurance Law). Social insurance. *Public expenditure ratio: 45.1%*	First law: 1950. Current law: 1958, as amended 1988; 1994 (National Health Insurance). Social insurance.	First laws: 1968 (employer liability) and 1971 (social assistance). Current law: 1997. Dual employer liability and social assistance system.	First laws: 1968 (employer liability); 198 (provident fund). Current laws 1996 (employer liability); 198 (provident fund). Multiple employer liability, provident fund and social assistance systems. *Public expenditure ratio: 36.4%*
Work injury	First law: 1911. Current law: 1947, 1980, 1986 and 1995. Social insurance.	First law: 1953. Current law: 1963 as amended through 1997. Compulsory insurance with public carrier.	First laws: 1929, 1950. Current law: 1958, as amended 1988 and 1994. Social insurance.	First laws: 1953 (employer liability) and 1971 (social assistance). Current law: 1995. Dual employer liability and social assistance system.	First law: 1933. Current law: 1990. Employer liability/ compulsory insurance with private carrier.

Welfare states in East Asia 313

Thailand	Malaysia	Indonesia	Philippines	China
First and current law: 1990. Revised 1999. Social insurance. *Contributors/ Labour force: 18.0%*	First law: 1951 (provident fund). Current law: 1969 (disability insurance); 1991 (provident fund) amended 1995. Dual provident fund (lump-sum benefits and periodic payments) and social insurance systems (disability only). *Contributors/ Labour force: 50.0%*	First law: 1951. Current law: 1977. Provident fund (lump-sum benefits only). *Contributors/ Labour force: 10.6%*	First and current law: 1954, as amended 1997. Social insurance. *Contributors/ Labour force: 21.0%*	First law: 1951. Current laws: 1953, 1978, 1996 and 1997. Local government social insurance (basic pension) and individual pension accounts systems. *Contributors/ Labour force: 12.3%*
First and current law: 1990. Revised 1994. Social insurance. *Public expenditure ratio: 31.7%*	First law: 1951. Current law: 1991. Dual provident fund (lump-sum benefits and periodic payments). *Public expenditure ratio: 58.3%*	First law: 1957. Current law: 1992. Social insurance. *Public expenditure ratio: 46.7%*	First and current laws: 1954 as amended in 1997 (sickness benefits); 1969 as amended in 1996 (medical care); and 1977 as amended in 1997 (maternity). Social insurance. *Public expenditure ratio: 45.9%*	First law: 1951. Current laws: 1953, 1978, 1986, 1988, 1994 and 1998. Local government social insurance (medical fund pools) and/or employer-provided (medical savings accounts) programs.
First law: 1972. Current law: 1994. Compulsory insurance with public carrier.	First law: 1929. Current law: 1969. Social insurance.	First law: 1939. Current law: 1992. Social insurance.	First and current law: 1974, as amended 1996. Social. insurance	First law: 1951. Current laws: 1953, 1978, 1986. Local government social insurance (work-injury fund pools) and/or employer-provided (medical savings accounts) programs.

continued

Table 12.1 continued

	Japan	Korea	Taiwan	Hong Kong	Singapore
Unemployment	First law: 1947. Current laws: 1975 and 1998. Social insurance.	First law: 1995.	First law: 1968. Current law: 1968, effective January 1999. Social insurance.	First and current law: 1977. Social assistance (not specialized in unemployment).	none.
Family allowances	First law: 1971 (children's allowance). Current laws: 1981, 1985, 1991 and 1994. Dual employer liability and assistance systems.	none.	none.	First and current law: 1971. Social assistance (not specialized in family allowance).	none.

Sources: U.S. Social Security Administration (1999), *Social Security Programs Throughout the World 1999*; as for Contributors/Labour force (1996): World Bank, 2000, *Pension Systems in East Asia and the Pacific: Challenges and Opportunities*, 65; as for Japan's Contributors/Labour force: *Japan Statistical Yearbook 2002*; as for Taiwan's Contributors/Labour force: *Statistical Yearbook of The Republic of China 2000*; as for Public expenditure ratio (as % of total health expenditure, 1998): UNDP (2001), *Human Development Report 2001*.

out. 1) As for work injury compensation, every country has introduced it in the early period. 2) Most countries have also introduced certain kinds of health security policies. But in some countries (Thailand and Singapore, especially), the ratio of public expenditure to the total cost for health care is low. 3) As for old age income security, many countries adopt provident fund systems, which often provide only lump-sum benefits. Only Japan has a universal pension system. 4) Only four countries have an unemployment insurance system. Except for Japan, however, these were only recently introduced.

We can classify the countries according to the characteristics of their pension systems.

1. Early introduction and extensive coverage: Japan, Taiwan, Singapore, Malaysia.
2. Late introduction and extensive coverage: Korea.
3. Early introduction and minimal coverage: Indonesia, the Philippines, China.
4. Late introduction and minimal coverage: Thailand.

The extent of coverage must be determined by the size of the agricultural sector in each country. Indonesia, the Philippines, China and Thailand all have large agricultural sectors. Meanwhile, what determines the timing of introduction? I will explain this point in the next section.

Thailand	Malaysia	Indonesia	Philippines	China
Included under the 1990 Social Security Act, implementation pending. Royal Decree	none.	none.	none.	First law: 1986. Current law: 1999. Local government social insurance.
First and current law: 1990 (implemented in 1998). Revised 1999. Social insurance.	none.	none.	none.	none.

A single trajectory?[13]

While we often talk about the "East Asian model" of economic development, can we also identify a single trajectory of welfare development that can be labeled as the "East Asian welfare model"?

Differences with the three worlds

As we have seen in the previous section, although East Asian countries (except Japan) are roughly similar in that they have relatively young populations and low social expenditure, we also observe considerable variation among them. How can we understand this diversity?

As for the diversity among Western countries, Esping-Andersen (1990) distinguished the three welfare models, that is, liberal, conservative and social democratic. Learning much from Polanyi (1944), he argued that the patterns of historical class coalition determined the characteristics of each welfare state. According to Polanyi, in the nineteenth century, the trading class supported economic liberalism which was aimed at the establishment of a self-regulating market, while the working and the landed classes supported the principle of social protection against the destructiveness of the market (ibid. 138). While the landed classes sought a solution in the maintenance of the past (i.e. conservatism), the workers borrowed a solution from the future (i.e. socialism) (ibid. 162). Esping-Andersen also examined the classes that led the formation of welfare states. But he noted that the structure of class coalitions in parliament, rather than the power of any single class, is decisive (Esping-Andersen 1990: 30). According to him, in the Nordic countries, the coalition of the working class and farmers led to the formation of the "social democratic" welfare state that would promote an equality of the highest standards with the principles of universalism. In contrast, in the continental European countries, the conservative forces successfully formed "reactionary" alliances, which developed the "conservative" welfare state that preserved status differentials in the labor market. In the Anglo-Saxon countries, such a coalition did not appear. Thus, there emerged the "liberal" welfare state, in which only a modest level of benefits would be provided (ibid. 27).

Unfortunately, this kind of story does not fit the reality of East Asia. I argue this, stressing the cases of the Asian NIEs (Korea, Taiwan, Hong Kong and Singapore). First, in the regime formation[14] period of all four countries, there were no strong capitalists who favored the formation of "liberal" welfare states. Since Korea and Taiwan were still very much agricultural countries, powerful industrial capitalists had not yet emerged. While there were commercial capitalists in Hong Kong and Singapore who were engaged in transit trade, they never took the initiative in politics. As happened in Korea, capitalists in the Asian NIEs were created in the process of state-led industrialization, and did not create the regime by themselves. Second, there were no powerful landed classes to favor the formation of "conservative" welfare states. Since Hong Kong and Singapore were city states, and therefore had minimal agricultural sectors, there were no landed classes from the very beginning. While there had been landed classes in Korea and Taiwan, early land reforms effectively removed them. Third, there was no possibility in the Asian NIEs of a coalition combining the working class and farmers, which might have favored the formation of "social democratic" welfare states. As Hong Kong and Singapore had insignificant agricultural sectors, this hypothesis was unrealistic for them. In Korea and Taiwan, the state incorporated farmers in order to block the influence of communists. In all cases, there were no opportunities for labor parties to lead welfare regime formation. In sum, it is hard to apply Esping-Andersen's model to the Asian NIEs.

Relationship between state and labor

What then, led welfare regime formation in these countries? And, what factors determined the character of their welfare systems? My answers to these questions are that state-labor relations are decisive. It was the state, relatively independent of any social forces, that nurtured capitalists, dismissed the landed classes, suppressed workers' excessive demands and at the same time could introduce some measures for people's welfare. State-labor relations were crucial then, because other social forces, such as capitalists and landlords, were weak. I shall argue in the rest of this section that the difference in state-labor relations in the regime formation period explains the character of the social security systems (stressing pensions for workers) of each country during its rapid industrialization.

When we examine the state-labor relations in the regime formation period of each country, we notice that three countries other than Hong Kong had the character of "state corporatism" in Schmitter's terminology (Schmitter and Lehmbruch 1979).

> Corporatism can be defined as a system of interest representation in which the constituent units are organized into a limited number of [1] singular, [2] compulsory, [3] noncompetitive, [4] hierarchically ordered and functionally differentiated categories, [5] recognized or licensed (if not created) by the state, and [6] granted a deliberate representational monopoly within their respective categories in exchange for [7] observing certain controls on their selection of leaders and articulation of demands and supports.
> (Schmitter 1979: 13. The numbering was added by me.)

According to this definition, state-labor relations in each country could be described as follows (also see Table 12.2).

First, in the case of Taiwan, 1) there was only the Chinese Federation of Labor (CFL) of Taiwan Province as the national center of labor unionization. 2) Unions joined the CFL as a matter of course, though not by legal obligation. 3) There were no organizations that could rival the CFL. 4) The CFL was established to be centralized upon the federations of each prefecture and city, the Federation of Industrial Unions of Taiwan Province and the prefectures and the Federation of Occupational Unions of Taiwan Province and the prefectures (Wakabayashi 1992: 114). 5) The CFL was not only established by the government, but also subsidized by it (ibid.). 6) The leaders of the CFL were also executive members of the Kuomintang (KMT, the Nationalist Party). Most of the officials of lower level unions were also members of the KMT (ibid.). 7) Although the CFL was the quasi-governmental organization for controlling unions, it certainly had the monopolistic privilege of direct interaction with the government.

Table 12.2 State–labor relations in the regime formation periods

	Taiwan	Singapore	Korea	Hong Kong
1 Singular	yes	yes	yes	no
2 Compulsory	yes	yes	yes	no
3 Noncompetitive	yes	yes	yes	no
4 Hierarchically ordered	yes	yes	no	no
5 Recognized by state	yes	yes	yes/no	no
6 Representational monopoly	yes	yes	yes	no
7 Controls on leadership selection and interest articulation	yes	yes	no	no

Source: Kaminura 1999: 239.

Second, in the case of Singapore, 1) although there had been two national labor centers, the leftist one was weakened by the government. By 1965, unions were integrated by the National Trade Union Congress (NTUC). 2) Unions were expected to join the NTUC as a matter of course and did, though not by legal obligation. 3) There were no other organizations that could oppose the NTUC. 4) The NTUC was highly centralized to the extent that lower level unions could not oppose it. The NTUC also developed grassroots movements like a cooperative society of consumption for penetrating into the rank and file member communities (Rodan 1989). 5) The NTUC was not only established by the government, but was also subsidized by it, even being given civil servants as staff (Kimura 1990: 12). In the late 1960s, about 80 percent of the NTUC's revenue was from government subsidies (Kobayashi *et al.* 1993: 30). 6) The leaders of the NTUC were also executive members of the People's Action Party. In those days Devan Nair was the secretary general of the NTUC. He had converted from the leftist labor movement, then was a member of the Party's central committee, and eventually became the third president of Singapore in 1981 (Takeshita 1995). 7) The NTUC was the monopolistic representative of labor's interest. Later the NTUC joined the tripartite National Wage Council, established in 1972, from which they extracted some social policies from the government in exchange for agreements on wage restraint and cooperation in the improvement of productivity (ibid.; Shimodaira 1986: 44).

Third, in the case of Korea, 1) there was only the Federation of Korean Trade Unions (FKTU) as the national center of labor unionization. 2) Unions were expected to join the FKTU as a matter of course, though not by legal obligation. 3) Anti-mainstream factions that might rival the FKTU were made illegal. 4) The FKTU had, however, a decentralized character, the leaders of which could not control the lower level unions fully. President Park saw the FKTU as a target of repression, rather than as the counterpart of cooperation, because it was not a monolithic organization. 5) The FKTU was developed from its predecessor, which was reorganized by President Park. So he only used the existing structure, but did not create the new body by himself. His government provided money for the FKTU (Choi 1989: 83), but the police sometimes interfered in the establishment of new unions (Shin 1993: 183). 6) The leaders of the FKTU were selected from among labor movement activists, and trained by the government. But they were not sent from within Park's circle. That is, none of them were military personnel who had joined the revolution, nor executive members of the ruling party (Choi 1989: 233). 7) Although the FKTU certainly represented labor's interest to the government monopolistically, it did not have a strong say. It could not join deliberative councils of the government through the 1960s, nor could it send its representatives to the national assembly until 1972 (Choi 1989: 233).

Finally, the situation in Hong Kong was quite different from the other three countries. 1) There were two national labor centers, the Federation of Trade Unions (FTU) and the Trade Union Congress (TUC). The former was affiliated with the Communist Party of Mainland China, while the latter with the KMT (the Nationalist Party) of Taiwan. 2) There were many unions that did not join either of these organizations. 3) The FTU and the TUC were in a competitive relationship. 4) There were myriad craft unions arising from their guild origin, which the national centers could not control fully. The FTU and the TUC were more political groups than integrated bodies of lower level unions. Thus, the nature of Hong Kong's labor movement was highly decentralized and fragmented (England and Rear 1981: 136). 5) Although the FTU and the TUC were legitimized by the Colonial Office, they developed with the aid of the Communist Party of mainland China and the KMT of Taiwan respectively. They were not established or subsidized by the Colonial Office (England and Rear 1981: 136, 141). 6) The Colonial Office strictly controlled the political activities of the national centers, but did not care about their selection of leaders or expression of opinions. 7) Neither of the two national centers was regarded as the counterpart of negotiation by the Colonial Office. That means they did not have any representational right before the Office.

Inclusionary corporatism

Thus we can see that, while Taiwan and Singapore fulfil all the features of corporatism, Korea's corporatism seems to be different. How can we sub-categorize these cases? Stepan (1978) developed Schmitter's concept, and distinguished two "policy poles" within state corporatism by examining several Latin American regimes. He says,

> Near the "inclusionary pole" the state elite can attempt to forge a new state-society equilibrium by policies aimed at incorporating salient working-class groups into the new economic and political model. Near the "exclusionary pole" the attempt to forge a new state-society equilibrium can rely heavily on coercive policies to deactivate and then restructure salient working-class groups.
>
> (Stepan 1978: 74)

He also noted that the same regime can shift from one pole to another.

> The state elite attempts to exclude from the political arena a variety of relatively autonomous, largely working-class based, institutional structures capable of resisting their political design, and then seeks to reintegrate the excluded groups into associational organizations designed and controlled by the state.
>
> (ibid. 79)

And he observes that in inclusionary corporatism, distributive, symbolic and group-specific welfare policies are used to encapsulate salient worker and peasant groups into state corporatist associational structures (ibid. 76).

As for Taiwan, Singapore and Korea, each state's elites seemed to choose an "exclusionary" policy at first. The Taiwanese and Singaporean governments harshly eradicated anti-governmental labor unions, and established their own conformist labor organizations. The Korean government was also antagonistic to labor organization, but could not eradicate it. This is the line that divides Korea and the other countries. Since the Taiwanese and Singaporean governments effectively excluded anti-governmental unions, they inevitably shifted to "inclusionary" policies. On the other hand, the Korean government could not do that, and therefore it remained near the "exclusionary pole." As for Hong Kong, although there were two major labor organizations, the colonial government of Hong Kong did not see them as partners in negotiation. So we may describe Hong Kong's regime as "exclusionary pluralism."

Thus we see that only Taiwan and Singapore shifted to "inclusionary" corporatism, in which pension schemes for workers were introduced prior to full-scale industrialization. In Taiwan, Labor Insurance was set up in 1950, which included sickness, disability, maternity, death and old age benefits (only in lump sum). While those who were covered were mainly workers in public enterprises in the beginning, coverage was gradually extended to workers in the private sector, which included medium-sized and small businesses. In Singapore, the Central Provident Fund (CPF), which was founded before independence, was improved after 1968 when the People's Action Party monopolized parliament. CPF was a mandatory saving scheme for old age income security, which was later extended to other purposes, including housing, medical care and education.

In Korea and Hong Kong, in which a shift to the "inclusionary" pole did not occur, pension schemes for workers were not adopted until recent years. Most workers in Korea and Hong Kong, therefore, had to survive the industrialization period without a reliable social security system. In Korea, although Industrial Injury Insurance was introduced in 1964, and Medical Insurance was implemented in 1977, these were not extended to a wide range of workers until the late 1980s. Moreover, the pension scheme was not started until 1988. In Hong Kong, welfare had been left to charity and mutual aid until the social assistance system was set up in 1971. After long discussion, the Mandatory Provident Fund (MPF) was finally legislated in 1999.

To sum up, we can distinguish at least two paths in regard to welfare state formation of the Asian NIEs. One is the early introduction path of Taiwan and Singapore, which results from "inclusionary corporatism." The other is the late introduction path of Korea and Hong Kong. Therefore, one can hardly maintain that there is only one trajectory in East Asia.

Where are they headed?

Which direction(s) are the welfare systems of East Asian countries marching in? How are they located in relation to the reform trajectories of the advanced welfare states? In this section, I will continue to focus on four countries – Korea, Taiwan, Hong Kong and Singapore – though I can only outline a story as to the recent situation.

Beyond democratization and economic crisis

East Asian countries were pushed toward the construction (or restructuring) of their welfare systems by democratization from the late 1980s and by the economic crisis of the late 1990s. The circumstances of democratization, however, were considerably different across countries. As for Asian NIEs, it was Korea and Taiwan that underwent typical democratization. The colonial office of Hong Kong also promoted a certain degree of "democratization," while regime shift did not occur in Singapore. The impact of the economic crisis also differed among countries. Korea was hardest hit, while the influence on Hong Kong and Singapore was also considerable. Considering this variation, I would like to sketch out the character of changes that were brought about by democratization and the economic crisis.

In Korea, the introduction of a social security system was delayed because of the absence of inclusionary corporatism. However, the change came dramatically during the process of democratization in the late 1980s. The government of President Chun Doo-hwan announced the "Three Measures for the Promotion of Social Welfare" just before the presidential election, against a surging democracy movement pushed by the opposition party, labor unions and students. These measures included 1) the implementation of the minimum wage law, 2) the introduction of the national pension scheme, and 3) the expansion of the medical insurance scheme to the entire nation (Chung 1992: 295). This was the preemptive concession of the Chun government, for the democracy movement had not yet pushed the introduction of specific social security schemes. These policy commitments were implemented around the 1987 Declaration of Democratization.

Korea was hit directly by the East Asian economic crisis. The crisis, however, turned out to be a promoter of welfare reform in Korea. President Kim Dae-jung, who was inaugurated soon after the outbreak of the crisis, spurred welfare reform, putting forward his idea of "productive welfare." According to him, productive welfare is comprised of four factors, that is, 1) primary distribution through the establishment of fair market order, 2) redistribution by government, 3) social investment for self-reliance support in the realm where the state and the market overlap, and 4) enhancement of people's quality of life (Kim Dae-jung 2002: 35).

Based on these ideas, the Kim government made considerable achievements, such as 1) accomplishment of universal pensions by extending coverage to urban self-employed workers, 2) solidaristic reform of medical insurance integration, 3) an expanded employment insurance scheme, which had been introduced in 1995, and 4) enactment of the National Basic Livelihood Security Law.

In Taiwan, the social security system was introduced prior to full-scale industrialization because of the formation of inclusionary corporatism. This system, however, has come to be criticized along with democratization in the late 1980s because of the unfairness of the various schemes, for the schemes vary according to occupation, like Labor Insurance for workers, Military Servicemen's Insurance, Government Employees Insurance, Insurance for Teachers and Staff of Private Schools and Farmer's Insurance. As for health, National Health Insurance was introduced in 1995. As a result, all people have come to be covered by the same scheme. And, because of electoral competition between the KMT (the Nationalist Party) and the DPP (the Democratic Progressive Party), income security for social groups, which had been left in the cold, was partly realized by the introduction of the Living Subsidy for Low-Income Seniors in 1993 and Old-age Farmers Allowance in 1995.

Recently, unemployment problems have come to be aggravated in Taiwan with the change of the global economic environment and the shift of production bases to mainland China, though Taiwan was not directly hit by the economic crisis. The KMT government coped with the problem by adding an unemployment benefit scheme to Labor Insurance in 1999. Then, Chen Shui-bian, whose Democratic Progressive Party (DPP) has long advocated the establishment of a welfare state, won the 2000 presidential election, which was the first instance of partisan alternation in Taiwan's government. The Chen government reformed the unemployment benefit scheme to Employment Insurance in 2003, which put stress on support for reemployment (Tsen 2003). On the other hand, a National Pension Scheme has also been discussed, but has not yet been introduced. The reasons may be as follows (Kamimura 2002; Huang 2003). 1) It is difficult to coordinate the existing schemes which are divided by occupation. 2) There already exist various allowances that have been introduced through the election campaign. 3) The economic climate is worsening. 4) The DPP's minority government cannot pass bills effectively.

In Hong Kong, the introduction of a social security system was delayed because of the absence of inclusionary corporatism. After the Sino–British Joint Declaration of 1984 that started the process of returning Hong Kong to China, the Colonial Office promoted "democratization" of its territory, gradually increasing the directly elected seats of the Legislative Council. As the last Governor, Christopher Patten, who arrived at his post in 1992, instituted the electoral reform. As a result, social workers and union leaders gained a greater voice in politics (Sawada 1997: 251). Subsequently, the Comprehensive Social Security Assistance (CSSA) scheme, which had been implemented in 1971, was expanded in terms of benefit amounts and the number of recipients in 1993. In addition, the Mandatory Provident Fund, which is an individual account scheme for compulsory saving, was enacted in 1995 and implemented in 2000.

The impact of the Asian economic crisis on Hong Kong was second only to Korea in severity among the Asian NIEs. The Government of the Hong Kong Special Administrative Region, which succeeded the British administration in 1997, tried to address the crisis principally with existing schemes. The number of recipients of CSSA amounted to 230,000 in 1998–9 as a consequence of deepening unemployment. Among them, 120,000 were elderly, and 30,000 were unemployed. In 1999, the government implemented the Support for Self Reliance Scheme, which obliged unemployed recipients of CSSA to go to an employment agency every two weeks, and to participate in community service at least once a week. As a result, the number of unemployed recipients has declined (Chan 2001). On the other hand, the government is considering introducing the Health Protection Account, which is a compulsory individual saving scheme for health expenses after the age of 65, for the purpose of reducing public expenditure (ibid.).

Lastly, in Singapore, the social security system, which was introduced before independence, was expanded prior to full-scale industrialization because of the formation of inclusionary corporatism. As the inclusionary corporatism of Singapore's PAP government continues to operate, the development of the social security system has taken the form of a functional extension of CPF. In 1984, CPF added the Medisave scheme, which allows individual members to withdraw money from their own accounts to pay for hospitalization expenses incurred by family members. In 1987, the Minimum Sum scheme was introduced to encourage members to keep the minimum old age provision in their accounts or to buy private life annuities after reaching maturity at the age of 55 (Low and Aw 1997: 24, 58).

The impact of the economic crisis to Singapore was also significant, though it was not at the same level as in Korea and Hong Kong. Nonetheless, the PAP government did not push radical reforms like Korea and Taiwan, nor did it permit unintended expansion of public assistance like Hong Kong. The number of recipients of public assistance benefits in Singapore is severely limited in comparison with other countries. In September 2002, only 8,000 people received public benefits. In the 2001 general election, the Singapore Democratic Party, which did not have any seats in parliament, advocated the following policies but lost the election:[15] 1) establishment of a minimum wage system, 2) introduction of an unemployment allowance, 3) limitation of CPF to old age provision, and 4) extension of government subsidies for medical expenses. On the other hand, in the same year, the PAP government implemented the Economic

Downturn Relief Scheme for a one year trial, which provided needy people with 200 Singaporean dollars per month for three months only.

As observed above, the situation in each country looks considerably different when we examine the welfare reforms in the Asian NIEs. First of all, in Korea, the development of a welfare system started quite dramatically in line with democratization, and the later economic crisis promoted consolidation of the welfare system. Second, in Taiwan, the restructuring of the welfare system started with democratization, but the pace of reform was not as quick as in Korea, being trapped in the legacy of inclusionary corporatism. Third, in Hong Kong, even limited democratization promoted the development of a welfare system, though it took a passive attitude in response to the economic crisis. Finally, in Singapore, as inclusionary corporatism continues to operate, the restructuring of the welfare system has made little progress, even during the economic crisis. In essence, the change was substantial in the countries 1) which became democracies, and 2) where the legacy of inclusionary corporatism did not exist. Combining these two factors, we can order the countries according to the magnitude of the change. That ordering is Korea, Taiwan, Hong Kong and Singapore.

Future of welfare state and civil society

Do the evolving welfare systems in these countries represent a common march towards a European-type welfare state, though with some degree of variation in pace? Here I would like to switch gears to examine how the idea of the "welfare state" is discussed in the political discourse of each country.

We should consider the influence of new philosophies developed within the advanced welfare states. For, in the context of these advanced countries, "welfare state" has already become a negative phrase in some literature. The welfare state has been criticized by new social democrats and by advocates of "the Third Way" during the late 1990s, in addition to suffering harsh attacks from neoliberals during the 1980s. Civil society is replacing the notion of the "old" welfare state. The ideas of Professor Anthony Giddens, leading advocate of the Third Way, echo through the political spaces of East Asia. For example, one can feel undisputed input from Giddens in the book of Korea's ex-President Kim Dae-jung, *The Road to Productive Welfare*[16] (Kim Dae-jung 2002). Taiwan's President Chen Shuibian was honest when he wrote that his "New Middle Road" was inspired by Tony Blair's *New Britain* and Giddens' *The Third Way* (Chen 2000).

Here I would like to summarize Giddens as his arguments pertain to the present discussion (Giddens 1994, 1998). First, he declares that "the welfare state cannot survive in its existing form" (Giddens 1998: 174). He makes three key points. 1) The welfare state assumes the permanent full-time employment of male workers in an industrial society. This assumption obviously contradicts the present condition of post-industrial society, where women have entered the paid labor force in very large numbers and modes of work organization have been diversified. 2) The welfare state is inextricably connected with the consolidated nation state and undemocratic bureaucracy. These are altogether undermined gradually by the tide of globalization. 3) The welfare state is based on the risk management and ex-post benefits of social insurance. This kind of approach cannot deal with the new risks, which arise from various factors like technological innovation, social exclusion and the growth of single parent families. Therefore, according to Giddens, in place of the traditional welfare state we should construct the "social investment state," operating in the context of a "positive welfare society." Concretely speaking, we should work out policies to enable people to recognize risks as opportunities, rather than constructing policies only for redistributing income. He says that we need to foster an "active civil society" and a partnership between government and civil society.

I will not examine here whether his diagnosis and prescription for the advanced welfare states is right or wrong. A noteworthy point is the impact of his idea on the emerging countries. These countries, while just about building a welfare state, are strongly influenced by his argument that the traditional welfare state is no longer sustainable as the role of civil society becomes more important. It may be said that it is an example of "the intellectual precocity common to all backward countries to a certain extent"[17] (Maruyama and Kato 1998: 172). We should recognize that the welfare reforms underway in East Asian countries cannot be immune from the ideologies transmitted from the advanced welfare states, whether considering it as an advantage or a disadvantage of backwardness.

Moreover, one must clarify what kind of welfare state or civil society one is talking about, when talking about moving "from the welfare state to civil society" or "a partnership between the welfare state and civil society." For these terms can imply several different meanings. I would like to sketch out the four models of this relationship between the welfare state and civil society by pairing two models of each.

First, as for welfare state, it is well known that there are two contrasting concepts: the "residual model" and the "institutional model"[18] (Wilensky and Lebeaux 1965: 138; Titmuss 1974: 30). The residual model holds that the welfare state should provide minimum benefits only when the normal structures of satisfying the needs of individuals, the family and the market, break down. The institutional model, by contrast, sees the welfare state as a formal function of modern complex society, which provides services according to the needs of individuals with the objective of realizing social equality.

Second, I turn to civil society. According to Professor Takeshi Ishida, Masao Maruyama seldom used the term civil society, though he has long been regarded as a proponent of the "civil society school" in post-war Japan. Professor Naoaki Hiraishi, though accepting this point, explained

326 *Yasuhiro Kamimura*

that Maruyama used this term with two different meanings. The first example is civil society as a translation of *bürgerliche Gesellschaft*, which is a system of needs (*System der Bedürfnisse*) that Hegel (1770–1831) described as the character of modern society. The second example is civil society as a phrase that indicates a dynamic society in which intermediate groups independent of the state compete with each other, which Guizot (1787–1874) described as the character of European civilization. The former is an image of a market society based on exchange and contract among atomic individuals, while the latter is an image of democratic society in which people are organized in various types of voluntary groups. I would like here to call the former the "Hegelian model" of civil society and the latter the "Guizotian model" (Hiraishi 2003: 184).

Figure 12.7 presents a combination of the above models. First, the upper left is what Giddens criticized as the traditional welfare state. It can be said that this resembles the "iron cage" in which atomic individuals are entrapped in the paternalistic protection of bureaucracy, the coming of which Max Weber pessimistically predicted. Second, the lower left is the model in which the market, with rare exceptions, is dominant. One may find at the edge of this quadrant the "satanic mill" which crushes the people's communal life into crumbs, which was how Karl Polanyi characterized England after 1834. Third, the lower right is the model in which

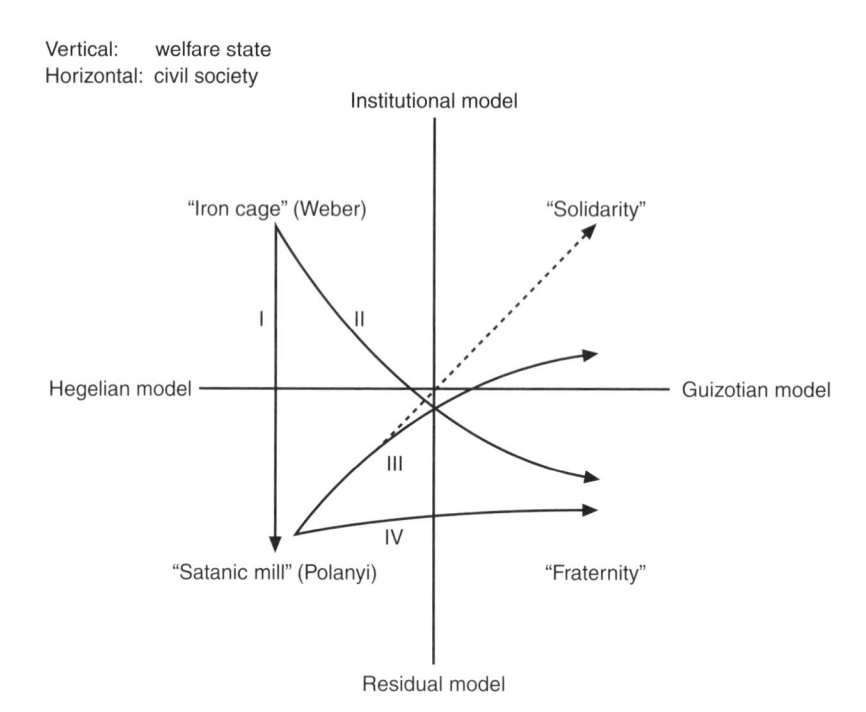

Figure 12.7 Diagram of welfare state–civil society trajectories.

people help each other without relying on the state. It may be illustrative to imagine a friendly society or the "fraternity," which flourished in Britain in the latter half of the nineteenth century. In this model there inevitably emerges a divide between those who have enough resources to help each other and those who do not.[19] Finally, the upper right is the model in which competitive complementarity is established between the welfare state that aims at social equality and the voluntary organizations that secure people's freedom and spontaneity. I would like to tentatively call this the "solidarity" model.[20]

We can place some thoughts from the advanced countries on this chart as follows. First, ideas like those that Thatcherism has advocated, the dismantlement of the welfare state and the revival of market, or neoliberalism that has spread among governments all over the world, can be represented as the arrow from the upper left to the lower left (I). Second, the proponents of the Third Way insist on moving the transition from the upper left to the lower right (II). The reasons why they do not want to move to the upper right are, on the one hand, that they have no sympathy for the traditional welfare state (what the "old" social democrats want to preserve), and on the other hand that they have to counter neoliberalism.[21]

How, then can we locate ex-President Kim Dae-jung's idea of "productive welfare" in Korea or President Chen Shui-bian's policy of the "New Middle Road" in Taiwan within this chart? Their starting points are undoubtedly not the consolidated welfare state like the iron cage of the upper left. Their course should be more like the arrow from the lower left towards the upper right. The arrow seems, however, to be bent downward by the influence of new beliefs sent out from the advanced welfare states (III). In fact, Kim detaches himself from "the advanced welfare states of the West," though he advocates the expansion of state welfare (Kim 2002: 6, 107). He emphasizes "the role-sharing between government and the private sector by voluntary participation of the people, as well as the principle of the government's responsibility" (ibid. 115). Chen also says "the ideal of social welfare should not be too high" in the era of global capitalism (Chen 2000: 230), pushing forward the idea of "Volunteer Taiwan" (ibid. 185), while he advocates the establishment of social security system.

On the other hand, the "welfare state" (that is, the "institutional model" of the welfare state in this text) is still taboo in the politics of Hong Kong and Singapore. Chief Executive Tung Chee-hwa of Hong Kong spoke on the issue of social policy at unusual length at the policy address of 2000. After a few days, however, he made a speech at the Business Community Luncheon and said, "Yet do let me assure you that we are NOT going down the slippery slope towards a welfare state." By contrast, he emphasized that "the Third Sector" is welcome, and said, "It is only when the Third Sector is strong, aside from the market being free, that the government really can be small."[22] Former Prime Minister Goh

Chok-tong of Singapore, when he was talking at the Swearing-In Ceremony of Mayors in 2002 about increasing the resources of the Community Development Councils which are responsible for regional welfare activities, declared "This does not mean that we are moving toward becoming more of a welfare state." As for civil society, he made very favorable comments in a speech in 2000, saying "The more the people can organize themselves to look after their own interests, the better it is for Singapore. Self-reliance will contribute to an enduring Singapore."[23]

Appreciation for civil society coincides with a negative attitude toward state welfare within the political discourse of Hong Kong and Singapore. So that means the idea is represented as arrow IV in the chart.

In conclusion, I would like to summarize the points of this chapter. 1) The East Asian economic crisis promoted debate on welfare systems across the region. The policy prescriptions of international agencies, however, split between the one-size-fits-all approach and the country-specific approach. To overcome this problem, we should develop a comparative framework. 2) It was because of their young population structure that East Asian countries have been able to keep the cost of social welfare low. Low expenditure does not mean that the welfare systems are embryonic. There have been a variety of social security schemes in East Asian countries. 3) It is, however, difficult to identify an "East Asian model" connecting all countries in the region. Taking Asian NIEs before the 1980s as an example, there was a wide difference in the development of social security schemes. This division essentially was determined by whether inclusionary corporatism had been established or not. 4) The welfare systems of East Asian countries are changing, stimulated by democratization and economic crisis. The magnitude and direction of the change, however, seems to vary considerably across countries, depending on the character of democratization and the legacy of inclusionary corporatism.

Notes

1 The direct attention of these international agencies was initially directed to the five hardest hit countries, that is, Thailand, Indonesia, Korea, Malaysia and the Philippines.
2 On the other hand, the ILO discussed the long-term issues in the same period of time, such as the introduction of unemployment insurance, in its report titled *The Asian Financial Crisis: The Challenge for Social Policy* (Lee 1998).
3 The Asia–Europe Meeting (ASEM) was started in 1996 for strengthening the partnership between East Asian countries and European countries. Thereafter, the summit meeting is held every other year.
4 There are also ADB and World Bank (2000), UNESCAP (2001), and OECD (2002).
5 There are already a considerable amount of books on the issue. See Goodman, White and Kwon eds (1998), Jacobs (1998), Tang (2000), Tang ed. (2000), Ramesh and Asher (2000), Aspalter ed. (2002), Holliday and Wilding eds (2003), Rieger and Leibfried (2003) and Ramesh (2004).

6 Based on ADB (Asian Development Bank), *Key Indicators of Developing Asian and Pacific Countries 2001*. It seems that it does not include the expenditure for pension payment.
7 Note that prior to 1995 the figure for Thailand includes education, health, housing and community amenities, which means it is not comparable with other years and other countries.
8 This kind of international statistics often excludes the expenditure of local governments. For more accurate comparison, we should explore the national data sources of each country.
9 Real GDP Per Capita (in constant US dollars, international prices, base year 1985) is based on World Bank (William Easterly and Mirvat Sewadeh), 2002, *Global Development Network Growth Database* (http://www.worldbank.org/research/growth/GDNdata.htm). Social expenditure is based on ILO, *Cost of Social Security 1990–96* (http://www.ilo.org/public/english/protection/socsec/publ/css/cssindex.htm). Note that the definition of expenditure is different from those of Figure 12.1. The amount of CPF withdrawals in Singapore is based on Asher (2000: 35). As for Taiwan, the figures are taken from DGBAS, *Statistical Yearbook of the Republic of China 2000*.
10 The case of Singapore is complicated. If we include the withdrawals of the Central Provident Fund into "social expenditure" (indicated as "Singapore (+CPF)" on the diagram), the amount is fairly high. It must be noted, however, that the CPF scheme is based on individual accounts, and have neither the function of income redistribution among rich and poor, nor that of social risk pooling.
11 The ageing ratio is based on UN, *Demographic Yearbook 1997*. As for Taiwan, the figures are taken from DGBAS, *Statistical Yearbook of the Republic of China 2000*. Public health expenditure is taken from UNDP, *Human Development Report 2001*.
12 The differences among rich countries remain, however.
13 This section is based on Kamimura (1997; 1999).
14 Here, "regime formation" means the establishment of power which preceded the industrialization of each country; Park Chung-hee's military government of Korea in the 1960s; the Kuo Ming Tang (KMT, the Nationalist Party) government of Taiwan in the 1950s; the People's Action Party government of Singapore in the 1960s; and in Hong Kong, we find that the new state-labor relation formed around 1949.
15 See the website of the Singapore Democratic Party (http://www.singaporedemocrat.org/informations/ge2001).
16 The author also admitted that "the idea of productive welfare basically shares an interest with the Third Way, [which is being proposed in the advanced welfare states like Sweden, the Netherlands, Britain and Germany]" (Kim Daejung 2002: 21).
17 This phrase is used by Masao Maruyama, when he points out the fact that the dangerousness of socialism and communism Japanese elites had already been well-informed about in late 1870s, long before its industrial revolution.
18 Titmuss (1974) proposed three models, adding the "industrial achievement-performance model." Esping-Andersen (1990) also follows the three models in his famous comparative study. I would like here to omit the third model to be able to make a two-dimensional diagram.
19 The sharpest criticism of this model is found in the volume of Ralph M. Kramer, who compared voluntary agencies helping disabled people in the Netherlands, England, the United States and Israel.

> Voluntarism is no substitute for services that can best be delivered by government, particularly if coverage, equity, and entitlements are valued. ...there is a danger that those who have jumped on the bandwagon of the

era of limits, signaling the end of the welfare state by advocating more volunteerism, are being coopted by others who have less concern with social justice than with tax reduction.

(Kramer 1981: 283)

20 This diagram somewhat reflects European taste. In reality, both "welfare state" and "civil society" are conceptualized differently according to the local context of each country.
21 The arrows indicate the direction of policy ideas. Therefore, an actual policy which is led by one of these ideas will not necessarily reach the tip of the arrow.
22 See "2000 Policy Address by Chief Executive" (http://www.info.gov.hk/gia/general/200010/11/1011140.htm) and "CE's speech at Hong Kong Business Community Luncheon" (http://www.info.gov.hk/gia/general/200010/16/1016122.htm).
23 See "Speech by Prime Minister GOH Chok Tong at the Swearing-In Ceremony of Mayors of Community Development Council Districts" (http://www.cdc.org.sg/data/speeches/speeches1.html) and "Speech by Prime Minister GOH Chok Tong at the NUSS Millennium Lecture" (http://app10.internet.gov.sg/data/sprinter/pr/2000110404.htm).

References

ADB and World Bank (2000) *The New Social Policy Agenda in Asia: Proceedings of the Manila Social Forum*, Manila: Asian Development Bank.
Asher, M.G. (2000) "Social Security Reform Imperatives: The Southeast Asian Case," Draft.
Aspalter, C. (ed.) (2002) *Discovering the Welfare State in East Asia*, Westport, CT: Praeger.
Chan, R. (1996) *Welfare in Newly-Industrialised Society: The Construction of the Welfare State in Hong Kong*, Aldershot: Avebury.
—— (2001) "The Sustainability of the Asian Welfare System after the Financial Crisis: Reflections on the Case of Hong Kong," Working Paper No. 7, Hong Kong: Southeast Asia Research Centre of the City University of Hong Kong.
Chen, S. (2000) *The Son of Taiwan*, translated into Japanese by T. Oikawa, Tokyo: Mainichi Shinbunsha.
Choi, J. (1989) *Labor and the Authoritarian State: Labor Unions in South Korean Manufacturing Industries 1961–1980*, Seoul: Korea University Press.
Chung, M. (1992) *State Autonomy, State Capacity, and Public Policy: The Development of Social Security Policy in Korea*, Ph.D. thesis, Indiana University.
England, J. and Rear, J. (1981) *Industrial Relations and Law in Hong Kong*, Hong Kong: Oxford University Press.
Esping-Andersen, G. (1990) *The Three Worlds of Welfare Capitalism*, Cambridge: Polity Press.
Giddens, A. (1994) *Beyond Left and Right: The Future of Radical Politics*, Cambridge: Polity Press.
—— (1998) *The Third Way: The Renewal of Social Democracy*, Cambridge: Polity Press.
Goodman, R., White, G. and Kwon, H. (eds) (1998) *The East Asian Welfare Model: Welfare Orientalism and the State*, London: Routledge.
Gupta, S., McDonald, C., Schiller, C., Verhoeven, M., Bogetic, Z. and Schwartz, G. (1998) "Mitigating the Social Costs of the Economic Crisis and the Reform Programs in Asia," Papers on Policy Analysis and Assessments, Washington, DC: IMF.

Hiraishi, N. (2003) "Masao Maruyama's Argument on 'Civil Society,'" in M. Kobayashi (ed.) *Essays on Masao Maruyama: Voluntary Action, Fascism and Civil Society*, Tokyo: University of Tokyo Press (in Japanese).

Holliday, I. and Wilding, P. (eds) (2003) *Welfare Capitalism in East Asia: Social Policy in the Tiger Economies*, Basingstoke: Palgrave.

Holzmann, R. and Jorgensen, S. (1999) "Social Protection as Social Risk Management: Conceptual Underpinnings for the Social Protection Sector Strategy Paper," *Journal of International Development*, 11: 1005–27.

Huang, M. (2003) "The National Pension Scheme in Taiwan," in Y. Kamimura and A. Suehiro (eds) *Welfare System in East Asia*, Institute of Social Science, Tokyo: University of Tokyo (in Japanese).

Jacobs, D. (1998) "Social Welfare Systems in East Asia: A Comparative Analysis Including Private Welfare," CASE Paper No. 10, London: Centre for the Analysis of Social Exclusion, LSE.

Kamimura, Y. (1997) "Welfare State Formation in the Asian NIEs," Master's thesis (in Japanese).

—— (1999) "The Extension of the Theory of Welfare State to Asian NIEs," *Sociologos*, 23: 232–48 (in Japanese).

—— (2001) "Social Policy in the Asian Countries: Issues and Research Agenda," in A. Suehiro and A. Komorida (eds) *Comparative Studies of Liberalization, Economic Crisis and Social Restructuring in Asia, Latin America and Russia/Eastern Europe: Part 1: New Perspective on Critical Issues*, Tokyo: Institute of Social Science, University of Tokyo (in Japanese).

—— (2002) "A Sketch of Taiwan's National Pension Debate: Late Welfare State Formation in the Global Economy," in Society for the Study of Social Policy (ed.) *Economic Disparity and Social Change* (*The Journal of Social Policy and Labor Studies*, No. 7), Kyoto: Horitsu Bunka Sha (in Japanese).

—— (2004) "Welfare states in East Asia: Towards a Comparative Study," in M. Osawa (ed.) *Welfare Strategy of Asian Countries*, Kyoto: Minerva Shobo (in Japanese).

Kamimura, Y. and Suehiro, A. (eds) (2003) *Welfare System in East Asia*, Tokyo: Institute of Social Science, University of Tokyo (in Japanese).

Kim, D. (2002) *The Road to Productive Welfare*, translated into Japanese by M. Tauchi, Tokyo: Mainichi Shinbunsha.

Kimura, M. (1990) "The Development Regime of the Small City State," in T. Hayashi (ed.) *The Industrialisation of Singapore: the Business Center of Asia*, Tokyo: The Institute of Developing Economies (in Japanese).

Kobayashi, H., Kwak, Y. and Sofue, R. (1993) "The East Asian Economic Development and the Change of Industrial Relations," *Journal of Ohara Institute for Social Research*, 410: 13–40 (in Japanese).

Kramer, R.M. (1981) *Voluntary Agencies in the Welfare State*, Berkeley: University of California Press.

Ku, Y. (1997) *Welfare Capitalism in Taiwan: State, Economy and Social Policy*, Basingstoke: Macmillan.

Lee, E. (1998) *The Asian Financial Crisis: The Challenge for Social Policy*, Geneva: ILO.

Low, L. and Aw, T.C. (1997) *Housing a Healthy, Educated and Wealthy Nation through the CPF*, Singapore: Times Academic Press.

Marshall, K., Butzbach, O. (eds) (2003) *New Social Policy Agendas for Europe and Asia: Challenges, Experience, and Lessons*, Washington, DC: World Bank.

Maruyama, M. and Kato, S. (1998) *Translation and Japanese Modernity*, Tokyo: Iwanami Shoten.
OECD (ed.) (2002) *Towards Asia's Sustainable Development: The Role of Social Protection*, Paris: OECD.
Ortiz, I. (ed.) (2001) *Social Protection in Asia and the Pacific*, Manila: Asian Development Bank.
Polanyi, K. (1944) *The Great Transformation*, Boston, MA: Beacon Press.
Ramesh, M. (2004) *Social Policy in East and Southeast Asia: Education, Health, Housing, and Income Maintenance*, London: Routledge.
Ramesh, M. and Asher, M. (2000) *Welfare Capitalism in Southeast Asia: Social Security, Health and Education Policies*, London: Macmillan.
Rieger, E. and Leibfried, S. (2003) *Limits to Globalization*, Cambridge: Polity Press.
Rodan, G. (1989) *The Political Economy of Singapore's Industrialization: National State and International Capital*, London: Macmillan.
Sawada, Y. (1997) "Laissez-faire and Social Welfare," in Y. Sawada (ed.) *The Structural Change of Colonial Hong Kong*, Tokyo: The Institute of Developing Economies.
Schmitter, P.C. and Lehmbruch, G. (eds) (1979) *Trends toward Corporatist Intermediation*, London: Sage.
Shimodaira, Y. (1986) "Social Security System of a Developing Country: An Experiment in Singapore," *Overseas Social Security News*, 74: 38–58 (in Japanese).
Shin, D. (1993) *Korean Politics Now: Dynamics towards Democratisation*, Tokyo: Yuhikaku (in Japanese).
Stepan, A. (1978) *The State and Society: Peru in Comparative Perspective*, Princeton, NJ: Princeton University Press.
Takeshita, H. (1995) *Singapore: The Era of Lee Kuan Yew*, Tokyo: The Institute of Developing Economies (in Japanese).
Tang, K. (2000) *Social Welfare Development in East Asia*, London: Palgrave.
Tang, K. (ed.) (2000) *Social Development in Asia*, Dordrecht: Kluwer Academic Publishers.
Titmuss, R.M. (1974) *Social Policy: An Introduction*, London: Allen and Unwin.
Tsen, M. (2003) "The Formation and Development of Unemployment Insurance in Taiwan: An Image of Welfare State in the Era of Globalization and Democratization," in Y. Kamimura and A. Suehiro (eds) *Welfare System in East Asia*, Tokyo: Institute of Social Science, University of Tokyo (in Japanese).
UNESCAP (2001) "Strengthening Policies and Programmes on Social Safety Nets: Issues, Recommendations and Selected Studies," Social Policy Paper No. 8, Bangkok: UNESCAP.
Wakabayashi, M. (1992) *Taiwan: Divided States and Democratisation*, Tokyo: University of Tokyo Press (in Japanese).
Wilensky, H.L. (1975) *The Welfare State and Equality: Structural and Ideological Roots of Public Expenditures*, Berkeley: University of California Press.
Wilensky, H.L. and Lebeaux, C.N. (1965) *Industrial Society and Social Welfare: The Impact of Industrialization on the Supply and Organization of Social Welfare Services in the United States*, New York: Free Press.
World Bank (1999) "Towards an East Asian Social Protection Strategy," Washington, DC: Human Development Unit, East Asia and Pacific Region, World Bank, Draft.
—— (2001) *Social Protection Sector Strategy: From Safety Net to Springboard*, Washington, DC: World Bank.

13 Characteristics of the Central European welfare system

Takumi Horibayashi

Introduction

There are different perspectives on the emerging social policy and welfare system in Central Europe. While some authors emphasize their inclinations to neoliberal residualism, others point to their similarities to the European model. There is also a view that stresses the still-existing legacies of the communist era in the present Central European welfare system.

This chapter attempts to characterize the present Central European welfare systems, that is, those of three countries, Poland, Hungary and the Czech Republic. It also deals with the issue of globalization in a limited dimension: the impact of international organizations on the Central European welfare system.

This chapter is divided into three sections. The next section summarizes the main features of the communist social policy and welfare system. The third section traces the process of formation and transformation of welfare systems in the three Central European countries since the political change of 1989, examining several determinants of the emerging welfare system in the region. The fourth, concluding section defines the present Central European welfare system. The subject of the impact of international organizations on the region is examined in the final two sections as well.

Social policy and welfare system in the communist era

Until 1989 a similar social policy and welfare system existed in Central and Eastern Europe and the former USSR. To summarize Deacon's accurate view (Deacon 2000), its basic features could be enumerated as follows:

- The welfare system was an inseparable part of the whole political and economic system, which was controlled by monopolized power, that is the communist party-state, and had minimal market mechanism and political democracy. In return for political subjugation, people were provided by the party-state with highly subsidized food, housing, transportation and basic necessities, as well as free education and health care services (although patients actually had to pay a gratuity to doctors to receive good treatment).

- The communist regime (party-state) also guaranteed employment and an egalitarian wage system with hidden privileges of the power elite, that is nomenklatura. Thus, there existed a distribution according to job status as well as political status. Regarding gender issues, females received favorable treatment such as a three-year childcare leave with partial wages (grants) and the right of resumption of their previous job, but the communist regime did not guarantee gender equality. Among other things, only females – not both genders – had the double burden of maintaining a paid job in the workplace and providing unpaid family care.
- The party-state monopolized decision making on the allocation of the national product and freely shifted resources between accumulation and consumption, and between individual consumption and socialized provisions such as pensions and health care. Universal social insurance funds for pension and health care were not separated from the state budget. The pension system guaranteed subsistence for the elderly; however it was eroded due to the lack of a suitable index-linking benefit system.
- Pensions and other benefits were related to a wage system in which some categories of workers (in particular, employees in the heavy industry sector) were given privileges.
- Another feature of the communist welfare system was that state enterprises provided several cash and in-kind benefits and services to their employees, employees' families and retirees, such as several sorts of allowances, subsidized recreational facilities, vacations and day-care facilities. Trade unions played a role in the provision of benefits and services.

Esping-Andersen simply summarizes the above features of the communist welfare system: "the old communist regime was characterized by three basic pillars: full and quasi-obligatory employment; broad and universalistic social insurance; and a highly developed, typically company-based, system of services and fringe benefits" (Esping-Andersen 1996: 9).

In defining the communist welfare system, Deacon *et al.* call it a "state bureaucratic collectivist regime," and take it to be "a particular product of the expropriation of capital and the paternalistic management of the state" (Deacon *et al.* 1997: 42–3). At the same time, they suggest that the communist welfare system had, to some extent, common features with "the European conservative corporatist tradition" in which "the workplace and a contract between government and trade unions dominated the entitlement system" and "the benefits reflected acknowledged status differences between workers" (ibid.: 91). Moreover, the communist welfare system, in our view, had common features with the social democratic regime too, because it brought a high degree of decommodification and female participation in the workforce (regarding the well-known classification of welfare regimes into liberal, conservative and social democratic, see Esping-Andersen 1990; 1999).

The communist welfare system had its achievements and defects. With regard to the former, Ferge, a well-known Hungarian expert on social policy, indicates that:

> [D]espite all its inhuman features and tragic failures, state socialism was not unqualified evil. Unlike its political or economic system, its social (societal) policy was not an artificial construct, forced in an inorganic way on the country ... By developing, and assuring access on a mass scale to the health system, to education, and to stable incomes, it contributed to the eradication of practically feudal social distances, the very significant reduction of utmost poverty, and the development of human capital.
>
> (Ferge 1997a: 108)

At the same time, she refers to the defects of the communist welfare system:

> The main defect of social policy in these states [state socialism] was that it was permeated with the totalitarian logic of the former political system. To mention just a few corollaries, because the legal system was arbitrarily dominated by politics, (1) rights remained illusory; (2) social policy, like everything else, was ideologically loaded, and; (3) all measures were developed without citizen's participation or control or any attempts of consensus building.
>
> (Ferge 1997b: 301)

Kornai, the best-known Hungarian economist, criticizes the "premature welfare state" created in his country. He argues:

> What I meant and still mean by premature welfare state is a country ahead of itself by comparison with its realistic economic potentials ... The [Hungarian] welfare state has outgrown its desirable extent. It needs cutting back and reforming, and at the same time preserving to the extent that [it] is desirable and needful ... Underlining the principle of need means that the state should refrain if possible from giving money to those who are not in need.
>
> (Kornai 1997: 95–6)

Kornai criticizes not only the "premature welfare state" but also the monopolistic welfare state:

> The trouble with the welfare system developed in this country is that it has a monopoly. It used to be an exclusive state monopoly ... I am convinced that monopolies are not a good thing, for several reasons. First they reduce efficiency ... The individuals supplied by monopolies are at their mercy, without any freedom of choice.
>
> (Kornai 1997: 95–6)

Although both scholars mainly describe the communist welfare system in Hungary, seemingly they present their own evaluations of the communist welfare system in general. In relation to those evaluations, some (mainly experts of social policy) proposed democratization of the welfare state, while others (mainly neoliberalism-oriented economists) insisted on a reduction of the welfare state in the transformation period following the collapse of communism.

Changes to social policy and the welfare system after 1989 in Central Europe

The characteristics of the communist social policy and welfare system described above were also essentially valid for three Central European countries: Poland, Hungary and the Czech Republic.

Since 1989, several factors have influenced the formation and transformation of social policy and the welfare system in Central Europe. Among them, important determinants existed, as follows:

- social costs of transformation,
- traditional European welfare system,
- neoliberalism as the dominant orientation in the world before and after 1989,
- advice and commitments of international organizations such as the World Bank and the International Labor Organization (ILO),
- legacies of the communist era.

This part analyzes the social policy and welfare system in Central Europe after 1989, examining these determinants.

Social cost of transformation and "emergent" social policy

The Central and East European countries have replaced the communist party-state system with a system governed by the rules of market and parliamentary democracy since 1989. Politics with freedom and democracy is, to varying degrees, now in operation across almost all post-communist countries. In general, three Central European countries, Poland, Hungary and the Czech Republic, are the top runners of democratization among post-communist countries.

On the other hand, after a heavy depression due to economic transformation ("transformational recession"), the countries have entered onto the path of growth, starting in 1992 in Poland, and in 1994 in Hungary and the Czech Republic. Economic growth has continued in Hungary. In Poland the GDP growth rate was moderate in 2001 and 2002, but then it went up to 3.8 percent in 2003. The Czech Republic, despite having once overcome the transformational depression in 1994, experienced recession again from 1997 to 1999, but then resumed economic growth (KOPINT-DATORG 2002; 2004).

As a result of a relatively smooth transformation of the political and economic system, Poland, Hungry and the Czech Republic gained membership in the EU in May 2004 together with seven other countries: Slovakia, Slovenia, Estonia, Latvia, Lithuania, Malta and (south) Cyprus. However, from the viewpoint of social policy-making it is important that social (societal) costs of transformation, that is negative phenomena or "sacrifices" due to the system change (Szamuely 1996: 55), have been heavy in all post-communist countries, including those of Central Europe, and they required "emergent" social policy in the region. The main social costs of transformation were represented in such phenomena as excessive mortality, mass unemployment, an increase in the economically inactive population, a rise in poverty and an increase of income inequalities.

Life expectancy had already been declining since the 1960s in the USSR and across Central and Eastern Europe, mainly due to insufficient funding and inadequacy of the medical systems, and underdevelopment in the preventive approach to health care (Ellman 1997: 356–62). In addition to those defects, stress brought about by the drastic system change caused high mortality and a decline in life expectancy, particularly for males of working age, after the collapse of communism in the region.

While life expectancy at birth of males drastically fell in Russia from 64.2 to 58.2 years, it fell slightly also in Hungary from 65.4 to 64.8 years during the period of 1989–94. Also, it fell slightly in Poland during the years 1990–2. In the Czech Republic, the same phenomenon occurred, but only in 1990 (Szamuely 1996: 66).

The transformational depression caused unemployment in post-communist countries, and negated a basic component of the communist welfare system, full employment. In Poland, after the unemployment rate peaked in 1993 (16.4 percent), it gradually declined until 1998 (10.4 percent); however it had risen again to 19.8 percent by 2003. During the years of transformational depression of 1990–3 in the Czech Republic, the unemployment rate was relatively low (3.5 percent, 1993), and it rose significantly from 1997 and reached 9.4 percent in 1999. However, it had slightly decreased to 7.8 percent by 2003 (KOPINT-DATORG 2002; 2004).

In Hungary, the unemployment rate registered 12.1 percent in 1993, and then it gradually declined to 5.9 percent in 2003 (KOPINT-DATORG 2002; 2004). However, the recovery of the employment rate is slow in comparison with the decrease in unemployment. It means that there are many economically inactive people, more than 2 million, among the 6 million of working age in Hungary. The Roma ethnic minority, unskilled and less educated workers and the inhabitants of undeveloped areas are over-represented among the unemployed, while the economically inactive population is mainly composed of students, early retired pensioners and housewives withdrawn from the labor market and provided with child-care allowance in the country (Frey 1998: 4–17).

While the percentage of females in the total unemployed is higher than that of males in Poland and the Czech Republic, it is less than 50 percent in Hungary (ECE 1996). However, the decline of the economically active population was more drastic among females than males after 1989 in Hungary. Thus, it could be said that the gender gap (bias) in the labor sphere that already existed in the communist era (see above) has grown, to varying degrees, in the respective post-communist countries.

Poverty is not a new phenomenon in the region. It already existed under the communist regime. Sociologists dealt with the issue of poverty, for instance, in the Czech Republic and Hungary (Adam 1999: 155–6; Andorka 1997: 75–6). In Hungary, the dissidents set up SZETA, the Foundation to Support the Poor, to assist the poor in 1978 (Lomax 1999: 175). Andorka reveals that about 1 million Hungarians, 10 percent of the population, lived on a per capita household income lower than the subsistence minimum (a poverty line which is defined as the value, per capita household income, of a basket of certain goods and services needed by an average household in order to maintain a minimum standard of living) in the 1980s (Andorka 1997: 76).

The poor in communist Hungary were composed of unskilled workers, peasants and inhabitants of villages and small towns. In addition to the old poor, the new poor appeared; both strata increased rapidly during the years of economic transformation in the 1990s. The proportion of the poor to the total population increased threefold by the middle of the 1990s in Hungary, applying the subsistence minimum as the poverty line. Even if another poverty line such as classifying as poor those with 50 percent of the average net income is used, the existence of increasing widespread poverty could not be denied. The new poor were families with three or more children, the unemployed and the economically inactive population. The Roma ethnicity, whose majority fell into unemployment, also was over-represented among the poor after the economic transformation in the country (Andorka 1997: 81–2).

Likewise, poverty spread rapidly in Poland and the Czech Republic during the years of system change. The proportion of the poor to the total population is higher in Poland than in the other two countries (Adam 1999: 155–70).

As system change, including marketization and privatization, was in motion in post-communist countries, the social structure changed, as reflected in the growth of income differentials. In the case of Hungary, in 1988, the year preceding the system change, the income of the highest household decile was 5.8 times higher than that of the lowest household decile, while in 1994–5 the former was 7 times higher than the latter (Kolosi and Sági 1999: 52–4).

Likewise in the Czech Republic, the income ratio between the lowest and highest household deciles increased from 2.6 in 1988 to 3.2 in 1996 (Potůček 2001: 86). According to a report by the World Bank, the income differential on the basis of Gini coefficient was widest in Poland in 1993 (World Bank 1996: 68).

Some researches suggest that quite a number of the new rich (or new elite) appeared from the old elite, at least in the first stage of system change, and the winners, in general, were persons with "cultural capital," or the well-educated (Eyal *et al.* 1997; Kolosi and Sági 1999).

Unlike economic policy which was carried out on the basis of *ex ante* designed and more or less systematic programs, which were strongly influenced by Bretton Woods institutions inspiring neoliberalism, social policy of the first stage of the system change had the character of "emergency responses" in the region (Cichon ed. 1995; Cichon *et al.* 1997: 19). To put it another way, emergency measures were introduced to deal with the social costs of transformation such as mass unemployment, widespread poverty and deteriorating living standards.

All the countries in the region rapidly introduced unemployment benefits and social assistance benefits and modified their pension provision strategy to fight rampant inflation.

In the three countries under discussion, decrees on employment were enacted and unemployment insurance was introduced in the beginning phase of the system change. The unemployment benefit plans were initially generous and wage related, but later became limited in terms of the replacement rate and length of entitlement because of budgetary pressure, as well as permeating neoliberalism in the region. For instance, in Hungary the length of entitlement of benefits was reduced from two years to one year in 1993 (and then to nine months in 2000). Likewise, in the Czech Republic unemployment benefits were paid for one year in 1991: 90 percent of salary for the first six months and 60 percent of salary for the next six months in 1991. Later, the length of entitlement of benefits was reduced to six months, and in 1999 only 50 percent of salary was paid for the first three months and 40 percent of salary for the next three months (Potůček 2001: 90).

The Czech Republic, from the beginning stage of the system change, attached much importance to its active employment policy, including organizing professional training and requalification programs and supporting small-scale business. Thus the proportion of expenditure on active employment policy to total expenditure on employment policy was more than two-thirds in 1994 in the Czech Republic, while in Poland, this proportion was only 12 percent on average in 1993–5 (Adam 1999: 100). Such a difference in policy approach could be explained partly from the different unemployment rates in two countries in the early stage of the system change. At the same time, it could be speculated that the Czech Republic drew lessons from the experiences of active employment policies in advanced countries, for instance in Sweden.

Pension provision strategies were modified, mainly aimed at improving the living standard of pensioners and preventing an increase in unemployment in the early stage of the system change in Poland and Hungary. In Poland, automatic indexation of old-age benefits to wage increases was introduced in 1990, while in Hungary pensions were adjusted twice a year, following wage levels, as a result of parliamentary action in 1992. Moreover, both countries applied generous eligibility conditions to old-age and disability pensions in order to promote early retirement. Early retirement was considered to be an alternative to unemployment. But this measure had a side effect of increased system independency ratio due to the increase in the number of pensioners of working age, and led to financial difficulties in the pension system in both countries.

All three countries, in the early stage of the system change, enacted decrees regulating social assistance that were intended as a safety net for those who were no longer able to support themselves. Social assistance is a means-tested benefit for poor people. Ferge, analyzing the practice of social assistance in Central and Eastern Europe, argues:

> There are also widespread shortages of funds at local level. Responsibility for some types of assistance may be shared with central authorities, but very often the locality is solely responsible ... Since there are many competing claims for these funds, the locality may not be able to provide for all needy ... [A]s many as 50 to 60 percent of the eligible poor are not receiving assistance.
>
> (Ferge 1997b: 305–6)

In Hungary, a new subsidy for parents, in addition to the existing family allowance and childcare leave, was introduced in 1992. This was means-tested support, directed at families that had three or more children and lived below the poverty line. Although it was also a component of the social assistance system, at the same time it created disincentives for mothers to work outside the home (Goven 2000: 291).

To sum up, the initial social policy after 1989 could be characterized to be an "emergent response" to the social costs of transformation.

Shift to a traditional European welfare system

According to a publication of ILO-CEET (the International Labor Organization, Central and Eastern European Team), the social security system in

Central Europe by the mid-1990s was characterized by an emergent response to the outcomes of economic transformation, while developing a shift to the three-tier social security system prevalent in Western Europe, which had existed in the region prior to 1950 (Cichon ed. 1995; Cichon *et al.* 1997: 10).

The three-tier system consists of social insurance plans, universal benefits and social assistance policies. Certainly, such a shift occurred, to varying degrees, in the region by the mid-1990s. Alongside the creation of the three-tier system, European-style tripartite institutions were also established. Thus, it could be said that, in parallel with the emergent response, to some extent, the Europeanization of social policy occurred in the region.

With regard to social insurance policies, Hungary was the most advanced example of a social insurance-based social security system in the region by the mid-1990s. In Hungary, the social insurance fund was separated from the state budget in 1989 and an employment insurance fund was introduced, following the enactment of the Employment Act in 1991. After the legislation of another law, which established elected boards for pension and health care funds, the representatives of the employees were elected by vote in 1993. The board of the pension fund was composed of the representatives of contributors, that is the employer and the employee, and also delegates of the retired. Ferge notes, "The establishment and election of the social security self-governments is one of the most important achievements" (Ferge 1995: 156), although the right wing cabinet abolished self-government of social insurance in 1998.

The Czech Republic (the then Czechoslovakia) introduced a health care insurance system with competing insurance funds in 1991. There, besides one general insurance company, a number of NPO-style insurance funds were created on the basis of industrial sector, profession and firm. Although the main contributors are the employer and the employee, the government also pays contributions for the unemployed, the retired, women on maternity leave and children without support (Adam 1999: 144–5). Because hospitals, except some small ones, have not been privatized, the government has financed their investment costs and medical education. Therefore, health care funding in the Czech Republic is a combination of the Bismarckian style of insurance and Beveridgean style of state funding. One problem that occurred by the mid-1990s in the country was the growth of expenditure in health care. Its percentage of GDP rose from 5.4 percent in 1991 to 8.1 percent in 1995 (OECD 1996: 93).

Poland also introduced a health care insurance system with a number of insurance funds. However, unlike the Czech Republic, the reform of the health care insurance system was delayed and not carried out until 1999. As for pension funding in Poland, although the pension fund was separated from the state budget in 1986, the state budget transferred resources into the pension fund to balance its account in the 1990s. The same occurred in Hungary. Such financial situations and the strong presence of the World Bank in both countries (Poland and Hungary) caused the partial privatization of the pension system in the late 1990s (see below).

The shift to an insurance-based social security system in the region is considered to be a return to the Central European (or European) tradition as well as an easy way of institutional restructuring for ex-communist countries. Deacon notes:

> The logic of post-communist development was towards a conservative, corporatist kind of welfare policy. Workplace entitlement to welfare and existing workplace status differentials inherited from state-socialist days could be readily converted into insurance-based, wage related and differentiated benefit entitlements of the Austro-German, Bismarckian kind.
>
> (Deacon 2000: 151–2)

As for universal benefits, there were legacies of the communist era. Through the retention of the family allowance and childcare leave with partial wages, the principle of universal provision was maintained (or enhanced, as in the case of Hungary where the family allowance was made universal in 1990) in the early stage of the system change in the region.

On the other hand, the right to return to one's previous job after childcare leave was eroded by the narrowing labor market and often strengthened gender-bias. Moreover, universal benefits were converted into means-tested ones as a result of permeating neoliberalism and strong pressure from the World Bank in the mid-1990s in the region (see below).

The ILO, whose branch was established in Budapest in 1992, has provided post-communist countries with the technical assistance to set up the institutional framework of industrial relations and social dialogue prevalent in continental Europe. Tripartite bodies at the national level were established in the three countries in the early stage of the system change.

In Hungary, the Interest Reconciliation Council was established in 1990 as an institution for social dialogue among the government, employers and employees. Likewise, a tripartite body was established in the Czech Republic (then Czechoslovakia) in 1990 and in Poland in 1993–4. These bodies were initially established to mitigate social tensions such as the Hungarian taxi drivers' demonstration against inflation and the massive and chaotic wave of strikes in Poland. Nevertheless, these bodies have not always functioned well because of the frequent antagonism between the government and trade unions or among rather fragmented trade unions (especially in Hungary and Poland).

In the Czech Republic, a tripartite body functioned relatively well even under the neoconservative Klaus government. This can be attributed partly to the tactics of the government to keep wages low in return for low unemployment through negotiation with trade unions (Orenstein 1996: 177–8) and partly to the less fragmented structure of the trade unions. Moreover, a publication of the ILO considers that the tripartite dialogue in the Czech Republic has become an integral part of government since 1998, the year when the social democratic party came into office (Casale *et al.* 2001: 14–15).

The number of workers and employers covered by collective bargaining at the sectoral level has recently increased in the Czech Republic, while the decentralization of bargaining at the firm level is one of the recent developments in Hungarian industrial relations. The latter development could be considered a sign of the shift of industrial relations toward the Anglo-Saxon model.

Last but not least, some parts of German or other Western European-style corporate governance were introduced in the Czech Republic (participation of employees' representatives on the supervisory board) and Hungary (work councils at the firm level). This is another example of a certain degree of Europeanization of the institutional setting in the region.

While some international organizations, especially the ILO and UNICEF, encouraged post-communist countries to establish a European-style welfare system, the European-based actors did not necessarily play such a role (except the Council of Europe).

UNICEF has provided post-communist countries with technical advice for child welfare. It proposed the maintenance of universal benefits and services and opposed the residual approach to welfare policy.

The EU directed a part of its PHARE program to advise on social security policy (Fagin 1999: 189), but its policy advice to post-communist countries did not have a systematic orientation toward the European style of welfare. Deacon *et al.* maintain that the battle between the Euroliberals and the Eurocorporatists within the EU was one reason for its inconsistent policy recommendations to the East (Deacon *et al.* 1997: 98). Rys notes that in the enlargement process the EU generally gave Central and Eastern European countries policy recommendations in which social protection issues were reduced to their economic aspect (Rys 2001: 185). Although the EU required improvements in the protection of human rights (e.g. those of ethnic minorities) to post-communist countries, it didn't necessarily stress the safeguarding of social rights (Ferge 2001: 14). Orenstein and Haas (2002) note that the "Europe Effect" made Central Europe maintain relatively high levels of welfare spending. In our view, there is no clear evidence that the EU itself intentionally intensified this effect, even if the concept of the "European social model" gave "indirect" influence to social policy making of national governments in the region (Guillén and Palier 2004: 204).

The EBRD initially attempted to play a role in the sphere of social security in post-communist countries. But in order to avoid overlapping with the role of the World Bank, it was limited to providing assistance to the private sector in the region.

The OECD, which the three Central European countries joined in the mid-1990s, took a stance seeking to reconcile economic and social requirements. Its stance is, to some extent, similar to the idea of "the Third Way" (Giddens 1998; 2000; Giddens ed. 2001) in terms of policy emphasis on social investment. (Its stance is called social-liberalism: see Deacon *et al.* 1997.)

To sum up, the European-based actors such as the EU and EBRD didn't exert direct influence on the Europeanization of the welfare system that occurred in the early stage of system change in Central Europe. It was the World Bank that had the strongest influence on the restructuring of the ex-communist welfare system, as revealed below.

Permeation of neoliberalism into the Central European welfare system, with the World Bank as its promoter

Widespread neoliberalism was one of the remarkable phenomena from the beginning of the system change in the post-communist region. Its signs were seen in economic policy more than in social policy and welfare systems in the early stage of system change.

Orenstein and Haas attribute this time lag to the lower priority of social policy among a set of transformation policies for domestic decision-makers in the region, and for Bretton Woods institutions by the mid-1990s (Orenstein and Haas 2002). Their explanation is partly true. It is certain that the domestic decision-makers in the region and the Bretton Woods institutions, in particular the IMF, gave the highest priority to economic policies in which economic stabilization and privatization were the main purposes.

On the other hand, one of the neoliberalism-inclined Bretton Woods institutions, the World Bank, imposed social conditionality such as tightened eligibility conditions for social security on post-communist countries in return for granting structural adjustment loans. For instance, the World Bank advised Hungary to scale down maternity and childcare benefits in 1992 (Goven 2000: 291).

Accordingly, Orenstein and Haas do not adequately describe social policy-making in the early period of the system change, because their description omits the above fact. Another fact to be noted was that the first post-communist governments in the region hesitated in drastically reducing social expenditures, out of fear of losing popularity.

Ferge expressed well such a complexity of the early period of the system change in Hungary:

> It is to the credit of the Antall government [the first post-communist government] that welfare benefits did not deteriorate faster ... The

entire period [1990–94] was characterized by a contradictory mixture of gaining ground of neoliberal ideals enhanced by conservative elements, the inadequate fulfillment of needs growing as a result of impoverishment, the temporary patching up of problems and *ad hoc* popularity seeking ideas.

(Ferge 1995: 157)

Around the middle of the 1990s, the neoliberal approach to social policy became more visible than before in the region. It occurred in the environment of a rapidly deteriorating state budget and external balance both in Hungary and Poland. Even in the Czech Republic, which did not face a severe imbalance, social policy shifted toward neoliberalism by the middle of the 1990s.

The core of the neoliberal social policy inspired by the World Bank was comprised of the following two elements: first, limiting the provision of welfare benefits to the "truly needy," thus reducing social expenditure, and second, privatization of the pension system (Deacon 2000: 154).

Around the mid-1990s, universal benefits and services such as family allowance and paid childcare leave were converted into means-tested benefits, and the principle of free education and health care was eroded by the introduction of co-payments for dental care and university tuition in Hungary. The austerity program, including these measures, was called the "Bokros Package" after the then financial minister of Hungary. Kornai supported this austerity program and criticized the "premature welfare state." In his view, overspending on welfare continued under the first post-communist government in Hungary (Kornai 1997: 95), while the Hungarian majority stood against the "Bokros Package." Although this "package" was modified to some extent and Bokros was forced to resign in 1996, the essential parts of the austerity program were put into operation in the country. As a result, the percentage of welfare expenditure in the budget in GDP decreased to 20.9 percent in 1996, from 26.3 percent in 1994 (Andorka and Tóth 1999: 66).

Likewise, in Poland the universal family allowance was converted into a means-tested one in 1995. Then, only families whose household incomes per capita were less than 50 percent of the average were entitled to the allowance. Also, in the Czech Republic, those whose income was above 1.8 times more than the established minimum were not entitled to a family allowance after a conversion to means-tested benefits.

As noted above, eligibility for unemployment benefits was also gradually narrowed in the region. Thus, the number of benefit recipients as a percentage of the unemployed declined in Hungary from 77 percent in 1991 to 29 percent in 1996; in Poland from 79 percent to 54 percent; and in the Czech Republic from 72 percent to 50 percent (Adam 1999: 98).

As for the pension system, its reform was carried out with the paradigm shift in Hungary in 1998 and in Poland in 1999. The original idea of pension reform was suggested to both countries by the World Bank. The reform process was led by each country's Ministry of Finance, which cooperated with the World Bank. The main concern of the World Bank was to limit the public PAYG scheme to a minimum scale (first pillar), to introduce the mandatory and individually funded, privately managed and non-solidaristic second pillar, and to establish the additional voluntary third pillar as well. Hungary introduced such a new pension system, composed of three pillars, in 1998, but the proportion of the second pillar to total contributions was smaller than initially proposed by the Ministry of Finance. The reason for this was that the Ministry of Finance was obliged to a compromise with the Welfare Ministry that, at least initially, stuck to the Bismarckian–Beveridgean tradition (Müller 1999: 76). A number of social policy experts also stood against the idea of the World Bank concerning the pension reform, as expressed in a publication entitled "Averting the Old Age Crisis" (World Bank 1994). The new Polish pension system introduced in 1999 was essentially similar to the Hungarian one, but it had more insurance elements because, in addition to having an individually funded second pillar, the "notional defined contribution" (NDC) plan was also arranged in the first pillar to enhance the contribution–benefit link.

In contrast with the Hungarian and Polish cases, the Czech Republic maintained its public PAYG scheme, although voluntary pension funds were allowed after 1993. Müller explains this bifurcation in the pension systems of Central Europe from the constellation of the main actors (the World Bank, the Ministries of Finance and the Welfare Ministries) and the structural conditions (the pension funds, state budgets and external balances) in the three countries concerned. On one hand, the deteriorating financial situation of the existing PAYG plan led to its dependence on budgetary subsidies as well as to the commitment of the Ministry of Finance to pension reform. Moreover, the fiscal crises made the Ministries of Finance strong actors in pension reform in Hungary and Poland. On the other hand, the high external debt in both countries created a situation in which the World Bank imposed social conditionality in return for funding. In such an environment, both the World Bank and the Ministries of Finance, which were inclined toward neoliberalism, could carry out pension reform with the paradigm shift in Hungary and Poland. As the Czech Republic, where a PAYG plan was sustainable, did not face serious problems regarding the state budget and external imbalance, the main driving force of pension reform was the Welfare Ministry, which was traditionally inclined toward Bismarckian–Beveridgean paradigms. Thus, the Czech Republic maintained its public PAYG structure (Müller 1999: 149–74).

The ILO-CEET supports pension reform within a PAYG structure and gathers research on pension reform (Cichon *et al.* 1997; Fultz ed. 2002a; 2002b; 2004). Interestingly, the former Senior Vice-President and the

Chief Economist of the World Bank suggest that a shift to an individually funded and privately managed pension system is not always the best solution (Orszag and Stiglitz 2001). And the following description by Deacon *et al.* is also noteworthy:

> Within the World Bank it is perhaps most evident that a heated and hard fought struggle of ideas and policy prescriptions is under way. Here we identified a "camp" associated with European wage related state funded social security systems and a "camp" associated with a flat rate – possibly means and assets tested – residual pensions policy.
> (Deacon *et al.* 1997: 148)

Legacies of the communist era in post-communist welfare systems

Although neoliberalism has become a notable element of post-communist social policy, especially since the mid-1990s, it has failed to permeate deeply into society due to the legacies of the communist era. Esping-Andersen describes how:

> East and Central Europe is clearly the most under-defined region, a virtual laboratory of experimentation. If it is at all possible to generalize, there is at least clear one trend: where neoliberal welfare policies (often inspired by the Chilean model) were pursued most vigorously, they were punished in subsequent democratic elections ... [S]o neoliberal welfare policies in Eastern Europe seem to revitalize socialism.
> (Esping-Andersen 1996: 267)

Certainly, neo-liberal economic policy "revitalized" socialism and helped ex-communist (presently the Social Democratic or Socialist) parties regain office in Poland (1993) and Hungary (1994). But the Social Democratic and Socialist Party-led coalition governments were also punished by people in "subsequent elections" in 1997 (Poland) and 1998 (Hungary) and lost their majorities because their governments adopted policies reducing welfare expenditures.

In Hungary, the subsequent conservative government abolished tuition at the universities and re-universalized the family allowance to maintain its popularity among the electorate. Nevertheless, in the 2002 general election, the conservative parties were defeated by the Socialist Party that was in cooperation with a liberal party, the Alliance of Free Democrats. The Socialist party promised the electorate many welfare measures such as an extra provision for pensions and an increase in wages for public employees, including low-paid school teachers and health care providers. As in Hungary, the Social Democratic Party came back into office in 2001 in Poland. In the Czech Republic, the Social Democratic Party, which is more generous with welfare expenditures than conservative parties, has remained in power since 1998 (Potůček 2004: 254). All the examples described above show that the majority of the population in the region expect a deep commitment from the state with regard to social protection. According to Ferge, people in the ex-communist region "would turn more willingly to public authorities when in need than to churches, non-governmental organizations, or charitable institutions" (Ferge 1997b: 315). Kornai refers to the relation between such an attitude and (lack of) "tax awareness" in the region (Kornai 1997: 240). Without details, it could be confirmed that the vast majority of the people in post-communist countries expect a strong welfare commitment from the state and that this attitude is a legacy of the communist era.

As already noted, Orenstein and Haas attribute a significant level of social expenditure in contemporary Central Europe to the "Europe Effect" (Orenstein and Haas 2002). However, we consider the above legacy as a more important factor in explaining the relatively strong welfare commitment of the state in Central Europe.

Thus, the weak movement toward privatization of health care and education in the region could be considered as a "Legacy Effect." In fact, the primary care (GP) facilities have almost exclusively privatized, but the hospitals have been predominantly managed by the central and local governments in the region. Privatization of education was mostly concentrated on the tertiary level and the percentage of secondary school pupils enrolled in private schools was still 8 percent in Hungary, 7 percent in the Czech Republic and 4 percent in Poland in 1996–7 (Deacon 2000: 155).

The informal sector (hidden economy) and, in general, informality are also legacies from the past regime, especially in countries where the second economy prevailed, as in the case of Hungary. While the informal sector plays the role of a hidden safety net for the unemployed, for the involuntarily economically inactive population and lower income earners, it narrows the taxation base. Equally important, those working only in the informal sector are not entitled to social insurance benefits such as public pensions and health care.

The informal sector, to some extent, is related to the dual structure of a labor market, which reflects a gender gap in the region:

> [T]he labor market is bifurcating in multiple ways: into public and private, to be sure, but within this into regular and secure jobs, coded as male, and into unstable, part-time work and multiple jobs occupied mostly by women. While equally a part of the private sector and potentially lucrative, these latter jobs offer neither security nor social benefits.
>
> (Gal and Kligman 2000: 61)

Social capital or social network resources also play the role of a safety net. But distribution of social capital is dependent on the past social structure (legacy from the communist era). As already described, many representatives of the old elite became the new rich on the basis of the old social network resources. Likewise, the old poor are largely overlapped with the new poor. It should be noted that the new poor tended to be excluded from social networking in the 1990s (Angelusz and Tardos 1999). This suggests that there exist those who can access neither a formal nor an informal safety net.

Conclusion

We could sum up the above description as follows:

- The transformation of the welfare system in Central Europe was determined by several factors: the social costs of the economic transformation, the traditional European model of welfare, neoliberalism, the influence of international organizations and legacies from the communist era.
- Social policy in the early years of the system change in Central Europe had the character of "emergent response" to the social costs of the economic transformation such as mass unemployment, widespread poverty and decreasing living standards. Emergent policy measures were composed of the establishment of unemployment benefits and social assistance, and the adjustment of pension benefits to wage increases.
- The process of instituting emergent social policy overlapped with a transition to the traditional European model of welfare. By the mid-1990s, three tiers of welfare system were established in Central Europe: social insurance, universal benefits and social assistance. In addition, the European model of corporatism, tripartism, was introduced to promote social peace. The ILO and UNICEF encouraged Central Europe to introduce a traditional European-style welfare system. The European or Europe-based organizations had a minimal impact on the creation of the traditional European-style welfare system in Central Europe. Advice of the EU to post-communist countries focused on the economic aspects of social policy and not much on safeguarding social rights.
- Although the permeation of neoliberalism and the presence of Bretton Woods institutions were significant from the beginning of the system change in Central Europe, their influence on social policy-making has been enhanced since the mid-1990s. Neoliberal social policy was promoted by the Ministries of Finance in cooperation with the World Bank. The key to the neoliberal social policy was the conversion of universal benefits into means-tested ones and the privatization of the pension system. The principle of universal provision was eroded in the three Central European countries. The privatization of

the pension system was partially implemented in Hungary and Poland, while the Czech Republic maintained its PAYG pension system.
- The legacy of the communist era still remains. People continued to expect a strong commitment to welfare from the state and have resisted attempts by post-communist welfare regimes to move toward a more residualist welfare state.

The above summary leads to two questions: first, what type of welfare system has appeared or is appearing in Central Europe? Second, to what extent could we attribute the formation or transformation of Central European welfare systems to external factors such as the intervention of international organizations?

As for the first question, there are several answers whose differences are caused by the complexity of the features of the welfare systems after the political change. As noted above, the ILO-CEET suggests that the welfare systems of Central European countries have come to resemble those of traditional systems in Western Europe. Orenstein and Haas stress the "Europe effect" in the formation of post-communist Central European welfare systems (see above).

On the other hand, some experts of social policy such as Ferge (Ferge 1997a) and Standing (Standing 1996) – the latter was the first director of the ILO Budapest office – maintain that neoliberalism has largely influenced social policy-making in the region. Ringold (Ringold 1999) and Kornai (Kornai 1997) emphasize the large effect of the legacies of the communist era on post-communist welfare systems.

In our view, the welfare systems in Central Europe are now still in their formative stage and it is too early to define their type. Nevertheless, our view is close to Deacon's well-balanced one:

> [S]ome of the countries were slowly reforming their social policies in the direction of one or other variant of Western welfare policy. A tension between the aspiration towards a European-style social market economy (or conservative corporatism) and a budget-induced and IMF–World Bank-backed residualism was evident and continuing in the late 1990s. There was remarkable continuity and stability in the provision of state social security, health and education services, although in some countries some private provision was appearing at the margins.
>
> (Deacon 2000: 156)

In our view, the Central European welfare system in the early stage of the system change resembled that of continental Europe, and since the mid-1990s it has developed into a (neo-) liberal model. But it has not become a residualist welfare system yet due to the resistance of the majority of society, in which the legacy of the communist era still remains. The tension between "a European-style social market" and "IMF–World Bank-backed residualism" was expressed in the tension between "budget-induced" austerity plans by the governments and resistance of the people to these plans, resulting in repeated power (governmental) alternations.

As for the degree of the effect of international organizations on the welfare system in Central Europe, Bretton Woods institutions were most influential. Deacon calls this increasing, ideologically motivated, influence by global actors on national welfare policy "political globalization," and distinguishes it from economic globalization (Deacon 2000: 157–9). To use this terminology, the main actors of "political globalization" were the Bretton Woods institutions, and the ILO emulated them in Central Europe.

The strength of intervention of the World Bank varied from one country to another. It depended on the degree of foreign debt of the respective countries. While Hungary and Poland, having faced serious external imbalances, were exposed to strong intervention from the World Bank in the formation of their welfare systems, the Czech Republic was not so strongly influenced by it. The attempts of the World Bank faced resistance from the people. It sometimes accomplished its policy objectives, but sometimes failed, or at least, was obliged to compromise with the people's wishes in the region. It could be said that the World Bank was a very strong actor but not always a winner in the region. As already pointed out, attention should be paid also to different views on welfare policies within the World Bank.

The impact of the EU was weak on welfare system transformation in Central Europe in the 1990s, in spite of increasing economic relations, and geographical and cultural closeness between them. This resulted partly from policy priorities and partly from a change of the EU social policy (or model). The policy priority of the EU was to establish a single market and to introduce a single currency in the 1990s, which resulted in enhanced economic competition and restricted fiscal policy within its member countries (Chapon and Euzéby 2002).

On the other hand, under the new situation of the creation of a single market and a single currency, the corresponding "European social model" has not been clearly conceptualized (Rys 2001). Guillén and Palier argue:

> While Brussels was more oriented towards the development of public social policies in 1980s, the discourse of "economically-oriented actors" ... who were partially in charge of the accession procedure for the CEE countries, has become more similar to the discourse of the international financial organizations ... At the current stage, there is no clear European social model promoted at the EU level, but conflict between "economically oriented actors" ... and "socially oriented actors" trying to find new perspective for a productive approach to

social policy, linking them positively to economic and employment policies.

(Guillén and Palier 2004: 206)

In such circumstances, the World Bank tended to be involved with the preparations for Central Europe's entry into the EU (Orenstein and Haas 2002; Funck and Pizzati eds 2002). However, in Central Europe, social impact from the EU has strengthened over recent years. The EU began to influence the debate and some policies such as gender equality and anti-discrimination policies as well as the fight against social exclusion in the region (Guillén and Palier 2004: 205; Ferge and Juhász 2004).

Now the three countries under discussion are members of the EU. The future social policy and welfare systems of these countries depend not only on their own choices but also on the EU's choices: whether they seek a "European social model" or aim only to be the winner in global economic competition.

References

Adam, J. (1999) *Social Costs of Transformation to a Market Economy in Post-Socialist Countries: The Cases of Poland, the Czech Republic and Hungary*, London and New York: Macmillan Press and St. Martin's Press.

Andorka, R. (1997) "The Development of Poverty during the Transformation in Hungary," in I.T. Berend (ed.) *Long-Term Structural Changes in Transforming Central & Eastern Europe (The 1990s)*, Südosteuropa-Gesellshaft in cooperation with the Center for European and Russian Studies, University of California.

Andorka, R. and Tóth, I.Gy. (1999) "Society," in *Encyclopedia of Hungarian Economy '99*, Budapest: The Central European Business Center.

Angelusz, R. and Tardos, R. (1999) "Changing Patterns of Social Network Resources in the Nineties," in T. Kolosi, I.Gy. Tóth and Gy. Vukovich (eds) *Social Report 1998*, Budapest: TÁRKI.

Casale, G., Kubinkoba, M. and Rychly, L. (2001) *Social Dialogue: The Czech Success Story*, InFocus.ILO, Programme on Strengthening Social Dialogue, Working Paper, No. 4, Geneva: ILO.

Chapon, S. and Euzéby, C. (2002) "Towards a Convergence of European Social Models?" *International Social Security Review*, 55(2): 37–56.

Cichon, M. (ed.) (1995) *Social Protection in the Visegrad Countries: Four Country Profiles*, ILO-CEET Report 13, Budapest: ILO-CEET.

Cichon, M., Hagemejer, K. and Ruck, M. (1997) *Social Protection and Pension Systems in Central and Eastern Europe*, ILO-CEET Working Paper No. 21, Budapest: ILO-CEET.

Deacon, B. (2000) "Eastern European Welfare State: The Impact of the Politics of Globalization," *Journal of European Social Policy*, 10(2): 146–61.

Deacon, B., Hulse M. and Stubbs, P. (1997) *Global Social Policy: International Organizations and the Future of Welfare*, London, Thousand Oaks and New Delhi: SAGE Publications.

ECE (1996) *Economic Survey of Europe in 1995–1996*, New York and Geneva: United Nations.

Ellman, M. (1997) "Transformation as a Demographic Crisis," in S. Zecchini (ed.) *Lessons from Economic Transition: Central and Eastern Europe in the 1990s*, Dordrecht, Boston and London: Kluwer Academic Publishers.

Esping-Andersen, G. (1990) *The Three Worlds of Welfare Capitalism*, Cambridge: Polity Press.

—— (1996) "After the Golden Age? Welfare State Dilemmas in a Global Economy" and "Positive-sum Solutions in a World of Trade-offs?" in G. Esping-Andersen (ed.) *Welfare States in Transition: National Adaptations in Global Economies*, London, Thousand Oaks and New Delhi: SAGE Publications.

—— (1999) *Social Foundations of Postindustrial Economies*, Oxford and New York: Oxford University Press.

Eyal, G., Szelényi, I. and Townsley, E. (1997) "The Theory of Post-communist Managerialism," *New Left Review*, 222: 62–92.

Fagin, A. (1999) "Eurogovernance and Eastward Expansion of the EU: Formal versus Substantive Democratic Reform," in F. Carr and A. Massey (eds) *Public Policy in the New Europe: Eurogovernance in Theory and Practice*, Cheltenham and Northampton: Edward Elgar.

Ferge, Z. (1995) "Challenges and Constraints in Social Policy," in C. Gombár, E. Hankiss, L. Lengyel and G. Várnai (eds) *Question Marks: The Hungarian Government 1994–1995*, Budapest: Korridor Books.

—— (1997a) "Is the World Falling Apart? A View from the East of Europe," in I.T. Berend (ed.) *Long-Term Structural Changes in Transforming Central & Eastern Europe (The 1990s)*, Südosteuropa-Gesellschaft in cooperation with the Center for European and Russian Studies, University of California.

—— (1997b) "Social Policy Challenges and Dilemmas in Ex-socialist Systems," in J.M. Nelson, C. Tilly and L. Walker (eds) *Transforming Post-communist Political Economies*, Washington, DC. National Academy Press.

—— (2001) "European Integration and the Reform of Social Security in the Accession Countries," *European Journal of Social Quality*, 3(1–2): 9–25.

Ferge, Z. and Juhász, G. (2004) "Accession and Social Policy: The Case of Hungary," *Journal of European Social Policy*, 14(3): 233–51.

Frey, M. (1998) "The Position of Women in the Labour Market after Change of Political System," in *Women in the World of Work: Women Workers' Rights in Hungary*, Budapest: ILO-CEET.

Fultz, E. (ed.) (2002a) *Pension Reform in Central and Eastern Europe – Volume 1. Restructuring with Privatization: Case Studies of Hungary and Poland*, Budapest: ILO-CEET.

—— (2002b) *Pension Reform in Central and Eastern Europe – Volume 2. Restructuring of Public Schemes: Case Studies of the Czech Republic and Slovenia*, Budapest: ILO-CEET.

—— (2004) "Pension Reform in the EU Accession Countries: Challenges, Achievements and Pitfalls," *International Social Security Review*, 57(2): 25–46.

Funck, B. and Pizzati, L. (eds) (2002) *Labour, Employment, and Social Policies in the EU Enlargement Process: Changing Perspectives and Policy Options*, Washington, DC: World Bank.

Gal, S. and Kligman, G. (2000) *The Politics of Gender after Socialism*, Princeton, NJ: Princeton University Press.

Giddens, A. (1998) *The Third Way*, Cambridge: Polity Press.

—— (2000) *The Third Way and Its Critics*, Cambridge: Polity Press.

—— (ed.) (2001) *The Global Third Way Debate*, Cambridge: Polity Press.

Goven, J. (2000) "New Parliament, Old Discourse? The Parental Leave Debate in Hungary," in S. Gal and G. Kligman (eds) *Reproducing Gender: Politics, Publics, and Everyday Life after Socialism*, Princeton, NJ: Princeton University Press.

Guillén, A.M. and Palier, B. (2004) "Introduction: Does Europe Matter? Accession to EU and Social Policy Developments in Recent and New Member States," *Journal of European Social Policy*, 14(3): 203–9.

KOPINT-DATORG (2002) *Economic Trends in Eastern Europe*, 11(2).

—— (2004) *Economic Trends in Eastern Europe*, 13(2).

Kolosi, T. and Sagi, M. (1999) "System Change and Social Structure," in T. Kolosi, I.G. Tóth and G. Vukovich (eds) *Social Report 1998*, Budapest: TÁRKI.

Kornai, J. (1997) *Struggle and Hope: Essays on Stabilization and Reform in a Post-socialist Economy*, Cheltenham and Northampton: Edward Elgar.

Lomax, B. (1999) "The Inegalitarian Nature of Hungary's Intellectual Political Culture," in A. Bozóki (ed.) *Intellectuals and Politics in Central Europe*, Budapest: Central European University Press.

Müller, K. (1999) *The Political Economy of Pension Reform in Central-Eastern Europe*, Cheltenham and Northampton: Edward Elgar.

OECD (1996) *Economic Surveys 1995–1996: The Czech Republic*, Paris: OECD.

Orenstein, M.A. (1996) "The Czech Tripartite Council and Its Contribution to Social Peace," in A. Ágh and G. Ilonszki (eds) *Parliaments and Organized Interests: The Second Steps*, Budapest: Hungarian Center For Democracy Studies.

Orenstein, M.A. and Haas, M.R. (2002) "Globalization and the Development of Welfare States in Postcommunist Europe," presented in the 3rd MDI Workshop at Tokyo, 24–5 March.

Orsazg, R.P. and Stiglitz, J.E. (2001) "Rethinking Pension Reform: Ten Myths about Social Security Systems," in R. Holzmann and J.E. Stiglitz (ed.) *New Ideas about Old Age Security: Toward Sustainable Pension Systems in the 21st Century*, Washington, DC: World Bank.

Potůček, M. (2001) "Czech Social Reform after 1989: Concepts and Reality," *International Social Security Review*, 54(2–3): 81–105.

—— (2004) "Accession and Social Policy: The Case of the Czech Republic," *Journal of European Social Policy*, 14(3): 253–66.

Ringold, D. (1999) "Social Policy in Post Communist Europe: Legacies and Transition," in L.J. Cook, M.A. Orenstein and M. Rueschemeyer (eds) *Left Parties and Social Policy in Post Communist Europe*, Boulder, CO: Westview Press.

Rys, V. (2001) "Transition Countries of Central Europe Entering the European Union: Some Social Protection Issues," *International Social Security Review*, 54(2–3): 177–89.

Standing, G. (1996) "Social Protection in Central and Eastern Europe: A Tale of Slipping Anchors and Torn Safety Nets," in G. Esping-Andersen (ed.) *Welfare States in Transition: National Adaptations in Global Economies*, London, Thousand Oaks and New Delhi: SAGE Publications.

Szamuely, L. (1996) "The Social Costs of Transformation in Central and Eastern Europe," *The Hungarian Quarterly*, 37(144): 54–69.

World Bank (1994) *Averting the Old Age Crisis: Policies to Protect the Old and Promote Growth: Toward Sustainable Pension System in the 21st Century*, New York: Oxford University Press.

—— (1996) *From Plan to Market, World Bank Report 1996*, New York: Oxford University Press.

Index

Abbott, K.W. 104n15
ABN Amro 151
absolute gains 89
Accounting Act and the Auditing Act (Thailand) 207
active employment policy 339–40
adjustable peg 18
advantages of economic backwardness 196
adverse selection 24
Advisory Center on WTO Law 99
African Development Bank (AfDB) 42, 47
agency cost 225–6, 227
agency problem(s) 8, 217, 218
agglomeration economies 261, 262
Alliance for Prosperity 128
Anderson, T.W. and Hsiao, C. 272
Andorka, R. 338
Annan, Kofi 82n8
antidumping duty (AD) 97, 102, 113, 114, 120
Aoki, Masahiko 23
Arellano, M. and Bond, S. 8, 269
Argentina 144
Argentinean crisis 239
Article VIII Parties of the IMF 200
Article XIV Parties of the IMF 200
ASEAN Surveillance Process 30
ASEAN Swap Arrangement (ASA) 31
Asia–Europe Meeting (ASEM) 307, 328n3
Asian crisis 142
Asian Currency Unit (ACU) 32
Asian Development Bank (ADB) 38, 42, 47, 306, 307
Asian Financial Crisis 162, 257
asset management companies (AMCs) 181
asymmetric information 22
Azis, Iwan. J. 24–5

balance of payments 90, 146
Balassa, Bela 212n3
Bank for International Settlements (BIS) 37, 140, 146, 166, 167, 170, 202, 207
Bank of Korea 173
Bank of Thailand (BOT) 204, 208
Bank of Tokyo-Mitsubishi 151
banking sector 142
Basel Committee 37
Basle Accord 24
BBVA 151
Bebchuk, L. 217, 225–6
Berger, P. and Ofek, E. 222
Berle, A.A. and Means, G.C. 217
Bevan, A. and Estrin, S. 282n8
Blair, Tony 324
Bokros Package 345
Bond Stabilization Fund 172
bonds 148
Borensztein, E. 276–7
Boulding, K. 234
Brazil 144
Bretton Woods 17
Bush, George 116, 130
Bush, George W. 130

Cairns Group 100
Canada and US Free Trade Agreement (CUSFTA) 112, 115, 116, 117, 121, 123, 124, 133n2, 133n3,
capacity building 98
capital adequacy 166, 170
capital adequacy ratio(s) 152, 184
capital adequacy standard 202, 207
capital flight 20
capital markets 148
Caribbean Basin Initiative (CBI) 132, 134n7
Central America Free Trade Agreement (CAFTA) 132, 134n8

356 *Index*

Central European welfare system 333
chaebol(s) 7, 147, 163–4, 165, 166–7, 173, 176–7, 179, 180, 187, 189n8, 217, 218, 220–1, 223–4, 225–30, 231n1
Chen, L. and Kwan, Y. 268
Chen Shui-bian 322, 324, 326–7
Chiangmai Inititative 4, 30, 31, 32
childcare leave 334, 340, 342
China 158
Chuan 208, 209
Chuan Leekpai 206
Chun Doo-hwan 321
Citibank 151
civil society 302, 303, 324, 328, 329n17; Hegelian model 326
CLIE 272
Clinton, Bill 117, 126, 130
Coalition for Fair Lumber Imports (CFLI) 133n3
collective action problems 176
Collier, P. and Dollar, D. 64
Colombia 144
commercial papers (CP) 167
Commonwealth of Independent States (CIS) 265, 274, 280, 283n29
communist welfare system 334, 336
Company Bankruptcy Act (Thailand) 207
comparative advantage(s) 95, 100, 196, 223, 261, 262, 265, 273
comparative institutional analysis 23
Comprehensive Development Framework (CDF) 4, 69
conditionality 28, 35, 50, 59, 61, 71, 73, 74, 75, 83n17, 162, 169, 187, 204; social 344, 346
consumer lending 154
contagion 20, 31, 39n6
controlling minority structure (CMS) firm 217–18, 225–8, 230
convergence 110
corporate governance 29, 31, 32, 36, 50, 145, 166, 201, 206, 209
Corporate Reorganization Law 183
Corporate Restructuring Accord (CRA) 189n10
Corporate Restructuring Co-ordination Committee (CRCC) 189n10
Corporate Restructuring Promotion Act 183
corporate restructuring vehicle (CRV) 181, 185
Corporate Restructuring Vehicle Act 181

corporatism 316–17, 349, 350; inclusionary 10, 319–20, 321, 323, 324; state 317
corporatist 300
corruption 264, 271
Council for Mutual Economic Aid (COMECON) 46
Council for Mutual Economic Assistance (CMEA) 262
countervailing duty (CVD) 113, 114, 120, 121
Country Assistance Strategy (CAS) 71
coverage 292
Credit Swiss First Boston 167
Cullet, P. 105n22
cultural capital 339

Deacon, B. 333, 334, 342, 343, 346, 350, 351
debt crisis 236, 257
debt-equity ratio 173, 177, 182
debt-equity swaps 168, 181–2
debt forgiveness 168
debt relief 168
debt rescheduling 36
debt-workout program 176
democratic deficit 126
deposit insurance 146
Depositor Protection Act 185–6
deregulation 58, 62, 66, 199, 200, 201, 218, 230, 231, 257
Deutsche and Dresdner 151
development banks 140
development policy loan (DPL) 72, 73, 74
"developmentalist" regime 197, 198
diversification premiums 221–4
Doha Development Agenda 12n4
Dollar, D. 56, 82n9
Dunning, J. 263

early retirement 340
East Asia 142
East Asian Miracle 143
East Asian welfare model 315
Easterly specification 283n32
Easterly, W. 276, 277, 279
economic partnership agreements (EPA) 213n14
economy of scale 164, 263
Eichengreen, Barry 22, 39
Employers-Employees Consultative Council 197
empowerment 49

Enabling Clause 92
Enhanced Structural Adjustment Facility (ESAF) 81n5
Enterprise for the Americas Initiative (EAI) 116
equity markets 148
Esping-Andersen, G. 290, 315, 316, 329n15, 334, 335, 347
Ethyl Corp. v. Canada 125
EU 343, 344, 349, 351, 352
Europe 158
European Bank for Reconstruction and Development (EBRD) 2, 42, 47, 343–4
European social model 351, 352
Europeanization 343; of social policy 341
Everything but Arms (EBA) 99
evolutionary economics 4, 17
Extraordinary Challenge Committee (ECC) 121

family allowance 340, 342, 345, 347
Fauver, L. 222
Ferge, Z. 335, 340, 341, 344, 348, 350
Ferraz, J.C. 203
financial depth 143
financial liberalization 228–30, 236
Financial Supervisory Commission (FSC) 170, 185
fixed capital formation 240
FleetBoston 151
flexible industrial relations 300
flexible labor contracts 297
foreign banks 150
foreign exchange reserve 169
formal sector 292, 293, 295, 298, 299
Fox, Vicente 128
Frankel, J. 1, 103n2
free trade agreements (FTA) 213n14
Free Trade Area of the Americas (FTAA) 130, 131, 134n9
Frieden, J.A. and Rogowski, R. 104n16
FSC (Financial Supervisory Commission) 165

G7 21, 30, 75
G20 105n25, 131
G22 21
Gagné, Gilbert 122
gender gap 338, 348
generalized method of moments (GMM) 261, 269, 272, 274, 279, 283n28

generalized system of preferences (GSP) 92, 193
Gerlach, M. 220
Giddens, Anthony 324–5, 326
Gini coefficients 82n9, 339
global governance 3, 5, 109
globalization 199, 202, 210, 211, 212, 223; "fractured" 19
Goh Choktong 327
gold standard 17, 18, 23
Goldman Sachs 167
Goldstein, Morris 29
good governance 29, 76, 77
Goto, A. 218, 220
governance 109, 111
government procurement 115
Government Savings Bank 207
Granovetter, M. 217
Great Depression 19, 206, 239
Greater Mekong Sub-Regional Program 78
greenfield investment 239
Guillén, A.M. and Palier, B. 351
Guizot, F. 326
Gupta, S. 306
Gurria, José Angel 83n21
Gylfason, T. and Zoega, G. 282n17

harmonization 96, 98, 99
Harrod–Domar model 62
Hart, Michael 116
Hausman test 282n26
Head, K., Ries, J. and Swenson, D. 268
health care 293, 297, 298, 334, 348
health care insurance system 341
hedge funds 201, 204
Hegel, G.W.F. 326
hegemonic stability 88, 103n5
Helms Burton Act 122
herd 264, 272
herd behavior 20
Hiraishi, Naoaki 325
Holliday, I. and Wilding, P. 212n5
Holzmann, R. 306
Horisaka, K. 196
Hosono, A. 212n7
HSBC 151
Huber, E. 295

ILO 328n2, 336, 342–3, 349, 351
import substitution 193, 236
import substitution industrialization (ISI) 9, 90, 196, 253, 289, 294, 295, 299, 303

Indonesia 19, 26, 143
Industrial Bank of Korea 151
industrial restructuring plan (IRP) 207
informal employment 299
informal sector 292, 293, 298, 348
information symmetry 21
innovation 234–5, 258
institutional economics 109
institutional investors 149
institutional model 325
institutional voids 218, 219, 220, 226, 230
Integrated Framework (IF) 99
intellectual precocity 325
intellectual property rights 96
Inter-American Development Bank (IDB) 42, 46, 129, 144
Inter-American Investment Corporation (IIC) 46
interest coverage ratio (ICR) 167–8
International Development Association (IDA) 43
International Finance Corporation (IFC) 46
internationalization 87
intra-firm trade 252
Ishida, Takeshi 325

Japan 158
Japan Bank for International Cooperation (JBIC) 207
Joh, S.W. 227

Kali, R. 228
Kaminsky, Graciela L. and Reinhart, Carmen M. 24
Kang Bong-Kyun 189n12
keiretsu 220–1
Keohane, R.O. and Milner, H.V. 103n2
Keohane, Robert 88, 110
Khanna, T. 217, 228
Khanna, T. and Palepu, K. 219, 221
Kim Dae-Jung 71, 176, 321, 324, 326–7
Kim, C. 227
Kindleberger, Charles P. 88, 103n3
Korea 38
Korea Asset Management Corporation (KAMCO) 181, 185
Korea Deposit Insurance Corporation (KDIC) 170, 171, 184–5
Korea Development Institute 189n3
Korean Development Bank 151
Korean Export-Import Bank 151
Kornai, J. 335, 345, 348, 350

KOSDAQ 188
Kramer, Ralph M. 329n16
Krasner, Stephen D. 103n5, 104n7, 133n1
Kravis, I.B. and Lipsey, R. 281n3
Krugman, P. 282n12
Kwon, J. and Nam, J. 167–8

La Porta, R. 217
labor union(s) 297, 300, 302, 303
Latin America 142
Lee, G. 222
Lee, J., Lee, Y. and Yoo, J. 231n6
Lee, K. 227
Lee, K., Ryu, K. and Yoon, J. 221
Leff, N. 218, 220
legacy of the communist era 348, 350, 351
Letter of Development Strategy (LDS) 77
Liberal-Institutionalism 88
Lieberman, I.W. and Mako, W. 164
life expectancy 337
Lincoln, J.R. 220
London Rules 189n10
Lucas, R.E.Jr. 281n3, 282n12

Maddison, A. 234
Manila Framework Group 30
Manila Framework Group Meeting 4
Mankiw, G. 277
market failure 217–19, 220, 221, 230
market-oriented model 303
Marshall, Katherine 307
Maruyama, Masao 325, 329n14
means-tested benefits 345
medical insurance 297, 298, 302
Meltzer Commission 75, 76
Meltzer report 22
MERCOSUR 110, 131, 254
mergers and acquisitions (M&A) 202, 212n8, 235, 239–40, 242–3, 250, 253, 254–5
Mesa-Lago, C. 292, 296
Mexico 144
Milgrom, P. and Roberts, J. 219, 226
Millennium Developmental Goals (MDGs) 52, 77, 82n8
Ministry of Economy, International Trade and Industry (METI) 213n10
Ministry of International Trade and Industry (MITI) 213n10
Mizutani mission 207
Moody's Investor Services 163

Index 359

moral hazard 24, 33, 176, 184, 217
mortgage lending 154
Most-Favored-Nation treatment (MFN) 91, 112, 123, 124
Müller, K. 346
Mulroney, Brian 115
Multilateral Investment Guarantee Agency (MIGA) 46
mutual gains 89

National Committee on Social Policy 207
National Competitiveness Plan 209
"notional defined contribution"(NDC) 346
National Economic and Social Development Board (NESDB) 213n12
National Trade Union Council (NTUC) 197
national treatment 123, 124
nationalization 125
neoliberal economic policy 296, 299
neoliberal economic reform 300
neoliberal policy 289
neoliberalism 336, 339, 342, 344–7, 348, 349, 350
New Middle Road 327
Newly Industrializing Countries (NICs) 101, 192, 193
newly industrializing economies 142
nomenklatura 334
non-bank financial institutions (NBFIs) 162, 171–3, 229
non-performing loans (NPLs) 6, 145, 152, 163, 165–8, 170, 172, 179, 181, 183, 202, 206, 207, 208
non-reciprocity 91, 94
Noorbakhsh, F. and Youssef, A. 271
North American Free Trade Agreement (NAFTA) 5

official development assistance (ODA) 59, 67, 83n14
offshore banking 230
Omnibus Trade and Competitiveness Act of 1988 97, 113
one village [tambon] one product (OTOP) 209–10
Ordinary Least Squares (OLS) regression 268, 269, 272, 273, 274
Orenstein, M.A. and Haas, M.R. 343, 344, 348, 350
Organization of Economic Cooperation and Development (OECD) 147, 223, 344
Ortiz, Isabel 307
Overseas Economic Cooperation Fund (OECF) 207
Ownership 150

Pagano, M. 187
panel data 261
Park Chung-hee 318, 329n11
parliamentary democracy 336
path dependence 21, 22–3, 37
Patten, Christopher 322
PAYG 346, 350
pension reform 346
pension system 345–7; privatization of 345, 349–50
pension(s) 292, 296–7, 298, 322, 334, 340, 347, 348
People's Bank 210
performance requirements 124
Peron 197
Peron Administration 9
Peru 144
PHARE 343
Philippines 143
Polanyi, Karl 315, 326
policy coherence 59
political globalization 351
populism 294
populist 295
populist administrations 295
populist government 295
populist regime 212
poverty line 338
Poverty Reduction and Growth Facility (PRGF) 81n5
Poverty Reduction Strategy Papers (PRSP) 4, 71, 72, 77, 80
Poverty Reduction Support Credits (PRSCs) 71, 73
preferential treatments 87, 92, 98
premature welfare state 335
principle of subsidiarity 81n4
Prisoners' Dilemma 89
private health care services/insurance 293–4
privatization 58, 187, 199, 200, 206, 235, 236, 242, 248, 250, 253, 254, 257, 262, 299, 342, 348
Public Fund Committee 184–5
Public Fund Management Act 184
Public Fund Overseeing Committee 186
public hospitals 293, 297, 298, 299

Index

Public Limited Company Act (Thailand) 207, 208
public social expenditure 290
public-sector banks 150
Purchase and Assumption (P&A) formula 170

R&D 256
random effects model 282n26
reciprocity 91, 94, 95
red tapes 271
regional cooperation 101
regional trade agreements 5
regulation and supervision 145
relative gains 89
rent-seeking 94
residual character 292, 293
residual model 325
residualist welfare state 350
Resmini, L. 274, 282n8
return on equity (ROE) 152
return on total assets (ROA) 152
Ringold, D. 350
Roma 338
rule of law 280
Rys, V. 343
S.D. Mayers v. Canada 125
Sachs, Jeffrey 201
safeguards 97, 102
Salinas de Gortari 117, 124
Santander 151
Sargan test 269, 272, 274
Sarit 197
Savings & Loans crisis 188n2
Schelling, Thomas 103n4
Schlegel, J. 234
Schmitter, P.C. and Lehmbruch, G. 317, 319
Scotia Bank 151
SDR 33, 40n29
second oil crisis 192
secondary market 149
Section 301 97, 112–13, 122
sectoral structural adjustment loans (SECALs) 73
Securities and Exchange Act 186
September 11 128, 133
Sharfstein, D.S. 227
single undertaking 97
small and medium-size enterprises (SMEs) 6, 46, 139, 141, 177–9, 187, 188, 207, 209, 210
Small Industries Finance Corporation (SIFO) 210

SME Development Bank 210
social assistance 197, 340
social costs of transformation 336, 337, 339, 340
social dialogue 342
social insurance 197, 292–6, 298, 300, 306
Social Investment Plan (SIP) 207, 213n12
social protection 306–7
social risk management 306
social safety nets 58
social security 327
social structure 338, 348
Solow model 276
sovereignty 109
special and differential treatment(s) 92, 99
Standing, G. 350
state enterprises 196, 199, 200, 202, 206
state owned companies 250
state-led industrialization 316
Steers, R. 220
Stepan, A. 319
Stiglitz, J. 171, 188
Stock and Exchange Commission of Thailand (SEC) 207
Stock Exchange of Thailand (SET) 207
structural adjustment loan(s) (SAL(s)) 50, 73, 83n17, 200, 206
structural adjustment programs 199
structural reforms 199
Summers, Lawrence 36
Super 301 113, 114
system change 339

tariffication 96
tariffs 263
technical assistance 98
Thai Bankers Association (TBA) 208
Thailand Assets Management Corporation (TAMC) 208
Thaksin Shinawatra 208–12, 213n14
Thaksinocracy 210
Thatcherism 327
Third Way 324, 327, 344
Titmuss, R.M. 329n15
Tobin tax 34, 36
Tobin's Q 227
Tokyo Round 101, 112
total factor productivity (TFP) 261
Trade Act of 1974 112–13, 122
Trade Policy Review Mechanism (TPRM) 97

Trade Promotion Authority (TPA) 126, 130, 134n6
trade unions 197, 342
traditional European welfare system 336, 340
transformational recession 337
tripartite body 342–3
Tung Chee-hwa 327
two-gap model 62
Twu Jaw-yann 193

unemployment benefit 339
unemployment insurance 297, 339
unfair trade practices 112, 113, 121
UNICEF 343, 349
United Nations Development Programme (UNDP) 78
universal medical system 294
universal system 294, 298, 303
universalization of social security 294
Uruguay Round 91, 96
Usami, K. 197
US–Chile free trade agreement (FTA) 131, 132

Valgas Administration 9

Venezuela 144
Volcker, Paul 83n21
voluntary export restraints (VERs) 97

Wade, R.H. 82n7
Washington Consensus 2, 5, 12n1, 17, 21, 22, 28, 37, 58, 59–62, 69, 79, 82n10, 129, 199, 201, 203, 206, 236; first generation 7; post- 12n1, 62; second generation 7
Weber, Max 326
welfare economics 21
Wheeler, D. and Mody, A. 268
Wilensky, H.L. 290, 310
Williamson, John 12n1, 21, 82n10, 83n15
Wolfensohn, James 69
World Development Indicators (WDI) 269
WTO Cancún Ministerial Conference 12n4

Yoon, J.I. 223

zaibatsu 220

eBooks – at www.eBookstore.tandf.co.uk

A library at your fingertips!

eBooks are electronic versions of printed books. You can store them on your PC/laptop or browse them online.

They have advantages for anyone needing rapid access to a wide variety of published, copyright information.

eBooks can help your research by enabling you to bookmark chapters, annotate text and use instant searches to find specific words or phrases. Several eBook files would fit on even a small laptop or PDA.

NEW: Save money by eSubscribing: cheap, online access to any eBook for as long as you need it.

Annual subscription packages

We now offer special low-cost bulk subscriptions to packages of eBooks in certain subject areas. These are available to libraries or to individuals.

For more information please contact webmaster.ebooks@tandf.co.uk

We're continually developing the eBook concept, so keep up to date by visiting the website.

www.eBookstore.tandf.co.uk